THE ART OF
Culinary Cooking

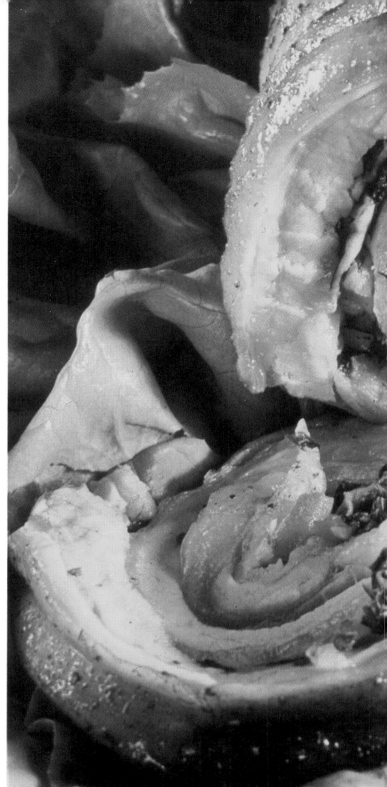

THE
ART OF
CULINARY

COOKING

Editorial Director Donald D. Wolf
Design and Layout Margot L. Wolf

Lexicon Publications, Inc.
95 Madison Avenue, New York, N.Y. 10016

Copyright © 1991 by
Lexicon Publications, Inc.
95 Madison Avenue
New York, NY 10016

ISBN: 0-7172-4615-9

CONTENTS

NOTE: Recipes for microwave cooking are indicated by this symbol:

APPETIZERS and FIRST COURSES

Avocado Cocktail Dip

ABOUT 1 CUP

1 large ripe avocado	¼ cup mayonnaise
2 teaspoons lemon juice	6 drops Tabasco
1 small slice onion	Salt to taste
	Potato chips

1. Halve and peel avocado, reserving 1 shell. Cube avocado and put into container of an electric blender. Add lemon juice, onion, mayonnaise, Tabasco, and salt. Process until puréed.
2. To serve, pile avocado mixture into reserved shell; place on a serving dish and surround with potato chips for dipping.

Chili con Queso Dip

3¼ CUPS DIP

1 cup chopped onion	1 pound process sharp Cheddar cheese, cut into chunks
2 cans (4 ounces each) green chilies, chopped and drained	
	1 teaspoon Worcestershire sauce
2 large cloves garlic, mashed	¼ teaspoon paprika
	¼ teaspoon salt
2 tablespoons cooking oil	½ cup tomato juice

1. Sauté onion, green chilies, and garlic in oil in cooking pan of chafing dish over medium heat until onion is tender.
2. Reduce heat to low, and add remaining ingredients, except tomato juice. Cook, stirring constantly, until cheese is melted.
3. Add tomato juice gradually until dip is the desired consistency. Place over hot water to keep warm.
4. Serve with corn chips.

Party Spread

MAKES ABOUT 1⅓ CUPS

1 package (8 ounces) cream cheese	2 teaspoons capers, drained
¼ cup butter, softened	1 teaspoon prepared mustard
1 teaspoon paprika	2 teaspoons minced onion
¼ teaspoon dry mustard	
½ teaspoon onion salt	
1½ teaspoons caraway seeds	

1. Blend cream cheese and butter together.
2. Blend in remaining ingredients and chill several hours to blend flavors.
3. Spread on thinly sliced pumpernickel or rye bread or crackers.

Appetizer Kabobs

40 APPETIZERS

8 large precooked smoked sausage links	1 tablespoon brown sugar
	2 tablespoons soy sauce
1 can (16 ounces) pineapple chunks, drained	1 tablespoon vinegar

1. Arrange sausage evenly around edge of roasting rack set in a glass dish or directly on glass plate and cook 2 to 3 minutes, rotating dish one-quarter turn halfway through cooking time. Drain sausage and cut each sausage link into 5 pieces.
2. Make kabobs, using 1 sausage piece and 1 pineapple chunk threaded on a round wooden pick. Arrange evenly in a large shallow dish.
3. In a 1-cup glass measure, blend brown sugar, soy sauce, and vinegar and pour over kabobs. Refrigerate 1 or 2 hours until serving time.
4. Arrange 20 kabobs on a large glass plate and cook 2 to 3 minutes, rotating dish one-quarter turn and spooning sauce over top halfway through cooking time.
5. Cook additional kabobs as needed. Serve warm.

Tuna with Béarnaise Sauce.

Tuna with Béarnaise Sauce

SERVES 6

6 (4 ounce) cans tuna
3 hard-cooked eggs
½ cup Béarnaise
   sauce (below)

1 ounce caviar
Bunch of dill

1. Open and drain each can of tuna and arrange on a serving dish layered with fresh dill.
2. Place a teaspoon of Béarnaise sauce on top of each tuna round.
3. Shell the hard-cooked eggs; cut in half and arrange each half on the sauce.
4. Put a small dollop of caviar on top of each egg and serve with freshly heated bread.
5. Serve extra Béarnaise sauce on the side.

Béarnaise Sauce:
¼ cup tarragon
   vinegar
¼ cup white wine
2 teaspoons tarragon
1 tablespoon shallot or
   onion, chopped

⅛ teaspoon pepper
1 tablespoon parsley
3 egg yolks
4 ounces butter

1. Combine vinegar, wine, tarragon, shallot, pepper, and parsley. Bring to a boil in a saucepan. Reduce heat and simmer uncovered for about 8 minutes.
2. Strain and cool.
3. Cook egg yolks and 2 tablespoons cold water in the top of a double boiler. Beat with a whisk until blended and thick, about 1 minute.
4. Add butter, 1 tablespoon at a time, beating continuously.
5. Beat in tarragon and serve.

7

Hot Tuna Canapés

48 CANAPÉS

1 can (6¹/₂ or 7 ounces) tuna	¹/₄ teaspoon Worcestershire sauce
¹/₄ cup mayonnaise	1 cucumber
1 tablespoon ketchup	Paprika (optional)
¹/₄ teaspoon salt	48 melba toast rounds
Few grains cayenne pepper	12 pimiento-stuffed olives, sliced
2 teaspoons finely chopped onion	

1. Drain and flake tuna. Add mayonnaise, ketchup, salt, cayenne pepper, onion and Worcestershire sauce.
2. Pare cucumber and slice paper-thin (if desired, sprinkle with paprika).
3. For each canapé, place cucumber slice on toast round, pile tuna mixture in center and top with olive slice.
4. Put 8 canapés in circle on individual paper plates. For each plate, cook uncovered in microwave oven 30 to 60 seconds.

Feta Cheese Triangles

ABOUT 100 PIECES

1 pound feta cheese, crumbled	Dash finely ground pepper
2 egg yolks	³/₄ pound butter, melted and kept warm
1 whole egg	
3 tablespoons chopped parsley	1 pound filo

1. Mash feta cheese with a fork. Add egg yolks, egg, parsley, and pepper.
2. Melt butter in a saucepan. Keep warm, but do not allow to brown.
3. Lay a sheet of filo on a large cutting board. Brush with melted butter. Cut into strips about 1¹/₂ to 2 inches wide. Place ¹/₂ teaspoon of the cheese mixture on each strip about 1 inch from base. Fold to form a triangle. Continue until all cheese mixture and filo have been used.
4. Place triangles, side by side, in a shallow roasting pan or baking sheet.*
5. Bake at 350°F about 20 minutes, or until golden brown. Serve at once.

*Pan must have four joined sides, otherwise butter will fall to bottom of the oven and burn.

Note: Feta Cheese Triangles freeze well. Before serving, remove from freezer and let stand 15 to 20 minutes. Bake at 325°F until golden brown.

Shrimp Mousse as First Course

SERVES 6

1 can cod roe caviar paste (7 ounces)	1 cup heavy cream
About ¹/₄ pound shelled and deveined shrimp	1 package unflavored gelatin
	1 small yellow onion
	1 head lettuce

1. Sprinkle the gelatin in ¹/₂ cup of cold water. Heat until dissolved.
2. Chop the onion finely. Cut the shrimp in pieces, saving a few for decoration.
3. Mix the caviar paste and the dissolved gelatin. Whip the cream to a stiff peak. Mix all ingredients.
4. Rinse a bowl or mold with cold water. Pour the mixture into the mold and let it set in the refrigerator about 3 hours.
5. Place the shrimp mousse in the center of a serving dish. Place whole shrimp on top of the mousse and place lettuce, cut in strips, around the outside.

Smoked Trout Pâté

SERVES 6-8

3 smoked trout	2 tablespoons butter
Salt to taste	2 tablespoons heavy cream
Pepper to taste	
Juice of ¹/₂ lemon	2 bay leaves
2 tablespoons white wine	4 ounces butter, melted
¹/₂ pound flounder fillet	*Garnish:*
¹/₂ cup fresh white bread crumbs	2 hard-cooked eggs
1 egg yolk	1 tin caviar
	Lettuce

1. Remove heads, tails, skin, and bones from the trout. Cut the flesh of 2 fish into finger-length pieces and place in a bowl.
2. Mix salt, pepper, lemon juice, and wine and pour over fish. Marinate for 2 hours, turning occasionally.
3. Preheat oven to 325°F.
4. Grind 1 trout and the flounder. Add bread crumbs, egg yolks, butter, and cream.
5. Remove the trout from the marinade. Pour the marinade over the flounder mixture and season.
6. Cover the bottom of a mold with a layer of flounder mixture. Add a layer of trout and continue layering, finishing with a layer of bread crumbs and flounder mixture.

(continued)

Smoked Trout Pâté.

Shrimp Mousse.

7. Place the bay leaves on top of the pâté, cover with foil, and cover. Cook in a water bath for 45 minutes. Cool.

8. Remove the cover and foil and cover pâté with wax paper. Put on a 2-pound weight and chill overnight.

9. Remove bay leaves and pour a little melted butter over the pâté to seal. Serve on a bed of lettuce with hard-cooked egg wedges, caviar (optional), and melba toast.

Tomato Aspic

SERVES 8

3¹/₂ cups tomatoes	2 tablespoons gelatin
1 teaspoon salt	¹/₄ cup celery, chopped
¹/₂ teaspoon paprika	¹/₄ cup green pepper, chopped
1¹/₂ teaspoons sugar	
2 tablespoons lemon juice	¹/₄ cup carrots, chopped
3 tablespoons onion, chopped	1 avocado, sliced
1 bay leaf	1 pound shrimp, cleaned and deveined
4 ribs celery	
1 teaspoon tarragon	Fresh dill

1. Simmer first nine ingredients for 30 minutes and strain.

2. Place gelatin in ¹/₂ cup cold water and pour into hot tomato mixture.

3. Chill aspic. Just before it sets add celery, green pepper, carrots, and avocado.

4. Chill aspic until firm. Unmold and serve with mayonnaise and shrimp. Decorate with fresh dill.

Stuffed Mushrooms

25 TO 30 APPETIZERS

1 bunch green onions, chopped	¹/₂ cup bulk pork sausage
¹/₄ cup sour cream	1 pound fresh mushrooms, washed, drained, and stemmed
¹/₂ teaspoon Worcestershire sauce	
¹/₂ teaspoon oregano	

1. In a 1-quart casserole, blend green onions, sour cream, Worcestershire sauce, oregano, and sausage. Cook 2 to 3 minutes, stirring halfway through cooking time.

2. Stuff mushroom caps with filling. Place stem in top of filling and secure in place with wooden pick.

3. Arrange 10 to 12 mushrooms evenly around the edge of a glass pie plate and cook, covered, 6 to 8 minutes.

4. Serve warm.

Crabmeat Quiche

16 APPETIZERS

1 unbaked 9-inch pie shell	³/₄ cup (3 ounces) shredded Gruyère cheese
2 eggs	
1 cup half-and-half	1 tablespoon flour
¹/₂ teaspoon salt	1 can (7¹/₂ ounces) Alaska king crab, drained and flaked
Dash ground red pepper	

1. Prick bottom and sides of pie shell. Bake at 450°F 10 minutes, or until delicately browned.

2. Beat together eggs, half-and-half, salt, and red pepper.

3. Combine cheese, flour, and crab; sprinkle evenly in pie shell. Pour in egg mixture.

4. Bake, uncovered, at 325°F 45 minutes, or until tip of knife inserted 1 inch from center comes out clean. Let stand a few minutes. Cut into wedges to serve.

Tomato Aspic.

Coquilles St. Jacques
au Vin Blanc.

Coquilles St. Jacques au Vin Blanc

SERVES 6

1¹/₂ pounds large sea scallops	2 egg yolks
2 tablespoons butter	2 ounces heavy cream
¹/₄ pound mushrooms, sliced	Salt
1 shallot, chopped	Pepper
2 tablespoons chopped parsley	Fresh lemon juice (¹/₂ lemon)
2 cups white wine	6 scallop shells or ramekins
1 cup fish stock or 1 cup clam juice	

1. Put the scallops in a saucepan, pour on the white wine, chopped shallot, and parsley. Bring to a boil and simmer 4-5 minutes. Remove the scallops and cut in slices. Set aside.
2. Sauté the mushrooms in butter.
3. Reduce fish stock to ¹/₂ cup. Thicken the fish stock with the cream mixed with the egg yolks and stir until mixed.
4. Add the scallops and mushrooms and season with fresh lemon juice, salt, and pepper.
5. Fill the scallop shells with the mixture and serve with fluffy mashed potatoes.

Greek Meatballs

50 TO 60 MEATBALLS

1 pound ground lamb	¹/₄ teaspoon ginger
1 egg	¹/₄ teaspoon garlic powder
¹/₃ cup cracker crumbs	¹/₈ teaspoon cumin
¹/₃ cup soy sauce	¹/₂ cup slivered almonds or pinenuts
¹/₂ cup water	

1. In a medium mixing bowl, blend lamb, egg, and cracker crumbs. Add soy sauce, water, ginger, garlic powder, cumin, and almonds or pinenuts. Mix thoroughly. Shape in 1-inch meatballs.
2. Arrange 10 meatballs in a circle in a 9-inch glass pie plate. Cook, covered, 3 to 4 minutes, rotating dish one-quarter turn halfway through cooking time. Cook longer if needed.
3. Serve hot on wooden picks.

Avocado Cream

SERVES 4

2 ripe avocado pears	chopped onion
1 tablespoon white wine vinegar	Cayenne pepper
	1 teaspoon sugar
4 anchovy fillets, finely chopped	$\frac{1}{2}$ cup whipping cream
2 teaspoons finely	Paprika

1. Cut the pears in half and remove the seed.
2. Scoop out all the flesh, being careful not to break the skin. Reserve the empty shells. Put the flesh into a bowl and mash well. Add vinegar, anchovy, and onion and season with salt, Cayenne pepper, and sugar.
3. Chill. Just before serving fold in the whipped cream. Fill the pear shells and sprinkle with paprika.

Shrimp Canapés

SERVES 8

8 cooked jumbo shrimp split from head to tail	16 toast rounds
	4 tablespoons lemon mayonnaise
$\frac{1}{2}$ cup French dressing	$1\frac{1}{2}$ ounces caviar
	Parsley

1. Marinate shrimp in French dressing for 1 hour.
2. Spread toast rounds with lemon mayonnaise.
3. Place shrimp, flat side down, on toast.
4. Fill curve formed by shrimp with caviar.
5. Garnish with tiny sprig of parsley at the head of shrimp.

Spicy Beef Dip

ABOUT 3 CUPS DIP

1 pound ground beef	1 teaspoon sugar
$\frac{1}{2}$ cup chopped onion	1 package (3 ounces) cream cheese
1 clove garlic, minced	
1 can (8 ounces) tomato sauce	$\frac{1}{3}$ cup grated Parmesan cheese
$\frac{1}{4}$ cup ketchup	
$\frac{3}{4}$ teaspoon oregano, crushed	

1. In a $1\frac{1}{2}$-quart casserole, sauté ground beef, onion, and garlic 4 to 6 minutes, stirring twice.
2. Spoon off excess fat. Stir in tomato sauce, ketchup, oregano, and sugar.

3. Cover and cook 5 to 6 minutes, stirring twice.
4. Add cream cheese and Parmesan cheese, and stir until cream cheese has melted. Serve warm.

Swedish Meat Balls

ABOUT 3 DOZEN MEAT BALLS

1 cup (3 slices) fine, dry bread crumbs	$\frac{1}{2}$ teaspoon brown sugar
1 pound ground round steak	$\frac{1}{4}$ teaspoon pepper
	$\frac{1}{4}$ teaspoon allspice
$\frac{1}{2}$ pound ground pork	$\frac{1}{4}$ teaspoon nutmeg
$\frac{1}{2}$ cup mashed potatoes	$\frac{1}{8}$ teaspoon cloves
	$\frac{1}{8}$ teaspoon ginger
1 egg, beaten	3 tablespoons butter
1 teaspoon salt	

1. Set out a large, heavy skillet having a tight-fitting cover.
2. Set out bread crumbs.
3. Lightly mix together in a large bowl $\frac{1}{2}$ cup of the bread crumbs and steak, pork, potatoes, egg and a mixture of salt, brown sugar, pepper, allspice, nutmeg, cloves, and ginger.
4. Shape mixture into balls about 1 in. in diameter. Roll balls lightly in remaining crumbs.
5. Heat the butter in the skillet over low heat.
6. Add the meat balls and brown on all sides. Shake pan frequently to brown evenly and to keep balls round. Cover and cook about 15 minutes, or until meat balls are thoroughly cooked.

Corn Fritters

ABOUT 30 FRITTERS

1 cup fresh corn kernels	flour
	4 eggs
$\frac{1}{2}$ cup butter	Corn oil for frying, heated to 365°F
1 cup all-purpose	

1. Cook corn until soft in boiling salted water in a saucepan; drain thoroughly, reserving 1 cup liquid. Melt butter with corn liquid in saucepan, add flour, and cook, stirring rapidly, until mixture is smooth and rolls away from the sides of pan.
2. Remove from heat and add the eggs, one at a time, beating well after each addition. Stir in cooked corn.
3. Drop batter by spoonfuls into heated oil and fry until golden and well puffed. Drain on absorbent paper. Serve hot.

Avocado Cream.

Grapefruit with Crab

SERVES 2

2 grapefruit	A little mayonnaise
1 cup (8 ounces) crabmeat	Parsley or lemon slices for garnish

1. Mix the flesh from 2 grapefruit with 1 cup crabmeat.
2. Bind with a little mayonnaise, season to taste, and serve in the grapefruit shells, garnished with parsley or lemon slices.

Swedish Liver Pâté

SERVES 6

2 pounds calf's liver	2 cups heavy cream
1 medium yellow onion, finely chopped	2 eggs, beaten
1 pound pork fat	2 teaspoons anchovy paste
1/4 cup butter	1/2 teaspoon salt
1/4 cup all purpose flour	1 teaspoon pepper
	1/2 teaspoon dill

1. Preheat oven to 325°F.
2. Grind liver and pork fat.
3. Melt the butter in a skillet and stir in the flour with a whisk. Gradually stir in the cream. Cook over low heat, stirring constantly till thickened.
4. Add pork fat and stir till fat has melted.
5. Remove from heat.
6. Add liver, eggs, anchovy paste, salt, pepper, and dill and blend thoroughly.
7. Spoon into a pâté mold or crock.
8. Place mold in a baking pan and fill with water 1/2

Swedish Liver Pâté.

way up mold. Bake for 1 1/2 - 2 hours till a knife inserted in the center comes out clean. If pâté browns too quickly, cover with aluminum foil. Cool and serve.

Liver Pâté Balls

SERVES 8-10

1 pound chicken livers	2 teaspoons tarragon
Sherry	1 clove garlic, minced
2 tablespoons butter	1/4 teaspoon salt
2 tablespoons rendered chicken fat	1/2 teaspoon pepper
1/2 cup onion, minced	1/4 cup heavy cream
	Parsley

1. Preheat oven to 325°F. Place chicken livers in a dish and pour in sherry to cover. Marinate 2-4 hours.
2. Drain and sauté in butter and fat. Add onions,

Grapefruit with Crab.

Liver Pâté Balls.

Ham Mousse with Asparagus.

tarragon, and garlic. Cook for 4 minutes. Chicken livers should be pink inside.

3. Place mixture in a blender and add salt, pepper, and cream. Purée.

4. Butter a 4-cup baking dish and pour in purée. Cover tightly with heavy foil and place in roasting pan. Fill roasting pan with water halfway up side of baking dish. Bake for 1 1/4-1 1/2 hours till set. Remove foil. Cool. Cover and chill thoroughly.

5. Remove pâté in large tablespoons and roll into balls. Roll balls in parsley. Serve with melba toast.

Ham Mousse with Asparagus

SERVES 4

1/2 pound lightly smoked ham	Paprika powder
1 envelope unflavored gelatin	3 ounces finely chopped aromatic herbs (dill, parsley, thyme)
3/4 cup heavy cream	*Garnish:*
2 egg whites	Lettuce leaves
1 teaspoon dry mustard	1 can asparagus tips
1/2 teaspoon salt	Sliced fresh cucumber
Pepper	

1. Chop the ham finely and mix with the mustard, pepper, paprika, salt, and the chopped aromatic herbs.

2. Beat the egg whites to very stiff peaks and whip the cream. Sprinkle the gelatin in 1/2 cup cold water. Heat over low heat till gelatin dissolves. Mix with the cream. Add the ham mixture and the egg white foam. Pour the batter in a greased ring mold and put in a cold place to set. Place on a serving dish; garnish with lettuce leaves and asparagus tips. Put sliced cucumber in the hole in the middle. Serve with toasted pumpernickel rounds.

Vegetable Mélange with Mustard Sauce

SERVES 6

1 large yellow squash or zucchini, pared and minced	1/3 cup prepared mustard
3 medium carrots, minced	1/3 cup dill pickle juice
1/4 cup minced onion	1 teaspoon sugar
1/4 cup minced dill pickle	1/2 teaspoon curry powder
4 ounces Swiss cheese, minced	1 garlic clove, minced
	Lettuce cups

Combine squash, carrot, onion, pickle, and cheese in a medium bowl. Mix remaining ingredients, except lettuce cups; pour over vegetables and stir to coat well. Refrigerate until well chilled. Serve in lettuce cups.

Flybanes

8 FLYBANES

8 hard-cooked eggs	Mayonnaise
4 small tomatoes	Lettuce
Salt and pepper	

1. Peel the eggs. Cut off both ends so eggs will stand evenly. Stand the eggs on a small tray; they will serve for mushroom stems.

2. Cut the tomatoes in halves lengthwise. Remove cores. Sprinkle with salt and pepper. Put each tomato half over an egg as a mushroom cap. Dot the caps with mayonnaise. Garnish the tray with lettuce.

Ham Appetizer.

Broiled Fish Quenelles

SERVES 8

2 pounds skinned fish fillets (all trout or a combination of trout, whitefish, or pike)	oil
	1¹/₂ teaspoons salt
	1¹/₂ teaspoons matzo meal or white cornmeal
¹/₂ cup chopped onion	3 tablespoons ice water
¹/₃ cup chopped carrot	Watercress
1 egg, beaten	
2 teaspoons vegetable	

1. Place all ingredients except 1 tablespoon of the ice water and watercress in a blender or food processor; purée until the consistency of a paste. Add remaining ice water if necessary (mixture should hold together and be easy to handle).
2. Form fish mixture into oval patties, using ¹/₂ cup for each. Place on a lightly oiled cookie sheet.
3. Broil 4 inches from heat until patties are well browned and slightly puffed (8 to 10 minutes on each side). Serve immediately. Garnish with watercress.

Taste Teasers

Select an attractive array of Taste Teasers from these recipes. All are delightful bits of finger food, though some may be easier to serve if they have stems of wooden or plastic picks.

Meat 'n' Cheese Wedges—With a round cutter, cut 2¹/₂- to 3-inch rounds from slices of **ham,** canned **luncheon meat, ready-to-serve meat, bologna,** or other **sausage.** Repeat the process with thin slices of **Swiss** or **Cheddar cheese.** Alternately stack the meat and cheese rounds, using five in all. Wrap in waxed paper and chill in refrigerator until time to serve. Cut stacks into small wedges. Insert picks.

Bacon-Wrapped Olives—Wrap **pimiento-** or **almond-stuffed olives** in pieces of **bacon.** Fasten with picks. Put in shallow baking dish. Bake or broil until bacon is done.

Biscuit Bites—Dot toasted bite-size **shredded wheat biscuits** with **peanut butter.** Thread on picks alternately with thin slices of **sweet pickle.**

Pecan Sandwiches—Lightly brush large **pecan halves** with **butter** and spread one layer deep on baking sheet. Toast at 350°F about 20 minutes, or until delicately browned. Grate **Swiss cheese;** blend in **cream** to spreading consistency. Spread one side of one pecan half with cheese mixture and top with a second half. Press gently together.

Pineapple Delights—Wrap drained **pineapple chunks** each in one third of a slice of **bacon;** secure with a whole **clove** or wooden pick. Arrange in shallow baking dish and bake or broil until bacon is done.

Smoked Cheese Blossoms—Soften **smoked cheese** and mix with chopped **pimiento, sweet pickle** and crisp crumbled **bacon.** Roll into small balls and chill in refrigerator. Or pack mixture into a small pan, chill and cut into squares. Insert picks.

Caviar with Egg—Cut **hard-cooked eggs** into halves lengthwise or cut forming sawtooth edges. Remove yolks and set aside for use in other food preparation. Fill whites with chilled **caviar,** black or red. Garnish with small piece of **lemon.**

Cheese Popcorn—Sprinkle **salt** and ¹/₂ cup (2 ounces) grated sharp **Cheddar** or **Parmesan cheese** over 1 quart hot buttered **popped corn.**

Dried Beef Tasters—Flavor **cream cheese** with a small

amount of **prepared horseradish.** Roll into small balls. Then roll and press balls in minced **dried beef.** Insert picks.

Olive Teasers—Coat large **stuffed olives** with softened **cream cheese.** Roll in finely chopped **nuts.** Chill in refrigerator; insert picks.

Stuffed Celery Spears—Blend together softened **cream cheese** and **milk.** Mix in a few grains **celery salt,** few drops **Worcestershire sauce** and very finely chopped **radish** and **green pepper** or **pimiento** and **parsley.** Stuff cleaned **celery** with the cheese mixture.

Apple Sandwiches—Wash and core but do not pare small **apples.** Cut crosswise into thin slices, forming rings. Dip in **lemon, orange** or **pineapple juice** to prevent darkening. Spread **peanut butter** or a **cheese spread** on one ring; top with a second ring. Cut into thirds.

Fruit and Ham "Kabobs"—Alternate cubes of cooked **ham** or canned **luncheon meat** on picks with seedless **grapes** or cubes of **melon** or **pineapple.**

Stuffed Prunes or Dates—Pit and dry plump soaked **prunes** and pit **dates.** Stuff with a tangy **cheese spread.** If desired, add chopped **nuts,** drained **crushed pineapple** or chopped **maraschino cherries** to cheese.

Ham Appetizer

SERVES 4

2 tablespoons finely chopped green pepper	mustard
	2 teaspoons lemon juice
2 tablespoons finely chopped celery	2 teaspoons olive oil
	4 slices cooked ham
2 tablespoons finely chopped pimiento	Stuffed olives or gherkins for garnish
¼ teaspoon Dijon	

1. Mix the green pepper, celery, and pimiento together.
2. Mix the mustard with the lemon juice and oil. Add salt and pepper to taste. Pour over the vegetables, and mix well.
3. Divide equally between the four slices of ham, fold over and secure with wooden picks.
4. Arrange on a serving dish, and garnish with stuffed olives or gherkins cut into fan shapes.

SOUPS and SANDWICHES

Cream of Corn Soup

SERVES 4-6

3 tablespoons butter
1 onion, chopped
1 medium potato, finely sliced
1½ cups fresh or canned corn
3½ cups milk
1 bay leaf
3-4 sprigs of parsley
¼ teaspoon mace
1 chicken bouillon cube

Garnish:
4-6 tablespoons heavy cream
1 tablespoon chopped chives or parsley (or a sprinkling of paprika)
Fried bread croutons*

*Check index for recipe

1. Melt the butter and cook the onion and potato gently, covered, for 5 minutes, shaking the pan occasionally to prevent sticking. Add 1 cup of the corn. Stir well. Then add the milk, bay leaf, parsley, salt, pepper, and mace. Bring to simmering heat, add bouillon cube, and cook until vegetables are tender.
2. Put soup into electric blender and blend until smooth, or put through fine food mill.
3. Return soup to the pan with the remaining corn (which if fresh should be simmered until tender in salted water). Reheat soup until nearly boiling, and adjust seasoning.
4. Serve in soup cups with a spoonful of cream in each cup, a sprinkling of chopped chives, parsley, or paprika, and fried bread croutons.

Curried Corn Soup

SERVES 4-6

1. Using the recipe for Cream of Corn Soup *(see above)*, add 2 teaspoons of curry powder to the onion and potato mixture, and cook with those ingredients. If using canned corn use mixed corn and pimiento rather than plain corn.
2. Garnish the soup with paprika.

Creole Bouillabaisse

SERVES 6

1 pound red snapper fillets
1 pound redfish fillets
2 teaspoons minced parsley
1 teaspoon salt
¾ teaspoon thyme
½ teaspoon allspice
⅛ teaspoon pepper
2 bay leaves, finely crushed
1 clove garlic, finely minced or crushed in a garlic press
2 tablespoons olive oil

1 large onion, chopped
1 cup white wine
3 large ripe tomatoes, peeled and cut in ¼-inch slices
3 or 4 lemon slices
1 cup hot Fish Stock (see below) or hot water
¾ teaspoon salt
⅛ teaspoon pepper
Dash cayenne pepper
Pinch of saffron
6 slices buttered, toasted bread

1. Thoroughly rub into fish fillets a mixture of parsley, salt, thyme, allspice, pepper, bay leaf, and garlic. Set fillets aside.
2. Heat olive oil in a large skillet over low heat; add onion and fillets. Cover and cook over low heat 10 minutes, turning fillets once.
3. Remove fish fillets from skillet; set aside and keep warm. Pour wine into skillet, stirring well; add tomato slices and bring to boiling. Add lemon slices, hot fish stock, salt, pepper, and cayenne pepper. Simmer about 25 minutes, or until liquid is reduced by almost one half.
4. Add fish fillets to skillet and continue cooking 5 minutes longer.
5. Meanwhile, blend several tablespoons of the liquid in which the fish is cooking with saffron. When fish has cooked 5 minutes, spread saffron mixture over fillets. Remove fillets from liquid and place on buttered toast. Pour liquid over fish. Serve at once.

Fish Stock: Combine **1 quart water, 1 tablespoon salt,** and **1 pound fish trimmings** (head, bones, skin, and tail) in a large saucepan. Cover and simmer 30 minutes. Strain liquid and use as directed.

ABOUT 1 QUART STOCK

Curried Corn Soup.

18

Brussels Sprout Soup

SERVES ABOUT 20

4 packages (10 ounces each) frozen Brussels sprouts	2 teaspoons salt
	1/2 teaspoon pepper
7 bouillon cubes	1 package (10 ounces) frozen peas and carrots
5 cups boiling water	
8 slices bacon, diced	
2 cloves garlic, minced	1 teaspoon salt
6 cups milk	2 cups water
3/4 cup uncooked rice	2/3 cup shredded Parmesan cheese
1 teaspoon oregano leaves, crushed	Assorted crackers

1. Set out a large saucepot or Dutch oven and a saucepan.
2. Partially thaw frozen Brussels sprouts.
3. Make chicken broth by dissolving bouillon cubes in boiling water. Set aside.
4. Fry in saucepot or Dutch oven the bacon and garlic.
5. Add 3 cups of the broth to saucepot with milk, uncooked rice, and a mixture of oregano leaves, salt, and pepper.
6. Bring to boiling; reduce heat and simmer covered 15 minutes.
7. Add to saucepot the frozen peas and carrots. Bring to boiling; reduce heat and simmer about 10 minutes, or until vegetables are tender.
8. Meanwhile, coarsely chop the partially thawed Brussels sprouts. Combine in saucepan the remaining 2 cups of broth, salt, and 2 cups water.
9. Bring to boiling and add the chopped Brussels sprouts. Return to boiling and simmer uncovered 10 minutes, or until tender.
10. Add Brussels sprouts with their cooking liquid to rice mixture. Stir in shredded Parmesan cheese. Serve with assorted crackers.

Stromboli Sandwich

SERVES 6

1 pound ground beef	1/4 teaspoon oregano
2 tablespoons finely chopped onion	1/2 teaspoon garlic powder
1/2 cup tomato sauce	1/4 cup butter
1/2 cup ketchup	6 French rolls
2 tablespoons grated Parmesan cheese	6 slices Mozzarella cheese
1/2 teaspoon garlic salt	

1. In a 1 1/2-quart casserole, combine ground beef and onion. Cook 4 to 5 minutes, stirring halfway through cooking time. Spoon off drippings.
2. Stir in tomato sauce, ketchup, Parmesan cheese, garlic salt, and oregano. Cook, covered, 5 to 6 minutes, stirring halfway through cooking time.
3. In a 1-cup glass measure, combine garlic powder and butter; heat 30 seconds. Stir to blend. Pour melted butter evenly over inside of top half of each roll.
4. Divide meat mixture evenly and spread on bottom halves of rolls. Top with 1 slice Mozzarella, place tops on rolls, and wrap each in a napkin.
5. Cook as follows, rotating one-quarter turn halfway through cooking time: 30 to 45 seconds for 1 sandwich; 1 1/2 to 2 minutes for 3 sandwiches; and 3 to 4 minutes for 6 sandwiches.
6. Serve warm.

Tacos

SERVES 4

1 package taco shells (8), dried or frozen	1/2 cup lettuce, shredded
1 pound ground beef	1/4 cup Cheddar cheese, grated
1/4 cup water	
1 package taco seasoning	1 tablespoon hot sauce (optional)
1/2 tablespoon vegetable oil	

1. In a skillet heat the oil and add the ground beef, crumbled, along with the packaged seasoning and water.
2. Let the beef brown over low heat, stirring occasionally, about 15 minutes.
3. Heat the taco shells in a warm oven for 3-4 minutes; remove and fill the base with about 2 tablespoons meat.
4. Top the meat with the shredded lettuce, then sprinkle with some grated Cheddar cheese. If desired, add a few drops of hot sauce. Serve immediately.

Note: Tacos can also be served filled with meat and shredded lettuce on the side.

Tacos.

Scotch Broth.

Scotch Broth

SERVES 6-8

3-4 tablespoons pearl barley	3 carrots, one sliced for the soup, 2 diced for garnish
1¹/₂-2 pounds neck or breast of mutton or lamb	4 stalks celery, 2 whole for the soup, 2 diced for garnish
6-8 cups water	
1 teaspoon salt	¹/₂ small turnip, diced for garnish
¹/₄ teaspoon pepper	
1 bay leaf	1 leek, sliced for garnish
2 large onions, one to add whole, the other diced for garnish	2 tablespoons chopped parsley
1 clove	

1. Soak barley for several hours, preferably overnight, in cold water.

2. Remove as much fat as possible from the lamb or mutton and put into a soup pot with the water and the drained barley. Add salt and pepper, the bay leaf, herbs, a whole onion stuck with a clove, a sliced carrot, and 2 stalks of celery. Bring slowly to a boil and simmer for 1¹/₂ hours, skimming off the fat and scum occasionally.

3. If time allows let soup cool and skim off fat; if not, skim carefully while hot, removing the bay leaf and celery and carrot as far as possible.

4. Add the diced vegetables and cook for 20-30 minutes or until they are tender. Adjust seasoning of soup, and if too much liquid has evaporated add a little extra to make up quantity. Remove the bones, leaving the meat in the soup. Reheat and serve hot, sprinkled with chopped parsley.

Volhynian Beet Soup

ABOUT 2¹/₂ QUARTS

¹/₄ cup dried navy or pea beans	1 can (16 ounces) tomatoes (undrained)
2 cups water	1 small head cabbage (about 1¹/₂ pounds)
2 cups Bread Kvas (below)	1 small sour apple
2 cups meat broth, bouillon, or meat stock	Salt and pepper
	1 tablespoon butter (optional)
6 medium beets, cooked and peeled	Sour cream

1. Bring beans and water just to boiling in a large kettle. Remove from heat. Let stand 1 hour. Then boil for 20 minutes, or until beans are tender. Add kvas and meat broth.
2. Slice beets. Mash tomatoes or make a purée by pressing through a sieve or using an electric blender. Add beets and tomatoes to beans.
3. Cut cabbage into sixths; remove core. Pare apple, if desired; core and dice. Add cabbage and apple to beans.
4. Season to taste with salt and pepper. Stir in butter, if desired. Cook soup over medium heat 30 minutes.
5. To serve, spoon a small amount of sour cream into each bowl. Ladle in hot soup and stir.

Bread Kvas

ABOUT 3 CUPS

1 quart hot water	1 rye bread crust
1 pound beets, pared and sliced	

1. Pour hot water over beets in a casserole. Add bread. Cover with a cloth. Let stand 3 to 4 days.
2. Drain off clear juice and use as a base for soup.

Quick Canned Soup with a Zest

SERVES 2

1 can (10¹/₂ ounces) condensed meat and vegetable soup, any flavor	²/₃ cup beer
	²/₃ cup water

Combine ingredients in a saucepan; heat to simmering. Simmer 2 to 3 minutes.

Mixed Vegetable Soup

SERVES 4

3 cups beef broth or 3 beef bouillon cubes dissolved in 3 cups boiling water	¹/₂ cup shredded cabbage or ¹/₂ cup sliced zucchini
1 small potato, diced	¹/₂ teaspoon Beau Monde seasoning or seasoned salt
2 carrots, diced	
1 tomato, chopped	1 tablespoon minced parsley
1 green onion, sliced	

1. Combine broth, potato, and carrot in a saucepan; bring to boiling. Simmer 30 minutes.
2. Add remaining ingredients; cook 5 minutes, or until cabbage is crisp-tender.

Four Seasons Pizza

SERVES 2

Dough:	6 ounces Bayonne ham
1 cup flour	¹/₂ red pepper
2 ounces tepid water	¹/₂ green pepper
1 ounce yeast	1 small yellow onion
1 tablespoon salad oil	10 black or pimiento-stuffed olives
Filling:	
2 tablespoons tomato purée or chili sauce	1 can anchovies
	1 tomato
6 ounces shrimp and 1 can mussels	7 ounces Porte Salut cheese
6 ounces fresh mushrooms	1 teaspoon oregano

1. Stir the yeast with some of the water in a bowl. Stir in the rest of the water, flour, and oil and make a smooth dough, working it with a wooden fork until the dough is so firm that it lets go of the bowl. Let the dough rise in the bowl to double its size.
2. Meanwhile prepare the fillings. Shell and devein the shrimp and drain the mussels. Slice the mushrooms and cut the ham in strips.
3. Slice and cut the peppers in small pieces. Chop the onion and slice the olives. Slice the tomato, divide the anchovies in small pieces, and cut the cheese in thin slices.
4. Flatten the dough on an oiled baking sheet into one large or two smaller round pies about 1-inch thick.
5. Spread on the tomato purée or chili sauce and divide the surface into 4 parts.
6. Cover each part with a different filling. Crumble oregano all over the pizza and cover with several layers of cheese slices. Bake in a 450°F oven for about 15 minutes.

Four Seasons Pizza.

Apple Chicken Soup.

Pioneer Potato Soup

SERVES 4-6

1 quart chicken stock	**half**
4 potatoes, chopped	**2 tablespoons flour**
(about 4 cups)	*Garnishes:*
2 cups sliced carrots	**Paprika, sliced green**
$^1/_2$ cup sliced celery	**onions, crisply**
$^1/_4$ chopped onion	**cooked crumbled**
1 teaspoon salt	**bacon, chopped**
$^1/_2$ teaspoon marjoram,	**pimiento, snipped**
dill weed, or cumin	**chives or parsley, or**
$^1/_8$ teaspoon white	**grated Parmesan**
pepper	**cheese**
1 cup milk or half-and-	

1. Combine all ingredients except milk, flour, and garnishes in a large saucepan. Bring to boiling; simmer 30 minutes.
2. Gradually add milk to flour, stirring until smooth. Stir into soup.
3. Bring soup to boiling; boil 1 minute, stirring constantly.
4. Garnish as desired.

Potato Soup with Sour Cream: Follow recipe for Pioneer Potato Soup. Before serving, stir in $^1/_2$ **cup sour cream.** Heat; do not boil.

Puréed Potato Soup: Follow recipe for either Pioneer Potato or Potato Soup with Sour Cream, omitting the flour. Purée in an electric blender before serving. Reheat, if necessary.

Apple Chicken Soup

SERVES 4

4-5 apples	**1 tablespoon flour**
2 tablespoons lemon	**2 egg yolks**
juice	**1 cup heavy cream**
1$^1/_2$ tablespoons butter	**Pepper to taste**
1 onion	**Salt to taste**
1 teaspoon curry	*Garnish:*
2$^1/_2$ cups chicken stock	**Watercress**

1. Peel and dice apples. Pour the lemon juice over the apples.
2. Chop the onion and sauté in butter with apples.
3. Add the curry, stir and brown the apples. Sprinkle with flour and add stock. Let the soup cook over high heat for 10 minutes. Strain.

Jellied Gazpacho.

4. Whip the egg yolks with the heavy cream and add to the hot soup. Turn heat down and add pepper and salt to taste.

5. Cool soup and chill. Serve with watercress on top.

Jellied Gazpacho

SERVES 6-7

1 can (1 quart 14 ounces) tomato juice	dice
	¼ cup grated onion
2 envelopes unfla- vored gelatin	4 tablespoons olive oil
4 tomatoes, peeled, seeded, and chopped	4 tablespoons wine vinegar
	1 clove garlic, crushed
1 cucumber, peeled, seeded, and chopped	6-8 drops hot pepper sauce
	Freshly ground black pepper
½ green pepper, seeded and cut into	Salt

1. Heat the tomato juice, add the gelatin, stir until dissolved, and set aside to cool.

2 Combine the tomatoes, cucumber, green pepper, and onion and add to the tomato juice

3 Stir in the oil and vinegar, add garlic, hot pepper sauce, and salt and black pepper to taste Mix well and chill thoroughly, preferably overnight

4 Serve in small bowls set in beds of crushed ice

Cream of Turkey Soup

SERVES ABOUT 6

½ cup butter	3 cups turkey or chicken broth
6 tablespoons flour	
½ teaspoon salt	¾ cup coarsely chopped cooked turkey
Pinch black pepper	
2 cups half-and-half	

1 Heat butter in a saucepan Blend in flour, salt, and pepper Heat until bubbly

2 Gradually add half-and-half and 1 cup of broth, stirring constantly Bring to boiling, cook and stir 1 to 2 minutes

3 Blend in remaining broth and turkey Heat, do not boil Garnish with grated carrot

Creole Soup

SERVES 4

3 tablespoons butter, oil, or bacon fat	Pinch of Cayenne pepper
1/2 cup chopped green and red peppers	1/4 teaspoon paprika
1 onion, chopped	1/4 teaspoon sugar
2 tablespoons flour	1 teaspoon vinegar
2 teaspoons tomato purée	2-3 teaspoons grated fresh horseradish (or 1 teaspoon dried horseradish)
4 large ripe tomatoes (or 3/4 cup canned tomatoes)	*Garnish:*
4 cups Beef Stock*	1 tablespoon chopped parsley
1 bay leaf, 4 sprigs of parsley, 1 sprig of thyme, tied together	Garlic croutons*
	*Check index for recipe

1. Melt butter, oil, or bacon fat. Cook the peppers and onions gently for 5-6 minutes without browning. Stir in flour and blend well; add tomato purée, chopped, de-seeded fresh or canned tomatoes, stock, bay leaf, herbs, and seasoning. Bring to a boil, stirring constantly. Then reduce heat and simmer for 25-30 minutes.
2. Remove the bay leaf and herbs and adjust seasoning. Add freshly grated or dried horseradish and vinegar. If soup is not a good enough color a little more tomato purée can now be added. Serve hot, sprinkled with chopped parsley and garlic croutons.

Frankfurter Reuben

SERVES 6

12 slices rye bread	1 cup sauerkraut, well drained
Butter	6 slices Swiss cheese
6 large frankfurters	
1/3 cup Thousand Island dressing	

1. Toast bread, and butter each piece on 1 side. Split frankfurters in half lengthwise and place on buttered side of 6 slices toast. Spread dressing on frankfurters, and top each sandwich with about 2 tablespoons sauerkraut. Top each with remaining bread slice, buttered side toward cheese.
2. Cook as follows, rotating one-quarter turn halfway through cooking time: 45 to 60 seconds for 1 sandwich; 2 to 2 1/2 minutes for 3 sandwiches; and 3 to 4 minutes for 6 sandwiches.
3. Serve warm.

Baked Minestrone

SERVES 10-12

1 1/2 pounds lean beef for stew, cut in 1-inch cubes	seasoning
1 cup coarsely chopped onion	1 can (16 ounces) tomatoes (undrained)
2 cloves garlic, crushed	1 can (15 1/4 ounces) kidney beans (undrained)
1 teaspoon salt	1 1/2 cups thinly sliced carrots
1/4 teaspoon pepper	1 cup small seashell macaroni
2 tablespoons olive oil	2 cups sliced zucchini
3 cans (about 10 ounces each) condensed beef broth	Grated Parmesan cheese
2 soup cans water	
1 1/2 teaspoons herb	

1. Mix beef, onion, garlic, salt, and pepper in a large saucepan. Add olive oil and stir to coat meat evenly.
2. Bake at 400°F 30 minutes, or until meat is browned, stirring occasionally.
3. Turn oven control to 350°F. Add broth, water, and seasonings; stir. Cover; cook 1 hour, or until meat is tender.
4. Stir in tomatoes, kidney beans, olives, carrots, and macaroni. Put sliced zucchini on top. Cover; bake 30 to 40 minutes, or until carrots are tender.
5. Serve with grated cheese.

Minestrone

SERVES ABOUT 6

6 cups water	1 medium potato, pared and diced
1 1/4 cups (about 1/2 pound) dried navy beans, rinsed	1 tablespoon chopped parsley
1/4 pound salt pork	1/2 teaspoon salt
3 tablespoons olive oil	1/4 teaspoon pepper
1 small onion, chopped	1 quart hot water
1 clove garlic, chopped	1/4 cup package pre-cooked rice
1/4 head cabbage	1/2 cup frozen green peas
2 stalks celery, cut in 1/2-inch slices	1/4 cup tomato paste
2 small carrots, pared and cut in 1/2-inch slices	Grated Parmesan cheese

1. Bring the 6 cups water to boiling in a large saucepot. Gradually add the beans to the boiling water so the boiling does not stop. Simmer the beans 2 minutes, and remove from heat. Set aside to soak 1 hour.
2. Add salt pork to beans and return to heat. Bring to

(continued)

Creole Soup.

boiling, reduce heat, and simmer 1 hour, stirring once or twice.

3. While beans are simmering with salt pork, heat the olive oil in a skillet, and brown the onion and garlic lightly. Set aside.

4. Wash the cabbage, discarding coarse outer leaves, and shred finely.

5. After the beans have simmered an hour, add the onion, garlic, celery, carrots, potato, cabbage, parsley, salt, and pepper. Slowly pour in 1 quart hot water and simmer about 1 hour, or until the beans are tender.

6. Meanwhile, cook the rice according to package directions. About 10 minutes before the beans should be done, stir in the rice and peas. When the peas are tender, stir in the tomato paste. Simmer about 5 minutes. Serve sprinkled with cheese.

Roman Egg Soup with Noodles

SERVES 4

4 cups chicken broth	**¹⁄₈ teaspoon salt**
1¹⁄₂ tablespoons semolina or flour	**¹⁄₈ teaspoon pepper**
1¹⁄₂ tablespoons grated Parmesan cheese	**4 eggs, well beaten**
	1 cup cooked noodles
	Snipped parsley

1. Bring chicken broth to boiling.

2. Meanwhile, mix semolina, cheese, salt, and pepper

together. Add to beaten eggs and beat until combined.

3. Add noodles to boiling broth, then gradually add egg mixture, stirring constantly. Continue stirring and simmer 5 minutes.

4. Serve topped with parsley.

Roman Egg Soup with Spinach: Follow recipe for Roman Egg Soup with Noodles; omit noodles. Add ¹⁄₂ **pound chopped cooked fresh spinach** to broth before adding egg mixture.

French Onion Soup

SERVES 4-6

3-4 tablespoons butter	**3-4 sprigs of parsley**
4-5 medium onions, peeled and finely sliced	**1 sprig of thyme**
	Pinch of nutmeg
1-2 cloves garlic, crushed	**4-6 slices French bread (long flute or yard of bread type)**
¹⁄₂ teaspoon sugar	
2 tablespoons flour	**4-6 tablespoons grated mixed Gruyère or Emmentaler and Parmesan cheese or other strong hard cheese**
5 cups water	
¹⁄₂ cup white wine (optional)	
1 bay leaf	

1. Melt the butter; add the onions and garlic and a

French Onion Soup.

Chicken and Curry Mayonnaise Sandwich.

sprinkling of sugar. Brown slowly, stirring constantly to prevent burning. Sprinkle in the flour and brown this slightly. Add the water, and the wine if using; otherwise add an equivalent amount of water. Bring to a boil, stirring constantly. Add herbs and seasoning and simmer for 20-30 minutes.

2. Meanwhile, cut the French bread into slices and put into the oven to dry and brown slightly.

3. Remove bay leaf from soup. Put the slices of bread into ovenproof soup bowls or a large tureen. Pour the soup over the bread, sprinkle thickly with cheese, and put into a hot oven for 15-20 minutes or under broiler for 7-10 minutes to brown the cheese.

Chicken & Curry Mayonnaise Sandwich

SERVES 1

¼ pound chicken, cooked	½ teaspoon mustard
2 tablespoons mayonnaise	½ teaspoon curry
	Sliced pineapple
1 tablespoon sour cream	1 slice dark bread or toast
	2 olives, sliced

1. Slice chicken.

2. Mix mayonnaise and sour cream with mustard and curry. Spread on bread.

3. Place chicken, pineapple, and olives on top.

Norwegian Fruit Soup

ABOUT 3½ CUPS SOUP

1 quart water	fruit syrup
2 tablespoons rice	¼ cup lemon juice
½ cup finely chopped apple	2-inch piece stick cinnamon
1 cup pitted dark sweet cherries and juice	1 tablespoon cold water
½ cup red raspberry	1 teaspoon cornstarch

1. Bring 1 quart water to boiling in a deep saucepan.

2. Add 2 tablespoons rice to water so boiling does not stop. Boil rapidly, uncovered, 15 to 20 minutes, or until a kernel is entirely soft when pressed between fingers. Drain rice, reserving liquid.

3. Rinse and finely chop enough apple to yield ½ cup.

4. Put cherries into a bowl.

5. Add fruit syrup and lemon juice.

6. Return the rice water to the saucepan. Add the apple and cinnamon stick.

7. Cook over medium heat 4 to 5 minutes, or until apple is tender. Add the drained rice and the cherry mixture. Remove the cinnamon. Simmer 5 minutes.

8. Blend together cold water and cornstarch to form a smooth paste.

9. Blend cornstarch mixture into soup. Bring to boiling. Continue to cook 3 to 5 minutes. Cool soup slightly.

10. Serve soup warm or cold. If serving soup cold, garnish with **whipped cream.**

Raisin Fruit Soup: Follow recipe for Norwegian Fruit Soup. Omit cherries. Increase red raspberry syrup to 1 cup. Add to the syrup mixture 1 cup (about 5 ounces) dark seedless **raisins.**

Open Shrimp Sandwich au Gratin.

Shellfish Soup-Provençale.

Hot Seafood Hero Sandwich.

Open Shrimp Sandwich au Gratin

SERVES 1

1 slice white bread	3 tablespoons Cheddar
1 teaspoon butter	cheese, coarsely
1/3 pound shrimp, cooked	grated
1 tablespoon mayonnaise	*Garnish:*
2 teaspoons cod roe	Shrimps
2 teaspoons chopped dill	Chopped parsley

1. Spread butter on the bread slice and add the cooked shrimp.
2. Stir the mayonnaise with the cod roe and spread it on. Sprinkle with the grated cheese.
3. Bake in a 350°F oven for about 8 minutes. Garnish with shelled and deveined shrimps and chopped parsley.

Shellfish Soup Provençal

SERVES 8

4 tablespoons salad oil	1 pound shrimp
1/2 leek, chopped	1 pound halibut
1 yellow onion, chopped	2 quarts water
2 cloves garlic, crushed	2 bottles (8 ounces)
1/4 teaspoon saffron	clam juice
1 pound can peeled	1 teaspoon oregano
tomatoes	1/2 teaspoon thyme
1 pound mussels,	Juice of 1/2 lemon
cleaned	1/3 cup white wine

1. Cut the halibut into 1-inch cubes. Salt lightly.
2. Shell the shrimp and boil the shells in 2 quarts water for about 8 minutes.
3. Heat the oil in a thick casserole, add saffron, leek, onion, and garlic. Sauté lightly without allowing to change color.
4. Pour in the tomatoes with their liquid, strained shrimp liquid, and seasonings. Let simmer covered for 15 minutes.
5. Add the halibut and simmer for 2 minutes. Add mussels and shrimp and cook for an additional 5 minutes.

Tortilla Sandwiches

12 SANDWICHES

12 corn tortillas	6 slices Monterey Jack
Salad oil	cheese

1. Fry tortillas in small amount of hot oil on range until

Peapod Soup.

limp. Fold in half and hold slightly open with tongs; continue to fry until crisp, turning to fry on both sides. Drain on paper towel.

2. Place ¹/₂ slice cheese in each tortilla. Arrange tortillas in shallow glass dish in microwave and cook 1 to 1¹/₂ minutes, rotating dish one-quarter turn halfway through cooking time.

3. Serve hot; reheat if needed.

Hot Seafood Hero Sandwich

SERVES 4

1 long loaf French or Italian bread	1 pound shrimp
Filling:	1 can mussels
5 tablespoons butter	1 small can peas
5 tablespoons all-purpose flour	³/₄ teaspoon salt
	¹/₄ teaspoon pepper
2 cups milk	¹/₄ cup grated Monterey Jack cheese

1. Cut top off a loaf of French bread and scoop out most of dough.

2. Clean and devein shrimp and cook for 5 minutes in boiling water. Cool.

3. Mix together all filling ingredients and stuff bread.

4. Sprinkle bread with grated cheese and bake in a 450°F oven till cheese has melted, about 10 minutes. Cut into slices and serve with a green salad.

Pea Pod Soup

SERVES 4

2 pounds peapods	2 tablespoons margarine
1 onion, peeled and sliced	1¹/₂ tablespoons flour
2-3 sprigs mint	Sugar
2-3 sprigs parsley	4 tablespoons cooked green peas (optional)
4 cups stock or 2 bouillon cubes and 4 cups water	Chopped mint

1. Wash the pods and put into a large kettle with the onion, mint, parsley, and stock. Bring to a boil, cover, and simmer for about 40 minutes.

2. When the outer flesh of the pods is tender, rub all through a sieve.

3. Melt the margarine in a pan, stir in the flour, and cook for 2 minutes. Add the purée and stir until boiling. Add salt, pepper, and sugar to taste.

4. Add peas, and serve sprinkled with a little chopped mint.

31

Ham-Bean Soup

ABOUT 4 QUARTS SOUP

2 quarts water	1 ham shank (about
1 pound (about 2 cups)	4 pounds) or 2 ham
dried Great North-	hocks (about 1½
ern or pea beans	pounds)
3 tablespoons butter	1 can (about 16 ounces)
2 cups finely chopped	tomatoes or 4 to 6
onion	medium-sized firm
½ cup finely chopped	ripe tomatoes, peeled
celery	and chopped
2 teaspoons finely	2 whole cloves
chopped garlic	1 bay leaf
3 cans (about 10 ounces	¼ teaspoon freshly
each) condensed	ground black pepper
chicken broth	2 cups shredded Cheddar
Water	cheese (about 8 ounces)

1. Bring water to boiling in a 6-quart saucepot. Add beans gradually to water so that boiling continues. Boil 2 minutes. Remove from heat and set aside 1 hour.
2. Drain beans, reserving liquid. Return beans to saucepot along with 4 cups of cooking liquid.
3. Melt butter in a large skillet. Add onion, celery, and garlic; cook 5 minutes, stirring occasionally. Turn contents of skillet into saucepot.
4. Combine chicken broth with enough water to make 6 cups. Pour into saucepot.
5. Peel skin from ham shank and cut off excess fat. Add shank and skin to saucepot along with tomatoes, cloves, bay leaf, and pepper. Bring to boiling, reduce heat, and simmer 2 to 2½ hours, or until ham is tender.
6. Remove ham shank and skin; cool. Transfer soup to a large bowl; remove bay leaf and cloves. Cut meat into pieces and return to soup. Refrigerate, then skim off fat.
7. Transfer soup to saucepot and bring to simmer. Add cheese and stir until melted.

Note: Soup may be stored in the refrigerator and reheated, or cooled and poured into freezer containers and frozen. Thaw and reheat over low heat.

Soup Paysanne

SERVES 4-5

3 tablespoons bacon	3 cups stock or water
or other cooking fat	1 cup canned toma-
½ cup diced carrot	toes
½ cup diced onion	½ cup diced potato
½ cup diced celery	1 tablespoon chopped
½ cup diced turnip	parsley

1. Heat the fat in a large kettle and sauté the carrot, onion, celery, and turnip for about 5 minutes.

2. Add stock or water, tomatoes, potato, and a little seasoning. Cover and simmer for 35 minutes.
3. Add parsley and adjust the seasoning before serving.

Note: If you use a pressure cooker, put all the ingredients into the cooker and cook for 3 minutes at 15 pounds pressure.

Lettuce Soup

SERVES 3

2 tablespoons butter or	cored and coarsely
margarine	chopped
2 tablespoons flour	¼ cup thinly sliced
1 can (about 10 ounces)	celery
condensed chicken	1 tablespoon chopped
broth	watercress
1 soup can water	Salt and pepper
½ small head lettuce,	

1. Melt butter in a saucepot; stir in flour and cook until bubbly.
2. Gradually stir in chicken broth and water; bring to boiling, stirring constantly. Cook 1 minute.
3. Stir in lettuce, celery, and watercress. Season with salt and pepper to taste. Cook until vegetables are crisp-tender, about 5 minutes.

Farm-Style Leek Soup

SERVES 6, ABOUT 1½ CUPS EACH

2 large leeks (1 pound)	2 cups uncooked
with part of green	narrow or medium
tops, sliced	noodles (3 ounces)
2 medium onions, sliced	1 can or bottle
1 large garlic clove,	(12 ounces) beer
minced	1½ cups shredded
¼ cup butter or	semisoft cheese
margarine	(Muenster, brick,
4 cups chicken stock or	process, etc.)
bouillon	Salt and pepper

1. Cook leek, onion, and garlic in butter for 15 minutes, using low heat and stirring often.
2. Add stock. Cover and simmer 30 minutes.
3. Add noodles. Cover and simmer 15 minutes, or until noodles are tender.
4. Add beer; heat to simmering. Gradually add cheese, cooking slowly and stirring until melted. Season to taste with salt and pepper.

Soup Paysanne.

Shrimp Bisque

SERVES 4-6

2 pounds shrimp	dried parsley)
3 cups Chicken Stock*	A squeeze of lemon
3 tablespoons butter	juice
1 onion, sliced	$1/4$ teaspoon ground
1 carrot, sliced	mace
1 stalk celery, sliced	1 cup heavy cream
3 tablespoons rice	3 tablespoons brandy
1 bay leaf	or sherry
3-4 sprigs of parsley	*Check index for
(or 1 tablespoon	recipe

1. Remove the shells from the shrimp, and wash in cold water. Reserve $1/2$ cup shrimp for garnish. Put the shells into a pan with the stock, and simmer gently for 20 minutes.
2. Melt the butter, and cook the onion, carrot, and celery for 4-5 minutes to soften. Add the rice, the shrimp, roughly chopped, the herbs, lemon juice, and seasoning. Cook together for a minute. Then strain over the stock. Bring to a boil, and simmer for 20 minutes.
3. Remove the bay leaf. Put the soup into an electric blender and blend until smooth, or put through a fine food mill or sieve.
4. Return soup to pan, add the reserved $1/2$ cup of shrimp. Reheat and adjust seasoning. Add the heated cream, and just before serving add the brandy or sherry.

Meatball Soup

SERVES 8

1 pound ground beef	$1/2$ cup uncooked barley
1 onion, chopped	2 teaspoons salt
$1^{1/2}$ quarts water	$1/2$ teaspoon crushed
1 can (16 ounces)	thyme or basil
tomatoes	$1/4$ teaspoon garlic
3 potatoes, cubed	powder
2 carrots, sliced	$1/4$ teaspoon pepper
2 stalks celery, sliced	1 bay leaf
3 sprigs fresh parsley,	1 teaspoon
minced, or 2 table-	Worcestershire sauce
spoons dried	1 beef bouillon cube

1. Shape beef into tiny meatballs. Brown meatballs and

Shrimp Bisque.

Creamy Cucumber Soup.

onion in a large saucepan, or place in a shallow pan and brown in a 400°F oven. Drain off excess fat.

2. Add remaining ingredients. Bring to boiling, simmer 1½ hours, or until vegetables are tender.

Creamy Cucumber Soup

SERVES 4-6

2-3 medium cucumbers	**1 teaspoon chopped dill**
4-5 spring onions (or 3 shallots) chopped finely	**A little green coloring (if necessary)**
3 tablespoons butter	**2 egg yolks**
2 tablespoons flour	**½ cup heavy cream**
4 cups Chicken Stock*	*Garnish:*
¼ teaspoon mace	**2 teaspoons chopped dill**
A pinch of sugar	**Fried croutons**
1 tablespoon chopped parsley	***Check index for recipe**

1. Peel and quarter the cucumbers; remove and discard seeds. Cut into small dice. Reserve 4-5 ta-blespoons of cucumber dice to use as garnish: sprinkle these with salt, and let stand for 20 minutes before washing and draining. Melt the butter and cook the onions (or shallots) very gently for 5 minutes to soften without browning. Add the larger amount of cucumber dice and cook gently for 2-3 minutes, stirring frequently.

2. Sprinkle in flour, blend smoothly before adding stock. Bring to a boil, stirring constantly. Add herbs and seasonings, then simmer gently for 15 minutes or until vegetables are tender.

3. Put soup into electric blender and blend until smooth, or put through food mill. Return to pot and reheat. Add a little green coloring and adjust seasoning to taste.

4. Make liaison: mix the egg yolks and cream well, add a few spoonfuls of hot soup, and mix well before straining into soup, whisking constantly. Heat soup gently, but do not boil, as this causes the egg yolk to curdle.

5. Just before serving add the raw, drained cucumber dice, and sprinkle each soup cup with a little chopped dill. Serve with fried croutons.

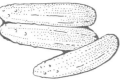

Yellow Pea Soup.

Chinese Cabbage Soup

SERVES 6

2 cups cooked chicken, cut into strips (about 1 chicken breast)	cabbage (celery cabbage)
7 cups chicken broth	1 teaspoon soy sauce
6 cups sliced Chinese	1 teaspoon salt
	$^1/_4$ teaspoon pepper

Combine chicken and chicken broth; bring to boiling. Stir in remaining ingredients; cook only 3 to 4 minutes, or just until cabbage is crisp-tender. (Do not overcook.)

Note: If desired, lettuce may be substituted for the Chinese cabbage. Reduce cooking time to 1 minute.

Yellow Pea Soup

SERVES 6-8

1 cup split yellow peas	sprigs of parsley, 1 sprig thyme, tied together
5 cups water	
1 ham bone	$^1/_2$-1 cup chopped ham
2 onions, sliced	
1 cup chopped celery or celeriac	2 tablespoons parsley
2 carrots, sliced	*Garnish:*
1 small potato, sliced	**Fried bread croutons (see end of soup section)**
1 bay leaf, several	

1. Wash and soak the split peas overnight if not using a quick-cooking variety. Drain and put into a pan, with 5 cups water, the ham bone, vegetables, bay leaf, parsley sprigs, and salt and pepper. Bring to a boil. Then simmer for $1^1/_2$-2 hours or until peas and vegetables are tender.

2. Remove the ham bone and herbs; put the soup into electric blender and blend until smooth. Measure soup and bring it up to the required quantity with water or stock. Taste and adjust seasoning. Reheat, adding the chopped ham.

3. Sprinkle with chopped parsley, and serve with fried croutons.

Creamed Onion Soup

SERVES 8

4 medium onions, sliced	cups boiling water
$^1/_2$ cup butter	1 to $1^1/_2$ teaspoons salt
$^1/_4$ cup flour	1 egg yolk
1 quart milk	1 tablespoon minced parsley
2 cups chicken broth or 2 chicken bouillon cubes dissolved in 2	$^1/_2$ cup croutons

1. In a 3-quart casserole, sauté onions in butter 4 to 5 minutes, stirring every minute. Stir in flour and cook until sauce bubbles, about 1 minute.

2. Add milk slowly, stirring gently. Cook until slightly thickened, about 6 to 8 minutes, stirring every 2 minutes.

3. Add broth and cook 5 minutes, stirring twice.

4. Stir in salt to taste. Blend some of the hot soup with egg yolk and return to remaining soup. Cook 1 minute, stirring every 15 seconds.

5. Serve topped with minced parsley and croutons.

Almond Cream Soup

SERVES 4

1 small potato, finely
 sliced
3-4 spring onions,
 finely sliced (or
 2-3 slices of ordi-
 nary onion)
3-4 stalks celery,
 finely sliced
3 cups Chicken Stock*
¹/₂-³/₄ cup almonds
1 small bay leaf
3-4 sprigs of parsley
2 tablespoons butter
1 tablespoon flour
A pinch of mace
4-5 tablespoons heavy
 cream
*Check index for
 recipe

1. Put the potato, onions, and celery in a pan with the stock, bay leaf, and sprigs of parsley. Simmer gently, covered, until the potato slices are tender.
2. Meanwhile, pour boiling water onto the almonds and let stand for a few minutes; then drain and pop almonds out of their skins. Reserve 10-12 whole almonds for garnish, and chop or finely grind the remainder. This can be done in an electric blender, but a little stock should be added to liquefy slightly. Add this paste to the pan, and cook for another 20 minutes.
3. Remove the bay leaf and sprigs of parsley. Pour soup into the electric blender and blend slowly until smooth. Strain through a fine sieve.
4. Melt the butter, add the flour, and stir until smooth. Add the strained soup slowly, stirring until smooth. Bring to a boil, stirring constantly. Add salt, pepper, and mace, being careful not to overpower the light almond flavor.
5. Cut the remaining almonds into slivers, brown lightly in a cool oven, and sprinkle with a little salt.
6. Add a spoonful of cream to each soup cup, and at the last moment sprinkle with the crisp brown almonds. The soup can also be served chilled.

Egg and Lemon Soup

SERVES 6

1¹/₂ quarts chicken
 stock (homemade or
 canned)
1¹/₂ cups uncooked
 parboiled rice
1 whole egg
3 egg yolks
Juice of 2 lemons
Salt and pepper to
 taste

1. Heat stock in a saucepan. Add rice and simmer, covered, until tender (about 20 minutes).

(continued)

Almond Cream Soup.

2. Beat egg and yolks until light. Beating constantly, slowly add lemon juice.

3. Measure 2 cups hot chicken stock and add, tablespoon by tablespoon, to egg mixture, beating constantly to prevent curdling. Add this mixture to the remaining hot chicken stock with rice. Season with salt and pepper.

4. Serve at once.

Chicken Stock

3 TO 3½ QUARTS

5 pounds chicken backs and wings, or stewing chicken, cut up	2 teaspoons salt
	Bouquet garni:
3 carrots, cut in 2-inch pieces	¾ teaspoon dried thyme leaves
2 medium yellow onions, quartered	¾ teaspoon dried rosemary leaves
1 stalk celery, cut in 2-inch pieces	1 bay leaf
	4 sprigs parsley
	2 whole cloves
	Water

1. Place chicken, vegetables, salt, and bouquet garni in an 8-quart Dutch oven. Pour in water to cover (about 4 quarts). Simmer covered 2 to 2½ hours.

2. Strain stock through a double thickness of cheesecloth into a storage container. Taste for seasoning. If more concentrated flavor is desired, return stock to saucepan and simmer 20 to 30 minutes, or dissolve 1 to 2 teaspoons instant chicken bouillon in the stock.

3. Store covered in refrigerator or freezer. Remove solidified fat from top of stock before using.

Note: Refrigerated stock is perishable. If not used within several days, heat to boiling, cool, and refrigerate or freeze to prevent spoilage. Stock can be kept frozen up to 4 months.

Beef Stock

2 TO 2½ QUARTS

1 pound lean beef stew cubes	1 stalk celery, cut in 2-inch pieces
1 pound lean veal stew cubes	1 garlic clove, minced
½ pound beef soup bones	1 teaspoon salt
3 carrots, cut in 2-inch pieces	*Bouquet garni:*
1 tomato, quartered and seeded	1 teaspoon dried thyme leaves
2 medium yellow onions, quartered	1 bay leaf
	2 sprigs parsley
	Water

1. Place meats, vegetables, garlic, salt, and bouquet garni in an 8-quart Dutch oven. Pour in water to cover

(about 3 quarts). Simmer covered 2 to 2½ hours. Cool slightly.

2. Strain stock through a double thickness of cheesecloth into a storage container. Taste for seasoning. If a more concentrated flavor is desired, return stock to saucepan and simmer 20 to 30 minutes, or dissolve **1 to 2 teaspoons instant beef bouillon** in the stock.

3. Store covered in refrigerator or freezer. Remove solidified fat from top of stock before using.

Note: Refrigerated stock is perishable. If not used within several days, heat to boiling, cool, and refrigerate or freeze to prevent spoilage. Stock can be kept frozen up to 4 months.

Fish Stock

ABOUT 1 QUART

2 pounds fresh lean fish with heads and bones, cut up	*Bouquet garni:*
	4 sprigs parsley
1 medium yellow onion, quartered	1 bay leaf
	½ teaspoon dried thyme leaves
½ teaspoon salt	1 sprig celery leaves
1 cup dry white wine	2 peppercorns
Water	

1. Rinse fish under cold water. Place fish, onion, salt, wine, and bouquet garni in a 3-quart saucepan. Pour in water to cover (about 1½ quarts). Simmer covered 2 hours. Cool slightly.

2. Strain stock through a double thickness of cheesecloth into a storage container. Taste for seasoning. Add a small amount of salt and lemon juice, if desired. If a more concentrated flavor is desired, return stock to saucepan and simmer 30 to 45 minutes.

3. Store covered in refrigerator or freezer.

Note: Use white firm-fleshed fish such as halibut, cod, flounder, or lemon sole. Frozen fish can be used if necessary.

Refrigerated stock is highly perishable. If not used within 2 days, heat to boiling, cool, and refrigerate or freeze to prevent spoilage. Stock can be kept frozen up to 2 months.

Brown Vegetable Stock

ABOUT 2 QUARTS STOCK

2 pounds mixed vegetables (carrots, leeks, onions, celery, turnips, etc.)	2½ quarts water
	½ teaspoon salt
	½ teaspoon thyme
	3 sprigs parsley
¼ cup butter or margarine	½ bay leaf
	Dash of pepper

1. Chop vegetables. Brown in butter.

Cabbage Soup.

2. Add water and seasonings. Cover.
3. Simmer 1½ hours or until vegetables are tender.
4. Strain and chill.

White Vegetable Stock: If a lighter, clearer stock is desired, omit butter and do not brown vegetables.

Cabbage Soup

SERVES 4-6

1 small green cabbage (or 2 cups of shredded green cabbage)	used, if not too salty)
1 large onion, chopped	2 tablespoons chopped parsley
2 small leeks, white part only, sliced	1 bay leaf
2 carrots, sliced	A pinch of nutmeg
1 potato, sliced	2 teaspoons chopped dill or 1 teaspoon dill seeds
2 slices fat bacon	*Garnish:*
1 tablespoon flour	3-4 frankfurters
4 cups brown stock (or water and bouillon cubes— ham stock can be	Fat for frying
	Fried bread and bacon croutons (see end of soup section)

1. Slice and wash the green cabbage, put into a pot of boiling salted water, and cook for 5 minutes. Then drain and rinse under cold water.
2. Meanwhile, chop the bacon and heat over gentle heat until the fat runs. Then add the onion, leeks, carrots, and potato and stir over heat for a few minutes. Sprinkle in flour, and blend well before adding stock (or water and bouillon cubes). Add parsley, bay leaf, salt, and pepper. Bring to a boil. Then reduce heat, and simmer for 10 minutes before adding cabbage. Cook for 20 minutes more, or until the vegetables are tender but not mushy.
3. Adjust seasoning, and add nutmeg and chopped dill, or a few dill seeds. Remove bay leaf.
4. For garnish, either fry frankfurters and cut in slices, putting a few slices into each serving, or prepare fried bread and bacon croutons to serve separately.

Beef Sub Gum Soup

SERVES ABOUT 6

½ pound beef round, cut into small cubes	each) condensed beef broth or bouillon
1 tablespoon cooking oil	2 cups water
1 can (20 ounces) Chinese vegetables, drained	¼ cup uncooked rice
	2 tablespoons soy sauce
	⅛ teaspoon pepper
2 cans (10½ ounces	1 egg, beaten

1. In a large wok, brown beef in hot oil. Chop vegetables and add to the browned meat with remaining ingredients, except egg.
2. Bring soup to boiling, stirring to blend. Cover and simmer 40 minutes.
3. Remove soup from heat and slowly stir in the egg. Let stand until egg is set.

Watercress Soup

SERVES 4-6

2 bunches fresh
  watercress
3 tablespoons butter
1 potato, sliced
1 small onion, finely
  chopped
1 tablespoon flour
3 cups white or
  chicken stock (or
  water)
3-4 sprigs of parsley
1 bay leaf

2 cups milk
¼ teaspoon mace
A little green coloring
  (optional)
Garnish:
Watercress sprigs
4-6 tablespoons
  cream
Fried bread croutons
  (see end of soup
  section)

1. Wash and pick over the watercress, discarding any yellow leaves. Reserve enough green top-sprigs to make the final garnish, and chop the remaining cress roughly. Melt the butter and cook the potato and onion together for 2-3 minutes before adding the chopped watercress. Continue cooking for 3-4 minutes, stirring constantly to prevent browning. Sprinkle in flour and blend well. Add stock and blend together before bringing to a boil. Add herbs and some seasoning, reduce heat, and simmer until the potato is tender, about 20 minutes.
2. Remove bay leaf. Put soup into electric blender and blend until smooth, or put through fine food mill or sieve. Return soup to pan and reheat gently. At the same time heat milk in a separate pan. When almost at boiling point, pour into watercress mixture—this makes texture of soup lighter and more delicate. Adjust seasoning, adding mace and a little green coloring if desired.
3. Serve with a spoon of cream in each cup and the reserved watercress sprigs on top. Fried bread croutons are also excellent with this soup.

Chili Soup

SERVES 8-10

½ pound ground beef
1 cup chopped onion
5 cups water
1 can (28 ounces)
  tomatoes
1 can (15 ounces)
  tomato sauce
1 clove garlic, crushed

1 tablespoon chili powder
1 teaspoon salt
1 teaspoon cumin
½ teaspoon oregano
1 cup uncooked
  macaroni
1 can (about 15 ounces)
  kidney or chili beans

1. Brown meat in a large saucepan; drain off fat. Stir in onion; cook 1 minute.
2. Add water, tomatoes, tomato sauce, garlic, chili powder, salt, cumin, and oregano. Simmer 30 minutes.
3. Add remaining ingredients; cook until macaroni is done (about 10 to 15 minutes).

Watercress Soup.

Mock Bouillabaisse.

Mock Bouillabaisse

SERVES 6-8

½ cup olive oil
2 medium onions, chopped
2 leeks, chopped
2 carrots, chopped
1-2 cloves of garlic, crushed
2 pounds mixed fish: red snapper, flounder, whiting, halibut, perch, red mullet, haddock, eel
4 ripe tomatoes (or ½ cup canned tomatoes)
1 bay leaf
1 tablespoon chopped fennel
A pinch of saffron soaked in boiling water

1 sprig of thyme
4-5 parsley stalks chopped
2-3 thinly peeled pieces of orange zest
2-3 cups fish stock or water
¾-1 cup shrimp, clams, and lobster meat
1 teaspoon lemon juice
1 cup white wine
6-8 slices of French bread
Garnish:
2 tablespoons butter
1 clove garlic, crushed
2 tablespoons chopped parsley

1. Heat the oil in a large pan. Add the onions, leeks, carrots, and garlic. Cook slowly until golden brown, stirring frequently to prevent burning.
2. Add the fish, which should be boneless and cut into chunks. Add the peeled, chopped tomatoes (or canned tomatoes), bay leaf, fennel, saffron, thyme, parsley, orange zest, fish stock or water, salt, and pepper. Cover the pan, and cook for 15-20 minutes.
3. Then add the shellfish, leaving the shrimp whole but cutting the clam or lobster meat into chunks (canned minced clams and canned lobster meat can be used). Bring to a boil, and cook for 6-8 minutes. Then add lemon juice and wine. Reheat for a few more minutes, and adjust seasoning.
4. While the soup is cooking, cut the French bread into ½-inch slices and put into a warm oven to bake hard. Mix the softened butter with a crushed clove of garlic; add pepper and salt. Spread this paste onto the bread slices.
5. Put a slice of bread into the bottom of each soup cup or plate. Carefully spoon the pieces of fish and shellfish into the soup cups, dividing equally; then spoon over the broth. Sprinkle with chopped parsley and serve at once.

French Tomato Soup

SERVES 4-6

2 large onions, finely
   sliced
2 slices of bacon,
   chopped
1 tablespoon butter
4-6 ripe tomatoes (or
   1 cup canned
   tomatoes), chopped
1 tablespoon tomato
   purée
2-3 strips of lemon
   rind
4 cups Chicken Stock*

1 teaspoon sugar
1 tablespoon parsley
1/4 teaspoon thyme
1 teaspoon basil
Garnish:
1 tablespoon chopped
   mixed parsley and
   basil
Fried garlic croutons
   (see end of soup
   section)
*Check index for
   recipe

1. Heat the bacon pieces in a pan. When the fat has run, add the butter. When it has melted, add the onions and cook gently for 5-6 minutes until tender and golden brown. Add the tomatoes and tomato purée, lemon rind, stock, salt, pepper, sugar, and herbs. Bring to a boil. Then simmer for 20 minutes or until tomatoes are tender.
2. Put soup through a food mill or blend in electric blender. Adjust seasoning and serve hot, sprinkled with chopped parsley and basil and with fried garlic croutons.

Consommé Madrilene

SERVES 4-6

1 pound ripe toma-
   toes
5 cups well-flavored,
   clear jellied chicken
   stock
1 cup chopped lean
   beef
1/4 cup sherry (or
   white wine)
1 tablespoon parsley
1 teaspoon basil

A pinch of sugar
2 egg whites and
   shells of two eggs
Garnish:
1 large tomato, peeled
   and cut into strips,
   if hot
Lemon quarters and
   cheese straws (see
   end of soup section)

1. Chop the tomatoes and put into an enamel or heat-proof glass pan. Add well-flavored jellied chicken stock, which has been skimmed to remove fat. Add chopped lean raw beef, sherry or white wine, herbs, sugar, and seasoning.
2. Beat the egg whites until frothy but not stiff. Add to the soup pan with the finely crushed egg shells. Bring the soup very slowly to a boil, whisking thoroughly the whole time. When soup is just reaching boiling point and is rising up in the pan stop whisking, remove pan from heat to allow the egg white

French Tomato Soup.

Consommé Madrilene.

Canned Pea Soup with Bacon.

crust to subside, then leave pan on very low heat for 30-40 minutes.

3. Put a piece of clean cloth over a fine sieve and strain soup carefully, allowing the egg white crust to slide onto the cloth. Pour soup through this filter again, by which time it should be clear. Adjust seasoning.

4. Prepare garnish: Dip 1 large tomato into boiling water for the count of ten and then in cold water. Remove skin and seeds, and cut the tomato flesh into strips. Add to soup just before serving. If serving cold, let cool, and set in refrigerator. Then stir with a fork. Serve in chilled soup cups with lemon quarters and cheese straws.

Canned Pea Soup with Bacon

SERVES 4-6

1 can condensed pea soup or two cans ordinary pea soup	1 tablespoon chopped mint
1 can water or milk	*Garnish:*
2 slices bacon	Fried bread crou-
4 tablespoons cooked peas	tons*
4 tablespoons heavy cream	*Check index for recipe

1. Chop the bacon slices and cook gently until crisp. Add the pea soup and can of water or milk. Stir over gentle heat until smooth. Then add the cooked peas. Heat to boiling point.

2. Pour into heated soup cups and put a spoonful of heavy cream into the center of each one. Sprinkle with chopped mint and serve at once with fried bread croutons.

Cheese Straws

SERVES 4

½ cup of butter or 1 stick	can cheese
1 cup of all-purpose flour	¼ teaspoon dry mustard
1 cup grated Ameri-	Cayenne pepper and salt to taste

1. Cut the butter into the flour that has been sifted into a bowl. Blend well. Add the grated cheese, dry mustard, pepper, Cayenne pepper, and salt if necessary. Shape the paste into a ball, wrap well, and refrigerate for at least 10 minutes.

2. Roll out paste on a floured board and cut into strips or rounds. Bake in a hot oven (400°) for 6-10 minutes or until golden brown and crisp.

Fried Bread Croutons

SERVES 4

2 large slices white bread	1 tablespoon butter
Oil	Onion powder (as desired)

1. Remove crusts from slices of bread and cut the bread into small cubes. Heat enough oil in frying pan to come at least half way up the sides of the bread cubes while cooking. When the oil is hot, add the butter. When this has melted and is foaming, add all the bread cubes at once.

2. Cook over a moderate-to-hot flame and stir constantly to ensure that the cubes brown evenly. When golden brown, place on kitchen paper to drain. Remove from pan when slightly less brown than the final color you want, as they continue to cook for a few seconds, because of the hot oil.

3. Season with salt and pepper, and onion powder if this will improve the soup for which the croutons are intended. Keep hot and serve separately.

Bacon Croutons

SERVES 4

2 slices bacon	cubes
2 large slices white bread cut into	Oil
	Pepper

1. Remove rinds from bacon slices and chop the bacon finely. Put into a dry frying pan and cook slowly to extract fat, then cook until crisp and golden. Remove bacon bits and reserve.

2. Add enough oil to bacon fat to cook the diced bread in same way as fried bread croutons. When golden brown, remove and drain. Add the bacon bits with pepper and serve hot.

Garlic Croutons

SERVES 4

1 clove garlic or ¾ teaspoon dried or powdered garlic	3 slices white bread
	Oil
	Cayenne pepper

1. Crush the garlic. Cut the crusts off bread slices and cut into cubes. Heat the oil. When hot add the bread cubes and cook, stirring constantly. When cubes start to turn color add the garlic and mix well. When cubes are golden brown remove and drain.

2. Sprinkle with salt and pepper and a touch of Cayenne pepper, and serve hot.

MEAT

Beef

Standing Rib of Roast Beef

SERVES 8-10

3-rib (6 to 8 pounds) standing rib roast of beef (have butcher saw across ribs near backbone so it can be removed to make carving easier)	**1¹/₂ teaspoons salt** **¹/₈ teaspoon pepper**

1. Place roast, fat side up, in a shallow roasting pan. Season with a blend of salt and pepper. Insert meat thermometer so tip is slightly beyond center of thickest part of lean; be sure tip does not rest on bone or in fat.
2. Roast at 300° to 325°F, allowing 23 to 25 minutes per pound for rare; 27 to 30 minutes per pound for medium; and 32 to 35 minutes per pound for well-done meat. Roast is also done when meat thermometer registers 140°F for rare; 160°F for medium; and 170°F for well done.
3. Place roast on a warm serving platter. Remove thermometer.
4. For a special treat, serve with *Yorkshire Pudding,* below.

Note: A rib roast of beef may be one of three cuts. From the short loin end of the rib section, a first-rib roast is cut. This is mostly choice, tender "rib eye" meat. From the center rib section, the center-rib roast is cut. It has less "rib eye" meat than the first-rib roast and is usually somewhat less expensive. From the shoulder end of the rib section, the sixth-and-seventh rib roast is cut. It has the least "rib eye" meat and is likely to be least tender of the three. It usually is the least expensive. When purchasing a rib roast, buy not less than two ribs for a standing roast; for a rolled rib roast, buy a 4-pound roast.

Rolled Rib Roast of Beef: Follow recipe for Standing Rib Roast of Beef. Substitute **rolled beef rib roast** (5 to 7 pounds) for standing rib roast. Roast at 300°F, allowing 32 minutes per pound for rare; 38 minutes per pound for medium; and 48 minutes per pound for well-done meat.

Yorkshire Pudding: Pour ¹/₄ **cup hot drippings** from roast beef into an 11 x 7 x 1¹/₂-inch baking dish and keep hot. Add **1 cup milk, 1 cup sifted all-purpose flour,** and ¹/₂ **teaspoon salt** to **2 well-beaten eggs.**

Beat with hand rotary or electric beater until smooth. Pour into baking pan over hot drippings. Bake at 400°F 30 to 40 minutes, or until puffed and golden. Cut into squares and serve immediately.

Beef Roast

SERVES 10-12

5- to 6-pound beef roast (rib, rump, or chuck)

1. Place roast on roasting rack in a 2-quart glass baking dish. Shield protruding corners or bone ends with foil. Do not allow foil to touch inside walls of oven.
2. Cook, using the following times: for rare meat, 6 to 7 minutes per pound; for medium, 7 to 8 minutes per pound; and for well-done, 8 to 9 minutes per pound. Turn roast over and rotate the dish one-quarter turn halfway through cooking time.
3. Rest 10 to 15 minutes before carving and serving.

Old-World Short Ribs

SERVES 4

3 to 4 pounds beef short ribs	**1 teaspoon caraway seed**
2 tablespoons oil	**¹/₂ teaspoon salt**
1 medium onion, chopped	**¹/₈ teaspoon pepper**
1 can (8 ounces) tomato sauce	**1 bay leaf**
1 can or bottle (12 ounces) beer	**¹/₄ cup flour**
	2 to 3 cups cooked noodles

1. Brown ribs slowly in oil in a Dutch oven or deep skillet. Remove as they are browned.
2. Add onion and sauté until golden. Add tomato sauce, 1¹/₄ cups beer, and seasonings. Return ribs.
3. Cover and simmer 1¹/₂ hours, or until tender.
4. Place ribs on platter; keep warm. Skim fat from cooking liquid (there should be about 2 cups liquid). Stir in paste made from flour and remaining ¹/₄ cup beer. Cook, stirring constantly, until thickened. Serve gravy over ribs and noodles.

Cold Roast Beef Vinaigrette

SERVES 4-6

1½ pounds cooked medium-rare roast beef, sliced ¼ inch thick and cut in 2-inch-wide strips
3 stalks celery, cut in ¼-inch pieces
1 medium tomato, chopped
2 sweet red or green peppers, chopped in ¼-inch pieces
1 tablespoon finely chopped red onion
1 tablespoon olive oil
2 tablespoons wine vinegar
¼ cup Beef Stock*
2 teaspoons snipped fresh or 1 teaspoon dried basil leaves
1 teaspoon snipped

fresh or ½ teaspoon dried coriander leaves (cilantro)
1 tablespoon snipped parsley
1 teaspoon salt
¼ teaspoon freshly ground Szechuan or black pepper (See Note)
1 teaspoon snipped fresh or ½ teaspoon dried oregano leaves
2 garlic cloves, finely minced
2 teaspoons Dijon mustard
*Check index for recipe

1. Arrange beef in a shallow glass dish. Mix remaining ingredients and pour over meat. Refrigerate covered 8 hours or overnight.
2. Taste meat and marinade; adjust seasoning, if desired. Let stand at room temperature 45 minutes before serving. Serve beef slices topped with marinade.

Note: Lightly roast Szechuan pepper over medium heat in a skillet before grinding.

Swiss Steak Mozzarella

SERVES 8

2 pounds beef round steak, ½ inch thick
3 tablespoons flour
½ cup butter or margarine
1 can (16 ounces) tomatoes, cut up

1¼ teaspoons salt
¼ teaspoon basil
½ cup chopped green pepper
1½ cups mozzarella cheese

1. Cut meat into serving-size pieces; coat with flour.
2. Melt butter in a skillet. Brown meat slowly on both sides. Put into a 12 x 8-inch baking dish.
3. Combine tomatoes, salt, basil, and green pepper. Pour over meat.
4. Bake, covered, at 350°F 1 hour, or until meat is tender. Remove cover. Sprinkle with cheese and bake an additional 5 minutes, or until cheese is melted.

Teriyaki Steak

SERVES 4-6

2 to 2½ pounds beef chuck or sirloin steak
¾ teaspoon ginger
2 tablespoons sugar

¼ cup salad oil
¼ cup soy sauce
2 tablespoons sherry
1 clove garlic, minced

1. Slice meat diagonally into ⅛-inch-thick strips. Meat will slice easier if placed in the freezer 30 minutes.
2. In a 2-cup glass measure, combine ginger, sugar, oil, soy sauce, sherry, and garlic. Stir to blend. Pour over meat strips and marinate from 1 hour to overnight.
3. Preheat browning dish 5 minutes. Reserving marinade, remove meat from marinade and add to hot dish: fry 2 to 3 minutes, stirring after every minute. (See Note.)
4. Pour marinade over meat and cook 4 to 5 minutes more, stirring after every minute.
5. Serve hot over fluffy rice.

Note: If desired, meat may be browned in a conventional skillet on top of the range and then transferred to a 2-quart glass baking dish.

Fillet of Beef with Sour Cream Sauce

SERVES 6

3 pounds fillet of beef or eye round, rolled and tied securely at 1-inch intervals
½ pound onions, sliced
1 cup celery, diced
⅔ cup carrots, diced
1 cup parsnips, diced
¼ cup bacon, diced
8 peppercorns
4 whole allspice

2 bay leaves
Salt & pepper to taste
¼ teaspoon thyme
1 tablespoon butter, melted
2 cups beef or chicken stock

Sauce:
1 tablespoon lemon juice
2 cups sour cream
2 tablespoons flour

1. Place the beef in a 5-quart casserole. Add the next 10 ingredients. Dribble the melted butter evenly. Marinate for 24 hours.
2. Preheat oven to 450°F. Bake the meat, uncovered, in the middle of the oven for 25 minutes. Turn the meat once.
3. Lower the temperature to 350°F. Bring stock to a boil and pour over meat and bake the meat for 1 hour, turning occasionally.
4. Place meat on a platter and keep warm in a 200° oven while you make sauce.

Fillet of Beef with Sour Cream Sauce.

5. Strain the contents of the casserole through a sieve, pressing the vegetables with a wooden spoon. Return the stock to the casserole.

6. Bring the sauce to a simmer over medium heat.

7. In a mixing bowl, add 2 tablespoons of the sauce to the sour cream. Beat in the flour with a whisk. Stir the mixture into the casserole. Cook 3-4 minutes without boiling.

8. Add the lemon juice. Taste for seasoning. Serve the beef sliced and the sauce separately.

Beef Wellington

SERVES 6-8

3¹/₂- to 4-pound beef tenderloin	Pastry (prepared from pie crust mix or
Salt and pepper	Buttery Pastry, *below*)
1 can (2 to 3 ounces) liver pâté or spread	1 egg yolk, fork beaten 1 teaspoon water

1. Set beef on a rack in a shallow roasting pan. Roast at 425°F 25 minutes (medium rare). Remove from oven and cool completely.

2. Discard any fat on roast. Sprinkle with salt and pepper and spread with liver pâté.

3. Meanwhile, prepare pastry (enough for the equivalent of three 9-inch pie shells).

4. On a lightly floured surface, roll out pastry large enough to wrap around the roast.

5. Place meat on one edge of pastry and bring other edge over meat to cover completely; reserve extra pastry for decorations. Moisten edges with water and pinch together firmly. Place on a baking sheet. Cut out a few small holes on top to allow steam to escape.

6. Cut out decorative shapes from reserved pastry. Moisten underside of each with water and place on top. Brush entire surface of pastry with a mixture of egg yolk and water.

7. Bake at 425°F 30 to 35 minutes, or until pastry is golden.

8. Let stand 5 to 10 minutes before carving into thick slices.

For Buttery Pastry: Prepare pastry as directed in step 3, roll out on a lightly floured surface into an 18-inch square, and dot the center portion with slivers of **butter** (6 tablespoons). Fold so the two sides meet in center and seal by pressing edges with fingers. Fold ends to center and seal. Wrap and chill 20 minutes. Roll out as directed in step 4.

47

Seasoned Joint of Beef

SERVES 8

2¹/₂ pounds thick flank of beef	10 corns allspice
2 tablespoons butter	1¹/₄ tablespoon molasses
Salt	1 tablespoon vinegar
Pepper	*Sauce:*
2 cups beef stock*	¹/₂ cup heavy cream
2 yellow onions	1¹/₂ tablespoons flour
8 anchovy fillets (and anchovy liquid)	Soy sauce
1¹/₂ bay leaves	*Check index for recipe
8 white peppercorns	

1. Season the beef with salt and pepper and brown in a stewpan.
2. Heat beef stock and add to the beef. Add onions and the other ingredients. Braise the meat, covered, on low heat for about 2 hours in an oven at 350°F.
3. Baste the meat a few times and add more liquid if necessary.
4. Remove the beef and strain the gravy. Stir in cream and soy sauce. Thicken with flour; taste and correct seasoning. Serve with boiled potatoes, boiled vegetables, currant jelly, and pickled cucumber or preserved tomatoes.

Filets Mignons Rossini

SERVES 8

2¹/₂ pounds filet beef (cut into 1-1¹/₂ inch thick slices)	caps
	2 cups beef stock (or water and beef bouillon cube)
1 tablespoon shortening (or lard)	¹/₄ cup red wine
2 tablespoons chopped onions	1 teaspoon chopped parsley and thyme
1 slice bacon	1 cup butter
¹/₂ tablespoon flour	1 cup cooking oil
1 teaspoon tomato purée	8 slices white bread
8 large mushroom	1 can pâté de foie gras

Preheat oven to 350°F.
1. First make sauce: Melt shortening. Add onion and diced bacon. Cook to golden color slowly. Stir well, add flour, and cook until just turning light brown. Add tomato purée, chopped mushroom stems, stock, wine, salt, and pepper. Bring to boil and simmer for 15 minutes. Now add parsley and thyme and cook a few more minutes. Strain through fine sieve into dish ready to serve, and keep warm.
2. Put mushroom caps in a buttered dish, with a small pat of butter and salt and pepper on each. Cook in oven for 10 minutes.

Seasoned Joint of Beef.

Filets Mignons Rossini.

3. Cut bread into slices the same size as the filets. Heat oil and add 1 tablespoon of butter. When foaming, fry bread until golden brown on both sides. Drain and keep warm.

4. Melt ¹/₂ cup of butter in large frying pan. When foaming, cook filets 4-6 minutes each side, according to taste. (Or brush with melted butter and broil 5-8 minutes each side.)

5. Place filets on the fried bread. Top each with a slice of pâté and a mushroom. Garnish with watercress and serve with French fried potatoes and a green vegetable.

becue Baste occasionally during the last 30 minutes cooking time.

3. For a 3¹/₂- to 5-pound roast, allow 35 to 40 minutes per pound. For a 6- to 8-pound roast, allow 30 to 35 minutes per pound.

4. For easier carving, allow roast to "stand" in a warm place 15 to 20 minutes after removal from oven. Since roast usually continues to cook after removal from oven, it is best to remove it about 5°F below the temperature desired.

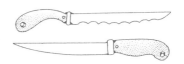

Beef Sirloin Tip Roast with Parmesan Barbecue Baste

SERVES 12-14

| 1 sirloin tip roast | Parmesan Barbecue |
| (3¹/₂ to 5 pounds) | Baste (below) |

1. Place roast, fat side up, in a shallow roasting pan. Insert meat thermometer so bulb is centered in the thickest part. Do not add water. Do not cover.

2. Roast at 325°F. Roast is done when meat thermometer registers 140°F for rare; 160°F for medium; and 170°F for well done. Brush with Parmesan Bar-

Parmesan Barbecue Baste

MAKES 1 CUP SAUCE

³/₄ cup ketchup	1 tablespoon Worces-
¹/₂ cup chopped onion	tershire sauce
¹/₄ cup water	
2 tablespoons Parme-	
san cheese	

Combine ketchup, onion, water, Parmesan cheese, and Worcestershire sauce in small saucepan. Cook slowly, for 5 to 10 minutes, stirring occasionally.

Steak Tartare.

Beef Stroganoff

SERVES 4

1-1½ pounds beef tenderloin	butter
1-2 onions	1 cup sour cream
8-10 medium-sized mushrooms	A grating nutmeg
	Salt
4-5 tablespoons	Pepper

1. Cut beef tenderloin into strips about 2½ inches long and ½ inch thick. Slice the onions and mushrooms finely. Melt 2 tablespoons of butter in a frying pan and cook the onions slowly until they are golden brown. Remove from pan and keep warm. Add a little more butter. Cook the mushrooms for about 5 minutes and add them to the onions.
2. Melt the remaining butter. When foaming put in about half the strips of steak and fry quickly for about 5 minutes, until they are brown on all sides. Remove and repeat with the remaining steak.

Beef Stroganoff.

3. Replace all meat and vegetables in the pan; shake over heat, adding salt, pepper, and nutmeg. Lastly, add the sour cream, heat until it nearly boils, and serve immediately with plain boiled rice.

Note: Do not start to cook this dish until you are ready to eat it. It can be cooked in a chafing dish at the table.

Steak Tartare

SERVES 4

1 pound extra finely ground beef	4 teaspoons ready mixed French mustard
1 can (4 ounces) capers	
2 yellow onions, chopped	4 raw egg yolks in their half-shells
4 teaspoons paprika	

1. Shape four round hamburgers of the ground beef and place each on a separate plate.
2. Arrange around each hamburger some chopped onion, drained capers, paprika, and mustard. Also add the egg yolks in their half-shells.

Serve with dark bread and butter and cool beer.

Roast Beef with Wine

SERVES ABOUT 8

1 beef rolled rump roast (5 pounds or more)	3/4 cup)
Salt and pepper	1 medium onion, quartered
2 garlic cloves, crushed in a garlic press	1/2 cup red wine
1 tablespoon oregano	1 package macaroni, cooked according to directions on package
2 tablespoons grated kefalotyri cheese	1 cup grated kefalotyri cheese
Chicken stock (about	

1. Sprinkle beef roast with salt and generously cover with pepper. Slit the meat with a small sharp knife in several places on a diagonal slant about 1 inch deep.
2. Mix garlic, oregano, and 2 tablespoons cheese. Fill each incision with some of this mixture. Pinch to close incision.
3. Place beef on a trivet in a roasting pan. Pour enough stock into the pan to barely reach top of trivet. Add the quartered onion.
4. Raost at 325°F until done to taste. (A meat thermometer will register 140°F for rare, 160°F for medium, and 170°F for well-done meat.)
5. During the last 15 minutes of roasting, pour in wine.
6. Remove meat to a platter. Keep warm. Remove fat from pan juices. Toss in cooked pasta. Sprinkle with remaining cheese. Serve hot.

Swiss Steak

SERVES 6-8

1 1/2 to 2 pounds beef round steak, cut in serving pieces and floured	1 soup can water
	Dash pepper
	1/4 teaspoon garlic powder
2 tablespoons salad oil	1 small onion, chopped
1 can (10 ounces) condensed cream of mushroom soup	1/2 cup chopped green pepper

1. Brown meat in hot oil on range in a conventional skillet or in microwave oven. To brown in microwave oven, preheat browning skillet 6 minutes. Pour oil in hot pan and cook meat 1 1/2 minutes, turn over, and cook for 1 minute. Place meat in a 2-quart glass casserole.
2. In a mixing bowl, blend soup with water, salt, pepper, and garlic powder. Pour over meat. Arrange onion and green pepper on top.

3. Cook, covered, 10 minutes; rest 5 minutes. Rotate dish one-quarter turn and cook 7 to 8 minutes; rest 5 minutes. Rotate dish one-quarter turn and cook 10 minutes.
4. Rest 10 minutes before serving.

Bachelor's Steak

SERVES 2

2 small single-serving steaks (rib, rib eye, strip, T-bone)	1/4 to 1/3 cup beer
	1 tablespoon flour
	1/4 teaspoon salt
1 garlic clove, halved	Dash pepper
1 can (2 to 2 1/2 ounces) sliced mushrooms	

1. Rub meat with cut surface of garlic. Broil 2 to 3 inches from heat until as done as desired.
2. Meanwhile, drain mushroom liquid into measuring cup. Add enough beer to measure 2/3 cup total liquid.
3. Pour 2 tablespoons steak drippings into a saucepan; stir in flour, salt, and pepper until smooth. Stir in beer mixture. Cook, stirring constantly, until thickened and smooth. Add drained mushrooms; heat through.
4. Pour beer-mushroom sauce over steak and potatoes.

Yankee Steak

SERVES 8

2 pounds beef round steak, 1/2 inch thick	2 medium onions, thinly sliced
1/2 cup flour	1 can (15 ounces) tomato sauce
2 teaspoons salt	1/8 teaspoon garlic powder
1/2 teaspoon pepper	
3 tablespoons vegetable oil	

1. Cut meat into serving-size pieces. Combine flour, salt, and pepper; pound into steak.
2. Heat oil in a skillet. Brown meat slowly on both sides. Place in a 13 x 9-inch baking dish. Top with onion slices.
3. Combine tomato sauce and garlic powder. Pour over meat.
4. Bake, covered, at 350°F 1 hour, or until meat is tender.

Creamy Baked Steak

SERVES 2-4

1 pound beef round tip steak	1 can (10$\frac{1}{2}$ ounces) condensed beef broth
4 tablespoons flour	
$\frac{1}{2}$ teaspoon salt	1 cup sour cream
2 tablespoons vegetable oil	2 tablespoons sherry
1 small onion, sliced	1 can (3 ounces) sliced mushrooms, drained
1 garlic clove, minced	

1. Cut steak into serving-size pieces. Sprinkle with 1 tablespoon flour and the salt.
2. Brown meat in oil in a skillet. Add onion and garlic.
3. Combine beef broth with remaining 3 tablespoons flour. Stir into skillet. Cook, stirring constantly, until mixture thickens. Put meat and sauce into a 12 x 8-inch baking dish.
4. Bake, covered, at 350°F 30 minutes, or until steak is tender. Remove cover. Combine sour cream, sherry, and mushrooms. Stir into meat mixture in baking dish. Bake an additional 5 minutes, or until heated through.

Parisian Hamburgers

SERVES 4

1 pound ground beef	3 tablespoons capers
2 tablespoons salad oil	2 tablespoons butter for frying
1$\frac{1}{2}$ teaspoons salt	*Trimmings*:
$\frac{1}{4}$ teaspoon black pepper	Green salad
3 ounces milk	Cucumber
1 medium yellow onion	Parsley
	Lemon slices
	Fried potatoes

1. Cut a few rings of the onion and chop the rest. Chop 1 tablespoon capers.
2. Mix the ground beef with salt, pepper, milk, chopped onion, and chopped capers. Work into a firm mass.
3. Shape into 4 large "parisians." Heat butter and fry until brown for about 4 minutes on both sides.
4. Transfer to a hot serving dish. Boil $\frac{1}{4}$ cup water in the frying pan and pour the liquid on the "parisians." Add the rest of the capers and the raw onion rings.

Serve with fried potatoes and the green salad.

Parisian Hamburgers.

Pepper Hamburgers Flambées

SERVES 6

1½ pounds ground
   beef
½ teaspoon paprika
1 egg yolk
1 teaspoon salt
2 ounces heavy cream
2 ounces water
2 tablespoons
   coarsely crushed
   green peppers
For frying:
1½ tablespoons
   butter

For flambé:
3 ounces good brandy
Seasoned sauce:
6 ounces heavy cream
1 teaspoon soy sauce
1 tablespoon chopped
   parboiled shallot
1 tablespoon chopped
   parsley
1 teaspoon chervil
1 teaspoon tarragon

1. Work the ground beef with egg yolk, salt, and paprika. Add the cream and water and work the mixture until smooth. Shape into round hamburgers.
2. Coat the hamburgers in the crushed peppers. Let them rest for a half hour to absorb seasoning. Heat the butter in a frying pan.
3. Fry the hamburgers quickly about 1½ minutes on each side.
4. Pour on the brandy, set aflame, and let burn out.
5. Take the hamburgers out of the frying plan. Pour on the cream, soy sauce, shallot, and herbs. Heat for a few minutes. Replace the hamburgers in the pan and heat through. Serve right from the pan with boiled potatoes and a green salad.

Hawaiian Hamburger

SERVES 4

1 pound ground beef
1 tablespoon oil
1 medium yellow
   onion
1 teaspoon salt
¼ teaspoon freshly
   ground black pep-
   per
½ teaspoon paprika
1 tablespoon corn-

starch
4 ounces pineapple
   juice
2 pounds canned
   pineapple (8-10
   slices)
About 4 ounces
   grated cheddar
   cheese

1. Brown the ground beef in the oil. Divide with a fork to make it grainy.

Hawaiian Hamburger.

2. Peel and chop the onion and let it fry with the beef.
3. Salt and season with pepper and paprika.
4. Stir the cornstarch in the pineapple juice and add to beef.
5. Let the pineapple drain and place the slices on a greased ovenproof dish. Distribute the beef on the pineapple slices and sprinkle with the grated cheese. Bake in a 400°F oven for 15 minutes.
Serve with rice and green salad.

Spanish Hamburgers

SERVES 6

1½ pounds ground
   beef
1 teaspoon salt
¼ teaspoon pepper
½ teaspoon paprika
1 egg
1 egg yolk
2 ounces heavy cream
2 ounces soda water
2 tablespoons all-
   purpose flour
2 large yellow onions,
   chopped
2 cloves garlic,

chopped
For Frying:
3 tablespoons butter
2 tablespoons
   Worcestershire
   sauce
3 dashes Tabasco
   sauce
2½ ounces brandy
4 ounces plain yogurt
3 ounces heavy cream
2 tablespoons chili
   sauce
Sliced olives

1. Work the ground beef, seasonings, eggs, and flour together. Add the cream and water and work the mixture until smooth. Taste and correct seasonings. Shape mixture into oval hamburgers.
2. Sauté the onions in butter over low heat till transparent.
3. Fry the hamburgers till golden brown. Transfer

Pepper Hamburgers Flambées.

Spanish Hamburgers.

them together with the fried onions to a serving dish.
4. Add the Worcestershire sauce and a few dashes of Tabasco sauce to the frying pan. Pour on brandy, set aflame, and let burn out. Pour over hamburgers.
5. Mix yogurt, cream, and chili sauce and pour on the hamburgers. Top hamburgers with the sliced olives.
Serve with boiled potatoes and a green salad.

stirring halfway through cooking time. Drain cooking juices into marinade.
4. Stir green pepper and onion into meat. Cook 3 to 4 minutes, stirring halfway through cooking time. Top with tomato wedges.
5. In a 1-cup glass measure, combine cornstarch and water, and blend with marinade. Cook 1 to 2 minutes, stirring halfway through cooking time, until thickened. Pour over meat and vegetables and heat 1 to 2 minutes.
6. Rest 5 minutes and serve over hot fluffy rice.

Chinese Tomato Beef

SERVES 8

2 pounds beef steak (sirloin, round, flank, or chuck)	3 green onions, cut in 1-inch pieces
2 tablespoons sugar	2 large tomatoes, peeled and cut in wedges
1/2 cup soy sauce	
1 clove garlic, minced	2 tablespoons cornstarch
1/4 teaspoon ginger	
3 tablespoons salad oil	1/4 cup water
2 large green peppers, cut in strips	

1. Slice steak diagonally across the grain in 1/8-inch-thick slices. Meat will slice easier if placed in the freezer 30 minutes.
2. In a 2-cup glass measure, combine sugar, soy sauce, garlic, and ginger. Pour over meat in a 9-inch baking dish. Marinate at least 30 minutes, turning meat occasionally.
3. Preheat browning dish 6 minutes. Remove meat from marinade; reserve marinade. Add oil and meat to dish. Fry meat 5 to 6 minutes in microwave oven,

Beef Stew

SERVES 6-8

3 tablespoons lard or vegetable oil	2 cans (4 ounces each) mild red chilies, drained and puréed
3 pounds lean beef, cut in 1/2-inch cubes	2 cups beef broth
1 large onion, finely chopped	2 teaspoons salt
1 clove garlic, minced	1/8 teaspoon pepper
3 fresh ripe tomatoes, peeled, seeded, and chopped	1/2 teaspoon oregano

1. Heat lard in a large skillet. Brown meat quickly on all sides. Remove beef from fat and set aside.
2. Add onion and garlic to fat in skillet; cook until onion is soft. Remove from fat and add to beef.
3. Cook tomato in fat in skillet, adding more fat if necessary. Return meat and onion to skillet. Add chili purée, beef broth, and seasonings; stir. Cover; bring to boiling, reduce heat, and cook over low heat about 2 hours, or until meat is tender.

Roast Beef in Red Wine with Green Pepper Sauce

SERVES 6

3 pounds roast beef	Salt
2 tablespoons butter	2 teaspoons soy sauce
3 ounces brandy	A few drops lemon
3/4 cup red wine	juice
1 tablespoon fresh	1/8 teaspoon dried
green pepper	finely pounded
1 1/2 cups heavy cream	tarragon

1. Trim and truss the beef if necessary. Heat 1 tablespoon butter in a stewpan and fry the beef quickly. Make certain it is well browned all over. Place beef in a 325°F oven till thermometer reads 140°F (rare) or 160°F (medium) for about 1 1/2 hours. Remove beef and let stand while making sauce.
2. Pour the brandy in the stewpan, heat for a few seconds and set aflame, standing well back. As soon as flames have died, add the red wine and the green pepper. Heat over medium heat while stirring. Pour in the cream a little at a time and stir the sauce occasionally.
3. Season with soy sauce, lemon juice, and tarragon. Lower the heat and reduce the sauce.
4. Taste and correct seasoning. Add the remaining butter and mix well. Pour the sauce in a sauce boat and keep warm.
5. Wash the stewpan, check how red the beef is inside, put more butter in the pan and continue to roast if beef is not ready.

Serve with boiled rice or potatoes, a green salad, and fried or fresh tomatoes.

Herbed Skirt Steak

SERVES 4-6

1 1/2 pounds lean beef	ground pepper
skirt steak	1 1/2 teaspoons salt
2 teaspoons clarified	1/2 cup Mock Crème
butter	Fraîche (below)
1 large yellow onion,	1/4 cup snipped fresh
finely sliced	dill or 2 tablespoons
1/2 cup Beef Stock*	dried dill weed
1 garlic clove, minced	*Check index for
1/4 teaspoon freshly	recipe

1. Slice steak in half lengthwise; cut pieces across the grain into paper-thin slices. Heat butter over high heat in a 12-inch skillet. Add meat slices, stirring quickly to coat meat with butter. Add onion; cook and stir 2 minutes. Add Beef Stock, garlic, pepper, and salt; simmer covered until onion is tender (about 3 minutes).

2. Stir 1/4 cup pan juices into Mock Crème Fraîche. Stir mixture back into pan; stir in dill. Serve immediately.

Mock Crème Fraîche

ABOUT 2 CUPS

1 1/2 cups Neufchatel	6 tablespoons low-fat
cheese	yogurt

1. Mix cheese and yogurt in a blender or food processor until smooth and fluffy. Place in small jars; cover tightly.
2. Set jars in a warm place (100°F) for 2 hours; see Note. Cool and refrigerate. Stir before using.
Note: Use an oven thermometer in making Mock Crème Fraîche, as temperature is very important. A gas oven with a pilot light will be about 125°F. Turn electric oven to as warm a setting as necessary to maintain temperature. Mock Crème Fraîche can be refrigerated up to 3 weeks.

Island-Style Short Ribs

SERVES 8

4 pounds lean beef	1/2 teaspoon lemon
short ribs	pepper seasoning
1/2 cup soy sauce	1/4 teaspoon garlic salt
1/3 cup sugar	1 large onion, finely
2 tablespoons vinegar	chopped
1 tablespoon vege-	1/4 cup butter or
table oil	margarine
1 teaspoon ginger	2 cups water

1. Cut meat from bones; reserve the bones. Trim off as much fat as possible. Cut meat into cubes. Put meat into a bowl.
2. Combine soy sauce, sugar, vinegar, oil, ginger, lemon pepper seasoning, and garlic salt. Pour over meat. Cover and refrigerate several hours or overnight.
3. Sauté onion in butter in a skillet. Remove onion; set aside.
4. Cook meat in skillet about 10 minutes. Add onion, marinade, and water. Put into a 2-quart casserole. Top with bones.
5. Bake, covered, at 325°F 1 1/2 hours. Remove bones and bake, uncovered, an additional 30 minutes, or until meat is tender. To serve, spoon broth over hot, cooked rice.

Roast Beef in Red Wine with Green Pepper Sauce.

Meatloaf on Potato Bed.

Meatloaf on Potato Bed

SERVES 6

1¹/₂ pounds ground beef	8-10 raw potatoes
³/₄ teaspoon salt	Salt
1¹/₄ teaspoons pepper	Black pepper
¹/₂ teaspoon paprika	Garlic salt
¹/₂ teaspoon garlic salt	³/₄ cup heavy cream
6 ounces parsley, chopped	*For Larding:*
1 egg and 1 egg yolk	¹/₂ pound bacon
3 ounces heavy cream	*For Baking:*
3 ounces water	Grated Cheddar cheese
For Brushing:	6 tomatoes
Vegetable oil	Salt
For the Potato Bed:	Pepper
Butter	Basil

1. Peel the potatoes and cut them in slices. Layer them in a greased pan or ovenproof dish with salt, pepper, and garlic salt between the layers.

2. Pour on the cream.

3. Work the ground beef with seasonings, parsley, egg and yolk, cream, and water.

4. Shape into 2 loaves and place them on the potato bed. Brush with vegetable oil and bake in a 325°F oven for 45 minutes.

5. Make gashes in the loaves and lard with a piece of bacon in each gash. Sprinkle with cheese. Place 3 tomatoes on each short side, cut a cross in their tops and dredge with salt, pepper, and basil. Replace the dish in the oven for about 15 minutes.

Serve with a green salad.

Meatloaf with Zucchini.

Meat Loaf with Zucchini

SERVES 4

6-8 boiled, cold, sliced potatoes	1 teaspoon salt
	$^1/_2$ teaspoon pepper
1 pound ground beef	2 large yellow onions
6 ounces milk	6 tomatoes
3 ounces water	1 zucchini, sliced
2 ounces fine bread crumbs	$^1/_2$ teaspoon salt
	$^1/_2$ teaspoon basil
1 egg	2 tablespoons butter

1. Soak the bread crumbs in the milk and water and let them swell.
2. Spread the potato slices at the bottom of a greased ovenproof dish.
3. Mix the ground beef with the egg, seasonings, and the bread crumb mixture. Spread the meat on the potatoes.
4. Fry the sliced onions golden yellow and distribute on the meat. Top the onions with sliced tomatoes and zucchini and season with salt and crumbled basil.
5. Dot with butter and bake in a 350°F oven for about 40 minutes.
Serve with a green salad.

Corned Beef

SERVES ABOUT 12

6-pound beef brisket corned, boneless	$^1/_2$ cup firmly packed light brown sugar
2 teaspoons whole cloves	$^1/_4$ cup sherry

1. Put the meat into a saucepot and add enough water to cover meat. Cover saucepot tightly and bring water just to boiling over high heat. Reduce

(continued)

heat and simmer about 4 hours, or until meat is almost tender when pierced with a fork.

2. Remove from heat and cool in liquid; refrigerate overnight.

3. Remove meat from liquid and set on rack in roasting pan. Stud with cloves. Put brown sugar over top and press firmly.

4. Roast at 325°F 1½ hours. After roasting 30 minutes, drizzle with sherry.

5. To serve, carve meat into slices.

Red Tulip Casserole

SERVES 4

1½ pounds ground beef	paste
3 tablespoons butter	1 tablespoon mustard
½ teaspoon paprika	1 cube chicken bouillon
2 onions or leeks, chopped	Salt to taste
¼ pound smoked ham	1 clove garlic, chopped
5 tablespoons tomato	½ cup water
	½ cup sour cream

1. Heat the butter in a skillet. Sauté onions till they are transparent, about 5 minutes. Add the paprika and beef. Cook over high heat till brown. Turn heat down and add ham. Simmer for 5 minutes.

2. Add the water and stir in the tomato paste and mustard.

3. Add the bouillon, salt, and garlic. Simmer 10 minutes.

4. Add sour cream just before ready to serve.

Red Tulip Casserole.

Full-Flavored Steak

SERVES 6-8

2½ tablespoons brown sugar	1 tablespoon tarragon vinegar
1½ tablespoons sugar	3 pounds beefsteak (sirloin, porterhouse, T-bone, or rib), cut 1½ inches thick
1 tablespoon ground ginger	
1 clove garlic, crushed	
½ cup soy sauce	

1. Combine the sugars, ginger, garlic, soy sauce, and vinegar.

2. Put meat into a large shallow dish and pour soy sauce mixture over meat. Allow to marinate at least 30 minutes, basting frequently and turning once or twice.

3. When ready to grill, remove meat from marinade, reserving marinade.

4. Place steak on grill about 3 inches from coals. Brushing frequently with marinade, grill about 6 minutes, or until one side is browned. Turn and grill other side about 6 minutes, or until done. (To test, slit meat near bone and note color of meat.) Serve immediately.

Marinated Ribs

SERVES 6

3 pounds ribs	black peppercorns
2 tablespoons butter	1½ tablespoons tomato purée or chili sauce
2 teaspoons salt	
Marinade:	
3 ounces vegetable oil	*For the Sauce:*
½ cup red or white wine	3 ounces juices from ribs
1 tablespoon soy sauce	1 cup heavy cream
¾ teaspoon ginger	2½-3 tablespoons flour
1 large clove garlic	½ teaspoon soy sauce
3 slices yellow onion	Salt
15 coarsely crushed	Pepper

1. Cut the garlic in thin slices and mix all ingredients for the marinade in a deep bowl, large enough to fit the ribs.

2. Loosen the meat a little along the bone to make it easier for the marinade to penetrate. It will also be easier to carve the meat when ready. Put the meat in the marinade with the bone side up. Set aside for at least four hours, but preferably longer, up to 12 hours.

3. Remove the meat and wipe it dry with paper towel.

Marinated Ribs.

4. Heat the butter in a stewpan and brown the meat.
5. Skin away most of the fat from the marinade. Pour ³/₄ cup into the stewpan.
6. Braise meat slowly in the stewpan, covered, for at least 1¹/₂ hours till thoroughly done, basting now and then.
7. Sauce: Skim the fat from the juices, add the cream, and thicken with flour. Boil for 5 minutes. Season with salt, pepper, and soy sauce. Serve dish with boiled potatoes and sliced cucumber.

Marinated Flank Steak

SERVES 6

¹/₃ cup soy sauce	1¹/₂ teaspoons ground ginger
2 tablespoons vinegar	
¹/₄ cup minced onion	2 tablespoons sugar
¹/₄ teaspoon garlic powder	2 pounds beef flank steak

1. In a 2-quart glass baking dish, blend soy sauce, vinegar, onion, garlic powder, ginger, and sugar. Dip meat in mixture and marinate 4 hours, turning occasionally.
2. Cut steak into serving pieces. Pound to tenderize.

3. Return to 2-quart dish with sauce and cook, covered, 12 to 14 minutes, rotating dish one-quarter turn halfway through cooking time.
4. Serve with hot rice.

Beef 'n' Peppers

SERVES 6

1 garlic clove, minced	2 cans (10¹/₂ ounces each) brown gravy with onions
1¹/₂ pounds lean beef, cut in 1-inch cubes	
2 tablespoons shortening	1 green pepper, cut in strips
1 cup sliced fresh mushrooms	

1. Sauté garlic and beef in hot shortening in a skillet. Put into a 1¹/₂-quart casserole.
2. Combine mushrooms and gravy in skillet with drippings. Pour over meat.
3. Bake, covered, at 350°F 2 hours, or until meat is tender. Remove cover. Add pepper strips. Bake an additional 15 minutes, or until pepper is tender but still crisp. Serve over hot, cooked rice or noodles.

Swedish Beef Stew

SERVES 6

3¹/₄ pounds beef
    chuck
3 tablespoons all-
    purpose flour
2 teaspoons salt
1 teaspoon white
    pepper
2 teaspoons juniper
    berries, crushed

5 small onions, peeled
    and halved
1³/₄ ounces margarine
2 cups beef stock
2 tablespoons cheese,
    grated
2 tablespoons black
    currant jelly
¹/₄ cup heavy cream

1. Cut meat into small pieces and turn in a mixture of flour, salt, pepper, and juniper berries.
2. Brown meat in margarine in frying pan. Remove from pan.
3. Add meat to onions in a pot and bring to boil with the beef stock. Let meat and onions simmer about 1¹/₂ hours.
4. Add jelly, cream, and cheese.
Serve with boiled potatoes.

Beef Ragout

SERVES 8

¹/₂ cup all-purpose
    flour
¹/₂ teaspoon salt
¹/₂ teaspoon pepper
3 pounds beef chuck,
    cubed
¹/₄ cup vegetable oil
1 medium yellow
    onion, chopped
3 stalks celery,
    chopped
1 green pepper,
    chopped
2 cloves garlic,
    minced

2 cans (10¹/₂ ounces)
    condensed beef
    consommé, undi-
    luted
1 can (1 pound)
    tomatoes
1 can (6 ounces)
    tomato paste
2 tablespoons parsley,
    chopped
2 teaspoons paprika
2 teaspoons Worces-
    tershire sauce

1. Mix flour, salt, and pepper. Dredge beef cubes. Reserve remaining flour mixture.
2. Heat 3 tablespoons oil in a heavy frying pan. Add beef cubes a third at a time. Remove as browned.
3. Add more oil if necessary and sauté onion, celery, garlic, and green pepper until tender. Remove from heat.
4. Stir in 2 tablespoons flour until well blended. Gradually stir in beef consommé. Add tomatoes, tomato paste, parsley, paprika, and Worcestershire sauce. Bring to a boil stirring constantly.
5. Add beef to a casserole and pour in sauce. Simmer covered 2¹/₂ hours until meat is tender.
Serve with boiled rice.

Favorite Meat Loaf

SERVES 4-6

1³/₄ pounds ground
    beef
³/₄ cup uncooked oats
¹/₄ cup finely minced
    onion
¹/₄ cup chopped celery

1¹/₂ teaspoons salt
¹/₂ teaspoon pepper
1 cup tomato juice
2 eggs
¹/₂ cup ketchup

1. In a large mixing bowl, combine ground beef, oats, onion, celery, salt, pepper, tomato juice, and eggs, blending evenly.
2. Turn mixture into a 9-inch glass pie plate with a glass, open end up, in center of dish, packing lightly.
3. Cook 6 to 8 minutes, rotating dish one-quarter turn halfway through cooking time.
4. Remove excess drippings. Pour ketchup over top, cover with waxed paper, and cook 6 to 8 minutes, rotating dish one-quarter turn halfway through cooking time.
5. Rest, covered, 10 minutes before serving.

German Meatball Stew

SERVES 6-8

1¹/₂ pounds ground
    beef
1 egg
1¹/₂ teaspoons salt
¹/₂ teaspoon pepper
1 large potato, pared
    and grated
¹/₂ teaspoon ginger
2 large onions, sliced
2 tablespoons salad
    oil

1 pound carrots,
    pared and sliced
1¹/₂ cups beer or beef
    broth
1¹/₂ cups water
¹/₄ cup flour
Fluffy Dumplings
    (optional)

1. In a large mixing bowl, combine ground beef, egg, salt, pepper, potato, and ginger, blending evenly. Shape 24 meatballs.
2. Arrange meatballs evenly in a 2-quart glass baking dish. Cook 10 to 12 minutes, stirring halfway through cooking time.
3. In a 3-quart glass casserole, combine onions and oil and cook 2 minutes. Stir in carrots and cook, covered, 5 to 6 minutes.
4. Add meatballs, beer, and 1 cup water to casserole. Bring to boiling and cook 10 to 12 minutes, rotating one-quarter turn halfway through cooking time.
5. In a 2-cup glass measure, combine ¹/₂ cup water with flour and stir to blend. Stir flour mixture into liquid in stew. If desired, drop dumpling dough on

(continued)

Beef Ragout.

stew. Cook, covered, 7 to 10 minutes, rotating one-quarter turn halfway through cooking time.

6. Rest, covered, 10 minutes before serving.

Fluffy Dumplings: In a small mixing bowl, combine **1 1/2 cups all-purpose flour, 1 tablespoon baking powder, 1/2 teaspoon salt,** and **1/4 cup chopped parsley.** Stir in **2/3 cup milk** until ingredients are moistened. Bring **2 1/2 cups stock** to boiling. Drop dough by rounded teaspoonfuls onto boiling stock. Cook, covered, 7 to 10 minutes, rotating dish one-quarter turn halfway through cooking time. Rest 5 minutes before serving.

Sauerbraten

SERVES ABOUT 8

1 beef round rump roast, boneless (about 3 pounds)	1 bay leaf
	2 juniper berries (optional)
2 cups water	1 tablespoon lard
1 cup vinegar	3/4 cup golden raisins
1 teaspoon salt	5 or 6 gingersnaps, crumbled
2 onions, peeled and sliced	
	1 tablespoon grated apple
1 carrot, pared and sliced	1 teaspoon salt
5 peppercorns	1/4 teaspoon pepper
2 whole cloves	1 cup sour cream

1. Trim excess fat from roast and put meat into a large glass bowl.

2. Combine water, vinegar, salt, onion, carrot, peppercorns, cloves, bay leaf, and juniper berries (if used) in a saucepan. Bring to boiling, then set aside to cool.

3. Pour cooled marinade over meat, cover, and refrigerate 2 or 3 days; turn meat over several times during marinating.

4. Remove meat from marinade and pat dry with paper towels. Reserve marinade.

5. Heat lard in a saucepot or Dutch oven; add meat and brown well on all sides. Put meat fat side up in an electric cooker. Strain marinade into cooker.

6. Cover and cook on low 2 to 3 hours.

7. Remove meat and keep warm. Turn cooker control to High.

8. Add raisins, gingersnap crumbs, apple, salt, and pepper to liquid in cooker; cook and stir until thickened. Blend in sour cream.

9. Cover and cook on High 30 minutes.

10. Slice meat and serve with gravy. Accompany with potato dumplings, if desired.

Chili con Carne

SERVES 4

1 large yellow onion, sliced	1 clove garlic, crushed
1 green pepper, sliced	1/2 teaspoon salt
2 tablespoons salad oil	3/4 teaspoon paprika
1 pound ground beef	1/4 teaspoon black pepper
1/3 cup red wine	1 1/4 teaspoons chili pepper
1 beef bouillon cube	
1 can (1 pound) white beans, drained	1 1/4 teaspoons basil
	1/4 teaspoon oregano
1 can (1 pound) peeled tomatoes	5 drops Tabasco sauce
2 tablespoons tomato purée	2 tablespoons parsley

1. Heat oil in a skillet. Add green pepper and cook till soft. Add ground beef while stirring with a wooden spoon. Cook without allowing the beef to become too crumbly. If dry add another tablespoon salad oil.

2. Add wine and bouillon cube and cook for a few minutes. Strain liquid from the tomatoes and set aside. Add the tomatoes, garlic, tomato purée, and

all dry seasonings. Bring mixture to a boil, reduce heat, and simmer, covered, for 45 minutes, now and then stirring well.

3. Add the beans and Tabasco and mix well. If additional liquid is needed add liquid from tomatoes. Garnish with chopped parsley and serve straight from the casserole with a green salad and French bread.

Tournedos

SERVES 6

6 slices beef loin tenderloin steak (1½ inches thick)	**¼ cup flour**
	¾ cup dry white wine
Salt and pepper to taste	**½ cup chopped parsley**
½ cup butter	**Juice of 1 lemon**

1. Season meat with salt and pepper on both sides.
2. Melt butter in a heavy skillet. Add meat and brown quickly on each side. Remove to a dish.
3. Using a whisk, stir flour into pan juices. Cook, stirring constantly, over low heat for 2 minutes.

4. Stir in wine and cover. Simmer 5 minutes.
5. Add meat, parsley, and lemon juice. Simmer 5 minutes.

Sukiyaki

SERVES 4-6

1 pound beef sirloin steak, diagonally sliced in very thin long strips	**2 cups sliced fresh mushrooms**
	2 cans (5 ounces each) bamboo shoots, drained
2 cups celery, diagonally sliced in ½-inch pieces	**½ cup soy sauce**
	¼ cup sugar
2 medium onions, cut in wedges	**½ cup saké or beef stock**
1 bunch green onions, including tops, cut in 1-inch lengths	

1. Stir-fry meat in conventional skillet on top of range, or using microwave oven, preheat browning dish 6 minutes, add meat, and fry 2 to 3 minutes until well browned.

(continued)

65

2. In a 2-quart glass casserole, combine celery, onion, green onion, mushrooms, and bamboo shoots with meat. Cook, covered, 6 to 8 minutes, stirring halfway through cooking time. Rest, covered, 10 minutes.

3. In a 1-cup glass measure, blend soy sauce, sugar, and saké. Cook 1 minute, stirring halfway through cooking time.

4. Pour sauce over vegetables and stir to blend.

5. Serve hot over fluffy rice.

Stuffed Beef Rolls

SERVES 4

8 thin slices of well hung thick flank of beef	*For diluting:*
	1 cup beef stock
Salt	*Sauce:*
Pepper	1 cup gravy
Stuffing (see below)	3 ounces heavy cream
For frying:	Soy sauce
3 tablespoons butter	*Thickening:*
	Potato flour stirred in water

1. Pound the beef slices lightly and season with salt and pepper. Place stuffing on top and roll up securely. Fasten with toothpicks.

2. Brown the rolls in the butter.

3. Transfer them to a casserole with a heavy bottom; add beef stock to half the height of the rolls. Simmer rolls slowly, covered, for 50 minutes.

4. Add the cream toward the end of the 50 minutes. Add soy sauce, taste the sauce and correct seasoning, and thicken it with flour stirred in water. Remove toothpicks, transfer the rolls to a serving dish, and pour on the sauce. Serve with boiled or fried potatoes and a green salad.

Suggestions for stuffings:

1. Bacon strips, onion strips, small halved tomato slices, chopped parsley.

2. Sweet corn, red pepper strips.

3. Strips of lard, anchovy fillet strips, thin onion rings, chopped parsley.

4. Cottage cheese, chopped red pepper, striped leek.

5. Capers, leek rings, chopped parsley.

6. Small half tomato slices, sliced mushrooms, chopped parsley.

7. Cream cheese, sliced pimiento olives, striped leek.

8. Thin green pepper slices, mango chutney.

9. Smoked bacon, paprika, and carrot in strips.

Stuffed Cabbage

SERVES 6

1 medium head cabbage	2 cloves garlic, diced
1 pound ground beef	1 tablespoon parsley
1 medium onion, finely chopped	¼ teaspoon horse-radish
1 cup cooked rice	Salt
	Pepper

1. Wash cabbage and cook in boiling water for approximately 5 minutes. Drain and separate large leaves (about 16).

2. Sauté onion, garlic, and spices in a skillet until golden, then add meat and cooked rice and continue to sauté for 6-8 minutes.

3. Fill 2 cabbage leaves with meat filling and roll into a cigar shape.

Stuffed Beef Rolls.

Stuffed Cabbage.

4. Put cabbage rolls on a greased baking sheet and bake for 20 minutes in a 350°F oven.

5. Remove and serve with a slice of pimiento, boiled potatoes, and sautéed cabbage.

Pot Roast Jardinière

SERVES 6

1 beef chuck pot roast (4 pounds)	1 teaspoon snipped fresh or ¹/₂ teaspoon dried thyme leaves
¹/₄ cup prepared horseradish	
1 tablespoon salt	1 teaspoon snipped fresh or ¹/₂ teaspoon dried marjoram leaves
1 medium tomato, chopped	
1 cup Beef Stock*	1 teaspoon salt
3 medium kohlrabi or turnips, pared and cut in ¹/₂-inch cubes	¹/₂ teaspoon pepper
	2 leeks, cut in 1-inch pieces
3 medium carrots, cut in ¹/₂-inch slices	2 teaspoons flour
	Cold water
1 pound fresh Brussels sprouts, cleaned (see Note)	*Check index for recipe

1. Rub meat on both sides with a mixture of horseradish and 1 tablespoon salt; place meat in a Dutch oven. Add tomato and stock to Dutch oven. Cover.

2. Cook in a 325°F oven about 3 hours, or until meat is tender.

3. Add vegetables, thyme, marjoram, 1 teaspoon salt, and ¹/₂ teaspoon pepper to Dutch oven during last 15 minutes of cooking time; cook just until vegetables are tender.

4. Remove meat and vegetables to platter. Skim fat from cooking liquid. If thicker sauce is desired, mix flour with a little cold water and stir into liquid. Simmer, stirring constantly, until sauce is thickened. Pass Sauce.

Note: 1 package (10 ounces) frozen Brussels sprouts can be substituted for the fresh. Add to Dutch oven for length of cooking time indicated on package.

Short Ribs, Western Style

SERVES ABOUT 6

4 medium onions, peeled and quartered	1 cup dried lima beans
2 teaspoons salt	3 tablespoons flour
¹/₄ teaspoon ground black pepper	1 teaspoon dry mustard
¹/₂ teaspoon rubbed sage	2 to 3 tablespoons fat
1 quart water	2 pounds beef rib short ribs, cut in serving-size pieces

1. Combine onions, salt, pepper, sage, and water in a large heavy saucepot or Dutch oven. Cover, bring to boiling, reduce heat, and simmer 5 minutes. Bring to boiling again; add lima beans gradually and cook,

(continued)

uncovered, 2 minutes. Remove from heat, cover, and set aside to soak 1 hour.

2. Meanwhile, mix flour and dry mustard and coat short ribs evenly.

3. Heat fat in large heavy skillet and brown short ribs on all sides over medium heat. Add meat to soaked lima beans. Bring to boiling and simmer, covered, 1½ hours, or until beans and meat are tender.

Ground Beef in Pastry Shell

SERVES 6

Pie:
2 cups all-purpose
   flour
1 teaspoon salt
1 cup butter
1 egg
Filling:
3 tablespoons butter
1½ pounds ground
   beef
½ cup yellow onion,
   finely chopped

½ cup mushrooms,
   chopped
2 tablespoons parsley,
   chopped
½ cup Cheddar
   cheese, grated
1 egg yolk
¼ cup milk
Salt
Pepper
Brushing:
1 egg, beaten

1. Make pie dough: Cut flour, salt, and butter together. Add egg and cream and work together quickly; place in a cold place for about 1 hour.

Meat Pudding à la Maison.

Ground Beef in Pastry Shell.

2. Cut the chilled dough in equal parts. Roll out two strips about 9" by 5".

3. Put one strip on a greased and floured baking sheet.

4. Heat butter in a skillet and add the mushrooms, onion, and beef.

5. Put the meat in a bowl, stir in parsley, egg yolk, milk, and seasonings. Mix.

6. Shape the meat into a loaf on the dough. Put the other dough half on top and fit together. Press the edges together with a fork.

7. Brush dough with beaten egg and slit holes on top with a knife. Bake in a 425°F oven for 45 minutes.

Serve with dry red wine.

Timbale Helleberg

SERVES 4

1 pound ground beef
2 egg yolks
1 egg white
2 large boiled pota-
   toes, mashed
3 ounces heavy cream
3 ounces water
Filling:
1 can (1 pound)
   tomatoes
Bacon strips to line
   the mold

Brussels sprouts
*Tomato, Onion, and
   Paprika mixture:*
1 green pepper
2 large yellow onions
4 tomatoes
Butter or salad oil
1-2 cloves garlic
1 chicken bouillon
   cube
Thyme
Salt and pepper

1. Mix the ground beef with egg yolks, egg white, mashed potatoes, water, and cream. Stir mixture until "thready" and season with salt and pepper.

2. Line an ovenproof mold at the bottom and partly up the sides with bacon strips. Pour on half the meat mixture. Distribute the drained and coarsely chopped

tomatoes on the mixture. Salt and pepper. Add the rest of the mixture. Cover the mold with foil and bake in double boiler in oven at 350°F for about 1 hour.

3. Peel the onions and remove the seeds from the pepper. Cut onions in slices, the pepper in strips and chop the tomatoes coarsely. Fry the onions, finely chopped garlic, and pepper in butter or oil for a while without letting ingredients brown.

4. Add the tomatoes and some chicken bouillon and simmer until everything is soft. Season with salt, pepper, and thyme. Serve with boiled Brussels sprouts.

Meat Pudding à la Maison

SERVES 6

1¹/₂ pounds ground beef	peeled tomatoes
¹/₄ cup milk	1 can (8 ounces)
¹/₃ cup bread crumbs	creamed mush-
Salt to taste	rooms
Pepper to taste	5 tomatoes
1 can artichoke hearts	Butter for the roast-
1 can (1 pound)	ing and baking pans

1. Mix the ground beef with milk and bread crumbs. Add salt and pepper to taste.

2. Spread on a roasting pan lined with greased aluminum foil.

3. Place artichoke hearts, tomato halves, and creamed mushrooms on the meat.

4. Bake in a 325°F oven for about 50 minutes.

Tenderloin Supreme in Mushroom Sauce

SERVES 16-24

1 whole beef loin tenderloin roast (4 to 6 pounds)	¹/₈ teaspoon pepper
	¹/₈ teaspoon thyme
	1¹/₂ cups beef broth
Mushroom Sauce:	³/₄ cup red wine, such
¹/₃ cup butter	as burgundy
³/₄ cup sliced mush- rooms	1¹/₂ teaspoons wine vinegar
³/₄ cup finely chopped onion	1¹/₂ tablespoons tomato paste
1¹/₂ tablespoons flour	1¹/₂ teaspoons
³/₄ teaspoon salt	chopped parsley

1. Place tenderloin on rack in roasting pan. Insert roast meat thermometer in center of meat so that tip is slightly more than halfway through meat.

2. Roast, uncovered, at 425°F 45 to 60 minutes. The roast will be rare when meat thermometer registers 140°F.

(continued)

Timbale Helleberg.

3. For Mushroom Sauce, heat butter in a skillet. Add mushrooms and cook over medium heat until lightly browned and tender, stirring occasionally. Remove mushrooms with a slotted spoon, allowing butter to drain back into skillet; set aside.

4. Add onion and cook 3 minutes; blend in flour, salt, pepper, and thyme. Heat until mixture bubbles. Remove from heat.

5. Gradually add, stirring constantly, beef broth, wine, and wine vinegar. Cook rapidly until sauce thickens. Blend in the mushrooms, tomato paste, and parsley. Cook about 3 minutes.

6. Serve slices of beef tenderloin with sauce spooned over individual servings.

Green-Pepper Beef

SERVES 4

2 pounds top round steak	1 tablespoon Chinese soy sauce
2 tablespoons yellow onion, finely chopped	1 cup heavy cream
	½ cup plain yogurt
	½-1 teaspoon salt
3 tablespoons green pepper	2-3 tablespoons butter, for frying

1. Chop the green pepper coarsely and mix with the onion. Pat in the mixture on both sides of the beef.

2. Heat a frying pan; add the butter and let it turn brown. Put in the beef and fry on high heat for 2-4 minutes on each side, depending on thickness and how well done the beef is desired. A good rule is to turn the beef slice when meat juice appears on the top side. When meat juice starts showing on the fried side the beef is ready and rosy inside.

3. Place the beef on a hot serving dish and salt lightly. Pour the soy and the cream in the frying pan and reduce by boiling for a few minutes until the sauce starts thickening. Remove the pan from the heat and stir in the yogurt. Season with salt and a few drops of fresh lemon juice. Serve with potatoes and a green salad.

Tongue with Mushrooms and Olives

SERVES 4

2 pounds smoked beef tongue, boiled	seed
	2 bay leaves
1 large onion, quartered	4 whole cloves
10 whole black peppercorns	½ pound mushrooms, sliced
¼ teaspoon mustard	6 pimiento-stuffed olives, sliced

1. Wash tongue and dry with paper towels.

Green-Pepper Beef.

Tongue with Mushrooms and Olives.

2. Place tongue in a large pot with 3 quarts of water and next 5 ingredients.
3. Bring to a boil over high heat. Reduce heat and simmer, covered, 3 hours till tender. Drain and put tongue in cold water.
4. Remove skin: Slit skin on underside from end to end with a sharp knife. Peel off skin and remove and discard root.
5. Slice tongue thinly and serve with mushrooms and olives.

Sweet-and-Sour Meatballs

SERVES 4

1 pound ground beef	drained (reserve
1 egg	juice)
2 tablespoons corn-	½ cup sugar
starch	3 tablespoons corn-
2 tablespoons finely	starch
minced green onion	1 tablespoon soy
1 teaspoon salt	sauce
Dash pepper	3 tablespoons vinegar
1 can (16 ounces)	4 cups cooked rice
pineapple chunks,	

1. In a medium mixing bowl, blend ground beef, egg, cornstarch, onion, salt, and pepper. Shape 1

tablespoon mixture around each pineapple chunk. Reserve remaining pineapple.
2. In a glass pie plate, arrange meatballs evenly around edge. Cook 5 to 7 minutes, stirring to rearrange meatballs halfway through cooking time.
3. In a 2-cup glass measure, blend sugar, cornstarch, soy sauce, vinegar, and reserved pineapple juice.
4. Cook sauce 2 to 3 minutes, or until mixture begins to boil, stirring after every minute.
5. Pour sauce and remaining pineapple chunks over meatballs, mixing gently.
6. Serve over cooked rice.

Kidney with Paprika Flavor

SERVES 4

1½ pounds kidneys	2 yellow onions,
1½ teaspoons salt	thinly sliced
1 teaspoon paprika	2 green peppers, cut
3 tablespoons butter	in strips
¾ cup red wine	4 tomatoes in wedges
Garnish:	
1 pound bacon	

1. Rinse the kidneys, dry with absorbent paper towel and cut in slices 1-inch thick. Cut the slices in rather thick pieces and season with salt and paprika.

(continued)

Fall Stew.

Braised Bacon Rolls.

2. Fry the kidney pieces till they are light brown.

3. Add the wine, lower the heat, and let the kidneys simmer, covered, about 10 minutes.

4. Meanwhile fry the bacon with the onion slices, the pepper strips, and the tomato wedges in another frying pan without any butter. Stir with a spatula until the mixture is soft but has not turned color.

5. Season with salt if necessary. Pour the kidneys in the middle of a hot serving dish and arrange the garnish around the edges.

Fall Stew

SERVES 4

1 pound ground beef	4 teaspoons green
1 yellow onion	pepper
1 head white cabbage	1 tablespoon all-
2 tablespoons butter	purpose flour
1 tablespoon parsley,	1¹/₂ cups beef bouillon
chopped	2 apples
¹/₂ teaspoon salt	

1. Peel and chop onion. Chop cabbage.

2. Heat butter in a casserole and brown meat. Remove to a heated dish.

3. Sauté onions and green pepper about 5 minutes. Remove from heat. Stir in flour, bouillon.

4. Add beef and cabbage. Cover and cook over low heat for 10 minutes.

5. Peel apples, core, and cut in wedges. Add to stew last 5 minutes of cooking time. Sprinkle with chopped parsley.

Beef Kabobs with Vegetables

SERVES ABOUT 6

3 tablespoons light	1 clove garlic, minced
brown sugar	1¹/₂ to 2 pounds beef
¹/₄ teaspoon dry	sirloin, cut in
mustard	1¹/₂-inch cubes
1 cup soy sauce	Tomato wedges
¹/₂ cup water	Green pepper squares
3 tablespoons dry	(about 1 to
sherry	1¹/₂ inches)
¹/₄ teaspoon Tabasco	Small onions, peeled
1 tablespoon grated	
onion	

1. Mix brown sugar, mustard, soy sauce, water, sherry, Tabasco, onion, and garlic in a bowl.

2. Place meat in glass baking dish, pour marinade over beef, and allow to marinate in refrigerator overnight. Remove meat and reserve marinade.

3. Alternate meat and vegetables on skewers.

4. Place kabobs on grill about 5 inches from hot coals. Brush generously with marinade. Grill 7 to 10 minutes, then turn and baste with more marinade. Continue cooking until meat is done as desired.

Note: The beef often requires a longer cooking period than the vegetables. If desired, place all beef on 2 or 3 skewers, and place all vegetables on other skewers. Place vegetables on grill toward end of cooking time of beef. Meat and vegetables may be rearranged on skewers for serving.

Mexican Meat Pie

SERVES 4

³/₄ pound ground beef	1 teaspoon salt
2 onions	White pepper
3 tablespoons butter	*Mashed potatoes:*
2 green peppers, cut in thin strips	4-5 medium potatoes
	water
1 can peeled tomatoes	1 teaspoon salt
1 garlic clove	1 tablespoon butter
³/₄ cup beef bouillon	2 egg yolks

1. Chop the onion and sauté in the butter.

2. Add the beef and brown. Then add the green peppers, tomatoes, crushed garlic, and bouillon and season with salt and pepper. Heat for about 5 minutes, stirring occasionally.

3. Peel potatoes and boil in lightly salted water about 20 minutes. Mash and add warm milk, egg yolks, and salt and pepper.

4. Place meat in an ovenproof dish and place the mashed potatoes on top. Bake in a 450°F oven for 10-15 minutes until the potatoes are golden brown.

Braised Bacon Rolls

SERVES 4

1 pound ground beef	The white of 1 leek
3 slices bacon	1¹/₂ tablespoons butter
For frying:	
2 tablespoons butter	³/₄ cup beef stock
For braising:	¹/₃ cup tomato juice
1 yellow onion	¹/₂ teaspoon salt
1 large fennel	¹/₂ teaspoon paprika
3 tomatoes	

1. Trim the vegetables and cut them into small cubes. Sauté the cubes in the butter over low heat.
2. Pour on the beef stock and the tomato juice. Season with salt and paprika to taste.
3. Spread the ground beef in a rectangle ¹/₂-inch thick on a water-rinsed cutting board.
4. Cut out 6 rectangle parts. Place ¹/₂ bacon slice on each part and shape into a roll.
5. Brown the rolls all over in butter.
6. Put the rolls in the vegetable mixture and braise covered over low heat for 40 minutes. Serve with boiled or baked potatoes and a green salad.

Mexican Meat Pie.

Veal

Festive Veal Dish

SERVES 4

2 pounds veal chops	*Sauce: (makes 1 cup)*
Salt	1 cup light cream
Freshly ground	3 tablespoons flour
pepper	stirred into 3 oz.
1 tablespoon butter	cold milk
$^1/_2$ cup beef stock	Salt
3 ounces light cream	Freshly ground
1 can mushroom soup	pepper
1 can artichoke	Finely crumbled
bottoms	oregano
1 can whole mush-	4 ounces grated
rooms	cheese
1 red pepper	

1. Sauté veal chops in a frying pan for 2-3 minutes on each side. Season with salt and pepper. Set aside.
2. Heat the mushroom soup in the frying pan with the beef stock and strain.
3. Add the cream and beat in the flour dissolved in the milk. Bring to a boil and simmer for a few minutes. Season with salt, pepper, and oregano to taste.
4. Arrange veal chops two by two and pour mushroom soup on top. Put an artichoke bottom and a pepper ring on top.
5. Sauté the mushrooms, browning them lightly, and add 3 ounces light cream. Let the mushrooms absorb the liquid.
6. Distribute the mushrooms on the artichoke bottoms, pour on the sauce, and sprinkle with grated cheese. Bake in a 450°F oven for 15 minutes or until the surface has turned light brown and the dish is thoroughly hot.
Serve with French fries and a crisp green salad.

Veal Chops Pizzaiola

SERVES 6

$^1/_4$ cup olive oil	2 cloves garlic, sliced
6 veal rib or loin	1 teaspoon oregano
chops, cut about	1 teaspoon salt
$^1/_2$ inch thick	$^1/_2$ teaspoon pepper
1 can (28 ounces)	$^1/_2$ teaspoon chopped
tomatoes, sieved	parsley

1. Heat oil in a large, heavy skillet. Add chops and brown on both sides.
2. Meanwhile, combine tomatoes, garlic, oregano, salt, pepper, and parsley. Slowly add tomato mix-

ture to browned veal. Cover and cook over low heat 45 minutes, or until meat is tender.

Beefsteak Pizzaiola: Follow recipe for Veal Chops Pizzaiola. Substitute **2 pounds beef round steak,** cut about $^3/_4$ inch thick, for veal chops. Cook about 1$^1/_2$ hours.

German Veal Chops

SERVES 4

4 veal loin or rib	1 cup dark beer
chops	1 bay leaf
Butter or margarine	$^1/_2$ teaspoon salt
2 medium onions,	Dash pepper
sliced	2 tablespoons flour

1. Brown veal in butter in a skillet; set meat aside. Sauté onion in same skillet until golden.
2. Add beer, bay leaf, salt, and pepper. Cover and simmer 15 minutes.
3. Transfer veal and onion to a platter. Make a paste of flour and a little water; stir into cooking liquid in skillet. Cook, stirring constantly, until thickened and smooth. Pour over veal and onion.

Note: If you do not have dark beer, add $^1/_2$ **teaspoon molasses** to light beer.

Veal Cutlet in Wine with Olives

SERVES ABOUT 6

1$^1/_2$ pounds veal	2 to 3 tablespoons
cutlet, cut about	butter or marga-
$^1/_4$ inch thick	rine
$^1/_4$ cup all-purpose	$^1/_3$ cup marsala
flour	$^1/_3$ cup sliced green
1 teaspoon salt	olives
$^1/_4$ teaspoon pepper	

1. Place meat on flat working surface and pound with meat hammer to increase tenderness. Turn meat and repeat process. Cut into 6 serving-size pieces. Coat with a mixture of flour, salt, and pepper.
2. Heat butter in skillet over low heat. Brown meat over medium heat. Add marsala and green olives. Cover skillet and cook over low heat about 1 hour, or until meat is tender when pierced with a fork.

Festive Veal Dish.

74

Stuffed Brisket of Veal.

Carbonada Criolla

SERVES ABOUT 10

2 pounds veal for stew (1- to 1½-inch pieces)	¼ teaspoon marjoram
½ cup flour	⅛ teaspoon cayenne pepper
1 teaspoon salt	6 peppercorns
Lard for frying	1 bay leaf
2 cloves garlic, crushed	1 cup white wine, such as sauterne
2 medium onions, peeled and chopped	1 cup beef broth
2 green peppers, cut in strips	1 can (about 8 ounces) whole kernel corn, drained
1 cup chopped celery	3 medium tomatoes, peeled and cut in wedges
4 potatoes, pared and cubed	
½ pound pared pumpkin meat, cubed (optional)	2 peaches, peeled and cut in wedges
2 apples, pared and cut in wedges	½ pound grapes, halved and seeded
¼ cup chopped parsley	½ pound zucchini, washed and thinly sliced
1½ teaspoons salt	
½ teaspoon thyme	

1. Coat veal with a mixture of flour and 1 teaspoon salt.
2. Heat a small amount of lard in a large skillet, add meat, and brown well on all sides.
3. Put browned meat into a large electric cooker.
4. Heat a small amount of lard in a skillet, add garlic, onion, and green pepper and cook until partially tender. Turn contents of skillet into cooker.

Add celery, potato, pumpkin (if used), apple, parsley, dry seasonings, wine, and broth; mix well.
5. Cover and cook on Low 8 to 10 hours.
6. Remove bay leaf. Add corn, tomatoes, peaches, grapes, and zucchini to mixture in cooker; stir.
7. Cover and cook on High 1 hour.
8. Accompany with fluffy hot rice.

Stuffed Brisket of Veal

SERVES 6

2 pounds brisket of veal, boneless	2 ounces water
½ teaspoon salt	¾ cup bread crumbs
½ teaspoon pepper	¼ cup raisins
Stuffing:	¼ cup brandy
¼ pound veal, minced	1 teaspoon salt
¼ pound pork, minced	¾ cup beef bouillon
	½ cup heavy cream

1. Wash the raisins in hot water, squeeze them, and put them to soak in the brandy.
2. Spread out the veal. Salt and pepper.
3. Mix the ingredients for the stuffing. Taste and correct seasonings and spread stuffing on the veal. Roll up and tie with string. Brush the roll with melted butter.
4. Preheat oven to 350°F. Place roll in baking pan and add beef stock. Lower the heat to 325°F when the roll has turned brown (about 25 minutes). Cook for another 45 minutes. Turn every half hour.
5. Remove veal from baking pan and keep warm. Meanwhile make sauce. To thicken pan drippings slowly add heavy cream. Serve with fried potatoes and vegetables.

Ossobuco

SERVES 6

3 pounds veal shank,
  sliced in 1-inch
  rounds
$^1/_2$ teaspoon salt
$^1/_2$ teaspoon pepper
$^1/_2$ cup flour
$^1/_2$ cup olive oil
$^3/_4$ cup dry white wine
1 cup onion, chopped
$^1/_2$ cup celery,
  chopped
2 small carrots,
  chopped
$2^1/_2$ cups tomatoes
1 cup chicken stock

1 clove garlic,
  crushed
1 sprig parsley
$^1/_2$ teaspoon thyme
1 bay leaf
Green of 1 leek
5 white pepper corns
Garnish:
3 tablespoons lemon
  juice
1 clove garlic,
  chopped
3 tablespoons parsley,
  chopped

1. Rub the veal slices with salt and pepper and coat them in flour. Heat $^1/_4$ cup oil in a large skillet and brown veal. Use more oil as needed. Set aside.
2. Pour the wine in the skillet and reduce to half over high heat.
3. In a casserole heat $^1/_4$ cup oil and sauté onion, celery, carrots, and garlic till slightly colored.
4. Place meat in casserole over vegetables. Pour wine on top. Add tomatoes, stock, parsley, thyme, bay leaf, leek, and peppercorns. Simmer for $1^1/_4$-$1^1/_2$ hours till meat is tender.
5. Taste and correct seasonings. Remove meat from casserole and strain sauce. Return meat and sauce to casserole and add lemon juice, garlic, and parsley. Simmer for an additional 5 minutes. Serve with risotto alla Milanaise.

Veal and Peppers Basilicata Style

SERVES 4

2 tablespoons butter
1 tablespoon lard
$1^1/_2$ pounds boneless
  veal leg, rump, or
  shoulder roast, cut
  in 1-inch pieces
1 teaspoon salt
$^1/_8$ teaspoon pepper
1 medium-size onion,
  sliced

4 large ripe tomatoes
1 tablespoon chopped
  basil leaves or
  1 teaspoon dried
  sweet basil
4 large firm green or
  red peppers
3 tablespoons olive oil

1. Heat butter and lard in skillet over medium heat.

(continued)

Ossobuco.

Add meat and brown on all sides. Stir in salt, pepper, and onion; cook 5 minutes.

2. Cut tomatoes in half, squeeze out seeds, chop pulp, and add with basil to meat. Cover and simmer 20 minutes.

3. Cut out stems, remove seeds, and clean peppers. Cut in quarters, lengthwise. Fry peppers in hot olive oil about 10 minutes, or until softened. Add to meat, cover, and simmer 30 minutes, or until meat is tender. Serve hot.

Veal St. Simon

SERVES 4

1¹/₄ pound boned veal shoulder	¹/₂ cup heavy cream
¹/₄ cup Madeira	¹/₂ teaspoon salt
¹/₄ cup butter	¹/₄ teaspoon pepper
2 shallots, chopped	¹/₂ teaspoon paprika
¹/₂ pound mushrooms	¹/₄ cup unsalted butter
4 medium tomatoes, skinned and quartered	12 puff paste crescents

1. Pound the veal thin, salt and pepper lightly. Place in a dish and pour on the Madeira; let stand for

about 2 hours, turning the veal a few times. Take out the veal and let it drain.

2. Brown 1 tablespoon butter in a frying pan and fry half of the veal quickly for about 2 minutes on each side. Remove to platter and keep hot. Repeat with remaining veal.

3. Put remaining butter in pan and sauté shallots and mushrooms for 5 minutes. Add tomatoes to the marinade and let the sauce boil slowly.

4. Add the cream and season. Finally stir in a pat of cold butter. Serve sauce over meat and place small puff paste crescents around the edges (baked with ready-made frozen puff paste dough or patty shells).

Saltimbocca

SERVES 4

4 large, thinly sliced veal cutlets	Dried sage leaves
Salt and pepper	Olive oil
4 large, very thin slices ham or prosciutto	¹/₄ cup (2 ounces) marsala

1. Place veal slices on a cutting board and pound with a mallet until very thin. Divide each slice into 2 or 3 pieces.

Veal St. Simon.

Veal and Mushroom Pancakes.

2. Season veal with salt and pepper.

3. Cut ham into pieces the same size as veal.

4. Place a sage leaf on each piece of veal and top with a slice of ham. Secure with a wooden pick.

5. Heat several tablespoons olive oil in a skillet; add the meat and cook slowly until golden brown on both sides. Remove meat to heated platter and keep warm.

6. Scrape residue from bottom of pan; add the marsala and simmer over low heat several minutes. Pour over meat and serve.

Veal and Mushroom Pancakes

SERVES 4-6

1½ cups chopped cooked veal	parsley
1¼ cups flour	A little cream
2 eggs	A pinch of mace or
1 egg yolk	ground nutmeg
1½ cups milk	A little oil
3 tablespoons butter	3 tablespoons grated
1 cup mushrooms	Parmesan cheese
½ cup corn	1½ tablespoons
1 tablespoon chopped	melted butter

Preheat broiler.

1. Sift 1 cup flour with salt and pepper into bowl. Make a hollow in center and drop in beaten eggs and 3-4 tablespoons of milk. Mix eggs and milk together with spoon before gradually drawing in flour. Add 6 tablespoons milk as mixture thickens; when it is smooth and like thick cream, beat for about 5 minutes. Then stir in 2 teaspoons of melted butter and another 3 tablespoons of milk. Leave batter in a covered bowl for about ½ hour before using.

2. Melt about 2 tablespoons butter and cook sliced mushrooms in covered pan for 3-4 minutes. Remove from stove. Stir in a scant tablespoon flour and add ½ cup of milk. Bring slowly to boil. Add chopped meat and corn, parsley, mace, seasoning, and cream. Keep warm while cooking pancakes.

3. Test thickness of batter, which should just coat back of spoon. If too thick, add remaining milk and stir well. Grease a 5-6 inch pancake or frying pan with a little oil. When hot, pour in enough batter to coat pan thinly. When browned on one side turn and cook on the other side. Pile up and keep warm. Allow 2 to 3 per person.

4. Put a spoonful of filling in center of each pancake and roll up. Arrange in overlapping rows in ovenproof dish. Sprinkle with grated cheese, spoon over melted butter, and broil until golden brown.

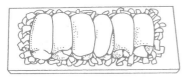

79

Wiener Schnitzel

SERVES 4

4 large thin veal scallops	1 hard-cooked egg
2-3 tablespoons flour	4 slices of lemon
1 egg	4 anchovies
5-6 tablespoons dried white bread crumbs	2 teaspoons capers
	2 teaspoons paprika
	4 olives
2-3 tablespoons butter	2 tablespoons chopped parsley

1. Beat out scallops between pieces of waxed paper until wafer thin. Toss in seasoned flour until completely coated. Shake to remove excess. Beat the raw egg with a few drips of oil and some salt. Brush each scallop with this, then toss in the dried white crumbs. (A paper bag is a good container for this process.)
2. Melt butter in frying pan. When foaming, cook scallops for 3-4 minutes on each side until they are golden brown and crisp.
3. Place on a hot dish and garnish the top of each scallop with 1 slice of lemon. In the center of this place an olive, and curl an anchovy filet around the olive. Surround this with a portion of chopped egg white, chopped capers, and paprika. Sprinkle all over with chopped parsley. Decorate with sieved egg yolk, if desired.

4. Serve at once, with the remaining butter from the frying pan as a sauce. (Extra butter can be added.)

Roast Stuffed Veal Roll

SERVES 6

2¹/₂-pound neck of veal	2 tablespoons vegetable oil
Salt	1 cup beef stock
Pepper	¹/₃ cup heavy cream
¹/₂ cup chopped parsley	1 tablespoon soy sauce
¹/₄ pound mushrooms, sliced	2 teaspoons flour mixed with a little cold water
¹/₂ red pepper, diced	
2 tablespoons butter	
³/₄ cup beef stock, heated	

1. Remove bones and filament from the meat. Season with salt and pepper and sprinkle on parsley and red pepper. Spread with the sliced mushrooms.
2. Roll together tightly and tie with string. Place the roll in a greased roasting pan. Brush with vegetable oil, season with salt and pepper, and insert a meat thermometer at the thickest part of the roll. Place in

(continued)

Wiener Schnitzel.

a 275°F oven and pour on the ³/₄ cup hot beef stock. Roast until thermometer reads 180°F.

3. Take the roll from the pan and keep hot. Whisk the pan with the cup of stock, stir in the cream, add the soy sauce, and thicken with the flour.

4. Serve the veal roll hot or cold.

Sunday Veal Burgers

SERVES 4

1¹/₂ pounds ground veal	1¹/₂ tablespoons salad oil
¹/₂ teaspoon salt	*Sauce:*
¹/₂ teaspoon pepper	1 cup Béarnaise sauce
¹/₄ teaspoon paprika	2 tablespoons tomato purée
1 egg yolk	*For Garnish and Serving:*
2 ounces cream	4 slices lean bacon
1 tablespoon sifted bread crumbs	1 box frozen green beans
3 ounces finely chopped parsley	1 tablespoon butter
For Frying:	Garlic salt
1¹/₂ tablespoons butter	

1. Mix the ground veal with seasonings, egg yolk, cream, bread crumbs, and chopped parsley. Shape mixture into hamburger patties.

2. Cook the green beans in butter, garlic salt, and salt.

3. Fry the hamburgers golden brown in the butter

and oil over medium heat, about 2¹/₂ minutes on each side.

4. Heat Béarnaise sauce.

5. Place the hamburgers on a hot serving dish. Garnish each hamburger with a crisp bacon slice. Mix the Béarnaise sauce with the tomato purée and pour it on the hamburgers. Place the green beans beside the hamburgers. Serve with fried or boiled potatoes and a green salad.

Wallenburgers

SERVES 4

1 pound ground veal	1¹/₂ tablespoons butter
1 cup heavy cream	¹/₄ teaspoon salt
4 egg yolks	¹/₄ teaspoon pepper
¹/₂ teaspoon salt	¹/₂ cup heavy cream
¹/₂ teaspoon freshly ground pepper	Dash of sherry (optional)
For Frying:	Paprika
2 tablespoons butter	
Mushroom Sauce:	
¹/₂ pound fresh mushrooms	

1. Work the ground veal with the cream, the egg yolks, and the seasonings.

2. Shape the mixture into four round hamburgers, and put them in the refrigerator for a while.

3. Fry the trimmed and washed mushrooms in the butter, salt, and pepper, pour on the cream, and reduce liquid by simmering to desired consistency.

4. Fry the hamburgers in the butter for 2-3 minutes on medium heat until golden brown on both sides. Place the hamburgers on a hot serving dish. Spread on the creamed mushrooms and sprinkle with paprika.

Serve with boiled or fried potatoes and a green salad.

Veal Paprika.

Veal Parmigiano

SERVES 4

1 pound veal steak or cutlet, thinly sliced	¹/₄ cup shortening
1 teaspoon salt	1 medium onion, finely chopped
¹/₈ teaspoon pepper	1 can (6 ounces) tomato paste
1 egg	
2 cups plus 2 teaspoons water	1 teaspoon salt
¹/₃ cup grated Parmesan cheese	¹/₂ teaspoon basil
	6 slices mozzarella cheese
¹/₃ cup fine dry bread crumbs	

1. Cut veal into 8 pieces; sprinkle with 1 teaspoon salt and the pepper.
2. Lightly beat together egg and 2 teaspoons water.
3. Combine Parmesan cheese and bread crumbs.
4. Dip veal in egg wash, then Parmesan mixture. Refrigerate at least ¹/₂ hour.
5. Brown veal on both sides in shortening in a skillet. Remove to a 1¹/₂-quart shallow baking dish.
6. Sauté onion in skillet. Stir in tomato paste, 1 teaspoon salt, and basil. Simmer 5 minutes. Pour three fourths of the sauce over veal. Top with mozzarella cheese. Pour remaining sauce over cheese.
7. Bake, uncovered, at 350°F 20 to 25 minutes, or until mixture is bubbly.

Veal Paprika

SERVES 4

1¹/₂ pounds veal steak, 1 inch thick	2 teaspoons prepared mustard
2 tablespoons bacon fat	1 can tomatoes (about 2¹/₂ cups)
2-3 onions, very finely chopped	1 teaspoon paprika
1 tablespoon flour	¹/₂ cup sour cream

Preheat oven to 350°F.
1. Brown the meat in the bacon fat, then put into a shallow casserole with a tightly fitting lid.
2. Brown the onion in the remaining fat, stir in the flour, add mustard, tomatoes, a little salt, and ¹/₂ cup water. Stir until boiling. Then pour over the meat just to cover. Add a little extra tomato juice if necessary.
3. Cover, and cook for about 45 minutes, or until the veal is tender.
4. Stir in paprika and cream, and mix well. Reheat without boiling. Adjust seasoning to taste before serving.

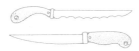

Veal Scaloppine with Mushrooms

SERVES 4

1 tablespoon flour	4 ounces fresh mush-
3/4 teaspoon salt	rooms, quartered
Pinch pepper	lengthwise
1 pound veal cutlets	1/2 cup sherry
2 tablespoons cooking	2 tablespoons finely
oil	chopped parsley

1. Combine flour, salt, and pepper; sprinkle over veal slices. Pound slices until thin, flat, and round, working flour mixture into both sides. Cut into 1/4-inch-wide strips.
2. Heat oil in a large wok. Add veal strips and stir-fry over high heat until golden.
3. Sprinkle mushrooms on top and pour sherry over all. Simmer, uncovered, about 15 minutes, or until tender.
4. Toss with parsley and serve.

Stuffed Veal Breast

SERVES 6

2 1/2 pounds boneless	1 teaspoon snipped
breast of veal	fresh or 1/2 tea-
Salt	spoon dried thyme
Freshly ground	leaves
pepper	1 1/2 teaspoons snipped
1 large onion,	fresh or 3/4 tea-
chopped	spoon dried basil
2 tablespoons	leaves
Chicken Stock*	1/2 teaspoon snipped
1/2 pound fresh spin-	fresh or 1/4 tea-
ach, washed and	spoon dried oreg-
stems removed (see	ano leaves
Note)	2 tablespoons snipped
3/4 cup low-fat ricotta	parsley
cheese	1 teaspoon salt
1/4 cup grated	1/4 teaspoon pepper
Jarlsberg or Par-	1/2 cup dry white wine
mesan cheese	or Chicken Stock*
2 garlic cloves,	
minced	*Check index for
	recipe

1. Trim excess fat from meat. Sprinkle meat lightly on both sides with salt and pepper.
2. Simmer onion in stock just until tender (about 5 minutes).
3. Place spinach with water clinging to leaves in a large saucepan; cook covered over medium heat just until wilted (about 3 minutes).
4. Drain onion and spinach well in a strainer, pressing moisture out with a wooden spoon. Mix onion, spinach, cheeses, garlic, thyme, basil, oregano, parsley, 1 teaspoon salt, and 1/4 teaspoon pepper. Spoon mixture on surface of meat; roll up and tie with string at intervals. Place meat in a roasting pan. Pour wine over roast. Cover.
5. Roast in a 325°F oven about 1 1/2 hours, or until tender.
6. Remove roast to a serving platter. Cover lightly with aluminum foil. Let stand 15 minutes before carving.

Note: 1 package (10 ounces) frozen spinach can be substituted for the fresh. Thaw and drain thoroughly in strainer.

Veal Rollettes

SERVES ABOUT 4

2 cloves garlic,	1 1/2 pounds veal
minced	round steak, cut
1 tablespoon grated	about 1/2 inch thick
Parmesan cheese	Mozzarella cheese,
2 teaspoons chopped	sliced
parsley	3 tablespoons olive oil
1/2 teaspoon salt	1/2 cup butter, melted
1/4 teaspoon pepper	1/4 cup water

1. Mix garlic, Parmesan cheese, parsley, salt, and pepper. Set aside.
2. Cut veal into 4 × 3-inch pieces. Put 1 slice mozzarella cheese on each piece of meat. Top each with 1 teaspoon garlic-cheese mixture. Roll each piece of meat to enclose mixture; tie with string, or fasten meat roll with wooden picks or small skewers.
3. Heat oil in a skillet. Add meat rolls and brown slowly on all sides. Put meat into a greased 2-quart casserole. Mix butter and water; pour over meat. Cover casserole.
4. Bake at 300°F about 1 hour, or until meat is tender. Remove string, wooden picks, or skewers.

Jellied Veal Loaf

SERVES 4-6

1 pound lean veal	2 cups well-flavored
1/4 pound bacon	Chicken Stock*
2 hard-cooked eggs	1 tablespoon gelatin
1 tablespoon chopped	*Check index for
parsley	recipe

Preheat oven to 320°F.
1. Cut veal into small strips, dice bacon, and bring to boil; drain and rinse with cold water.
2. Cut hard-cooked eggs into slices. Arrange meat

Jellied Veal Loaf.

and eggs in layers in a loaf pan or ring mold. Sprinkle each layer with parsley, salt, and pepper. Pour 1½ cups stock over meat. Cover with foil, cook in oven for about 1½ hours, and remove to cool.

3. Soak gelatin in remaining stock and melt over gentle heat. Pour over the meat and put in a cool place to set. When cold put in refrigerator for a short time or until needed.

4. Turn out the jellied veal and decorate dish with green salad, tomatoes, watercress, and cucumber.

Curried Veal and Vegetables

SERVES ABOUT 6

1 pound veal for stew (1-inch cubes)	3 tablespoons butter or margarine
2 cups water	2 tablespoons flour
1 teaspoon salt	½ teaspoon curry powder
3 medium carrots, pared and cut in quarters	¼ teaspoon salt
	Cooked rice
½ pound green beans	Fresh parsley, snipped
2 large stalks celery, cut in ½-inch slices	

1. Put veal into a large saucepan with water and 1

teaspoon salt. Cover, bring to boiling, reduce heat, and simmer 1 hour. Add carrots, green beans, and celery. Cover, bring to boiling, and simmer 1 hour, or until meat is tender.

2. Remove meat and vegetables from broth with a slotted spoon; set aside. Reserve broth.

3. Heat butter in a saucepan. Blend in flour, curry powder, and ¼ teaspoon salt. Heat until bubbly. Add reserved broth gradually, stirring until smooth. Bring to boiling, stirring constantly, and cook 1 to 2 minutes. Mix in meat and vegetables. Heat thoroughly.

4. Serve over rice. Sprinkle with parsley.

Sautéed Sweetbreads

SERVES 2

4 pairs sweetbreads from milk-fed calves	juice
	5 tablespoons butter or olive oil for frying
Ice water	
2 teaspoons salt	Flour seasoned with salt and pepper
1 teaspoon lemon	

1. Soak sweetbreads in ice water mixed with salt for 1 hour. Drain. *(continued)*

**Fried Kidneys
with Lemon Sauce.**

Veal Kidney Pie.

2. Place sweetbreads in boiling water to cover. Add lemon juice and simmer 10 minutes. Drain. Plunge at once into ice water. Remove membranes and connective tissue, and split into 2 pieces.

3. Melt butter or heat olive oil in a skillet. Dip sweetbreads into flour. Fry until golden brown on all sides.

Fried Kidneys with Lemon Sauce

SERVES 4

4 veal kidneys	1 egg, beaten
2 tablespoons butter	1 cup bread crumbs
$^1/_2$ cup flour	*Sauce:*
$^1/_2$ teaspoon salt	$^1/_4$ cup butter
$^1/_2$ teaspoon pepper	Juice of $^1/_2$ lemon

1. Skin the kidneys. Cut away the cores with scissors.

2. Coat kidneys with flour seasoned with salt and pepper. Dip in the beaten egg and roll in bread crumbs.

3. Heat 2 tablespoons butter in a heavy skillet, fry the kidneys over medium heat for 2-3 minutes on each side until lightly browned and pink in the center. Drain on paper towel and serve over rice.

4. Wipe out skillet and add $^1/_4$ cup butter and cook until light brown. Add lemon juice and mix. Serve over kidneys.

Veal Kidney Pie

SERVES 4

2 cups sifted all-purpose flour	3 tablespoons butter
6 ounces butter	$^1/_2$ pound mushrooms
4-5 tablespoons ice water	2 tablespoons chili sauce
2 pounds veal kidneys	$^3/_4$ cup heavy cream
$^1/_2$ teaspoon salt	$^1/_2$ teaspoon vinegar
$^1/_2$ teaspoon pepper	1 egg yolk, beaten

1. Cut butter into the flour with a pastry blender or two knives.

2. Quickly add the ice water, 1 tablespoon at a time.

3. Shape pastry into a ball. Wrap in waxed paper and refrigerate for 1 hour.

4. Roll out $^2/_3$ of the dough and place in a 9-inch pie pan. Cover the bottom and sides. Bake for 10 minutes in a 425°F oven.

5. Wash kidneys. Place them in lightly salted cold water and boil. Remove from pan and remove skin.

6. Remove fat from kidneys. Slice thinly, $^1/_4$-inch thick, and fry in 2 tablespoons butter. Set aside.

7. Rinse and clean mushrooms and sauté lightly in 1 tablespoon butter.

8. Add kidneys, chili sauce, cream, and vinegar and simmer for 10 minutes.

9. Roll out the rest of the dough.

10. Place kidneys in the baked pie crust and place remaining dough on top. Brush with egg and bake for 15 minutes until golden brown.

Serve with a green salad.

Calf's Liver with Curried Onions

SERVES 4

1 large yellow onion, sliced	$^1/_4$ cup golden raisins
$^1/_4$ cup sherry	2 teaspoons clarified butter
$^1/_2$ teaspoon curry powder	1 pound calf's liver
$^1/_2$ teaspoon salt	Clarified butter
Freshly ground pepper	

1. Simmer onion slices in wine in a medium skillet until onion is tender and wine is absorbed (about 10 minutes). Stir in curry powder, salt, pepper, raisins, and 2 teaspoons butter.

2. While onion is cooking, brush liver slices very lightly with clarified butter.

3. Broil 4 inches from heat until lightly browned (about 3 minutes on each side). Serve with onion.

Tongue in Almond Sauce

SERVES 8-10

2 veal tongues (about 2$^1/_2$ pounds each)	$^1/_2$ cup canned tomatoes with juice
1 medium onion, stuck with 2 or 3 cloves	$^1/_2$ cup whole blanched almonds
1 stalk celery with leaves	$^1/_2$ cup raisins
1 bay leaf	1 slice bread, torn in pieces
6 peppercorns	2 tablespoons lard or oil
2 teaspoons salt	2 cups tongue stock
Water	Salt and pepper
Almond Sauce:	$^1/_4$ cup blanched slivered almonds
2 fresh or dried ancho chilies	

1. Put tongues, onion stuck with cloves, celery, bay

(continued)

leaf, peppercorns, and salt into a Dutch oven or kettle. Cover with water. Cover Dutch oven, bring to boiling, and cook until meat is tender, about 2 hours. Allow to cool in liquid.

2. Remove skin from cooled tongues, trim off roots, and slice meat into 1/2-inch slices. Strain stock in which meat was cooked and save, discarding onion, celery, and bay leaf. Return sliced meat to kettle.

3. For almond sauce, first prepare chilies. Put chilies, tomatoes, the whole almonds, 1/4 cup of the raisins, and the bread into an electric blender. Blend to a thick purée.

4. Heat lard in a skillet. Add the puréed mixture and cook about 5 minutes. Stir in tongue stock and remaining 1/4 cup raisins. Cook about 5 minutes, stirring constantly. Season to taste with salt and pepper.

5. Pour sauce over sliced meat in Dutch oven and simmer until meat is heated through.

6. Transfer meat and sauce to platter and garnish with slivered almonds.

Veal Peasant Style

SERVES 6-8

2 tablespoons butter	3/4 cup beef broth
1 tablespoon olive oil	2 tablespoons butter
1 cup finely chopped onion	1 pound fresh green peas, shelled, or
1/3 cup finely chopped celery	1 package (10 ounces) frozen green peas
1 1/2 to 2 pounds veal, cubed	3 carrots, diced
1 teaspoon salt	1/2 teaspoon salt
1/4 teaspoon pepper	3/4 cup hot water
4 tomatoes, peeled and coarsely chopped	1 tablespoon minced parsley
Several basil leaves or 1/4 teaspoon dried basil leaves	

1. Heat 2 tablespoons butter and the olive oil in a Dutch oven or large saucepot. Add onion and celery; sauté 3 or 4 minutes.

2. Add meat and brown on all sides. Season with 1 teaspoon salt and the pepper. Stir in tomatoes and basil. Cover Dutch oven.

3. Cook at 275°F 1 1/4 hours, or until meat is almost tender. Add broth, a little at a time, during cooking.

4. Heat 2 tablespoons butter in a saucepan. Stir in peas, carrots, 1/2 teaspoon salt, and water. Cook, covered, until vegetables are tender (about 15 minutes).

5. Skim off fat from the meat. Stir in the cooked vegetables and parsley. Continue cooking in oven until meat is tender.

6. Serve meat surrounded with the vegetables and small sautéed potatoes on a heated platter. Pour sauce over all.

Sautéed Veal Brains in Browned Butter

SERVES 4

4 veal brains	1/2 cup butter
Juice of 2 lemons	2 tablespoons chopped fresh dill
1 teaspoon salt	1 lemon, cut in wedges
1/2 cup flour seasoned with salt and pepper	

1. Rinse brains thoroughly. Soak in water with ice cubes for 15 minutes. Drain; remove membranes.

2. Pour enough water into a saucepot to cover brains. Add lemon juice and salt; bring to boiling. Reduce heat and drop in brains. Simmer 15 minutes. Drain. Plunge into ice water to cool quickly.

3. Dip brains into seasoned flour.

4. Put butter into a skillet and heat until deep brown. Add brains and sauté briefly. Remove to a warm platter. Sprinkle with dill. Serve with lemon wedges.

Liver à la Nelson

SERVES 6

1 1/2 pounds sliced calf's liver	1/2 cup all-purpose flour
Milk	1/2 teaspoon salt
6 medium potatoes, pared	1/4 teaspoon pepper
1 onion, sliced	1 cup bouillon or meat broth
1/2 cup sliced mushrooms	1/2 cup sweet red wine or Madeira
1/4 cup butter	

1. Soak liver 45 minutes in enough milk to cover.

2. Cook potatoes in boiling water until tender; cut in thick slices.

3. Sauté onion and mushrooms in butter in a large skillet until tender, about 5 minutes.

4. Mix flour with salt and pepper. Drain liver; pat dry with paper towels. Coat liver with seasoned flour.

5. Quickly brown liver in skillet with onions and mushrooms. Add sliced potatoes, bouillon, and wine. Cover. Simmer just until liver is tender, about 10 to 15 minutes.

Sweetbread in Wine Sauce.

Sweetbreads in Wine Sauce

2 SERVINGS

³/₄ **pound sweetbreads**	**1 tablespoon tomato**
1 tablespoon butter	**purée**
1 sliced yellow onion	¹/₃ **cup white wine**
1 piece carrot, sliced	**Flour**
1 bay leaf	**8 mushrooms**
Few parsley sprigs	**1 egg**
10 black peppercorns	**3 tablespoons sea-**
1 teaspoon salt	**soned bread**
³/₄ **cup light bouillon**	**crumbs**
or canned con-	
sommé	

1. Put the sweetbreads in cold water for a while, then parboil them and remove as many filaments as possible.

2. Fry the onion and carrot in the butter. Add the sweetbreads and seasonings. Pour on the bouillon, tomato purée, and wine.

3. Cover the pot and let the sweetbreads simmer for about 10 minutes.

4. Take out the sweetbreads and let them get cold. Strain the liquid and reduce it by boiling for a few minutes. Season more if needed and thicken with flour.

5. Cut the sweetbreads in ¹/₂-inch thick slices and coat the slices in egg and bread crumbs.

6. Fry the slices attractively brown on both sides and put them on hot serving dish. Sprinkle with mushrooms that have been sautéed in butter. Pour on the sauce and garnish with chopped parsley.

Pork

Pork Chops Neapolitan Style

SERVES 4

1/2 cup olive oil	2 large sweet peppers
1 clove garlic, crushed	1 (1-pound) can tomatoes
8 loin pork chops	1/2 pound mushrooms, sliced
1/2 teaspoon salt	Parsley
1/2 teaspoon pepper	

1. Heat oil in a frying pan and sauté garlic until brown. Discard garlic and add pork chops.
2. Add more oil if necessary and brown on both sides till almost done, about 5 minutes on each side. Sprinkle lightly with salt and pepper and simmer gently.
3. Cut the peppers in half, discard cores and seeds, and cut the flesh into thin strips.
4. Take the meat from the pan and keep hot. Add peppers and tomatoes and cook over a medium heat for 20 minutes. Stir in the mushrooms, cover the pan, and simmer a few more minutes.
5. Return chops to sauce and heat thoroughly. Serve with parsley garnish.

Roast Suckling Pig

SERVES ABOUT 25

1 suckling pig, about 25 to 30 pounds	1/3 cup chopped parsley
Salt and pepper	1 potato
1 1/2 pounds stale bread, diced	Melted lard or salad oil
1 1/2 cups milk	1 small whole apple
2 eggs	Parsley sprigs or small fruits and leaves
2 apples, sliced	
2 onions, diced	

1. Wipe pig, inside and out, with a clean damp cloth. Sprinkle entire cavity with salt and pepper. If necessary to make pig fit into pan (and oven) cut crosswise in half just behind shoulders.
2. Put bread into a large mixing bowl. Add milk and let soak 20 minutes. Add eggs, sliced apples, onion, and parsley; mix well.
3. Spoon stuffing into cavity of pig. (There will not be enough stuffing to fill cavity entirely.)
4. Use metal skewers to hold cavity closed and lace with string.
5. Set pig belly side down in roasting pan. Tuck feet under body. Cover tail, snout, and ears with foil. Place whole potato in mouth.
6. Roast at 375°F 8 to 10 hours. Baste frequently with melted lard. When pig is done, juices run golden and skin is a crackling, translucent, golden-chocolate brown.
7. Set pig on platter. Remove potato from mouth; replace with apple. Make a wreath of parsley sprigs for neck or to cover joint behind shoulders.

Glazed Ham Steak

SERVES 6-8

1/2 cup buttermilk	1 teaspoon flour
1 smoked ham center slice, about 1 inch thick, cut in serving pieces	1/4 teaspoon pepper
	2 egg yolks
	1 cup buttermilk
1 teaspoon dry mustard	Paprika

1. Generously brush 1/2 cup buttermilk on both sides of ham slice. Arrange on roasting rack in a 2-quart glass baking dish.
2. Cook 7 to 8 minutes, rotating dish one-quarter turn halfway through cooking time.
3. In a 2-cup glass measure, combine mustard, flour, pepper, and egg yolks, blending well. Slowly add 1 cup buttermilk, stirring until combined.
4. Cook 2 to 3 minutes, stirring every 30 seconds, until mixture thickens.
5. Spoon over individual ham portions, arranged in serving dish. Sprinkle with paprika. Reheat 1 to 2 minutes if needed.

Tangy Pork Chops

SERVES 4-6

4 to 6 pork chops	1 can (10 1/2 ounces) condensed cream of celery soup
Prepared mustard	

1. Spread both sides of each pork chop with mustard and place in a 10-inch glass baking dish.
2. Cook pork chops 6 to 8 minutes, rotating dish one-quarter turn halfway through cooking time.
3. Remove drippings from pan. Pour soup over pork chops. Cook, covered, 5 to 6 minutes, rotating dish one-quarter turn halfway through cooking time.
4. Rest, covered, 5 minutes before serving.

Pork Chops Neapolitan Style.

Parsley-Stuffed Fillet of Pork.

Parsley-Stuffed Fillet of Pork

SERVES 6

2 pounds fresh fillet of pork	**¹/₄ teaspoon pepper**
¹/₂ pound butter	**1¹/₂ tablespoons butter**
1 bunch chopped parsley	**¹/₂ teaspoon salt**
¹/₂ teaspoon salt	**¹/₈ teaspoon pepper**
	¹/₂ cup bouillon

1. Trim the fillet and slit it lengthwise. Unfold and pound flat.
2. Mix butter, parsley, salt, and pepper and spread the mixture on the fillets.
3. Fold them together and tie with string.
4. Brown the fillet well all around in butter for 5 minutes.
5. Continue to cook covered for 5 minutes.
6. Remove the fillet from the pan, add bouillon, and boil. Serve the fillet with the bouillon and french fried potatoes.

Roast Loin of Pork

SERVES 5

3¹/₂-pound (8 ribs) pork loin roast	**¹/₂ teaspoon marjoram, crushed**
1¹/₂ teaspoons onion salt	**¹/₄ teaspoon pepper**

1. Rub roast with a mixture of the salt, marjoram, and pepper. Secure roast on spit. Insert meat thermometer. Adjust spit about 8 inches above prepared coals, placing aluminum foil pan under pork to catch drippings. If using a gas-fired grill, adjust flame size following manufacturer's directions.
2. Roast until meat thermometer registers 170°F or until meat is tender. About 30 minutes before roast is done, score surface.
3. Place roast on a warm serving platter. Garnish with parsley.

Note: To roast in the oven, place pork loin, fat side up, on a rack in a shallow roasting pan. Roast, uncovered, at 325°F about 2¹/₂ hours.

Roast Fresh Ham.

Roast Fresh Ham

SERVES 8

6-pound fresh ham
1 tablespoon salt
1 tablespoon dry
  mustard
$^{1}/_{2}$ teaspoon coarsely
  ground black
  pepper
3 yellow onions,
  chopped

6 carrots, sliced
3 cups beef stock
$1^{1}/_{2}$ tablespoons soy
  sauce
$^{1}/_{2}$ teaspoon salt
$^{1}/_{4}$ cup flour

1. Place the ham in a roasting pan and bake in a 300°F oven for 45 minutes.
2. Remove the ham from the oven and cut off the rind. Slit through the fat down to the meat in a lattice pattern.
3. Mix salt, dry mustard, and pepper and rub the ham with the mixture. Arrange the vegetables around the ham and return to the oven.
4. Bake for another 45 minutes. Add the beef stock mixed with soy and salt.

5. Continue roasting until a meat thermometer inserted into the thickest part of the ham registers 185° (about 4 to 5 hours total).
6. Make the sauce: strain the pan juices (there should be about 3 cups). Add the flour and bring the sauce to a boil while beating. Let boil for about 5 minutes. Season with salt and pepper if desired.

Fresh Ham

SERVES 10-12

5- to 6-pound cook-
  before-eating ham

1. Place ham on roasting rack in a 2-quart glass baking dish. Shield protruding corners or shank end with foil. Do not allow foil to touch walls inside microwave oven.
2. Cook 40 to 50 minutes, allowing 8 to 9 minutes

(continued)

93

per pound. Turn ham over and rotate dish one-quarter turn halfway through the cooking time.
3. Rest 10 to 15 minutes before carving or serving.
Cooked Ham: Follow recipe for Fresh Ham, but allow 6 to 7 minutes per pound cooking time, or 30 to 40 minutes for a 5- to 6-pound ham.
Fresh Pork Roast: Follow recipe for Fresh Ham, allowing 8 to 9 minutes per pound cooking time.

Indonesian Casserole

SERVES 8

2 pounds lean shoulder of pork	chopped
Salt	2 sour apples in wedges
Pepper	1 red and 1 green pepper, cut in strips
Ginger	
For Frying:	1 can bamboo shoots, sliced
1½ tablespoons butter	
1½ tablespoons salad oil	1½ cups beef stock
1 large yellow onion, sliced	4 ounces Chinese sweet and sour sauce
1 sliced leek	2 teaspoons soy sauce
2 cloves garlic,	1 banana, sliced

1. Cut the pork in large cubes and brown in butter and oil. Season lightly and transfer to a stew pan.
2. Fry onion, apple, and peppers in butter and oil and transfer to stew pan.
3. Whisk the frying pan with some of the beef stock and pour into stew pan.
4. Add the well-drained bamboo shoots, the sweet and sour sauce, and the soy sauce. Add the rest of the beef stock. Simmer covered for about 25 minutes.

Serve straight from the stew pan with sliced bananas and boiled rice.

Pork and Potatoes

SERVES 4

¾ pound lean pork, cubed	1 teaspoon mustard
¾ pound turnips, cubed	¼ cup water
2 tablespoons butter	1 tablespoon all-purpose flour
½ teaspoon salt	¼ cup heavy cream
¼ teaspoon pepper	Parsley

1. Brown the pork and turnip cubes in butter. Season with salt and pepper.
2. Add mustard and water; simmer covered until turnips are almost soft.

3. Sprinkle with flour, add cream, and stir.
4. Serve the hash on a platter, sprinkle with parsley. Serve with green beans.

Breakfast Kabobs

SERVES 6-8

8 ounces link pork sausage	16 maraschino cherries
6 ounces Canadian bacon, or 12 ounces canned luncheon meat	Maple syrup
	8 bamboo skewers
1 can (8 ounces) pineapple chunks, drained	

1. Cut each sausage link in 3 or 4 pieces. Cut bacon in small cubes.
2. Thread meat and fruit alternately on skewers. Arrange in a 2-quart glass baking dish and brush with maple syrup.
3. Cook, covered, 4 to 6 minutes, rotating one-quarter turn and basting with syrup halfway through cooking time.

Pork Pot Roast

SERVES 6-8

1 pork shoulder arm picnic or pork loin roast, boneless (3 pounds)	to taste: allspice, caraway seed, whole cloves, juniper berries, dried marjoram leaves, peppercorns (tie in cheesecloth)
2 tablespoons butter or lard	
2 tomatoes, peeled and cored	¼ cup water
1 celery root	½ cup bouillon or meat broth
1 parsley root	
1 onion, sliced	½ cup Madeira, marsala, or sherry
2 sprigs parsley	
2 tablespoons spices	

1. Rub meat with salt and pepper. Let stand 1 hour.
2. Brown meat in butter in a large, heavy skillet. Add vegetables, parsley, spice bag, and water. Cover tightly. Cook over medium heat 1½ hours, stirring as necessary and turning meat occasionally.
3. Sprinkle a small amount of flour over top of meat. Pour bouillon and wine over meat. Simmer 15 minutes.
4. Slice and arrange meat on a warm platter. Strain sauce and pour over meat.

Pork and Potatoes.

Indonesian Casserole.

Spareribs with Ginger Flavor

SERVES 4

2 pounds thick spare-ribs	1 teaspoon ginger
1¹/₂ teaspoons white or black pepper	¹/₄ cup beef stock

1. Rub the spareribs with the seasonings and place them on a rack in a roasting pan with the fat side up. Add ¹/₄ cup hot water to the pan.
2. Cook in a 325°F oven for about 1¹/₂ hours. Turn the ribs once while cooking. The meat juice can be seasoned with some beef stock. Serve the spareribs with red cabbage, apple, cheese, and prunes.

Spareribs

SERVES 4

1¹/₂ to 2 pounds lean spareribs	2 cups Barbecue Sauce
¹/₂ cup water	

1. In a covered 2-quart casserole, arrange spareribs in serving-size pieces toward edges of dish. Add ¹/₄ cup water, cover, and cook 6 minutes, rotating dish one-quarter turn halfway through cooking time. Pour off water and drippings.
2. Add another ¹/₄ cup water, cover, and cook again 6 minutes, rotating dish one-quarter turn halfway through cooking time. Pour off drippings.
3. Arrange spareribs in a 10-inch glass serving dish and cover with Barbecue Sauce.
4. Cook, uncovered, 4 to 5 minutes, rotating dish one-quarter turn halfway through cooking time.
5. Rest, uncovered, 5 minutes before serving.

Pork Loin Roast

SERVES 8-10

1 pork loin roast (4 to 6 pounds)	Salt and pepper Spiced crab apples

1. Have the butcher saw across the rib bones of roast at base of the backbone, separating the ribs from the backbone. Place roast, fat side up, on a rack in an open roasting pan. Season with salt and pepper. Insert meat thermometer in roast so the bulb is centered in the thickest part and not resting on bone or in fat.
2. Roast in a 350°F oven about 2¹/₂ to 3 hours, or until thermometer registers 170°F; allow 30 to 40 minutes per pound.

Spareribs with Ginger Flavor.

Spareribs.

3. For easy carving, remove backbone, place roast on platter, and allow roast to set for 15 to 20 minutes. Garnish platter with spiced crab apples, heated if desired.

Ham in Rye Crust

SERVES 12-15

Dough:
1 package active dry yeast
$\frac{1}{2}$ cup warm water
$\frac{1}{3}$ cup caraway seed
$\frac{3}{4}$ cup water
2 tablespoons molasses
3 cups rye flour (about)

Topping for ham:
$\frac{1}{2}$ cup firmly packed brown sugar
1 teaspoon dry mustard
$\frac{1}{4}$ teaspoon cloves
1 canned full cooked ham (5 pounds)

1. For dough, dissolve yeast in $\frac{1}{2}$ cup warm water and add caraway seed; let stand 10 minutes.
2. Stir in $\frac{3}{4}$ cup water, molasses, and half of the flour.
3. Turn out dough onto floured surface. Knead in remaining flour to make a stiff dough. Cover with plastic wrap. Let rest 20 minutes.
4. Mix brown sugar with mustard and cloves.
5. Remove gelatin and wipe ham with paper towels.
6. Roll out dough on a floured surface to form a 28 × 10-inch rectangle.
7. Sprinkle about 1 tablespoon brown sugar mixture

in center of dough. Place ham on sugar mixture. Sprinkle remaining sugar mixture over top of ham.
8. Fold dough over top of ham, cutting out corners to fit with only one layer of dough. Pinch edges to seal.
9. Set dough-wrapped ham on rack in pan lined with foil.
10. Roast at 350°F $1\frac{1}{2}$ to $1\frac{3}{4}$ hours, or until meat thermometer reaches 140°F. Remove from oven; let rest 10 minutes.
11. To serve, remove crust and discard. Slice ham.

Spareribs

SERVES 4

$3\frac{1}{4}$-$4\frac{1}{2}$ pounds spareribs
$\frac{3}{4}$ teaspoon salt

$\frac{1}{2}$-1 teaspoon ground ginger, rosemary, sage, or oregano

1. Rub meat with seasonings. Place bone down in open roasting pan with some water in the bottom.
2. Bake in 400°F oven about $1\frac{1}{2}$ hours. Add 1 bouillon cube and more water to meat juices to make more sauce if necessary. Sauce can be thickened with flour.

Serve with baked potatoes and red cabbage.

Curried Pork Steaks with Apple Onion

SERVES 4

4 slices (1 pound) boned thick flank of pork	¹/₂ teaspoon curry powder
3 tablespoons butter	*Apple onion:*
Coating:	1 large sour apple, chopped
1 egg, beaten	1 medium yellow onion, chopped
3 ounces finely sifted bread crumbs	1 tablespoon butter
1 teaspoon salt	Chopped parsley

1. Flatten the pork slices and coat them with the beaten egg. Dip in bread crumbs seasoned with salt and curry powder. Set pork aside until the coating dries.
2. Heat the butter in a heavy frying pan and fry the pork over medium heat for about 6 minutes on each side. Place the cooked pork on a heated serving dish.
3. Sauté the chopped onion until transparent. Add the chopped apple and sauté until the apple is soft. Stir in chopped parsley. Distribute mixture on the pork and place on a bed of boiled rice mixed with butter and curry powder.

Sauerkraut with Pork

SERVES ABOUT 6

2 pounds pig's feet or ham hocks	1 bay leaf
2 pounds neck bones or spareribs	¹/₂ teaspoon celery seed
3 tablespoons lard or margarine	1 quart (about 2 pounds) sauerkraut
1 large onion	¹/₄ cup barley
1 clove garlic, crushed	1 small apple, chopped
1¹/₂ quarts boiling water	¹/₂ teaspoon caraway seed
1 green pepper, diced	2 tablespoons salt
4 whole allspice	¹/₂ teaspoon pepper

1. Brown all meat in lard in a large kettle.
2. Add onion and garlic. Fry 1 minute.
3. Add boiling water, green pepper, allspice, bay leaf, and celery seed. Cover; cook 1 hour or until meat is tender.

Curried Pork Steaks with Apple Onion.

4. Remove meat; cool. Boil until broth is reduced to 3 cups.
5. Discard bones and gristle from meat. Drain and rinse sauerkraut.
6. Cook barley in the broth 15 minutes. Add meat, sauerkraut, apple, caraway seed, salt, and pepper. Cook 45 minutes longer.
7. Serve with potato dumplings, if desired.

Smoked Sausage Dinner

SERVES 4

1 medium onion, chopped	sausage, cut in ¹/₂-inch pieces
¹/₂ cup chopped green pepper	1 can (16 ounces) tomatoes, cut up
2 tablespoons butter or margarine	1 cup uncooked noodles
1 pound smoked	

1. Sauté onion and green pepper in butter in a skillet. Add sausage and brown lightly; drain off excess fat.
2. Stir in remaining ingredients. Put into a 1¹/₂-quart casserole.
3. Bake, covered, at 375°F 45 minutes, or until noodles are tender, stirring once.

Pork Roast with Olives and Rice

SERVES ABOUT 12

7-pound pork loin roast	¹/₂ teaspoon ground sage
3 cloves garlic, slivered	¹/₄ teaspoon pepper
1¹/₂ cups chicken broth	³/₄ cup sliced pimiento-stuffed olives
³/₄ cup dry vermouth	Special Gravy (below)
	Saffron Rice (below)

1. Score fat side of pork roast; insert garlic in slits. Place, fat side up, in a shallow roasting pan. Insert a meat thermometer in roast so that tip rests in thickest part of the meat.
2. Combine broth, vermouth, sage, and pepper; pour over meat.
3. Roast at 325°F until meat thermometer registers 170°F, basting occasionally. Total cooking time will be about 2¹/₂ hours. The last hour of cooking time, add ¹/₂ cup of the sliced olives to liquid in pan.
4. Transfer roast to a heated platter; keep warm.
5. Remove olives; reserve to add to rice along with remaining olives. Use liquid for the gravy.

(continued)

99

6. Spoon the Saffron Rice onto platter around the roast. Accompany with the gravy.

Special Gravy: Skim excess fat from reserved liquid. Measure liquid and add enough water to make 1³/₄ cups. Return liquid to pan or pour into a saucepan and bring to boiling. Stir a blend of **2 tablespoons cornstarch** and **¹/₄ cup water** into boiling liquid; boil 1 to 2 minutes, stirring constantly. Pour into a gravy boat.
About 2 Cups Gravy

Saffron Rice: In a large saucepan, combine **1 quart chicken broth, 2 cups uncooked white rice, 2 tablespoons butter or margarine, ¹/₂ teaspoon salt,** and **¹/₄ teaspoon crushed saffron.** Bring to boiling, stirring with a fork. Cook, covered, over low heat 15 to 20 minutes, or until rice is tender. Toss reserve olives with rice.
About 8 Cups

Glazed Roast Ham

SERVES ABOUT 20

10-pound whole smoked ham

1. Place ham on a rack in a shallow roasting pan. Roast at 300° to 325°F about 2 hours; remove from oven.

2. Cut off rind (if any) and score fat. Insert a **whole clove** in the center of each diamond.

3. Spread with one of **Glazes for Ham** (below), and continue roasting about 1 hour, or until internal temperature reaches 160°F.

Glazes for Ham

Cider: Combine and mix thoroughly ³/₄ **cup packed brown sugar, ¹/₂ teaspoon dry mustard,** and **2 tablespoons maple syrup.** Spread glaze over ham. Occasionally baste ham with about ³/₄ **cup apple cider.**

Apricot (using dried apricots): Pour 1¹/₃ **cups apple cider** over **8 ounces dried apricots** in a bowl. Cover and refrigerate overnight. Purée apricot mixture in an electric blender or force through a food mill. Stir in a mixture of **6 tablespoons brown sugar, ¹/₂ teaspoon ground cinnamon, ¹/₂ teaspoon ground allspice,** and **¹/₄ teaspoon ground cloves.** Spread ham generously with mixture before heating. Heat remaining sauce and serve as an accompaniment to the ham.

Mustard Glaze: Mix thoroughly in a small bowl **1 cup packed brown sugar, 1 tablespoon flour,** and **1 teaspoon dry mustard.** Stir in **2 tablespoons cider vinegar** to form a smooth paste.

Brown Sugar: Heat together in a saucepan, stirring until sugar is dissolved, **1 cup packed brown sugar** and ²/₃ **cup light corn syrup.** If desired, ²/₃ **cup spiced fruit juice or ginger ale** may be substituted for the corn syrup.

Festive Pork Fillet.

Festive Pork Fillet

SERVES 4

1 pound pork fillet	³/₄ pound mushrooms
2 tablespoons butter	2 tablespoons butter
1 teaspoon salt	¹/₂ cup red wine
1 teaspoon crushed	¹/₂ cup heavy cream
sage	1 small can olives
1 crushed clove garlic	

1. Cut the pork fillet in slices and brown in butter. Season and add the garlic.
2. Slice the mushrooms and sauté in the butter, seasoning lightly with salt and pepper. Put the fillet slices and mushrooms in an ovenproof casserole.
3. Heat the red wine and cream over medium heat and pour on the fillet slices. Simmer covered for 5 minutes.
4. Slice the olives and place on top of the fillet. Serve the dish with boiled rice and a green salad.

Oriental Pork Casserole

SERVES 6

2 pounds lean shoulder of pork	2 large yellow onions
Flour	5 tablespoons curry powder
5 tablespoons vegetable oil	1 quart beef stock

1. Cut the meat in large cubes and coat in flour. Brown in 3 tablespoons vegetable oil.

2. Peel the onions and cut coarsely. Brown in vegetable oil. Dredge with curry powder.
3. Mix meat and onions in a casserole and add the beef stock. Cook covered over low heat for 30 minutes.
Serve with rice, banana slices, raisins, apple pieces, peanuts, candied ginger, paprika, or mango.

Pork Casserole with Caraway Cabbage

SERVES 4

1 pound fresh shoulder of pork	2 carrots
1 onion	¹/₂ teaspoon salt
1 tablespoon butter	¹/₂ teaspoon pepper
¹/₂ head white cabbage (1 pound)	1 teaspoon pounded caraway
	1 cup beef stock

1. Cut away the rind if any and cut the meat in 1" × 1" pieces. Chop the onion.
2. Brown the butter in a heavy frying pan and add the pork. Sauté until brown.
3. Cut the white cabbage into strips. Scrape and slice the carrots. *(continued)*

Oriental Pork Casserole.

Pork Casserole with Caraway Cabbage.

4. Layer meat, cabbage, onion, and carrots with seasonings in a casserole.
5. Pour on the beef stock.
6. Simmer slowly, covered, for 30-35 minutes. Serve with boiled potatoes.

Place chops on platter. Stir flour paste, rest of beer, bouillon, and ketchup into cooking liquid. Cook, stirring constantly, until thickened. Season to taste, if desired. (Makes enough gravy to pour over meat and potatoes.)

Pork Chops Piquant

SERVES 4

4 pork loin chops, 1 inch thick	**$^1/_4$ cup dry white wine**
$^1/_4$ cup water	**1 green pepper, chopped**
$^1/_4$ teaspoon bottled brown bouquet sauce	**1 medium yellow onion, chopped**
$^1/_2$ teaspoon salt	**2 tablespoons capers, drained**
Freshly ground pepper	**Watercress or parsley sprigs**
$^1/_2$ cup Chicken Stock*	***Check index for recipe**

1. Trim excess fat from chops. Brush chops lightly with a mixture of water and brown bouquet sauce. Brown chops lightly on both sides in a nonstick skillet over medium heat. Sprinkle with salt and pepper.
2. Add stock and wine. Simmer, covered, 30 minutes. Skim fat from liquid. Stir in green pepper, onion, and capers. Simmer, uncovered, 10 to 15 minutes until vegetables are just tender. Taste vegetables and sauce; adjust seasoning.
3. Serve vegetables and sauce over chops; garnish with watercress.

Northwoods Pork Chops

SERVES 4

1 package ($2^3/_4$ ounces) instant wild rice	**4 pork chops, $^3/_4$ inch thick**
$^1/_4$ cup chopped celery	**$^1/_4$ cup flour**
$^1/_4$ cup chopped green pepper	**2 cups milk**
$^1/_4$ cup chopped onion	**$^1/_2$ teaspoon salt**
6 tablespoons butter or margarine	**$^1/_8$ teaspoon pepper**
	$^1/_2$ cup (2 ounces) shredded American cheese

1. Prepare wild rice according to package directions.
2. Sauté celery, green pepper, and onion in 4 tablespoons butter in a skillet. Combine with wild rice. Put into a $1^1/_2$-quart shallow baking dish.
3. Brown pork chops on both sides in skillet. Place on top of wild rice mixture.
4. Melt remaining 2 tablespoons butter in skillet. Blend in flour. Gradually add milk, stirring until thickened and smooth. Add salt and pepper. Pour over pork chops.
5. Bake, covered, at 350°F 1 hour, or until chops are done. Sprinkle with cheese.

Breaded Pork Chops with Beer Gravy

SERVES 4

4 pork chops, cut $^1/_2$ to $^3/_4$ inch thick	**$^1/_2$ teaspoon salt**
1 egg	**$^1/_4$ teaspoon paprika**
1 tablespoon water	**2 tablespoons oil**
$^1/_2$ cup fine cracker crumbs (from about 12 saltines)	**$^3/_4$ cup beer**
	2 tablespoons flour
	$^3/_4$ cup beef bouillon
	1 tablespoon ketchup

1. Dip chops in a mixture of egg and water, coating both sides. Mix crumbs, salt, and paprika. Dip egg-coated chops in this mixture, coating both sides well.
2. Brown chops slowly in oil, cooking about 15 minutes. Reduce heat; add $^1/_4$ cup beer. Cover and simmer 20 to 30 minutes, or until done.
3. Make a paste of flour and a little remaining beer.

Golden Pork Chop Bake

SERVES 6

6 pork chops, 1 inch thick	**golden mushroom soup**
2 tablespoons shortening	**$1^1/_3$ cups water**
$^1/_2$ cup sliced celery	**$1^1/_3$ cups packaged precooked rice**
1 garlic clove, minced	**$^1/_2$ cup chopped tomato**
2 cans ($10^3/_4$ ounces each) condensed	

1. Brown pork chops on both sides in shortening in a skillet. Remove chops from skillet; drain off excess fat.
2. Sauté celery and garlic in skillet. Combine with remaining ingredients. Spoon into a 2-quart shallow baking dish.
3. Arrange chops on top of rice mixture.
4. Bake, covered, at 350°F 1 hour, or until chops are tender.

California Pork Chops.

California Pork Chops

SERVES 4

4 large lean pork chops	*Sauce:*
Salt	³/₄-1¹/₄ cups water or bouillon
Pepper	1-2 teaspoons flour
Rosemary	2-3 teaspoons granu- lated sugar
1-2 tablespoons butter or marga- rine	2-3 tablespoons lemon juice
Parsley	Chinese soy sauce
Lemon	

1. Season pork chops with salt, pepper, and rosemary and brown in butter or margarine. Remove from pan and add water or bouillon to pan.
2. Add flour, lemon juice, sugar, and soy sauce to pan. Let pork chops simmer in sauce for 10-15 minutes, covered. Serve with lemon slices, parsley, and boiled potatoes.

Sausage Ring

SERVES 4-5

1 pound bulk pork sausage	¹/₂ cup bread crumbs
2 eggs	2 tablespoons parsley flakes
2 tablespoons minced onion	

1. In a 1-quart casserole, blend sausage, eggs, onion, bread crumbs, and parsley flakes. Mold into a ring and place a small glass, open end up, in the center of the ring. *(continued)*

103

Swedish Pork Chops.

2. Cook 5 to 6 minutes, rotating dish one-quarter turn halfway through cooking time.

3. Rest 5 minutes, remove glass from center, and invert ring on plate to serve. Center may be filled with cooked rice or noodles. If using for breakfast, center may be filled with scrambled eggs.

Note: Leftover Sausage Ring makes good sandwiches when reheated.

Fruited Pork Roast, Scandinavian Style

SERVES 8

1 pork rolled loin roast, boneless (3 to 3¹/₂ pounds)	**1 medium apple, pared and chopped**
8 to 10 pitted dried prunes	**1 teaspoon lemon juice**
1 can or bottle (12 ounces) beer	**¹/₂ teaspoon salt**
¹/₂ teaspoon ginger	**Dash pepper**
	¹/₄ cup flour

1. Make pocket down center of roast by piercing with a long, sharp tool such as a steel knife sharpener; leave string on roast. (Alternate method: Remove string. Using strong knife, cut pocket in pork by making a deep slit down length of loin, going to within ¹/₂ inch of the two ends and within 1 inch of other side.)

2. Meanwhile, combine prunes, beer, and ginger in a saucepan; heat to boiling. Remove from heat; let stand 30 minutes.

3. Mix apple with lemon juice to prevent darkening. Drain prunes, reserving liquid; pat dry with paper towels. Mix prunes and apple.

4. Pack fruit into pocket in pork, using handle of wooden spoon to pack tightly. (With alternate method of cutting pocket, tie with string at 1-inch intervals. Secure with skewers or sew with kitchen thread.)

5. Place meat on rack in a roasting pan.

6. Roast at 350°F 2 to 2¹/₂ hours, allowing 40 to 45 minutes per pound. During last 45 minutes of roasting, spoon fat from pan; baste occasionally with liquid drained from prunes.

7. Transfer meat to a platter. Skim fat from cooking liquid; measure liquid. Add a little water to roasting pan to help loosen brown bits; add to cooking liquid. Add salt, pepper, and enough additional water to measure 2 cups total. Make a paste of flour and a little more water. Combine with cooking liquid. Cook, stirring constantly, until thickened. Pass in a sauceboat for pouring over meat slices.

Swedish Pork Chops

SERVES 5

5 pork chops	**1 teaspoon Worcestershire sauce**
Salt	**1 bay leaf**
Pepper	**³/₄ cup Parmesan cheese, grated**
1 onion	
1¹/₂ cups tomato juice	
1 tablespoon vinegar	

1. Brown pork chops on both sides in hot frying pan with no butter added. Season with salt and pepper.

Ham and Mushrooms with Mashed Potatoes.

2. Place chops in ovenproof dish and boil frying pan off with ³/₄ cup water.

3. Add tomato juice, vinegar, and Worcestershire sauce. Slice onion and place on pork chops. Pour sauce over. Place bay leaf on top.

4. Sprinkle with cheese and bake in 475°F oven 15-20 minutes.

Serve with fried potatoes and a green salad.

Pork Slices in Mole Verde

SERVES 6-8

¹/₂ cup finely chopped onion	1 to 3 tablespoons minced canned green chilies
¹/₄ cup finely chopped blanched almonds	2 cups chicken stock, or 2 cups water plus 2 chicken bouillon cubes
2 tablespoons vegetable oil	
2 cans (10 ounces each) Mexican green tomatoes (tomatillos)	6 to 8 slices cooked pork loin roast
1 tablespoon minced fresh coriander (cilantro) or 1 teaspoon dried coriander	Salt
	Small lettuce leaves
	Whole pickled mild chilies
	Sour cream

1. Combine onion, almonds, and oil in a saucepan. Cook over medium heat until onion is soft.

2. Turn contents of cans of green tomatoes into an electric blender and blend until smooth (or force green tomatoes through a sieve).

3. Add purée to onion mixture and stir in coriander, chilies (to taste), and stock. Bring to boiling, reduce heat, and simmer, uncovered, until reduced to 2¹/₂ cups; stir occasionally.

4. Arrange meat in a large skillet, sprinkle with salt to taste, and pour sauce over meat. Cover, bring slowly to boiling, reduce heat, and simmer about 10 minutes, or until thoroughly heated.

5. Arrange sauced meat on a platter. Garnish with lettuce and chilies. Accompany with sour cream.

Ham and Mushrooms with Mashed Potatoes

SERVES 4

4 portions mashed potatoes	2 tablespoons butter
¹/₄ teaspoon nutmeg	1 tablespoon all-purpose flour
¹/₂ teaspoon salt	1 cup light cream
1 pound boiled ham, chopped	¹/₄ teaspoon pepper
¹/₂ pound mushrooms, quartered	¹/₂ cup sour cream
¹/₂ cup onion, chopped	¹/₄ pound Swiss cheese, grated

1. Preheat oven to 450°F.

2. Season potatoes with nutmeg and salt. Arrange in a ring in an ovenproof serving dish.

3. Sauté mushrooms and onion in butter. Stir in flour.

4. Add cream, salt, and pepper and stir until thickened. Remove from heat and stir in sour cream.

(continued)

5. Mix ham and mushrooms. Place in the center of the dish.

6. Sprinkle grated cheese on potatoes. Bake for 20 minutes.

Serve with a green salad.

Ham Ratatouille

SERVES 6

4 onions	2 cloves garlic,
2 leeks	pressed
6 carrots	1 can tomato paste
2 tablespoons vege-	1 teaspoon salt
table oil	Pepper to taste
1 cucumber	1 (1-pound) canned
6 tomatoes	ham

1. Rinse the vegetables. Cut the onions and tomatoes in wedges. Cut the leeks and carrots on the bias and the cucumber in the shape of half moons.

2. Warm the oil in a skillet. Add the onions and carrots and simmer without browning. Add the cucumbers and the tomatoes.

3. Stir in the garlic and tomato paste. Add salt.

4. Cover and simmer 10 minutes.

5. Add the gelatin from the canned ham.

6. Cut the ham in strips and add to mixture. Heat thoroughly. Serve with hot bread.

Ham Loaf en Brioche

SERVES ABOUT 8

Brioche Dough:	2 eggs, beaten
1 package	2 cups fine soft bread
(13³/₄ ounces) hot	crumbs
roll mix	³/₄ cup California
¹/₄ cup warm water	sauterne
¹/₃ cup milk	¹/₂ teaspoon dry
¹/₃ cup butter or	mustard
margarine	¹/₂ teaspoon salt
2 tablespoons sugar	¹/₄ teaspoon pepper
3 eggs, beaten	¹/₂ cup coarsely
Ham Loaf:	chopped ripe olives
2 cups ground cooked	¹/₄ cup diced pimiento
ham	1 tablespoon instant
1 pound ground veal	minced onion
or lean beef	

1. For brioche dough, combine yeast from packet in hot roll mix with warm water.

2. Scald milk and cool to lukewarm.

3. Cream butter and sugar. Add eggs and yeast; mix well. Stir in flour mixture from mix alternately with milk, beating until smooth after each addition. Cover tightly; let rise in a warm place until light (about 1

hour). Stir down and set in refrigerator until thoroughly chilled.

4. Meanwhile, prepare ham loaf.

5. For ham loaf, combine all ingredients and mix well. Turn into a greased fluted brioche pan, about 8¹/₂ inches across top and about 1-quart capacity; pack into pan and round up center.

6. Bake at 350°F 1 hour. Cool in pan about 10 minutes, then turn out of pan and cool thoroughly.

7. Divide chilled brioche dough in half. Roll each portion into a round about 10 inches in diameter. Turn cooled ham loaf upside down and fit a round of dough over bottom and sides. Trim off excess dough. Holding dough in place, quickly invert loaf and fit other round of dough over top and sides. Trim edges evenly.

8. Place dough-wrapped loaf in a well-greased brioche pan a size larger than one used for ham loaf, about 9¹/₂ inches in diameter across top and about 2-quarts capacity.

9. Shape dough trimmings into a ball and place on top of loaf. Let rise in a warm place about 30 to 45 minutes, or until dough is light.

10. Set on lowest shelf of 375°F oven. Bake 10 to 15 minutes, or until top is browned. Place a piece of brown paper or aluminum foil over top of loaf. Continue baking about 25 minutes, or until nicely browned and baked through (test brioche with wooden pick).

11. Turn loaf out of pan and serve warm or cold, cut in wedges.

Pork Casserole with Beans and Vegetables

SERVES 6

1 pound dried white	Pepper
beans (soaked	2 large carrots
overnight)	³/₄ pound small onions
3 pounds shank of	1 (1-pound) can
pork cut in 1-inch	peeled tomatoes
thick slices	2 bay leaves
3 tablespoons butter	1 teaspoon thyme
Salt	

1. Boil the white beans in plenty of salted water till half cooked.

2. Parboil the onions. Trim carrots and cut in slices.

3. Brown the pork slices in the butter. Season and transfer to a stew pan.

4. Fry onions and carrot slices in the remaining butter and transfer to stew pan.

5. Whisk the frying pan with some water and pour liquid over the pork.

6. Add the boiled white beans, the tomatoes with their liquid, bay leaves, and thyme.

7. Simmer, covered, until pork meat is tender, about 40 minutes.

Ham Ratatouille.

**Pork Casserole
with Beans and Vegetables.**

Whole Lomo of Pork in Tomato Sauce

SERVES 10-12

1 pork loin roast, boneless (3 to 4 pounds)
1 can (6 ounces) tomato paste
1/4 cup chopped onion
1 canned chipotle chili, very finely chopped; or 2 teaspoons chili powder

1 clove garlic, minced
1 teaspoon salt
1/4 teaspoon pepper
1 1/3 cups chicken stock, or 1 1/2 cups hot water plus 2 chicken bouillon cubes
1 cup sour cream

1. Put pork loin into a shallow baking pan; if necessary, cut in half so meat will fit into pan.
2. Combine tomato paste, onion, chili, garlic, salt, and pepper in a saucepan. Stir in chicken stock. Cook about 5 minutes.
3. Pour liquid over meat in pan.
4. Bake at 325°F about 1 1/4 hours. Occasionally spoon sauce over meat during baking, and check to see if additional water is needed to prevent drying.
5. When meat is tender, remove to serving platter.
6. Stir sour cream into sauce remaining in pan; warm slightly but do not boil. Pour over meat on platter.
7. To serve, slice meat about 3/4 inch thick.

German Pork Roast in Spicy Beer Sauce

SERVES 8

1 rolled pork loin roast, boneless (3 to 3 1/2 pounds)
2 to 3 cups beer
1 cup chopped onion
2 teaspoons grated lemon peel
2 teaspoons sugar
1 teaspoon tarragon

1 teaspoon salt
1/4 teaspoon each pepper, cloves, ginger, and nutmeg
3 bay leaves
1 carrot, diced
1 celery stalk, diced
1/4 cup flour

1. Place meat in a deep dish just large enough to hold it. Combine 1 can (1 1/2 cups) beer, onion, peel, and seasonings; pour over meat. Add a little more beer, if needed, to just cover meat. Marinate in refrigerator 1 to 2 days, turning occasionally.
2. Strain marinade, reserving solids and liquid. Place solids, carrot, and celery in bottom of a roasting pan. Place meat on top. Add a little liquid.
3. Roast in a 350°F oven 1 hour. Pour one quarter of remaining marinade liquid over meat. Continue roast-ing for 1 to 1 1/2 hours more, basting occasionally with drippings and more marinade, until meat thermometer registers 170°F.
4. Mix flour and 1/3 cup marinade or beer to a smooth paste. Place roast on a platter; keep warm. Skim fat from cooking liquid. Strain, pressing solids; add flour mixture and 1/2 cup beer plus water, if needed, to measure 2 cups total liquid. Cook in roasting pan or a saucepan, stirring constantly, until thickened. (For 3 cups gravy, use more beer and water plus 6 tablespoons flour.) Serve sauce over meat slices.

Savory Spareribs

SERVES 4-6

4 pounds pork spare-ribs
1 can or bottle (12 ounces) beer
1/2 cup honey
2 tablespoons lemon juice

2 teaspoons salt
1 teaspoon dry mustard
1/4 teaspoon pepper

1. Cut spareribs into 2-rib sections.
2. Combine remaining ingredients in a shallow glass or ceramic baking dish. Add ribs. Marinate in refrigerator at least 24 hours, turning and basting occasionally.
3. Arrange ribs in a single layer in a large baking pan; reserve marinade.
4. Bake at 350°F 1 1/2 hours, turning once and basting frequently with marinade.

Lomo of Pork with Pineapple

SERVES 6-8

1 tablespoon lard or oil
3 pounds pork loin, boneless, cut in 2-inch chunks
1 cup chopped onion
2 cups pineapple chunks (1 15 1/4-ounce can) with juice
1 cup beef stock, or

1 cup water plus 1 beef bouillon cube
1/4 cup dry sherry
1/3 cup sliced pimiento
1 fresh tomato, peeled and chopped
1/2 teaspoon chili powder
Salt and pepper
2 tablespoons flour

1. Heat lard in a large, heavy skillet. Add meat and brown well on all sides. Add onion and cook about 5 minutes, or until soft.
2. Add pineapple with juice, beef stock, sherry,

Pork Stew.

pimiento, tomato, and chili powder to the skillet; stir until well mixed. Bring to boiling, reduce heat to simmering, and add salt and pepper to taste. Cover and simmer until meat is tender, about 1½ hours; stir occasionally to prevent sticking.

3. Just before serving, sprinkle flour over simmering sauce and stir in; cook and stir until sauce is thickened. Serve over hot rice.

Pork Stew

4 SERVINGS

¾ pound lean pork, cubed	Pepper to taste
¾ pound turnips, cubed	1 teaspoon mustard
	¼ cup water
2 tablespoons butter	1 tablespoon flour
1 teaspoon salt	¼ cup light cream
	Parsley for garnish

1. Brown the pork and turnip cubes in butter.
2. Add the salt, pepper, mustard, and water. Stir to blend.
3. Simmer covered until the turnips are almost soft.
4. Sprinkle with flour, add the cream, and stir to mix.
5. Serve on a platter garnished with parsley and green beans.

Pork Roast Stuffed with Liver

SERVES ABOUT 8

1 teaspoon fennel seed	(about 3 pounds)
2 cloves garlic, peeled	½ pound pork, lamb, or beef liver, cut in slices ⅓ inch thick
1 teaspoon salt	
½ teaspoon sugar	
½ teaspoon coarsely ground pepper	1 tablespoon cornstarch
¾ teaspoon rubbed sage	1 cup cool beef broth
Boneless pork loin or loin end roast	

1. Using a mortar and pestle, crush the fennel seed. Add the garlic, salt, sugar, pepper, and sage. Crush until mixture becomes a rough paste.
2. Open pork roast and lay flat side down; cut the meat if necessary to make it lie flat. Rub surface of the roast with about half the garlic paste. Lay liver strips lengthwise over meat.
3. Roll the roast tightly lengthwise with seasoned surface inside. Tie with heavy string at 2-inch intervals. Rub remaining garlic paste on outside of roast. Place roast on a rack in a shallow baking pan.
4. Cook, uncovered, at 375°F until meat thermome-

(continued)

ter inserted in thickest part of the roast registers 170°F (about 1½ hours). Transfer roast to a serving platter and keep warm.

5. Remove rack from roasting pan and place pan over direct heat. Stir together the cornstarch and broth until blended. Stir into drippings in roasting pan. Cook over medium heat, stirring constantly, until sauce boils and thickens. Pour sauce into a serving bowl.

6. To serve, cut and remove strings from roast, and cut meat into thin slices.

Pork Medallions Flambés

SERVES 8

3 fillets of pork	½ pound mushrooms
½ teaspoon salt	1 tablespoon butter
½ tablespoon coarsely crushed black pepper	½ teaspoon salt
	½ teaspoon white pepper
1 tablespoon green pepper	*Hot Sauce:*
2 tablespoons butter	¾ cup heavy cream
3 ounces cognac	½ teaspoon garlic salt
	½ teaspoon soy sauce

1. Clean and prepare the meat. Cut each fillet into about 6 pieces. Salt. Dip the pieces thoroughly in pepper on both sides. Let rest for ½ hour.

2. Trim, wash, and fry the mushrooms lightly in butter. Season and remove from frying pan.

3. Fry the fillet in brown cooking fat for about 1 minute on each side. Pour on the cognac and put a flame to it immediately. Allow to burn until flame goes out.

4. Remove the meat and keep in a warm place. Heat the cream in the frying pan for a few minutes. Add seasonings and soy sauce.

5. Mix in the fried mushrooms.

6. Transfer the meat to a hot serving dish and pour on the hot sauce. Serve with french fries and a green salad.

Pork Casserole

SERVES 4

14 ounces pork fillet	1 bayleaf (crushed)
5 ounces chicken liver	Dash thyme
1 garlic clove	4 orange slices
3 onions	4 carrots
3 tablespoons butter or margarine	½ cup bouillon and ¾ cup red wine or 1¼ cups bouillon
Dash freshly ground pepper	Chopped parsley

1. Thaw chicken livers (if you use frozen) and chop. Cut pork in ¼-inch thick slices.

Pork Medallions Flambés.

2. Chop peeled onion and crush garlic. Peel carrots and cut in pieces.

3. Brown meat, onion, and liver separately in butter and then add carrots, seasonings, and orange slices with peel left on.

4. Pour bouillon and red wine on mixture and cook over low heat for 20 minutes. Add liver for last 10 minutes of cooking time. Stir carefully.

5. Serve garnished with chopped parsley.

Danish Pork Chops

SERVES 6

6 (2¹/₂ pounds) rib pork chops, 1-inch thick	¹/₄ pound light brown sugar
1¹/₂ teaspoons sage	¹/₂ cup heavy cream
¹/₂ teaspoon salt	1¹/₂ tablespoons flour
¹/₂ teaspoon pepper	2 tablespoons Dijon mustard
2 cups onion, sliced	Dash cayenne pepper
1 pound tart cooking apples, sliced	

1. Preheat oven to 350°F.

2. Trim fat from pork chops. Season chops with sage, salt, and pepper.

3. Place pork chops in a casserole. Top with onion and apples. Sprinkle with brown sugar.

4. Bake covered for 2¹/₂ hours. Remove cover, baste with pan juices. Bake 30 minutes till tender. Remove chops and vegetables from pan and keep hot.

5. Stir flour into drippings until smooth. Stir in cream, mustard, and cayenne pepper. Boil 1 minute, stirring. Place chops in serving dish, top with vegetables and sauce.

Pork Braised with Celery in Egg and Lemon Sauce

SERVES 8

¹/₄ cup butter	*Egg and Lemon Sauce:*
4 pounds lean pork, cut in 2-inch cubes	¹/₄ cup butter
1 large onion, minced	3 tablespoons flour
2 cups water	2 cups pork stock
2 bunches celery (stalks only), cut in 1-inch pieces	Juice of 2 lemons
	3 eggs, separated
	Salt and pepper to taste

1. Melt butter in a Dutch oven and sauté pork until golden brown. Add onion and cook until translucent. Add water. Cover and simmer 1 to 1¹/₂ hours or until meat is just tender. Add celery and simmer

(continued)

Danish Pork Chops.

about 15 minutes, or until tender. Drain off 2 cups stock and strain. Keep meat warm.

2. To make sauce, melt butter in a saucepan; add flour and cook about 1 minute, stirring constantly; do not brown. Add pork stock and lemon juice. Simmer, stirring constantly, until sauce thickens.

3. Separate eggs. Beat whites until soft peaks form. Beat yolks until thick. Fold yolks into whites. Using a wire whisk, slowly add sauce to eggs. Pour over pork mixture. Heat and serve at once.

Pork Shoulder with Sage

SERVES 4

14 ounces lean pork-shoulder	2 tablespoons all-purpose flour
1 package broccoli	1 bouillon cube
2 tomatoes	1 teaspoon paprika
Sage	1¼ cups water and meat juice
Salt	*Gratin:*
Pepper	3-4 slices cheese
Sauce:	
2 tablespoons margarine	

1. Slice pork and brown in saucepan. Season with salt, pepper, and sage. Place meat in buttered oven-proof dish. Add a little water to saucepan and save.

2. Blend butter and flour in saucepan and add bouillon cube, water, and meat juice. Season with paprika. Pour sauce over meat and place tomato slices between the slices.

3. Place cheese slices on top and bake in 425°F oven until cheese has melted.

Garnish with broccoli cooked in butter. Serve with boiled potatoes.

Ham Steak Barbecue

SERVES ABOUT 6

1 smoked ham slice, 1½ inches thick	2 tablespoons sugar
1 teaspoon grated grapefruit peel	1 teaspoon oregano
1 cup grapefruit juice	½ teaspoon salt
¼ cup soy sauce	¼ teaspoon pepper
2 tablespoons salad oil	2 tablespoons chopped parsley
	¼ cup chopped green onion

1. Put ham slice into a shallow dish. Mix remaining ingredients and pour over ham. Cover and refrigerate 2 hours.

2. Remove ham from marinade and place on grill over hot coals. Grill 25 minutes on one side, basting with marinade; turn and grill 20 minutes longer. Remove from grill and serve with Grapefruit Sauce (below).

Grapefruit Sauce

ABOUT 2½ CUPS SAUCE

½ cup sugar	1¼ cups grapefruit juice
2 tablespoons cornstarch	1 grapefruit, sectioned and sections halved
¼ teaspoon salt	
¾ cup water	

1. Mix sugar, cornstarch, and salt in a saucepan. Gradually add water and grapefruit juice, stirring to blend. Cook over low heat, stirring constantly, until mixture thickens and comes to boiling. Simmer 1 minute.

2. Remove from heat and stir in grapefruit pieces.

Pork and Green Tomato Sauce

SERVES 6-8

2¹/₂ pounds lean pork, cut in 1-inch cubes
1 tablespoon vegetable oil
1 onion, chopped
2 cloves garlic, minced
1 can (12 ounces) Mexican green tomatoes (tomatillos), drained and chopped

2 cans (4 ounces each) green chilies, drained, seeded, and chopped
1 tablespoon dried cilantro leaves
1 teaspoon marjoram
1 teaspoon salt
¹/₂ cup water
Cooked rice
Sour cream

1. Brown meat in oil in a large skillet. Push meat to sides of skillet; add onion and garlic and cook until onion is soft. Add green tomatoes, chilies, cilantro, marjoram, salt, and water; mix well. Cover; bring to boiling, reduce heat, and cook until meat is tender (about 2 hours).

2. Serve with rice and top with dollops of sour cream.

Ham Steak with Parsley Sauce

SERVES 3-4

2 bunches parsley, washed and stems removed
¹/₄ cup dry white wine
1 center-cut smoked ham steak, ³/₄ inch thick (about 1¹/₂ pounds)

²/₃ cup Mock Hollandaise Sauce*
Salt
Freshly ground white pepper
*Check index for recipe

1. Line bottom of a shallow baking dish with half the parsley; drizzle with half the wine. Lay ham steak on parsley. Cover ham with remaining parsley; drizzle with remaining wine. Lightly cover baking dish.
2. Bake at 325°F about 30 minutes, or until ham is thoroughly heated. *(continued)*

3. Make Mock Hollandaise Sauce while ham is baking; keep warm.

4. Place ham on platter; cover lightly with aluminum foil. Purée cooked parsley in a blender or food processor; stir mixture into Mock Hollandaise Sauce. Season sauce with salt and pepper. Heat sauce thoroughly; serve with ham.

3. Peel onions and potatoes and brown in a skillet, using the fat from the meat.

4. Add the onions and potatoes to the meat in the roasting pan and add enough water to half cover the vegetables.

5. Cover and roast in a 350°F oven for at least 1 hour. Cook until meat thermometer reads 180°F.

6. Meanwhile sauté mushrooms in butter.

7. Arrange meat on a platter and surround with vegetables.

Braised Loin of Pork

SERVES 8

1 loin of pork (about 5 pounds)	**1 clove garlic, crushed**
¹/₂ teaspoon oregano	**1 pound small onions**
2 tablespoons all-purpose flour	**2 pounds small potatoes**
¹/₄ cup onions, chopped	**1 pound mushrooms**
¹/₄ cup carrots, chopped	**2 tablespoons butter**

1. Rub loin of pork with oregano and flour, then put it in a deep roasting pan and bake in a preheated 450°F oven for 30 minutes.

2. Add the chopped onions, carrots, and garlic and cook for an additional 15 minutes; reduce heat to 350°F and continue cooking for 30 minutes.

Fruit-Stuffed Loin of Pork

SERVES 6

3¹/₂ pounds lean pork, boneless	**4 ounces crushed pineapple, drained**
1¹/₂ teaspoons salt	**8 prunes, finely sliced**
Pepper to taste	**1 apple, diced**
1¹/₂ teaspoons rosemary	**Soy sauce for basting**
	6 baking potatoes

1. Preheat the oven to 400°.

2. Rub the pork with salt, pepper, and rosemary.

3. Roll the pork out flat. Spread the pineapple, prunes, and apple over the meat.

4. Roll the meat together and tie with a string. Insert meat thermometer.

Braised Loin of Pork.

Fruit-Stuffed Loin of Pork.

5. Place pork roll on a rack in a baking pan.
6. Bake for 1½ hours or till meat thermometer reads 170°F.
7. Baste with soy sauce every fifteen minutes.
8. Place potatoes in oven 1 hour before cooking time is up. Serve with warm red cabbage.

Baked Spinach and Ham

SERVES 4

1 pound fresh spinach	6 slices smoked ham
1 tablespoon butter	6 slices Monterey
Nutmeg	Jack cheese
1 (1-pound) can	
asparagus	

1. Clean and wash fresh spinach and parboil in lightly salted water. Drain well and place at the bottom of a greased ovenproof dish.
2. Season with grated nutmeg.
3. Pour off the liquid from 1 can asparagus and put the asparagus on the spinach. Place 6 slices of smoked ham on the asparagus. Cover the ham with cheese slices. Bake in a 450°F until the dish is light brown, about 10-15 minutes. Serve with French bread.

Baked Ham Rolls

SERVES 3

1 large yellow onion	3 ounces Monterey
Butter	Jack cheese, grated
6 slices blue cheese	1 ounce fine bread
(3 ounces)	crumbs
6 slices smoked ham	

1. Peel the onion, slice and saute in the butter.
2. Put onion and blue cheese on the ham slices, roll up, and place rolls on a greased ovenproof dish.
3. Mix grated cheese and bread crumbs and sprinkle on the rolls. Bake in a 450°F oven until the cheese has melted and turned light brown, about 5-7 minutes.

115

Lamb

Roast Rack of Lamb with Anchovies

SERVES 4

1 rack of lamb with 8-9 bones	1 can of anchovy fillets
1 clove garlic	A little milk
Black pepper	2-3 tablespoons oil
	1 cup of brown stock

Preheat oven to 400°F.

1. Trim the rack of lamb by exposing the last inch of the bones and scraping these clean. Score the fat of the lamb in a trellis pattern and rub in the crushed clove of garlic and the black pepper.

2. Drain anchovies of oil, soak in milk for 10 minutes, rinse carefully and dry.

3. Heat oil in a roasting pan. When smoking put in the meat, baste with hot fat, and cook in oven for about 30-40 minutes, according to size and personal preference. Baste every 10 minutes. After 15-25 minutes place anchovy fillets in a crisscross design over the fat of the meat and continue cooking.

4. When cooked, remove and keep warm while heating roasting liquid with the stock to make gravy. Serve with potatoes and a green salad.

Crown Roast of Lamb

SERVES 8

2 racks of lamb (about 16 ribs)	butter or margarine
2 cloves garlic, cut into very thin slivers	1/2 cup chopped celery
Rosemary, lemon	1/2 cup chopped onion
Salt, black pepper	1/2 cup chopped carrot
1 cup breadcrumbs	2 teaspoons flour
1 teaspoon chopped parsley	2 cups chicken stock (or bouillon and water)
1 teaspoon chopped scallions	1 bay leaf
6 tablespoons melted	3-4 crushed peppercorns
	4 tablespoons cognac

Preheat oven to 375°F.

1. Have your butcher prepare the crown. Make small slits in the meat and insert slivers of garlic. Rub over the outside with rosemary and a cut lemon, and sprinkle with salt and pepper. Mix breadcrumbs, parsley, and scallions, add 4 tablespoons of the butter, mix well, and rub over the meat, coating the outside well. Wrap the tip of each rib bone with foil.

2. Put the vegetables and remaining butter into the bottom of a roasting pan and place the meat on top. Roast for about 1 hour. The meat should not be overcooked. A thermometer should register an internal temperature of 160°-165°, or 175°-180° if you prefer the meat really well cooked. Remove the lamb to a fireproof serving dish and keep warm.

3. Pour off excess fat from the roasting pan, stir in flour, and cook for 2 minutes. Add stock, bay leaf, and peppercorns, stir till boiling, and boil for 5 minutes. Strain, season to taste, and serve separately.

4. Remove the foil from the ribs of the roast and garnish the dish as required with vegetables cooked separately. A small potato or piece of carrot can be impaled on the tip of each rib bone.

5. Warm the cognac, pour it over the outside of the crown at the table and set alight.

(If the Crown of Lamb is served without the cognac, little paper frills can be put onto the rib ends—see picture.)

Pastichio

SERVES 8

3 tablespoons olive oil	tions on package and drained
2 pounds ground lamb	1 pound fresh kefalotyri cheese, grated
1 large onion, grated	
Few parsley sprigs, chopped	*Béchamel Sauce:*
1 tablespoon tomato paste mixed with 1/2 cup water	1/2 cup butter, melted
	7 tablespoons flour
1 pound elbow macaroni, cooked according to direc-	1 1/2 quarts milk, heated to lukewarm
	10 eggs, separated

1. Heat oil in a large skillet. Add meat and onion and cook until meat is brown. Add chopped parsley and diluted tomato paste. Cover and simmer for 30 minutes. If any liquid remains, cook meat uncovered until liquid has evaporated.

2. Spread half the cooked macaroni in an 18 X 12-inch baking dish and cover with all the meat mixture. Sprinkle top with three fourths of the cheese. Form a layer with remaining macaroni.

3. Meanwhile, to make sauce, melt butter in a large saucepan. Add flour and mix with a whisk for several minutes. Gradually add milk while stirring; simmer until sauce thickens, stirring frequently.

4. Separate eggs. Beat whites in a bowl until they pile softly. Beat yolks in another bowl. Fold yolks and whites together, then fold in sauce. Spoon over meat and macaroni. Sprinkle with remaining cheese.

5. Bake at 325°F about 45 minutes, or until golden brown. Cool slightly before serving.

Note: Pastichio may be prepared and baked in advance. To reheat, cover tightly with foil and heat in a 200°F oven.

Roast Leg of Lamb with Anchovies.

Crown Roast of Lamb.

117

Roast Leg of Lamb Dijon

SERVES 8-10

1 (6-pound) leg of lamb	1 teaspoon thyme
2 small cloves garlic, minced	½ cup Dijon mustard
1 teaspoon rosemary	¼ cup virgin olive oil
	1 teaspoon ground pepper

1. In a mixing bowl, combine the mustard, garlic, olive oil, and seasonings and mix thoroughly with a whisk until blended.
2. Coat the lamb with the marinade and let stand for 1-2 hours before cooking.
3. Preheat oven to 350°F and roast lamb for about 1 hour, or until center is pink.
4. Let stand for about 15 minutes before carving.
Serve with string beans and cooked cherry tomatoes.

Marinated Lamb Chops

SERVES 4

8 lamb chops	1 teaspoon rosemary
½ cup dry white wine	1 clove garlic, crushed
½ cup vegetable oil	½ teaspoon thyme
½ cup olive oil	

1. Mix oils, wine, and seasonings.

2. Remove and discard extra fat on lamb chops. Place lamb in a large, flat dish and pour marinade on top. Cover with Saran wrap. Marinate 8-10 hours, turning the chops once. Dry chops in paper towels and fry a couple of minutes on each side so they are pink in the center.
Serve with baked potatoes and vegetables.
Note: This marinade is suitable for meat such as lamb, veal, pork, and chicken.

Roast Lamb with Pungent Sauce

SERVES 10

1 joint of lamb (5 pounds)	2 tablespoons soy sauce
1 tablespoon salad oil	1½ tablespoons flour
1 teaspoon salt	6 ounces red wine
½ teaspoon pepper	4 ounces chopped pickles
2 yellow onions	1 bunch chopped parsley
1 large carrot	
Parsley sprigs	

Sauce:
2½ cups water

1. Preheat the oven to 325°F. Trim the bottom of the joint so that you get a good "handle" when carving.
2. Rub the meat with oil, salt, and pepper.
3. Trim and cut the vegetables in pieces.
4. Place the lamb on a rack in the roasting pan and

Roast Leg of Lamb Dijon

Roast Lamb with Pungent Sauce.

Roast Leg of Lamb with Caper Sauce.

put the vegetables in the bottom of the pan. Insert a meat thermometer at the thickest part of the joint.

5. Put the roasting pan in the oven. When the thermometer reads 160°F the meat is rosy inside. It takes about 2 hours. At 180°F the meat is well done. Pour in some water toward the end of the cooking time to prevent the vegetables from burning.

6. Remove the lamb and let rest for 5-10 minutes before carving.

7. Meanwhile dissolve the drippings in the pan with the water and strain into a saucepan.

8. Season with soy sauce. Thicken lightly with flour stirred in red wine.

9. Chop pickles and parsley and add to the sauce.

10. Carve the roast lamb.

Serve with boiled potatoes and cauliflower or Brussels sprouts. Also serve a large bowl of green salad with a mild dressing.

Lamb Roast

SERVES 8-10

**5- to 6-pound lamb
  leg roast**

1. Place roast, fat side down, on roasting rack in a 2-quart glass baking dish. Shield protruding corners or bones with foil. Do not allow foil to touch walls inside microwave oven.

2. Cook, using the following times: for medium, 7 to 8 minutes per pound; and for well-done, 8 to 9 minutes per pound. Turn roast over and rotate the dish one-quarter turn halfway through cooking time.

3. Rest 15 minutes before carving and serving.

Roast Leg of Lamb with Caper Sauce

SERVES 6

4-5 pounds leg of lamb	**1 teaspoon tarragon vinegar**
2 cloves garlic	**3 tablespoons all-purpose flour**
1 teaspoon rosemary	
1/2 cup olive oil	**1 teaspoon dry mustard**
Salt	
Pepper	**1 1/4 cups light cream**
Caper Sauce:	**2 tablespoons capers**
1 tablespoon olive oil	**1 egg yolk**
3 tablespoons sweet butter	**1 tablespoon dry sherry**
1/2 teaspoon tomato paste	**1/2 teaspoon cardamom seed, ground**
1/2 teaspoon meat glaze	

1. Rub lamb thoroughly with garlic, then with rosemary, salt, and pepper. *(continued)*

119

2. Pour olive oil into a roasting pan and preheat the oven to 350°F.

3. Place lamb in roasting pan and cook for 2-2¹/₂ hours or until center is pink.

4. Meanwhile make the caper sauce. Heat oil and 2 tablespoon butter in a saucepan. Remove from heat. Add tomato paste, meat glaze, vinegar, flour, and mustard. Mix to a smooth paste.

5. Add light cream. Stir over low heat until sauce comes to a boil. Stir in remaining butter, capers, egg yolk, sherry, and cardamom. Reheat slowly; do not boil.

Serve lamb with potatoes au gratin, cucumber salad, and caper sauce.

Barbecued Lamb Chops

SERVES 6

12 loin lamb chops	1 large onion,
2 tablespoons oil	chopped
10 onions	³/₄ cup ketchup
Sauce:	3 tablespoons brown
¹/₄ cup butter	sugar
3 large tart apples,	¹/₂ teaspoon salt
chopped	¹/₂ teaspoon pepper

1. Brush chops with oil and let stand for about 2 hours at room temperature.

2. Prepare sauce. Heat butter and sauté apples and onions. Add ketchup, sugar, salt, and pepper. Bring to a boil. Simmer 3 minutes.

3. Place chops in barbecue sauce and marinate for 30 minutes.

4. Alternate chops and onions on skewers and set over barbecue. Brush remaining sauce on chops and broil about 6 minutes until brown.

Party Lamb Chops

SERVES 6

6 lamb loin chops,	1 cup tomato juice
about 2 pounds	¹/₂ cup dry white
¹/₂ teaspoon salt	wine, such as
¹/₈ teaspoon pepper	sauterne
2 tablespoons butter	¹/₄ cup finely chopped
2 tablespoons pre-	parsley
pared mustard	
1 can (16 ounces)	
quartered hearts of	
celery	

1. Sprinkle chops with salt and pepper.

Barbecued Lamb Chops.

2. Brown chops on both sides in butter in skillet. Spread mustard on chops.

3. Add celery and liquid from can, tomato juice, and wine. Cover and simmer 1 hour over low heat until chops are tender. Place chops on platter and keep warm.

4. Pour pan juices into blender and whirl until smooth, or beat with a rotary beater in small bowl. Pour back into skillet and reheat until bubbly and thick. Spoon over chops. Sprinkle chops with parsley.

Lamb Chops with Oregano

SERVES 1

2 lamb chops (rib or	1 lemon, cut in half
loin) per serving	1 tablespoon olive oil
For each serving:	(optional)
1 tablespoon oregano	Pepper to taste
Salt to taste	

1. An hour before cooking, sprinkle lamb chops with oregano. Season with salt. Set aside.

2. Place lamb chops on a broiler rack and broil 7 minutes on each side.

3. Remove from broiler and squeeze lemon juice over the chops. Drizzle with salt. Season with pepper.

Lamb Crown Roast with Apricot Stuffing

SERVES ABOUT 8

3 tablespoons butter	3 tablespoons
¹/₂ package (4 ounces)	chopped dried
herb-seasoned	apricots
stuffing mix	1 lamb rib crown
¹/₄ cup water	roast (5 to
3 tablespoons	6 pounds)
chopped celery	

1. Melt butter in a 1-quart glass casserole in microwave oven. Add stuffing mix, water, celery, and apricots; mix well.

2. Place lamb crown roast on a roast rack set in a 2-quart glass baking dish. Fill center cavity with stuffing. Cover with waxed paper. Roast in microwave oven 10 minutes.

3. Rotate dish one-half turn. Shield meat and ribs as needed with foil. Roast covered in microwave oven set at 160°F.

4. Remove roast from oven. Cover with foil and allow to stand 10 minutes before serving.

Lamb Kabobs

SERVES 6

1¹/₂ pounds lamb (leg, loin, or shoulder), boneless, cut in 1¹/₂-inch cubes
¹/₂ cup vegetable oil
1 teaspoon lemon juice
2 teaspoons sugar
¹/₂ teaspoon salt
¹/₂ teaspoon paprika
¹/₄ teaspoon dry mustard
¹/₈ teaspoon ground black pepper
¹/₄ teaspoon Worcestershire sauce
1 clove garlic, cut in halves
6 small whole cooked potatoes
6 small whole cooked onions
Butter or margarine, melted
6 plum tomatoes

1. Put lamb cubes into a shallow dish. Combine oil, lemon juice, sugar, salt, paprika, dry mustard, pepper, Worcestershire sauce, and garlic. Pour over meat. Cover and marinate at least 1 hour in refrigerator, turning pieces occasionally. Drain.
2. Alternately thread lamb cubes, potatoes, and onions on 6 skewers. Brush pieces with melted butter.
3. Broil 3 to 4 inches from heat about 15 minutes, or until lamb is desired degree of doneness; turn frequently and brush with melted butter. Shortly before kabobs are done, impale tomatoes on ends of skewers.

Marinated Grilled Chops.

Marinated Grilled Chops

SERVES 4

4 large lamb chops
Marinade:
3 ounces salad oil
1¹/₂ ounces wine vinegar
1 tablespoon salt
5 crushed white or black peppercorns
1 small yellow onion, chopped
1 large bunch parsley
¹/₂ teaspoon thyme
1 crumbled bay leaf
Cumberland Sauce:
3 tablespoons red
currant jelly
1 cup port wine
1 teaspoon mustard powder
1 teaspoon finely chopped yellow onion
Cayenne pepper
Ginger
1 tablespoon very finely sliced orange rind
1 tablespoon very finely sliced lemon rind

1. Mix all the ingredients for the marinade. Place the chops in the marinade for at least 3 hours. Turn them occasionally.
2. Broil the chops for 5-6 minutes on each side.
3. Stir the currant jelly in the port wine and seasonings. Don't forget to cut away the white on the orange and lemon rinds.

Serve chops with boiled potatoes, the sauce, and a green salad.

Lamb-Stuffed Zucchini with Lemon Sauce

SERVES 4

8 medium straight zucchini
1 pound ground lamb
¹/₂ cup long-grain rice
1 small onion, minced
2 tablespoons chopped parsley
1 teaspoon chopped
mint
Salt and pepper
Water (about 2 cups)
Sauce:
2 egg yolks
Juice of 2 lemons
¹/₂ cup broth

1. Remove the ends and scrape the skins off the zucchini. With a corer, scoop out the zucchini center and discard. Soak the zucchini in cold water.
2. Meanwhile, mix meat with rice, onion, parsley, mint, salt, and pepper. Drain zucchini and stuff with meat mixture.
3. Arrange stuffed zucchini in a single layer in a Dutch oven. Add enough water to half cover the zucchini. Bring the water to a boil, reduce heat, and simmer, covered, about 35 minutes.
4. Before serving, beat egg yolks until frothy. Slowly add lemon juice, beating constantly. Add broth,

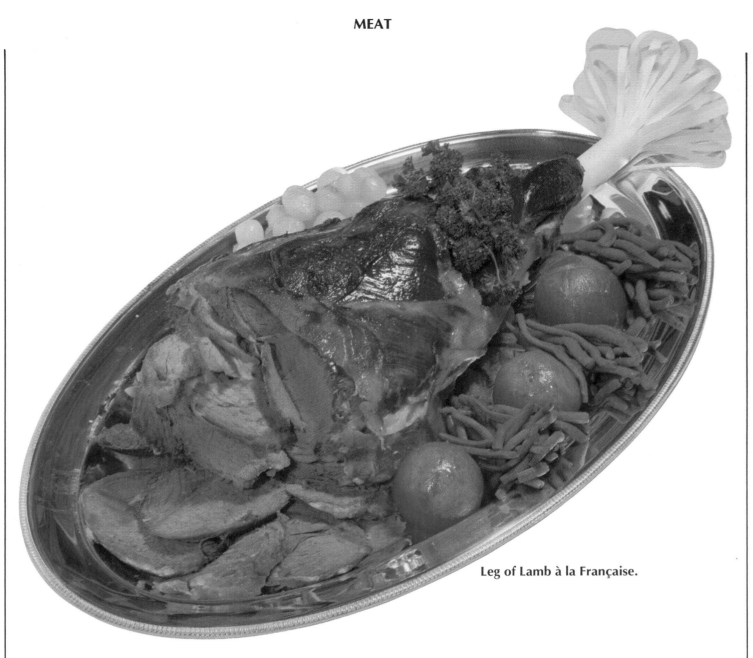

Leg of Lamb à la Française.

tablespoon by tablespoon, beating constantly. Heat thoroughly, but do not boil. Pour over zucchini. Serve immediately.

Roast Baby Lamb's Head

SERVES 1

1 head per serving, split in half and tied with a string to keep brains intact	2 tablespoons olive oil
	1 tablespoon oregano or more to taste
Juice of 1 lemon	Salt and pepper to taste

1. Soak head in cold salted water for 1 hour. Drain. Pat dry. Cut string and place halves in a shallow pan, brains up.
2. Combine lemon juice, olive oil, oregano, salt, and pepper. Drizzle over head.
3. Roast in a 350°F oven for about 20 minutes, basting frequently until brains are tender. Remove brains with a spoon and keep warm. Continue roasting about 45 minutes more, or until other parts are tender.

Leg of Lamb à la Française

SERVES 6-8

1 leg of lamb (6-7 pounds)	Fresh ground pepper
4 cloves of garlic (sliced thinly)	Salt
2 pounds small onions	4 tomatoes
2 tablespoons virgin olive oil	Parsley

1. With a small paring knife make tiny slits under the skin of the lamb and put garlic slivers in each slit.
2. Brush the lamb with the olive oil, season, and place in a roasting pan.
3. Roast lamb in a preheated 425°F oven, basting occasionally. Figure about 15 minutes per pound or until meat thermometer shows 160°F.
4. Peel the onions and place into the pan 25 minutes before cooking time is up.
5. Remove meat and serve with string beans and skinned tomatoes. Garnish with parsley.

Grilled Lamb Risotto.

Lamb Burgers.

Lamb Burgers with Dill Sauce

SERVES 4

1¹/₄ pounds ground lamb	3 tablespoons all-purpose flour
1 teaspoon salt	1¹/₂ cups beef stock
¹/₂ teaspoon pepper	2 tablespoons milk or cream
¹/₂ teaspoon thyme, crumbled	3 teaspoons vinegar
1 egg yolk	3 tablespoons sugar
3 ounces milk	¹/₂ teaspoon salt
3 tablespoons bread crumbs	1 large bunch or 2 teaspoons dried dill
2¹/₂-3 tablespoons margarine or butter	1 (1-pound) can white asparagus

Sauce:
2 tablespoons margarine or butter

1. Soften bread crumbs in milk.
2. Mix lamb with salt, pepper, thyme, and egg yolk. Add the crumb mixture a little at a time and mix until smooth. Shape into oval burgers.
3. Brown the burgers in margarine or broil for 8-10 minutes.
4. Melt margarine, add flour, and let bubble. Add beef stock and milk or cream and let simmer for a few minutes. Season with vinegar, sugar, and salt. Stir in chopped dill and drained asparagus.
5. Place the lamb burgers in a hot serving dish and cover with the sauce.

Lamb Burgers

SERVES 4

1 pound ground lamb	1 small clove garlic, crushed
1 medium onion, minced	1 teaspoon dill, chopped
1 teaspoon ground pepper	2 tablespoons butter

1. In a large bowl mix the lamb, onion, and seasonings.
2. Make 4 patties and sauté them in a skillet in which the butter has been melted.
Serve with mashed potatoes and pickled cucumbers.

Braised Lamb Shanks

SERVES 6

3 tablespoons olive oil	2 cups red wine
6 lamb shanks	¹/₄ cup dried oregano
Salt and pepper to taste	2 bay leaves
1 can (16 ounces) tomatoes (undrained)	¹/₄ cup minced parsley
	2 garlic cloves, minced
	2 onions, quartered

1. Heat olive oil until it begins to smoke. Brown lamb shanks on all sides. Season with salt and pep-

Lamb Burger with Dill Sauce.

per. Add tomatoes, wine, oregano, bay leaves, parsley, garlic, and onion. Cover. Simmer 2 to 2½ hours, or until meat is fork tender.

2. Remove from heat. Cool. Skim off fat. Reheat and serve hot.

Lamb Shish Kebob

SERVES 8-10

¾ cup dry red wine	2 tablespoons oregano, crushed
¼ cup lemon juice	
3 tablespoons olive oil	3 pounds leg of lamb, boneless, cut in 1½-inch cubes
1 teaspoon salt	
Freshly ground pepper to taste	
2 garlic cloves, crushed in a garlic press	Green peppers, cored and cut in squares
	Baby onions, peeled and left whole
1 onion, minced	Large mushroom caps
Bay leaf	Tomato wedges

1. Make a marinade of wine, lemon juice, olive oil, salt, pepper, garlic, onion, bay leaf, and oregano in a large bowl and add lamb cubes. Cover securely and refrigerate at least 6 hours. Turn lamb several times while marinating.

2. Remove meat from marinade and place on skewers with green pepper squares, onions, mushroom caps, and tomato wedges.

3. Barbecue over hot coals or boil about 20 minutes, or until done; baste with marinade during cooking.

Grilled Lamb Risotto

SERVES 6

2 pounds lamb, cubed	2 cloves garlic, chopped
Salt	
Pepper	8 black peppercorns
Grill Sauce:	1 bay leaf, crumbled
¼ cup olive oil	1 cup red wine
¼ cup vegetable oil	2 tablespoons tarragon vinegar
1 yellow onion, chopped	

1. Rub the lamb with seasoning. Mix all the ingredients for the grill sauce and place lamb in it for 2 hours. Place lamb on skewers over a barbecue grill, basting frequently with the grill sauce. Cook for about 4-5 minutes on each side.

2. Remove and add to rice *(below)* and serve.

Risotto

SERVES 6

1½ cups long-grain rice	powder
	1 teaspoon paprika
½ teaspoon curry	3 cups chicken stock

1. Heat chicken stock and add curry and paprika.

2. Add rice, cover, and cook for 20 minutes.

3. Drain and serve with grilled lamb.

Hotch-Potch Casserole

SERVES 4

1¼ pounds lamb without bones (shoulder, brisket, or saddle)	1 clove garlic
	10 ounces white cabbage
1½ cups water	2 carrots
½ teaspoon salt	1 piece celery root
5 white peppercorns	2 leeks
5 corns allspice	8 potatoes
	1 bunch parsley

1. Cut the meat in pieces and put in a casserole.
2. Pour in water and salt. Bring to a boil and skim the top.
3. Add the crushed white peppercorns and the crushed allspice corns. Simmer covered for about 40 minutes.
4. Meanwhile cut the white cabbage in wedges, the carrots in slices, the celery and leeks in pieces. Add the vegetables and boil for 15 minutes. Peel and slice the potatoes thinly.
5. Spread the potato slices on top of the casserole and sprinkle with a little salt. Simmer covered for another 20 minutes until the potatoes are ready. Do not stir.

Serve sprinkled with chopped parsley.

Stuffed Lamb Breasts

SERVES 6

5 strips bacon	½ teaspoon salt
½ cup finely chopped onion	¼ teaspoon pepper
	3 eggs, well beaten
6 cups bread cubes with crusts removed	½ cup milk
	2 lamb breasts with pockets (about 5 pounds)
⅓ cup chopped pepperoni	
	Brown Sauce (below)
3 tablespoons fresh parsley, or 1½ tablespoons dried parsley	2 tablespoons cornstarch
	½ cup water
1 teaspoon dried sweet basil	

1. Cook bacon in skillet until crisp; drain, then crumble and set aside. Sauté onion in bacon fat until tender, but do not brown.
2. In large bowl, combine bread, onion, pepperoni, parsley, sweet basil, salt, pepper, and bacon. Toss lightly until well mixed.
3. In small bowl, mix beaten eggs and milk; then add to bread mixture and toss lightly until well mixed. Spoon half of stuffing into each lamb breast; then close opening with skewers. Place lamb breasts on rack in shallow roasting pan. Sprinkle lightly with additional salt and pepper.
4. Roast in a 350°F oven 15 minutes. Meanwhile make Brown Sauce. Generously baste lamb with Brown Sauce and continue to roast for 2 hours longer, or until lamb breasts are tender, basting lamb with Brown Sauce about every 15 minutes.
5. Remove lamb to heated platter. Skim fat from pan juice; stir in cornstarch dissolved in water. Cook over medium heat, stirring continuously, until thickened, adding more water if needed.
6. Carve lamb into slices and serve with pan gravy.

Brown Sauce: In a 2-cup saucepan, mix **1½ cups water or bouillon** with **1 teaspoon prepared mustard, 1 teaspoon Worcestershire sauce, 1 teaspoon bottled steak sauce, ½ teaspoon celery salt, 1 bay leaf,** and **2 whole cloves.** Add **1 medium onion, halved,** and simmer over low heat for 15 minutes. Remove onion halves and place on top of lamb breasts. Baste meat with sauce.

Saddle of Lamb with Artichoke Purée

SERVES ABOUT 10

1 (5-pound) saddle of lamb (lamb loin roast)	8 to 10 thick grapevine leaves
	8 artichoke bottoms, cooked
2 tablespoons olive oil	1 pound mushrooms, cooked
Salt and pepper	
2 teaspoons oregano	2 tablespoons butter
4 garlic cloves, crushed in a garlic press	½ cup red wine
	½ cup water

1. Rub lamb with olive oil. Combine salt, pepper, oregano, and garlic. Rub over lamb. Cover with grapevine leaves. Seal with foil. Refrigerate overnight.
2. Purée artichoke bottoms and mushrooms. Combine with butter and heat.
3. Set roast in a roasting pan. Remove grapevine leaves and season with salt and pepper.
4. Roast in a 325°F oven 50 minutes. Remove from oven. Reserve juice in the pan. Separate each loin from the saddle in one piece. Cut the meat into slices. Spread each slice with some of the purée. Reassemble the loins and tie securely in place. Return the meat to the roasting pan and add wine and water. Continue roasting, basting frequently, for 15 minutes.
5. Remove to a serving platter and discard strings. Skim fat from the pan juices and strain juices over the meat.

Hotch-Potch Casserole.

Indian Lamb Curry

SERVES 4

1¹/4 pounds lamb, boned
1 large yellow onion
2 cloves garlic, finely chopped
3 tablespoons salad oil
2-3 teaspoons curry powder
Salt
Pepper
1-pound can whole tomatoes
2 teaspoons coriander
1 teaspoon turmeric
1 cup chicken stock
¹/2 teaspoon ginger
4 ounces plain yogurt
1 tablespoon butter
3 slices unsweetened pineapple, cubed

1. Cut meat in 1-inch cubes. Peel and chop the onion.
2. Brown onion, meat, garlic, curry, and oil in casserole. Salt and pepper lightly. Add tomatoes, spices, and stock.
3. Simmer the casserole covered for about 45 minutes, stirring occasionally.
4. Sauté the pineapple lightly in butter. Stir in the yogurt and pineapple. Serve with boiled rice.

Marinated Lamb Casserole

SERVES 4

1¹/2 pounds lamb without bones (brisket, saddle, or shoulder)
6 ounces white beans
3 yellow onions
4 carrots
Parsley
Marinade:
¹/2 bottle red wine
1 cup water
2 cloves garlic, crushed
1 teaspoon salt
2 teaspoons thyme
1 bay leaf
10 black peppercorns

1. Mix the ingredients for the marinade.
2. Cut the meat in pieces and place in the marinade for a few hours or overnight. Turn meat now and then if not fully covered by the liquid.
3. Boil the beans in lightly salted water for about 45 minutes.
4. Remove the meat from the marinade and brown in a frying pan. Transfer the meat to a casserole and add some of the marinade. Let the meat boil for about 30 minutes with the beans.
5. Peel the onions and cut in wedges. Scrape the carrots and cut in slices. Add to the casserole and boil covered for about another 20 minutes. Add the marinade. Taste and correct seasoning.

Serve sprinkled with parsley and boiled potatoes or rice.

Lamb Shank in Parchment Paper

SERVES 1

1 lamb shank per serving
For each serving:
1 garlic clove, peeled and slivered
1 slice hard mizithra cheese
1 small onion, sliced
1 small tomato, peeled and diced
1 teaspoon minced parsley
¹/4 teaspoon dill
¹/4 teaspoon mint flakes
¹/2 teaspoon oregano
Juice of ¹/2 lemon
Salt and pepper to taste
1 teaspoon olive oil
Parchment paper
Cotton string

1. Make several incisions in the meat, top and bottom. Insert sliver of garlic in each incision.
2. Place meat on a piece of parchment paper ample enough to seal meat and vegetables securely. Put cheese on meat, then arrange onion and tomato on top. Sprinkle with herbs, lemon juice, salt, and pepper. Drizzle with olive oil.
3. Wrap securely in parchment paper. Tie with string. Set in a roasting pan.
4. Bake at 350°F about 1¹/2 hours, or until meat is done. Serve package unopened.

Note: Oiled brown paper may be substituted for the parchment paper.

Hunter-Style Lamb with Fettuccine

SERVES ABOUT 6

2 pounds lamb (leg, loin, or shoulder), trimmed and cut in 1¹/2-inch cubes
³/4 to 1 teaspoon pepper
2 tablespoons butter
2 tablespoons olive oil
4 anchovies, chopped
1 clove garlic, minced
1 medium green pepper, cleaned and cut in pieces
Olive oil
1 teaspoon rosemary, crushed
1 teaspoon basil, crushed
¹/4 teaspoon sage, crushed
¹/2 cup red wine vinegar
¹/2 to ³/4 cup chicken broth
2 teaspoons flour
8 ounces fettuccine noodles, cooked and drained
Grated Parmesan cheese
Minced parsley

1. Season lamb with salt and pepper.

(continued)

Indian Lamb Curry.

Marinated Lamb Casserole.

2. Heat butter and 2 tablespoons oil in a large, heavy skillet; add meat and brown on all sides.

3. Meanwhile, cook anchovies, garlic, and green pepper in a small amount of oil in a small saucepan about 5 minutes. Add rosemary, basil, sage, and vinegar; mix well. Cook and stir until boiling.

4. Remove lamb from skillet with a slotted spoon; set aside. Add enough chicken broth to drippings in skillet to make ¾ cup liquid. Add herb-vinegar mixture and bring to boiling, stirring to blend. Return lamb to skillet, cover tightly, and simmer over low heat about 40 minutes, or until tender.

5. Combine flour with a small amount of water to make a smooth paste. Add to liquid in skillet; cook and stir until mixtures comes to boiling; cook 1 to 2 minutes.

6. Serve on a heated serving platter surrounded with fettuccine tossed with grated Parmesan cheese. Sprinkle with parsley.

Lamb Casserole

SERVES 6

2 pounds lamb (cut in 1-inch cubes)	**½ pound string beans**
¼ cup oil	**6 carrots, scraped**
2 onions, chopped	**½ head cauliflower**
1 clove garlic, minced	**3 cups stewed tomatoes**
½ pound peas	**¼ cup red wine**

1. In a skillet heat the oil and brown the lamb on all sides.

2. Add onions and garlic and heat until onions are soft.

3. In a separate saucepan blanch the peas, string beans, carrots, and cauliflower.

4. In a 2-quart casserole combine the wine, tomatoes, and meat and bake in a 325°F oven for 1 hour.

5. Add the vegetables and continue cooking covered for another 15 minutes.

Sofrito (a Greek specialty)

SERVES 4

1 pound joint of lamb, sliced	**1 cup wine vinegar**
½ teaspoon salt	**4 slices white bread**
½ teaspoon pepper	**2 pounds cold boiled and peeled potatoes**
Flour	**2 tablespoons butter**
2 tablespoons olive oil	**6 ounces half-and-half**
4 cloves garlic, sliced	**2 tablespoons chopped parsley**
1 bunch chopped parsley	

1. Pound the lamb slices. Season with salt and pepper and coat both sides with flour.

2. Fry slices quickly in hot oil and transfer to a casserole.

3. Fry the sliced garlic and parsley in hot oil, pour on the wine vinegar, add hot water and pour on the meat. The liquid should just cover the meat. Simmer the dish covered for about 20 minutes.

4. Cut the bread slices in triangles and fry in hot oil. Put the bread on a hot serving dish. Place the lamb on top.

Sofrito.

130

5. Cut the potatoes in small cubes and boil in the milk and butter. Serve the potatoes separately sprinkled with chopped parsley. Serve the meat sauce on the side.

Oven Lamb Stew

SERVES 6-8

2 pounds lean lamb shoulder, boneless, cut in 2-inch cubes	2 leeks, thinly sliced
1³/₄ teaspoons salt	2 medium onions, sliced
¹/₄ teaspoon thyme, crushed	1 cup sliced raw potatoes
1 bay leaf	4 cups water
4 whole allspice	8 small onions
2 tablespoons chopped parsley	4 carrots, cut in 2-inch pieces
1 clove garlic, minced	2 white turnips, quartered
¹/₄ small head cabbage, shredded	

1. Put lamb into a Dutch oven. Season with salt, thyme, bay leaf, allspice, parsley, and garlic. Add cabbage, leeks, sliced onions, and potatoes. Pour in water. Cover tightly and bring rapidly to boiling.
2. Cook in a 350°F oven about 1¹/₂ hours, or until meat is tender.
3. About 30 minutes before cooking time is ended, cook whole onions, carrots, and turnips separately in boiling salted water until tender. Drain.
4. Turn contents of Dutch oven into a food mill set over a large bowl. Return meat to the Dutch oven and add the cooked onions, carrots, and turnips. Discard bay leaf and allspice; force the vegetables through food mill into the bowl containing cooking liquid (or purée vegetables in an electric blender). Heat with meat and vegetables.

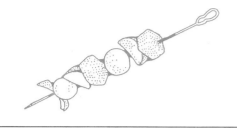

Grilled Lamb Kebabs

SERVES 4

4 skewers	2 teaspoons soy sauce
1 pound lamb without bones	¹/₂ teaspoon salt
4 small yellow onions	6 black peppercorns
8 cherry tomatoes	1 teaspoon rosemary
4 bay leaves	1 tablespoon lemon juice
Marinade:	
¹/₂ cup oil	

1. Mix oil, soy sauce, salt, peppercorns, rosemary, and lemon juice. Cut the meat in pieces and put them in the marinade for a couple of hours.
2. Peel the onions. Put on the skewers, alternating with the meat and tomatoes. Finish with a bay leaf.
3. Grill over fire for about 10-15 minutes. Turn often and brush with marinade. Serve with rice and a green salad.

Grilled Lamb Kebabs.

Mixed Meats

Meat Casserole

SERVES 8

2 pounds brisket of beef	1 pound tomatoes
¾ pound fresh ham or lean shoulder of pork	2 teaspoons salt
	2 teaspoons paprika
	2 teaspoons freshly ground black pepper
4 large yellow onions	
2 ounces salad oil	3-4 cloves garlic, pressed
1 pound green peppers	1 bunch parsley

1. Cut the meat in cubes 1 × 1-inches in size.
2. Chop the onions and fry in the oil.
3. Brown the meat cubes in the rest of the oil.
4. Cut the peppers in strips and the tomatoes in wedges and mix with the meat. Add the salt and the other seasonings.
5. Pour on cold water just to cover. Bring to boil and let boil until meat is tender, about 1 to 1½ hours. Serve the casserole sprinkled with chopped parsley.

Bollito Misto

SERVES 10-12

1 fresh beef tongue (3 to 4 pounds)	3-inch pieces
1 calf's head, prepared for cooking, or 2 pounds veal neck	2 large stalks celery, cut in pieces
	3 onions, peeled and quartered
2 pounds beef (neck, rump, or chuck roast)	4 turnips or parsnips, pared and quartered
2 pig's feet or 1 pound cotechino or other uncooked pork sausage	2 tablespoons chopped parsley
	1 teaspoon tarragon
1 stewing chicken (3 to 4 pounds)	1 teaspoon thyme
	Water
	Salt
4 medium carrots, pared and cut in	Salsa Verde (see below)

1. Combine meats, chicken, vegetables, parsley, tarragon, and thyme in a large saucepot. Pour in enough water to cover meat, and salt to taste.
2. Cover pot, bring to boiling, and simmer 3 to 4 hours, or until tongue is tender.
3. Remove skin from tongue. Slice meat, cut chicken in serving pieces, and arrange with vegetables on a large platter.

4. Serve with boiled potatoes, cooked cabbage, beets, pickles and Salsa Verde.

Note: A pressure cooker may be used. Follow manufacturer's directions for use of cooker and length of cooking time.

Salsa Verde: Finely chop **3 hard-cooked eggs;** set aside. Combine **½ cup salad oil** and **3 tablespoons wine vinegar.** Add **sugar, salt,** and **pepper** to taste. Mix well and combine with the chopped eggs. Blend in **6 tablespoons chopped herbs** such as **dill, tarragon, chervil, parsley, sorrel** and **chives.** Refrigerate several hours to allow flavors to blend.

Applesauce-Topped Beef and Sausage Loaf

SERVES 6

Meat Loaf:	½ teaspoon salt
1 pound ground beef	¼ teaspoon each sage, thyme, and garlic powder
½ pound pork sausage	
½ cup dry bread or cracker crumbs	⅛ teaspoon pepper
½ cup beer	*Topping and Sauce:*
1 small onion, minced	1⅓ cups applesauce
1 egg, slightly beaten	¼ cup beer

1. For meat loaf, mix ingredients. Shape into an elongated loaf. Place in a shallow roasting pan.
2. Bake at 350°F 50 minutes.
3. Spoon fat from pan. Spread ⅓ cup applesauce over meat loaf. Bake 10 minutes longer.
4. For sauce, heat 1 cup applesauce and beer to simmering; serve over meat loaf slices.

Corned Beef Hash

SERVES 3

1 medium onion	¼ pound smoked ham
¼ leek	
3 tablespoons butter	Salt
4 potatoes, cooked and peeled	Pepper
	Chive or parsley
¾ pound corned beef	3 egg yolks in shells
1 sausage, cooked	Ketchup

1. Chop onion and leek and sauté in 2 tablespoons butter.
2. Chop potatoes and mix with onion, leek, corned

(continued)

Corned Beef Hash.

132

beef, sausage, and ham. Season with salt and pepper.

3. Add more butter to skillet and add hash mixture. Pat down evenly with a spatula.

4. Cook over medium heat about 15 minutes until a brown crust forms on the bottom of the pan.

5. Sprinkle with chives and place egg yolks on top. Serve with ketchup

Scandinavian Meatballs

SERVES 4

1 pound ground beef	**2 teaspoons salt**
¹/₄ pound ground pork	**¹/₄ cup heavy cream**
1 egg yolk	**¹/₄ cup water**
¹/₂ teaspoon Cayenne pepper	**¹/₄ cup bread crumbs**
1 teaspoon basil	**¹/₂ cup onion, chopped**
	2-3 tablespoons butter or oil

1. Pour the bread crumbs into the cream and water mixture.

2. Mix the meat, egg yolk, and spices. Add the bread crumbs a little at a time and continue mixing. Finally add the onion and mix.

3. Shape into small meatballs for hors d'oeuvres or larger meatballs for a dinner course. Fry in butter

Meatballs with Fettuccine.

over a medium heat till golden brown. Shake the pan now and then to prevent sticking. Cook for 25 minutes.

Serve hot or cold with sliced pickled cucumbers.

Meatballs with Fettuccine

SERVES 6

1 pound ground beef	**¹/₂ teaspoon basil**
¹/₂ pound ground veal	**¹/₂ teaspoon oregano**
¹/₂ pound ground pork	**¹/₂ teaspoon ground pepper**
2 eggs	**1 bay leaf, crushed**
¹/₄ cup milk	**1 can (1 pound 13 ounces) tomato sauce**
¹/₄ cup Italian style bread crumbs	**1¹/₂ pound fettucine**
2 cloves garlic, minced	**¹/₂ cup Parmesan cheese, grated**
1 tablespoon parsley, chopped	**¹/₄ cup olive oil**

1. In a large mixing bowl combine the meat, eggs, milk, bread crumbs, garlic, and seasonings.

(continued)

Scandinavian Meatballs.

134

2. When thoroughly mixed, form into 1-inch balls and brown in a skillet in 2 tablespoons olive oil.

3. In a large saucepan heat the tomato sauce; put the browned meat balls into the sauce and cook over low heat for 35-40 minutes.

4. Boil 2 quarts of water and cook the fettucine *al dente.* Drain and arrange on a platter with meat balls. Sprinkle pasta with Parmesan cheese and serve immediately.

Serve with an endive and sliced red pepper salad.

Holiday Meatballs

SERVES 6

1 pound ground chuck	2 small onions, finely chopped
1/4 pound ground veal	2 cloves garlic, finely chopped
1/4 pound ground pork	1 teaspoon pepper
2 eggs	Salt
1/2 cup milk	2 tablespoons butter
1/2 cup bread crumbs	

1. Combine ground meats in a large mixing bowl. (Meats should be ground twice with a medium blade.)

2. In a large skillet melt 1 tablespoon of butter and sauté the onions and garlic until they start turning brown and transparent (about 5-6 minutes).

3. Let the onions and garlic cool for a few moments, then add to the meat.

4. Now add the eggs, milk, bread crumbs, and seasonings.

5. Mix all ingredients thoroughly in the bowl. The easiest way is with your hands.

6. Rinse hands in cold water and begin forming small balls (about the size of golf balls).

7. Heat the remaining butter in a skillet and sauté the meatballs until a slight crust begins to form on the balls and the insides are done.

8. Remove, pat dry, and serve with a horseradish cocktail sauce.

Saucy Ham Loaf

SERVES 8-10

Meat Loaf:

1 1/2 pounds ground cooked ham	2 tablespoons finely chopped parsley
1/2 pound ground veal	3/4 cup soft enriched bread crumbs
1/2 pound ground pork	3/4 cup apple juice
2 eggs, fork beaten	*Sauce:*
1/2 teaspoon salt	2/3 cup packed light brown sugar
1/8 teaspoon ground black pepper	2 teaspoons corn-starch
1/2 teaspoon ground nutmeg	1 teaspoon dry mus-tard
1/2 teaspoon dry mustard	1 teaspoon ground allspice
1/4 teaspoon ground thyme	2/3 cup apricot nectar
1/4 cup finely chopped onion	3 tablespoons lemon juice
1/2 cup finely chopped green pepper	2 teaspoons vinegar

1. Combine ham, veal, and pork with eggs, salt, pepper, nutmeg, dry mustard, and thyme in a large bowl. Add onion, green pepper, and parsley and toss to blend. Add bread crumbs and apple juice; mix thoroughly but lightly. Turn into a 9 × 5 × 3-inch loaf pan and flatten top.

2. Bake at 350°F 1 hour.

3. Meanwhile, prepare sauce for topping. Blend brown sugar, cornstarch, dry mustard, and allspice in a small saucepan. Add apricot nectar, lemon juice, and vinegar. Bring rapidly to boiling and cook about 2 minutes, stirring constantly. Reduce heat and simmer 10 minutes to allow flavors to blend.

4. Remove meat loaf from oven; pour off and reserve juices. Unmold loaf in a shallow baking pan. Spoon some of the reserved juices and then the sauce over loaf. Return to oven 30 minutes.

5. Place loaf on a warm platter and garnish as desired.

Holiday Meatballs.

Meatloaf with Mushroom Cream Sauce.

Baked Steak Patties

SERVES 6

1 pound ground beef	6 bacon slices
1/2 pound pork sausage meat	1 package (1³/8 ounces) dry onion soup mix
2 cups cooked white rice	3 cups water
1 egg	2 tablespoons flour

1. Combine ground beef, sausage, rice, and egg. Shape to form 6 patties. Wrap each with a bacon slice; secure with wooden pick. Place in an 11 × 7-inch baking dish.
2. Bake, uncovered, at 350°F 30 minutes; drain off excess fat.
3. Meanwhile, combine soup mix and 2¹/2 cups water in a saucepan. Cook, covered, 10 minutes.
4. Mix the remaining ¹/2 cup water and flour until smooth. Gradually add to soup mixture, stirring until thickened.
5. Pour over steak patties and bake an additional 20 minutes. Remove picks before serving.

Meatloaf with Mushroom Cream Sauce

SERVES 6

4 slices white bread	1/2 cup chopped celery
1¹/8 cup cream	1 bunch parsley
1¹/4 pound ground beef	2 eggs
1 pound ground veal	3 tablespoons tomato purée
¹/2 teaspoon salt	1 garlic clove
1¹/2 teaspoons black pepper	2 tablespoons butter or margarine

1. Crumble bread and let it soak in the cream about 10 minutes.
2. Work the meat with salt and pepper.
3. Chop celery and parsley and mix in the meat with eggs, tomato purée, and the soaked bread. Season with garlic.
4. Butter an ovenproof dish and put in the meatloaf. Bake in a 350°F oven for 50-60 minutes.

(continued)

Cheese Baked Bacon Loaf.

Casserole à la Nelson.

5. Baste with juice from meatloaf every 10 minutes.
6. Bake the potatoes in the same oven.

Serve with hot sauce, small carrots, cheese-potatoes, pickles, and a green salad.

Hot Sauce

Mix 1 can creamed mushroom soup, 1¹/₈ cups milk, and ¹/₂ cup cream with 1 can sliced mushrooms.

Potatoes with Cheese

Peel 10 large raw potatoes and cut in halves. Place them in a buttered baking dish, sprinkle with salt, and put a slice of cheese on top of each potato. Bake in a 350°F oven for about 50 minutes.

Casserole à la Nelson

SERVES 4

³/₄ pound ground beef	3 ounces water
4 ounces ground pork	3 tablespoons butter
¹/₂ teaspoon salt	3 yellow onions, sliced
¹/₂ teaspoon white pepper	6 uncooked sliced potatoes
1 boiled cold mashed potato	1 bottle of beer
1 egg	2 ounces meat juice
3 ounces cream	3 small laurel leaves
	5 peppercorns

1. Knead the meat together with salt and pepper.
2. Add the egg and the mashed potato. Dilute with the cream and the water. The mixture should be very smooth and fine.
3. Form the mixture into small oval patties.
4. Heat the butter in a skillet and brown the meat on both sides.
5. Brown the onion slowly in the remaining butter.
6. In an ovenproof casserole layer the meat, pota-

toes, and onions. Salt slightly and put the laurel leaves and pepper corns in the dish.
7. Pour a little water into the skillet in which the meat and onions were cooked, whip lightly, and pour the water together with the beer over the meat, potatoes, and onions. Cook in a 400°F oven for about 40 minutes. Serve directly from the dish with crisp bread and green salad.

Veal and Pork Rolls

SERVES 6

1 pound ground veal	Pepper
¹/₂ pound ground pork	1 teaspoon crumbled tarragon
1 egg	2 tablespoons chopped parsley
1 egg yolk	*For Frying:*
Salt	1¹/₂ tablespoons butter
Pepper	1¹/₂ tablespoons salad oil
3 ounces heavy cream	
3 ounces carbonated soda	*Sauce:*
3 ounces sifted bread crumbs	³/₄ cup beef stock*
Stuffing:	2 ounces heavy cream
4 slices smoked ham	1 teaspoon flour
3 ounces fresh mushrooms	Soy sauce
1 tablespoon butter	*Check index for recipe
Salt	

1. Pour the sifted bread crumbs into the cream and carbonated soda mixture.
2. Knead the ground veal with eggs, salt, and pepper. Add the bread crumb mixture a little at a time and work the mixture until smooth.

138

Veal and Pork Rolls.

3. Divide the mixture into 10 squares. Flatten the squares and sprinkle on a mixture of chopped mushrooms fried in butter, chopped ham, chopped parsley and seasonings. Roll together.

4. Fry the rolls in the oil and butter till golden brown, about 6-8 minutes, shaking the pan occasionally.

5. Place the rolls on a hot serving dish. Whisk the frying pan with the hot beef stock and thicken with cream and flour. Add a little soy sauce for coloring. Pour the sauce on the rolls.

Serve with boiled potatoes, pickled cucumbers, and currant jelly.

Cheese Baked Bacon Loaf

SERVES 4

1 pound ground beef	1 boiled mashed
1/4 pound ground	potato
pork	1/2 pound bacon
1 egg yolk	3 slices Cheddar
Salt	cheese
Pepper	1 package frozen
2 ounces heavy cream	broccoli
1/4 cup water	4 tomatoes

1. Combine the ground beef and pork with seasonings, egg yolk, heavy cream, and the mashed potato. Shape into a roll and put in a greased baking pan.

2. Cover the roll with bacon and bake in a 325°F oven for about 1 hour.

3. Cut the roll in even slices.

4. Cut each cheese slice in 4 triangles and put a cheese triangle between each meat roll slice. Bake in a 450°F oven until the cheese has melted.

Serve with tomatoes, broccoli, boiled potatoes, gravy, and a green salad.

Pâté à La Maison Grand Vefour

SERVES 6

Dough:	2 egg yolks
2 cups flour	Salt
1 egg	Pepper
3 ounces water	Chervil
7 ounces butter	Tarragon
Salt	Chopped parsley
Filling:	1/2 pound cooked ham
1 pound ground veal	Chopped truffles
1 pound ground pork	

1. Combine all ingredients for the dough and roll out to 1/3-inch thick. *(continued)*

139

2. For the filling make a mixture of the ground meat by grinding veal and pork together, add egg yolks, and season with salt and pepper and the other spices.

3. Add the cooked ham and the truffles, and place the mixture on the dough.

4. Roll the dough around the mixture (save a little for decoration) and pinch it together at both ends. Place it on a baking sheet. Cut a small strip of the dough and make a band. Place it on top of the roll where the dough sides are overlapping. Seal the band with a beaten egg. This band will keep the dough sealed.

5. Put two "chimneys" of waxed paper in the roll. This will allow all the liquid to evaporate and the paté will be firm.

6. Bake in a medium hot oven (350°-400°F) for about 1¹/₂ hours, for a paté of 4 pounds.

7. Remove the "chimneys." Cover the holes with small decorative lids made from leftover dough and brown.

Empanadas

24 TO 30 EMPANADAS

Picadillo:
¹/₂ **pound coarsely chopped beef**
¹/₂ **pound coarsely chopped pork**
¹/₂ **cup chopped onion**
1 **small clove garlic, minced**
¹/₂ **cup chopped raw apple**
³/₄ **cup chopped canned tomatoes**
¹/₄ **cup raisins**
³/₄ **teaspoon salt**

¹/₈ **teaspoon pepper**
Dash ground cinnamon
Dash ground cloves
¹/₄ **cup chopped almonds**
Pastry:
4 **cups all-purpose flour**
1¹/₄ **teaspoons salt**
1¹/₃ **cups lard or shortening**
²/₃ **cup icy cold water (about)**

1. For picadillo, cook beef and pork together in large skillet until well browned. Add onion and garlic and cook until onion is soft. Add remaining ingredients, except almonds, and simmer 15 to 20 minutes longer until flavors are well blended.

2. Stir in almonds. Cool.

3. For pastry, mix flour and salt in a bowl. Cut in lard until mixture resembles coarse crumbs. Sprinkle water over flour mixture, stirring lightly with a fork until all dry ingredients hold together. Divide dough in four portions.

4. On a lightly floured surface, roll one portion of dough at a time to ¹/₈-inch thickness.

5. Using a 5-inch cardboard circle as a pattern, cut rounds of pastry with a knife. Place a rounded spoonful of filling in center of each round. Fold one side over filling to meet opposite side. Seal by dampening inside edges of pastry and pressing together with tines of fork.

6. Place empanadas on a baking sheet. Bake at 400°F 15 to 20 minutes, or until lightly browned. Or fry in **fat for deep frying** heated to 365°F until browned (about 3 minutes); turn once.

Jambalaya

SERVES 10

2 **large yellow onions**
2 **cloves garlic**
5 **pounds chicken in pieces (quarters)**
2 **tablespoons cooking oil**
2 **tablespoons butter**
2¹/₂ **cups long-grain rice**
4 **cups chicken stock**
1 **green pepper, cut in strips**

1 **can peeled tomatoes**
1 **pound lightly cured cutlet of pork cut into cubes**
1 **pound shrimp**
Salt
Pepper
¹/₂ **teaspoon crumbled thyme**
¹/₂ **teaspoon oregano**
3 **ounces chopped parsley**

1. Peel and finely chop the yellow onions and garlic cloves.

2. Cut chicken into small pieces and fry in cooking oil with the onion and garlic. Add rice, tomatoes in juice, and chicken stock. Simmer covered for 25 minutes till chicken is tender.

3. Mix in pork, pepper, and shrimps. Add seasonings.

4. Allow to boil for a second. Turn heat down and cook till shrimps are pink. Sprinkle in chopped parsley.

Quick Sausage and Chicken Casserole

SERVES 4

1 **chicken cut in pieces or 2 packages chicken legs**
1 **pound small yellow onions**
1 **cup mushrooms**
1 **red and 1 green**

pepper
12 **small sliced sausages**
Salt
Pepper
Paprika
3 **ounces heavy cream**

1. Fry all ingredients separately. Combine everything in a casserole and add some water if necessary.

2. Season with salt, freshly ground pepper, and paprika. Bring to a boil and simmer for 20-30 minutes.

3. Add 3 ounces heavy cream and simmer till blended. Serve with a green salad and rice or potatoes.

Jambalya.

**Quick Sausage
and Chicken Casserole.**

POULTRY and GAME

Timetable for Roasting Turkey

QUICK METHOD   Preheat oven to 450°F

Turkey weighing 6-12 pounds, allow 15 minutes per pound and 15 minutes extra.

Turkey weighing 12 pounds and over, allow 10-12 minutes per pound and 10 minutes extra.

SLOW METHOD   Preheat oven to 325°F

Turkey weighing 6-12 pounds, allow 20 minutes per pound and 20 minutes over.

Turkey weighing 12 pounds and over, allow 16 minutes per pound and 20-30 minutes over.

FRENCH ROAST METHOD   Preheat oven to 350°F

Turkey weighing 6-12 pounds, allow 20 minutes per pound and 20 minutes over.

Turkey weighing 12 pounds and over, allow 15 minutes per pound.

Traditional Quick Roast Turkey

SERVES 8-10

1 fresh turkey unfrozen (8-9 pounds when plucked and cleaned)	Salt, ground pepper, and poultry seasoning
8-9 cups stuffing (*see below*)	8-10 strips fat bacon
1 onion	8 tablespoons oil
6-8 tablespoons butter	10-20 potatoes according to size
	1-2 cups stock

Preheat oven to 450°F.

1. Wash turkey inside and out with cold water. Dry thoroughly with kitchen towel. Rub surface all over with a cut lemon to keep flesh white. Fill the body cavity with sausage meat stuffing and the neck with chestnut stuffing, or if using other stuffings fill the neck first not too tightly and put remaining stuffing inside the body. (Recipes for stuffings below). Use wing tips to help hold neck skin in place under bird and sew down the neck skin to keep stuffing in place. Close the cavity as well as possible and put

Traditional Quick Roast Turkey.

an onion at entrance and tie or sew the leg bones together to keep it closed as much as possible. Rub breast and legs thickly with butter and seasoning, cover with strips of fat bacon and tie these in place. Weigh bird and calculate roasting time using table provided below.

2. Heat 8 tablespoons oil in roasting pan. When hot, put in bird and baste thoroughly. Place a large piece of foil over top and roast for $2^1/2$-$2^3/4$ hours, basting every 20 minutes and turning bird from one side to the other every 20 minutes to allow legs to cook without overcooking breast. For last 30 minutes place bird breast up and remove foil covering to brown breast.

3. Test if bird is done by running skewer into thickest part of leg. If juice is pink, cook longer; if clear, bird is done. Another indication is when the meat on the legs shrinks back on bones.

4. Parboiled potatoes can be roasted around turkey during last hour of cooking or in separate pan in same oven.

5. Remove from roasting pan and put on large serving dish. Keep warm. Pour off fat from pan. Add $^1/2$ tablespoon flour to juices in pan. Pour on stock. Bring to boil, stirring constantly. When well flavored, skim off any fat that has risen to surface and pour gravy into sauce boat to serve with turkey.

Chestnut Stuffing

STUFFING FOR TURKEY NECK

$1^1/2$ pounds raw chestnuts in shells, $2^1/2$ cups when peeled (or $2^1/2$ cups or large can of unsweetened chestnut purée)	1-2 cups milk or well-flavored stock
	2-3 tablespoons butter
	1 large onion
	2-3 slices bacon

1. If using raw chestnuts, bake in oven in dish of salt until skins come off cleanly, about 20 minutes, or bring to boil and cook for 5 minutes until skins are loose. Then remove all outer and inner skins, and cook chestnuts in milk or stock until tender. Drain and crush in liquidizer, reserving a few to chop roughly.

2. Melt butter and cook onion until tender. After a few minutes, add chopped bacon and cook. Stir into chestnut purée; add salt and pepper and as much milk or stock as is needed to make an easily molded stuffing. Do not make too wet. Add roughly chopped chestnuts last. Fill this mixture into neck of bird and

(continued)

143

sew up skin under back of bird or skewer securely, using wing tips to help hold in stuffing.

Note: Canned fresh puréed chestnuts can be used for this stuffing, but more onion and seasoning will be needed if the stuffing is not to be rather dull in flavor. Moisten with strongly flavored stock.

Sausage Meat Stuffing

STUFFING FOR BODY OF TURKEY

1 pound pork sausage meat	2 cups bread crumbs
1 cup chopped celery	2-3 tablespoons chopped parsley and thyme
1 large or two medium onions	1 egg
4 tablespoons butter	Juice of $^{1}/_{2}$ lemon
1 turkey liver	

1. Put sausage meat in a bowl with chopped celery. Melt butter and fry finely chopped onion and turkey liver for 2-3 minutes. Remove and let cool slightly.
2. Then cut into small pieces and mix into sausage meat. Add chopped herbs and bread crumbs. Add a beaten egg to moisten and a little lemon juice, and stuff inside turkey. Sew up opening carefully.

Turkey Tetrazzini

SERVES 6-8

8 ounces uncooked spaghetti	$^{1}/_{4}$ cup sherry
$^{1}/_{4}$ cup butter	$^{1}/_{4}$ cup grated Parmesan cheese
$^{1}/_{4}$ cup flour	2 cups cubed cooked turkey or chicken
1 teaspoon salt	
$^{1}/_{4}$ teaspoon nutmeg	$^{1}/_{4}$ pound green pepper, chopped
2 cups turkey broth or 2 chicken bouillon cubes dissolved in 2 cups hot water	$^{1}/_{2}$ pound fresh mushrooms, sliced
	1 egg yolk
1 cup evaporated milk	$^{1}/_{2}$ cup slivered almonds

1. Cook spaghetti following package directions. Drain well.
2. In a 4-cup glass measure, heat butter 30 seconds. Blend in flour, salt, and nutmeg. Stir until mixture is smooth.
3. Stir broth and milk into flour mixture. Cook until mixture boils, 6 to 8 minutes, stirring after every minute. Blend sherry and cheese into sauce and add sauce to cooked spaghetti.
4. In a 2-quart glass casserole, combine spaghetti, turkey, green pepper, mushrooms, and egg yolk; blend thoroughly. Sprinkle with almonds.
5. Cook, uncovered, 6 to 8 minutes, rotating dish

one-quarter turn halfway through cooking time. Rest 10 minutes before serving.

Conventional oven: Bake at 350°F 25 to 30 minutes.

Arroz con Pollo

SERVES 4

2 pounds chicken parts	$^{1}/_{4}$ teaspoon saffron or turmeric
2 tablespoons salad oil	$^{1}/_{8}$ teaspoon pepper
1 can (13$^{1}/_{2}$ ounces) chicken broth	1 bay leaf
	1 package (10 ounces) frozen peas
1 can (16 ounces) tomatoes, cut up	1 cup uncooked regular rice
$^{1}/_{2}$ cup chopped onion	$^{1}/_{4}$ cup sliced pimiento-stuffed or ripe olives
2 medium cloves garlic, minced	
1 teaspoon salt	

1. In a skillet, brown chicken in oil; pour off fat. Add broth, tomatoes, onion, garlic, salt, saffron, pepper, and bay leaf.
2. Cover; cook over low heat 15 minutes. Add remaining ingredients.
3. Cover; cook 30 minutes more or until chicken and rice are tender; stir occasionally. Remove bay leaf.

Chicken Livers in Madeira Sauce

SERVES 4

1 pound chicken livers	fat or butter
	$^{2}/_{3}$ cup all-purpose flour
Milk	
1 medium onion, minced	$^{3}/_{4}$ teaspoon salt
	$^{2}/_{3}$ cup chicken broth
2 tablespoons chicken	$^{1}/_{2}$ cup Madeira

1. Cover chicken livers with milk; soak 2 hours. Drain; discard milk.
2. Sauté onion in fat.
3. Mix flour with salt. Coat livers with seasoned flour.
4. Add livers to onions. Stir-fry just until golden, about 5 minutes.
5. Stir in broth and wine. Cover. Simmer 5 to 10 minutes, or just until livers are tender.

Exotic Chicken

SERVES 4

1 large or 2 small barbecued chickens	5 ounces sour cream
2 tablespoons butter	4 ounces light cream
1-2 cloves garlic, pressed	2 tablespoons ketchup
2 ounces water	2 ounces Monterey Jack cheese

1. Divide the chicken into 8-10 pieces. Brown the butter in a frying pan. Add the chicken parts and brown quickly.
2. Add the pressed garlic and the water plus the light cream.
3. Stir the cheese together with some of the sour cream until it becomes smooth. Add to pan together with the ketchup.
4. Cover and let simmer over a low flame for about 5 minutes. Add the rest of the sour cream, simmer, and season with salt and pepper.

Chicken Enchiladas

SERVES 6-8

1 onion, finely chopped	chicken soup
2 tablespoons butter	12 frozen corn tortillas
4 cups chopped cooked chicken or turkey	1 can (10½ ounces) condensed cream of celery soup
1 can (4 ounces) chopped green chilies	1½ cups sour cream
1 can (10½ ounces) condensed cream of	1 pound Cheddar or Monterey Jack cheese, shredded

1. In a large glass mixing bowl, cook onion in butter 2 minutes, stirring halfway through cooking time. Blend in chicken, chilies, and cream of chicken soup.
2. Defrost tortillas until soft and easy to roll, about 1

(continued)

Exotic Chicken.

minute. Spread about 3 tablespoons chicken mixture on each tortilla, roll, and secure with a wooden pick. Arrange in two 9-inch glass baking dishes.
3. In a small mixing bowl, blend cream of celery soup and sour cream. Pour over enchiladas.
4. Cook each dish 10 to 12 minutes, rotating one-quarter turn halfway through cooking time.
5. Sprinkle ¹/₂ pound of the cheese over top of each dish and heat for 1 minute.
6. Rest, covered, 10 minutes. Remove wooden picks and serve.

Roast Rock Cornish Hen with Wild Rice and Mushrooms

SERVES 4-8

1¹/₂ cups water	3 tablespoons melted
¹/₂ teaspoon salt	butter or marga-
¹/₂ cup wild rice	rine
2 tablespoons butter	2 tablespoons Ma-
or margarine	deira
¹/₂ pound mush-	4 Rock Cornish hens,
rooms, sliced	about 1 pound each
lengthwise through	2 teaspoons salt
caps and stems	¹/₄ cup unsalted
1 tablespoon finely	butter, melted
chopped onion	Watercress (optional)

1. Bring the water and salt to boiling in a deep saucepan.
2. Wash rice in a sieve. Add rice gradually to water so that boiling does not stop. Boil rapidly, covered, 30 to 40 minutes, or until a kernel of rice is entirely tender when pressed between fingers. Drain rice in a colander or sieve.
3. While rice is cooking, heat 2 tablespoons butter or margarine in a skillet. Add the mushrooms and onion; cook, stirring occasionally, until mushrooms are lightly browned. Combine mushrooms, wild rice, melted butter, and Madeira; toss gently until mushrooms and butter are evenly distributed throughout rice.
4. Rinse and pat hens with absorbent paper. Rub cavities of the hens with the salt. Lightly fill body cavities with the wild rice stuffing. To close body cavities, sew or skewer and lace with cord. Fasten neck skin to backs and wings to bodies with skewers.
5. Place hens, breast-side up, on rack in roasting pan. Brush each hen with melted unsalted butter (about 1 tablespoon).
6. Roast, uncovered, in a 350°F oven; frequently baste hens during roasting period with drippings from roasting pan. Roast 1 to 1¹/₂ hours, or until hens test done. To test, move leg gently by grasping end bone; drumstick-thigh joint moves easily when hens are done. Remove skewers, if used.
7. Transfer hens to a heated serving platter and garnish with sprigs of watercress if desired.

Guinea Stew

SERVES 2

Salt and freshly	¹/₄ cup soybean oil
ground pepper	¹/₂ cup amber rum
1 guinea fowl (2¹/₂ to	2 cups red wine
3 pounds)	1 cup Chicken Stock*
1 lime, halved	12 shallots
¹/₄ pound salt pork,	2 carrots, sliced
cubed	2 turnips, sliced
4 parsley sprigs	1 tablespoon butter
2 scallions or green	1 tablespoon corn-
onions, chopped	starch
2 garlic cloves	*Check index for
2 cloves	recipe
¹/₂ teaspoon salt	

1. Sprinkle salt and pepper over bird and refrigerate overnight. The next day, rub the skin with the cut side of the lime. Cut bird into pieces.
2. Render salt pork over medium heat in a Dutch oven. When crisp, remove the cracklings.
3. In a mortar, pound to a paste the parsley, scallions, garlic, cloves, and salt. Add the seasoning paste and oil to the Dutch oven.
4. Sauté the meat until golden brown on all sides.
5. Heat rum, ignite it, and pour it, still flaming, over the meat. Add wine and stock; reduce heat, cover, and simmer 30 minutes.
6. Add shallots, carrots, and turnips. Simmer until meat and vegetables are tender.
7. Place meat and vegetables on a serving platter.
8. Mix butter and cornstarch; add to liquid in Dutch oven and stir over high heat until sauce is slightly thickened. Season with salt and pepper, if necessary. Pour sauce over meat and vegetables.
Chicken Stew: Follow recipe for Guinea Stew, substituting **1 broiler-fryer chicken (about 2 pounds)** for guinea fowl.

Baked Pigeon

SERVES 1

1 pigeon	1 strip bacon, diced
Salt and pepper	Melted butter

1. Soak the pigeon about 2 hours in cold wter. Dry with paper towels.
2. Sprinkle cavity with salt and pepper.

Curried Chicken.

Chicken Florentine.

3. Make small slits in skin; insert pieces of bacon. Place in a roasting pan.
4. Bake at 350°F 30 to 40 minutes, or until tender; baste often with butter.

Curried Chicken

SERVES 4

1 cooked chicken	¹/₂ teaspoon salt
Curry Sauce:	¹/₂ teaspoon pepper
1¹/₂ tablespoons	*Rice:*
butter	1¹/₂ cups rice
3 tablespoons flour	3 cups water
2 cups Chicken	¹/₂ teaspoon salt
Stock*	1 (1-pound) can
2 teaspoons curry	peeled tomatoes
powder	*Check index for
1 egg yolk	recipe
2 tablespoons cream	

1. Boil the rice according to the package instructions.
2. Cut the chicken meat in pieces, removing all the skin. Heat the chicken in some of the stock.
3. In a skillet sauté the butter and flour and add chicken stock. Simmer the sauce while stirring for 3 minutes. Add the curry powder. Stir in more stock and thicken with the egg yolk stirred into the cream.
4. Place the heated chicken meat on a serving platter together with the boiled rice and the heated tomatoes. Pour on some of the sauce and serve the rest separately.

Chicken Florentine

SERVES 8

4 large chicken	¹/₂ teaspoon salt
breasts	¹/₂ teaspoon black
1 green pepper	pepper
1 cup dry white wine	2 packages frozen
³/₄ cup heavy cream	spinach
1 bunch dill	2 tablespoons butter
1 teaspoon paprika	

1. Thaw spinach.
2. Brown green pepper and dill in butter; add paprika but be careful not to burn it. Then add chicken and let it brown for 5 minutes, occasionally turning.
3. Pour in the wine and simmer over low heat for about 40 minutes.
4. Remove the chicken pieces and keep warm. Drain the sauce and let it boil down to half the amount. Pour in cream and simmer. Add chopped dill.
5. Melt butter in a heavy bottomed casserole and simmer with spinach for a couple of minutes. Season. Garnish chicken with spinach and pour sauce on top.

Serve with cooked rice.

Chicken à la King.

Chicken à la King

SERVES 4-6

1 large broiler chicken (3-4 pounds)	1 teaspoon curry powder
1 teaspoon salt	1 teaspoon paprika
15 black peppercorns	4 tablespoons flour
1 yellow onion, chopped	2 cups Chicken Stock*
1 piece of leek	1 chicken bouillon cube
1 bay leaf	½ cup heavy cream
4-5 cloves	1 tablespoon mango chutney or soy sauce
1 pound bacon	
1 pound shrimp	
1 red pepper	3 tablespoons dry white wine
1 green pepper	
Curry Sauce:	*Check index for recipe
4 tablespoons butter	

1. Place the chicken in a large saucepan. Pour on enough water to cover chicken. Add salt, peppercorns, onion, leek, bay leaf, and cloves. Bring water to a boil. Cover and simmer 1 hour.
2. Meanwhile cut the peppers into strips.
3. Shell and devein shrimp.
4. Let chicken cool and strain liquid. Remove skin and bones. Cut meat in small pieces.
5. Fry bacon till crisp. Set aside.
6. Make sauce. Heat butter in a skillet over low heat. Add curry and paprika and stir in the flour. Add chicken stock a cup at a time, stirring until smooth. Add the bouillon cube and heat for 5 minutes.
7. Add cream, chicken meat, peppers, and shrimp and cook for an additional 5 minutes till shrimp turn pink. Add mango chutney and wine. Top dish with crisply fried bacon.

Pheasant

SERVES 4

1 pheasant	3 tablespoons butter
1 to 1½ teaspoons salt	¾ cup heavy cream
½ teaspoon black pepper	1 ounce apple cheese
8 medium peeled raw potatoes	2 tablespoons soy sauce
1 to 1½ teaspoons salt	1 large bunch parsley sprigs

1. Rinse and wipe the pheasant inside and outside.

Chicken with Vegetable Sauce.

Season with salt and pepper, half inside and half outside. Brown the pheasant quickly all around in a frying pan in half the butter. Wrap in aluminum foil.
2. Preheat the oven to 325°F.
3. Cut the peeled raw potatoes in slices and fry them lightly on both sides in the remaining butter in the pan. Later add the rest of the butter. Sprinkle some salt over each round of potato slices before they are transferred to an ovenproof deep dish or casserole.
4. Distribute the potato slices evenly on the bottom and up towards the edge of the casserole; place the pheasant in the middle and pour on the gravy from foil if there is any.
5. Cover the casserole immediately. Put the casserole in the oven and roast the pheasant for about 30 minutes.
6. Whip together cream, apple cheese, and soy sauce. Taste and correct seasoning, adding more apple cheese if necessary.
7. Pour the cream mixture on pheasant and potatoes when the casserole has been in the oven for 20 minutes. Serve dish straight from the oven with the pheasant cut in four portion sizes, and garnish with fresh parsley sprigs.

Chicken with Vegetable Sauce

SERVES 6

2 pounds fresh chicken	**1 can (1 pound) peeled tomatoes**
Salt	**2 tablespoons tomato purée**
Pepper	
1 ounce butter	**3 ounces dry white wine**
1 tablespoon soy sauce	**1 cup of chicken bouillon**
Vegetable Sauce:	
6-8 stalks blanched celery	**1 teaspoon Italian salad seasoning, tarragon or oregano**
1 leek	
2 yellow onions	
3-4 tablespoons butter	**20 pimiento-stuffed olives**

1. Season chickens inside and out. Brush with melted butter and soy sauce. Place chickens with breast up on a rack in a roasting pan.
2. Bake in a 350°F oven for 45 minutes for small and 1 hour for large chickens.

(continued)

3. Vegetable sauce: Wash and cut celery and leek in narrow strips. Chop the onions. In a saucepan fry vegetables lightly in butter until they soften. Stir occasionally and add the canned tomatoes through a strainer.

4. Add the chicken bouillon, the tomato purée, and seasonings and let simmer, covered, for about 20 minutes. Dilute with 3 ounces dry white wine or tomato liquid.

5. Add the sliced olives; taste and correct seasoning. Carve the chickens in halves and place on a hot serving dish. Large chickens can be cut in four pieces. Pour on the hot chicken gravy and the hot vegetable sauce.

Loin of Venison

SERVES 4

2 pound boned loin of	diced
venison	1 stalk celery, diced
3 tablespoons oil	1 red pepper,
¼ cup red wine	chopped
½ teaspoon black	1 tablespoon flour
pepper	2½ cups Beef Stock*
¼ cup cashews	2 tablespoons parsley
⅓ cup raisins	1 bay leaf
2 tablespoons butter	½ cup red wine
Sauce:	2 tablespoons red
½ cup mushrooms,	wine vinegar
chopped	Salt
1½ teaspoons tomato	½ teaspoon pepper
paste	½ cup heavy cream
2 tablespoons oil	*Check index for
1 small yellow onion,	recipe

1. Cut venison into slices about ¼-inch thick. Lay on a plate and sprinkle with 1 tablespoon oil and pepper. Cover and let stand for at least 1 hour.

2. Make sauce: Heat the oil, add onion, carrot, red pepper, and celery and cook over low heat until they start to brown.

3. Stir in the flour and continue cooking to a rich brown. Add ⅔ of the stock, the mushrooms, tomato paste, parsley, and bay leaf and the wine. Bring mixture to a boil, stirring. Reduce heat and simmer with the lid half covering the pan for 20-25 minutes.

4. Add the remaining stock, bring to a boil again and skim. Strain sauce. Return to pan, add vinegar and continue to simmer 6-7 minutes.

5. Add cream and simmer for 5 minutes. Add nuts and raisins.

6. Heat remaining oil in a heavy frying pan and sauté venison over high heat for about 4 minutes on each side. Arrange on a warm platter and pour warm sauce on top.

Yesterday's Turkey Casserole

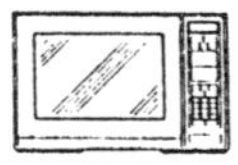

SERVES 4

¼ cup butter	cubes
⅓ cup flour	¾ teaspoon salt
½ cup chopped onion	8 small fresh mush-
¾ cup thinly sliced	rooms, sliced
celery	2 cups cooked diced
1½ cups water	turkey
2 chicken bouillon	

1. In a 2-quart casserole, cook butter 30 to 45 seconds. Add flour; blend until smooth. Stir in onion, celery, water, bouillon cubes, and salt.

2. Cook 5 to 6 minutes, until mixture thickens. Stir once halfway through cooking.

3. Add mushrooms and turkey; stir to blend.

4. Cook, covered, 3 to 4 minutes, rotating dish one-quarter turn halfway through cooking time.

5. Serve over toast, rice, or leftover stuffing.

Note: Chicken may be substituted for turkey. If no leftover cooked chicken is available, cook chicken breasts 7 minutes per pound. Cool chicken, remove meat from bones, and dice.

Stuffed Mini Turkey

SERVES 8-10

1 turkey (about	2 tablespoons butter
6½ pounds)	¾ cup cooked rice
½ teaspoon salt	5¼ ounces baked
½ teaspoon freshly	liver pâté
ground black or	¼ cup bouillon
white pepper	½ teaspoon salt
3 tablespoons butter	½ teaspoon pepper
Stuffing:	½ teaspoon sage
Giblets from turkey	
(not the neck)	*Gravy:*
1 chopped onion	Flour
3½ ounces sliced	Light cream
mushrooms	

1. Make stuffing: Dice giblets. Brown onion, mushrooms, and giblets in butter.

2. Mix with rice, liver pâté, and bouillon. Season with salt, pepper, and sage.

3. Brush turkey inside and out with salt and pepper. Stuff it and close with wooden picks. Tie the legs together and place turkey on a large piece of aluminum foil.

4. Brush the turkey with melted butter and wrap the turkey in the aluminum foil.

5. Place the turkey in a roasting pan in a 400°F oven and bake for about 1 hour. Open the foil and let the

Stuffed Mini Turkey.

turkey brown in 475°F oven for 15-20 minutes. Remove from oven and place on cutting board.
6. Add flour and cream to juices in pan.
7. Carve the turkey: start by cutting the thighs off. Cut breast meat loose and cut in slices.
8. Place the stuffing next to the meat on a serving dish and serve with boiled or browned potatoes and boiled vegetables.

Try this delicious lingonberry sauce: Mix together **1¹/₂ cups lingonberry jam with juice of 2 lemons, 3-4 tablespoons orange marmalade,** and **¹/₂ cup scalded, peeled, and chopped almonds.**

Wild Pigeons Perugian

SERVES 4

3 pigeons or Rock Cornish hens	¹/₄ teaspoon ground sage
4 to 6 tablespoons olive oil	¹/₂ teaspoon juniper berries
1 cup dry red wine	¹/₂ teaspoon salt
10 green olives	Dash pepper
4 fresh sage leaves or	

1. Brown pigeons in 2 tablespoons hot olive oil in a

Dutch oven, adding more oil if necessary. Stir in wine, 2 tablespoons olive oil, olives, sage, juniper berries, salt, and pepper.
2. Cook in a 300°F oven 50 to 60 minutes, or until pigeons are tender.

Capon in Cream

SERVES ABOUT 6

1 capon or chicken (5 to 6 pounds)	1 tablespoon melted butter
Salt	4 teaspoons flour
2 cups chicken stock or broth	2 cups sour cream
4 egg yolks	1 teaspoon salt
	¹/₄ teaspoon pepper

1. Sprinkle cavity of bird with salt. Place in a large kettle.
2. Add stock to kettle. Cover. Simmer until just tender (about 1 hour). Allow to cool.
3. Meanwhile, cream egg yolks and butter; add flour and blend thoroughly. Stir in sour cream. Season with 1 teaspoon salt and pepper. Beat at high speed until stiff. Cook until thickened in top of a double

(continued)

boiler, stirring constantly to keep from curdling or sticking (handle like hollandaise sauce). Cool.

4. Make cuts in capon as for carving, but without cutting through. Place in a shallow baking pan. Fill cuts with sauce, then spread remainder over the whole surface of the bird.

5. Bake at 425°F about 20 minutes, or until sauce is browned.

6. Meanwhile, boil liquid in which chicken was cooked until it is reduced to 1 cup of stock.

7. To serve, pour stock over capon. Carve at the table.

Ortolans on Croutons

SERVES 8

8 ortolans	1 tablespoon butter
¹/₂ lime	1 tablespoon corn-starch
Salt and freshly ground pepper	8 white bread slices with crusts trimmed
¹/₂ cup cubed salt pork	¹/₄ cup butter
¹/₄ cup amber rum	
¹/₂ cup red wine	

1. Truss ortolans. Rub the skin with the cut side of the lime half. Season with salt and pepper.

2. Render the salt pork over high heat in a Dutch oven. Sauté ortolans for 6 minutes, or until well browned.

3. Heat rum, ignite it, and pour it, still flaming, over the birds. Place birds on a serving platter.

4. Pour wine into Dutch oven to deglaze. Mix 1 tablespoon butter and cornstarch and add to wine. Stir until sauce is slightly thicker.

5. Make croutons by frying bread slices in butter until brown on both sides.

6. Serve each ortolan on a crouton, top with a slice of sautéed lier pâté, if desired, and pour sauce over all.

Turkey Roll Provençale

SERVES 6

1 turkey roll (2 pounds)	4 tablespoons chopped parsley
6 ounces butter	1 cup chicken bouillon
¹/₄ teaspoon salt	2-2¹/₂ pounds potatoes
¹/₄ teaspoon pepper	3 tablespoons butter
1 clove garlic, chopped	¹/₄ teaspoon salt
10 anchovy fillets	¹/₄ teaspoon white pepper
12 black olives	

1. Preheat oven to 350°F.

2. Peel and rinse potatoes. Slice potatoes and put them in very cold water. Remove and pat with paper towels. Heat butter in a skillet and brown potatoes quickly.

3. Spread the potato slices evenly on the bottom of an ovenproof dish. Salt and pepper.

4. Chop the anchovies and the olives finely.

5. Mix garlic, anchovies, and olives until smooth. Work into a roll and put in wax paper in a cool place.

6. Remove the skin from the turkey roll and cut the roll into thin slices. Brush with bouillon.

7. Place the slices of turkey on the bed of potatoes and brush again with bouillon. Cut the "aromatic" roll in thin slices and place between the turkey slices and on top.

8. Cover the ovenproof dish with foil and place in a 350°F oven for 20 minutes until the potatoes become soft.

Rock Cornish Hens with Fruited Stuffing

SERVES 4

1¹/₂ cups herb-seasoned stuffing croutons	2 tablespoons apricot nectar
¹/₂ cup drained canned apricot halves, cut in pieces	1 tablespoon chopped parsley
¹/₂ cup quartered seedless green grapes	¹/₄ teaspoon salt
¹/₃ cup chopped pecans	4 Rock Cornish hens (1 to 1¹/₂ pounds each), thawed if purchased frozen
¹/₄ cup butter or margarine, melted	Salt and pepper
	¹/₃ cup apricot nectar
	2 teaspoons soy sauce

1. Combine stuffing croutons, apricots, grapes, pecans, 2 tablespoons butter, 2 tablespoons apricot nectar, parsley, and ¹/₄ teaspoon salt in a bowl; mix lightly.

2. Sprinkle cavities of hens with salt and pepper. Fill each hen with about ¹/₂ cup stuffing; fasten with skewers and lace with cord.

3. Blend ¹/₃ cup apricot nectar, soy sauce, and remaining butter. Place hens, breast side up, on a rack in a shallow roasting pan; brush generously with sauce.

4. Roast in a 350°F oven about 1¹/₂ hours, or until hens are tender and well browned; baste occasionally with sauce during roasting.

Turkey Roll Provencale.

Chicken Basque

SERVES 5

5 chicken breasts	1 yellow onion,
4 tablespoons butter	chopped
2¹/₂ teaspoons tarra-	1 red pepper,
gon	chopped
2¹/₂ teaspoons oreg-	1 green pepper,
ano	chopped
¹/₂ teaspoon salt	2 zucchini, chopped
¹/₂ teaspoon pepper	2 tomatoes, chopped
¹/₄ teaspoon dried hot	¹/₄ cup all-purpose
red pepper	flour
2 tablespoons parsley	
2 stalks celery,	
chopped	

1. Preheat oven to 350°F.
2. Mix butter, 2 teaspoons tarragon, and 2 teaspoons oregano.
3. Rub butter mixture over chicken; season with salt and pepper. Place in casserole. Roast for 2 hours, basting several times.
4. Meanwhile cook vegetables. Heat 2 tablespoons butter in a frying pan. Add celery and onions and sauté till transparent. Add ¹/₂ teaspoon oregano, ¹/₂ teaspoon tarragon, red pepper, and parsley. Mix well.
5. Add peppers, zucchini, and tomatoes and pour over chicken 10 minutes before cooking time is up. Serve from casserole.

Chicken Basque.

Chicken Livers and Mushrooms

SERVES 4-6

1 to 1¹/₂ pounds	³/₄ teaspoon salt
chicken livers	¹/₂ teaspoon pepper
¹/₂ pound fresh mush-	¹/₂ cup burgundy
rooms, thinly sliced	¹/₄ cup butter
¹/₄ cup grated onion	6 slices toast or
2 tablespoons	3 English muffins,
chopped parsley	split and toasted

1. Dice livers coarsely. Combine with mushrooms, onion, parsley, salt, pepper, and wine in a large plastic bag. Marinate in refrigerator overnight.
2. In a 2-quart glass casserole, heat butter 30 to 45 seconds. Add chicken-liver mixture.
3. Cook, uncovered, 6 to 8 minutes, stirring every 2 minutes. Cover casserole and cook 3 to 4 minutes more.
4. Spoon onto toasted bread or muffins arranged on serving platter.

Curried Duck Martinique

SERVES 6

3 cups coarsely	3 tablespoons flour
chopped cooked	1 tablespoon curry
duck	powder
3 cups sliced mush-	¹/₂ teaspoon salt
rooms	¹/₄ teaspoon freshly
6 tablespoons butter,	ground pepper
melted	1 cup whipping cream
1 cup diced apple	¹/₂ cup duck stock
¹/₃ cup grated onion	(made from cooking
1 garlic clove,	the carcass)
crushed in a garlic	3 tablespoons Madeira
press	or sweet sherry

1. Cook duck and mushrooms in half the melted butter in a skillet over low heat, until the duck is slightly browned and the mushrooms are tender. Remove from heat and cover.
2. Sauté apple, onion, and garlic in remaining butter in a large skillet until soft. Remove skillet from the heat and stir in flour, curry, salt, and pepper.
3. Place skillet over low heat and blend in cream, stock, and Madeira. Stir constantly until the mixture thickens. Stir in the duck and mushroom mixture.
4. Serve with cooked white rice tossed with 1 cup diced banana.

Duck Stuffed
with Apricots.

Duck Stuffed with Apricots

SERVES 4-6

1 roasting duck (4-5 pounds)	3 tablespoons honey
1 pound fresh apricots (or 1 large can, drained)	1-1½ cups stock made with duck giblets (or a chicken bouillon cube)
1 orange	3-4 tablespoons apricot brandy
1 onion	
2-3 tablespoons oil	

Preheat oven to 400°F.

1. Stuff duck with half the seeded apricots and 3 strips of orange zest (the thin outer skin of orange), finely chopped onion, and seasoning. Prick skin of duck with fork to allow the fat to run out while cooking and season with pepper and salt.

2. Heat oil in baking pan. When very hot add duck and baste all over with oil. Roast in oven, allowing 20 minutes per pound. Half an hour before cooking is completed, spoon over the melted honey and juice of orange, which will give the skin a shiny crispness. Ten minutes before end of cooking, add rest of apricots to pan to heat through and brown slightly. Remove duck to a warm dish, and remove stuffing to a bowl. Arrange roasted apricots around duck.

3. Pour off fat from roasting pan, add stuffing to it with stock and bring to a boil, stirring all the time. When the sauce has a pleasant flavor, strain or blend in liquidizer or blender. Return to heat and add apricot brandy. Serve at once with duck and apricots.

155

Katrin's Chicken Pie

SERVES 4

Pie Dough:	strips
4 ounces soft butter	1 green pepper, cut in
1½ cups flour	strips
3 tablespoons icy cold	4 tablespoons butter
water and a few	½ teaspoon curry
drops of gin or	powder
brandy	3 tablespoons flour
Filling:	1 cup Chicken Stock*
1 boiled or fried	¾ cup heavy cream
broiler chicken	Salt
1 cup fresh mush-	Pepper
rooms	1 egg, beaten
1 small yellow onion	*Check index for
1 red pepper, cut in	recipe

1. Work together the ingredients for the pie dough till smooth. Let it rest wrapped in foil or plastic in the refrigerator for a few hours or overnight.
2. Rinse a 9-inch pie pan with cold water. Roll out the dough very thinly and line the bottom and sides of the pie pan. Bake the pie in a preheated 400°F oven for 20 minutes.
3. Divide the chicken in half and remove the skin. Remove the bones and cut the meat in pieces.
4. Sauté the mushrooms and peppers. Peel, slice, and sauté the onion.
5. Heat the butter and curry and stir in the flour. Stir in the Chicken Stock and cream.

6. Add chicken pieces, mushrooms, onions, and peppers and let the stew simmer for about 5 minutes. Salt and pepper and add cream or water if necessary.
7. Let the stew cool. Fill the pie pan with the stew. Roll out enough dough to cover the top and prick it with a fork. Roll the remainder of the dough into a narrow strip and work around the edge of the pie pan. Brush the pie with beaten egg and bake in a 400°F oven for about 25 minutes.

Chicken Baked in Salt Crust

SERVES 4

1 broiler chicken	1 teaspoon dried
(about 2½ pounds)	thyme
Rind from a large	1 teaspoon oregano
lemon, grated	4 pounds coarse salt
4 tablespoons butter	1½ cups water
1 small yellow onion	6-8 baking potatoes
4 cloves garlic	

1. Wash and dry the chicken inside as well as outside.
2. Preheat the oven to 400°F.
3. With a fork mix the butter, the grated lemon rind, thyme, and oregano.

(continued)

Katrin's Chicken Pie.

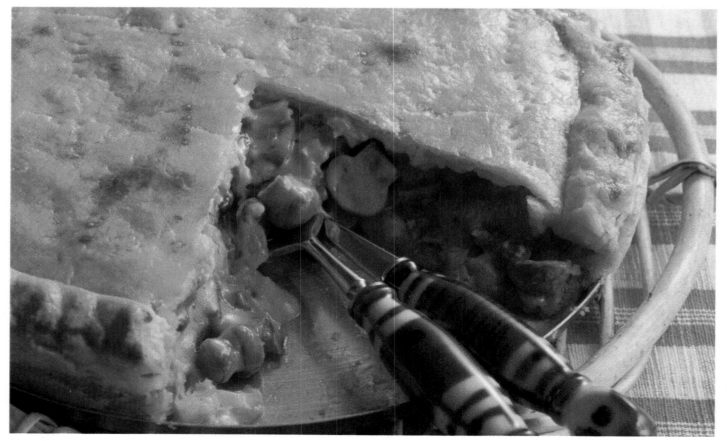

4. Place half the butter and the clove-studded onion inside the chicken and seal with a wooden pick.
5. Rub the chicken with the rest of the butter.
6. Spread about 1 pound of the coarse salt on the bottom of an ovenproof pan. Add enough water (about 3 ounces) to moisten the salt.
7. Place the chicken with the breast up on the salt bed.
8. Mix the rest of the salt (how much depends on the size of the pan) with water to moisten it.
9. Cover the broiler completely with salt.
10. Place pan in oven and bake for 1 hour 15 minutes. Add potatoes when one hour of the baking time remains.
11. Cut and lift the salt cover with a sharp knife.
12. Remove chicken to a cutting-board. Trim off salt that has stuck to the skin. Carve the bird.

Roast Goose with Rice and Pickle Stuffing

SERVES 6-8

3 cups cooked rice; or 1 package (6 ounces) seasoned white and wild rice mix, cooked following package directions	pickles, drained and chopped
	1/4 cup sweet pickle liquid
	1/2 to 3/4 cup butter or margarine, melted
1 package (7 ounces) herb-seasoned stuffing croutons	2 tablespoons brown sugar
2 medium navel oranges, pared and sectioned	1 goose (8 to 10 pounds)
	1 tablespoon salt
2 onions, chopped	1/4 teaspoon ground black pepper
1 cup cranberries, rinsed, sorted, and chopped	2 tablespoons light corn syrup
	1 1/2 cups orange juice
1 cup sweet mixed	1/2 cup orange marmalade

1. Combine rice, stuffing croutons, orange sections, onions, cranberries, pickles and liquid, butter, and brown sugar in a large bowl; toss lightly until blended.
2. Rinse goose and remove any large layers of fat from the body cavity. Pat dry with absorbent paper. Rub body and neck cavities with salt and pepper.
3. Lightly spoon stuffing into the neck and body cavities. Overlap neck cavity with the skin and skewer to back of goose. Close body cavity with skewers and lace with cord. Loop cord around legs; tighten slightly and tie to a skewer inserted in the back above tail. Rub skin of goose with a little salt, if desired.
4. Put remaining stuffing into a greased casserole and cover; or cook in heavy-duty aluminum foil. Set in oven with goose during final hour of roasting.

5. Place goose, breast side down, on a rack in a large shallow roasting pan.
6. Roast in a 325°F oven 2 hours, removing fat from pan several times during this period.
7. Turn goose, breast side up. Blend corn syrup and 1 cup orange juice. Brush generously over goose. Roast about 1 1/2 hours, or until goose tests done. To test for doneness, move leg gently by grasping end of bone; when done, drumstick-thigh joint moves easily or twists out. Brush frequently during final roasting period with the orange-syrup blend.
8. Transfer goose to a heated serving platter. Spoon 2 tablespoons drippings, the remaining 1/2 cup orange juice, and marmalade into a small saucepan. Heat thoroughly, stirring to blend. Pour into a serving dish or gravy boat to accompany goose.

Continental Roast Goose with Chestnut and Liver Stuffing

SERVES 6-8

1 goose, 8-10 pounds	thyme and marjoram
2 pounds chestnuts	Grated rind of 1/2 lemon
2 cups stock	2 tablespoon flour
6 apples	4-6 tablespoons oil
2 onions	2 tablespoons red currant jelly
1 goose liver	Juice of 1/2 lemon
1 tablespoon butter	1 1/2 cups cider or stock
2 cups bread crumbs	
2 tablespoons chopped parsley	
1 tablespoon mixed	

Preheat oven to 400°F.
1. Prepare stuffing: Put chestnuts in boiling water for 5-6 minutes or until skins will remove completely. Then cover peeled nuts with stock and simmer until tender. Drain and let cool. Reserve stock for moistening stuffing. Peel and chop apples, chop onions, and cook for 3-4 minutes, then mix in chestnuts. Cook goose liver in butter and when firm, chop and add to stuffing with 1-2 cups bread crumbs. Add chopped parsley, thyme, marjoram, lemon rind, salt, and pepper. Mix together, adding enough stock to make a moist but firm mixture.
2. Stuff goose and sew up opening. Prick goose all over lightly with sharp fork, sprinkle with 1 tablespoon flour and seasoning. Heat oil or fat in roasting pan. Put goose into pan, on a rack if possible to allow fat to drain, and cook for 20-25 minutes per pound, basting every 20 minutes, turning from side to side. Reduce heat slightly after first 20 minutes. For last 30 minutes pour off most of fat, place bird breast up and allow to brown, raising heat again if breast is not becoming crisp and brown. Test doneness with skewer in thick part of leg. When done,

remove to serving dish and keep warm while making gravy.

3. Skim off any remaining fat from roasting pan, sprinkle in 1 tablespoon flour and blend with roasting juices in pan. Add red currant jelly and lemon juice; stir in well. Add cider or stock and bring to boil. Cook for 2-3 minutes, strain, season to taste, and serve hot with goose.

Hens in Wine

SERVES 4

1 tablespoon rosemary	parsley
1 cup dry white wine	4 Rock Cornish hens, quartered
$^1/_3$ cup flour	$^1/_2$ cup butter or margarine
1 teaspoon salt	
$^1/_2$ teaspoon pepper	1 pound small fresh mushrooms
1 teaspoon snipped	

1. Soak rosemary in wine 1 hour.
2. Combine flour, salt, pepper, and parsley. Coat hen quarters with flour mixture.
3. Brown hen quarters in butter in a skillet. Place in a 12 × 8-inch baking dish. Add wine mixture.

4. Bake, uncovered, at 350°F 30 minutes.
5. Meanwhile, sauté mushrooms in butter in skillet. Add to baking dish. Bake an additional 15 minutes, or until hen quarters are tender.

Rabbit Stew

SERVES 8

2 rabbits, skinned, cleaned, and cut in four pieces each	2 tablespoons tomato paste mixed with 1 cup water
$1^1/_2$ cups mild vinegar	1 cup red wine
1 cup water	1 garlic clove, crushed in a garlic press
1 large onion, quartered	
2 teaspoons salt	1 bay leaf
1 teaspoon pepper	$^1/_8$ teaspoon cinnamon
2 bay leaves	Salt and pepper to taste
2 pounds whole baby onions	Water to cover
3 tablespoons olive oil	

1. Put rabbit pieces into a large bowl. Add vinegar,

(continued)

Continental Goose with Chestnut and Liver Stuffing.

Squab Stuffed with Orange Rice.

water, onion, salt, pepper, and bay leaves. Cover. Refrigerate 4 hours, turning occasionally. Pat dry.

2. Peel onions. Cut a small cross at the base of each (to keep onions whole during cooking).

3. Heat olive oil in a large Dutch oven and sear rabbits on all sides until reddened. Add all ingredients including onions and water to barely cover. Bring to a boil. Cover.

4. Bake at 250°F about 2 hours, or until rabbit is tender.

Note: If a thick sauce is desired, pour the sauce into a saucepan and simmer uncovered for ½ hour. Pour over rabbit.

Squabs Stuffed with Orange Rice

SERVES 4

4 tender squabs	onion
1 cup rice	2-3 tablespoons oil
3 oranges	1-2 teaspoons flour
½ cup seedless grapes	½ cup white wine
A little powdered	

Preheat oven to 400°F.

1. Prepare stuffing: Cook rice and let cool. Grate rind of 1 large orange; mix with 8-9 tablespoons cooked rice. Remove pith and skin from 2 oranges with a serrated knife and cut out segments; add these to rice. Dip grapes into boiling water for few

seconds, then into cold; peel and add to stuffing with salt, pepper, and little powdered onion. Stuff mixture into squabs.

2. Roast birds as in *Squabs Stuffed with Almonds and Raisins (see below)*.

3. Pour away oil and sprinkle in flour, blend with pan drippings and add wine and a little stock. Bring to a boil and simmer for 1 minute. Add juice of 1 orange and a few strips of peel, and serve with the squabs.

Squabs Stuffed with Almonds and Raisins

SERVES 4

4 tender squabs	4 tablespoons raisins
1 cup cooked rice	2-3 tablespoons sherry
2 onions	
3 tablespoons butter	4 slices fat bacon
3-4 tablespoons peeled flaked almonds	2-3 tablespoons oil
1 tablespoon chopped herbs	1-2 teaspoons flour
	½ cup red wine
	½ cup stock

Preheat oven to 400°F.

1. Prepare stuffing: Boil rice until tender. Drain and let cool. Chop 2 onions and cook in 3 tablespoons butter until soft. Add skinned sliced onions and cook until all are golden brown. Add 8 tablespoons rice to pan, cook for 1 minute; then remove. Add

Braised Quails with Risotto.

chopped herbs and raisins that have been soaking in sherry and seasoning. Stuff mixture into squabs.

2. Tie a slice of fat bacon around breast of each bird. Heat oil in oven, add squabs and baste thoroughly. Roast in oven for about 35-40 minutes, basting and turning every 10 minutes. Remove bacon for last 15 minutes to brown breast. Remove to a serving dish and keep warm.

3. Pour away oil and sprinkle in flour, blend into pan drippings, and add wine and stock. Stir until smooth and boiling, add seasoning, and pour into sauce boat.

Braised Quail with Risotto

SERVES 4

4 quail	*Risotto:*
4 vine leaves	2 tablespoons butter
3 tablespoons butter	1 onion
2 onions	1 cup rice
1 carrot	4 cups stock
2 stalks celery	2 tablespoons raisins
1/2 cup mushrooms	1 pimiento
1/2 cup stock	1 tablespoon chopped
2-3 tablespoons	herbs
sherry	8-10 olives
1 tablespoon chopped	2 tablespoons al-
herbs	monds

Preheat oven to 350°F.

1. Wrap quail in vine leaves and put a small piece of butter inside each one. Melt 2 tablespoons butter, and cook sliced onions, carrot, celery, and chopped mushrooms until golden brown. Place quail on top of vegetables in an ovenproof dish and add a little sherry, 3-4 tablespoons stock, a sprinkling of herbs and seasoning. Put into oven and braise for 25 minutes, or until tender.

2. Make risotto: Heat butter and cook chopped onion until golden brown. Add rice and cook for 1 minute. Pour on stock and add raisins, chopped pimiento, and herbs. Put in moderate oven for 20-30 minutes or until rice has absorbed all liquid. Mix in olives and browned almonds, and serve on dish with the quail on top, and with a sauce made from the pan gravy and remaining stock and sherry.

Dinner Chicken Wings

SERVES 5-6

2 to 3 pounds chicken wings	1/3 cup soy sauce
1 teaspoon ginger	3 tablespoons salad oil
1 teaspoon dry mus- tard	3 cloves garlic, quar- tered
1 tablespoon brown sugar	2 tablespoons sesame seed

1. Clip wing tips from each wing. Divide each wing

(continued)

at the joint, in two pieces. Place wing pieces in a 2-quart glass baking dish.

2. In a mixing bowl, blend ginger, mustard, brown sugar, soy sauce, oil, and garlic. Pour over chicken pieces and marinate overnight.

3. Remove the garlic pieces from the marinade. Cook the chicken in marinade 12 to 14 minutes, rotating dish one-quarter turn halfway through cooking time.

4. Rest, covered with waxed paper, 10 minutes. Pour off marinade. Sprinkle chicken with sesame seed and heat 1 minute.

Note: Dinner Chicken Wings may be served with rice for a main dish or used as an appetizer.

Chicken Cacciatore

SERVES 5-6

1 broiler fryer, cut up (2½ to 3 pounds)	1 tablespoon vinegar
¼ teaspoon salt	¼ teaspoon pepper
¼ teaspoon dry mustard	½ cup ketchup or chili sauce
3 tablespoons salad oil	1 tablespoon parsley flakes

1. In a 2-quart glass baking dish, arrange chicken pieces with meatier pieces toward the edge.

2. In a 2-cup measure, combine salt, dry mustard, oil, vinegar, pepper, ketchup, and parsley flakes; stir to blend. Pour sauce over chicken.

3. Cook, covered, 20 minutes, rotating dish one-quarter turn halfway through cooking time.

4. Rest, covered, 10 minutes before serving.

Roast Turkey

ABOUT 2 SERVINGS PER POUND

8- to 15-pound turkey	1 tablespoon bottled
2 tablespoons butter	brown bouquet sauce

1. Clean and prepare turkey for cooking as directed on turkey wrapper. Place turkey, breast down, on roasting rack in a glass baking dish; cover with waxed paper.

2. Estimate the total cooking time. For an 8- to 12-pound turkey allow 7 to 8 minutes per pound, and for a 12- to 15-pound turkey allow 6 to 7 minutes per pound. Cook the turkey for a fourth of the estimated cooking time.

3. Melt the butter in a custard cup and mix with the bottled brown bouquet sauce. Brush the turkey with the mixture. Cover the bottom half of wings and legs with small pieces of aluminum foil. Do not allow

foil to touch inside walls of microwave oven. Secure legs and wings close to body with string. Cover with waxed paper.

4. Place turkey on its side and cook a fourth of estimated roasting time. Turn turkey on its other side and cook for another fourth of estimated roasting time. Cut strings to allow legs and wings to stand free, remove foil, place turkey breast up and cook until turkey reaches internal temperature of 175°F. Each time turkey is turned rotate dish one-quarter turn and baste with drippings. Remove drippings as they accumulate, or additional cooking time will be needed.

5. When cooking time is up, rest the turkey 15 to 20 minutes; temperature should reach 190°F. Return to oven for additional cooking if needed.

6. Garnish with green grapes and serve.

Chicken Véronique

SERVES 8

2 chickens	1 yellow onion, chopped
½ lemon	*Sauce:*
6 tablespoons butter	½ cup cognac
1 cup red wine	3 cups seedless white grapes
Stuffing:	2 tablespoons flour
1 egg white	½ cup red wine
½ pound ground veal	½ cup chicken bouillon
1 cup light cream	
Salt	
Pepper	
¼ cup mushrooms	

1. Preheat oven to 350°F. Wash chickens inside and out. Rub with lemon.

2. Make stuffing: Mix egg white and veal. Beat in light cream. Season with salt and pepper.

3. Heat 2 tablespoons butter. Sauté onion and mushrooms and add to veal mixture.

4. Stuff chickens and tie them up. Brush chickens with melted butter.

5. Place chickens in a roasting pan, pour in 1 cup wine, and cover with aluminum foil. Roast about 2 hours till chicken is tender. Baste every 15 minutes with wine.

6. Remove foil after 1½ hours so skin can brown.

7. Make sauce: Remove chickens from pan, but leave in the oven with heat off to stay warm.

8. Place roasting pan over medium heat. When very hot add cognac and grapes and cook over low heat for 3 minutes.

9. Remove from heat and stir in flour. Add wine and chicken bouillon. Over low heat stir and bring to a boil. Simmer 2 minutes. Serve immediately with currant jelly.

Chicken Véronique.

Turkish Guinea Fowl

SERVES 4-6

1 guinea fowl	3 cups stock
2-3 tablespoons oil	4 tablespoons raisins
3 onions	1 teaspoon ground
Several parsley stalks	cinnamon
1 bay leaf	1 tablespoon chopped
8 peppercorns	herbs
3-4 tablespoons	3 tablespoons halved
butter	almonds
1 clove garlic	1 tablespoon chopped
1 cup rice	parsley

Preheat oven to 325°F.
1. Brown guinea fowl all over in oil. Then put into a large pan or casserole and barely cover with water. Add 2 sliced onions, parsley stalks, bay leaf, peppercorns, and salt. Cook gently until tender, about 1½ hours. Drain and let cool, reserving stock for cooking rice.
2. Heat 3-4 tablespoons butter in pan, cook one chopped onion and crushed garlic until golden. Add rice and cook for a few minutes. Pour in 3 cups stock and bring to a boil. Add raisins, herbs, cinnamon, and seasoning. Cut guinea fowl meat into good-sized chunks and add to rice mixture. Cover dish and cook in oven for 20-30 minutes until all liquid has been absorbed and guinea fowl is tender. Sprinkle top with browned almonds and chopped parsley, and serve hot.

Wild Duck, Goose, or Partridge

SERVES 4

2 partridges, 1 duck,	2 cups sliced red
or 1 goose	cabbage
12 peppercorns	1 large onion, sliced
1 onion, quartered	½ cup water
Salt	1 tablespoon corn-
14 to 20 juniper	starch or potato
seeds, ground or	starch
mashed	2 tablespoons water
2 tablespoons bacon	½ teaspoon sugar
drippings or butter	1 teaspoon vinegar
½ cup water	¾ cup red wine

1. Place partridges in a plastic bag with peppercorns and quartered onion. Refrigerate 3 days to age.
2. Discard peppercorns and quartered onion. Cut up bird. Sprinkle with salt and juniper. Let stand 1 hour.
3. Heat bacon drippings in a large skillet. Brown

Turkish Guinea Fowl.

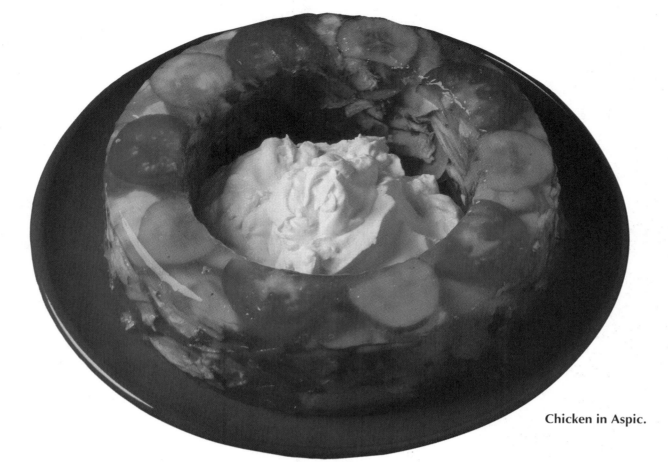

Chicken in Aspic.

bird in the drippings; add ¹/₂ cup water. Cover and simmer 1 hour.

4. Add cabbage, sliced onion, and ¹/₂ cup water. Cover and simmer 30 minutes. Remove the meat to a warmed platter.

5. Mix the cornstarch with 2 tablespoons water to make a smooth paste. Stir into drippings in pan.

6. Stir in sugar and vinegar; bring to boiling. Cook and stir 2 minutes. Remove from heat. Stir in wine.

Chicken in Aspic

SERVES 6

1 (3-pound) chicken	*Jelly:*
¹/₂ lemon	1 quart Chicken
¹/₂ teaspoon salt	Stock*
¹/₂ yellow onion, sliced	4 teaspoons gelatin
1 carrot, sliced	*Decoration:*
2 tablespoons parsley	1 cucumber, sliced
1 bay leaf	1 tomato, sliced
6 corns of allspice	Horseradish cream
12 white peppercorns	*Check index for
	recipe

1. Rinse the chicken and rub it with lemon inside and out. To a large kettle of boiling water add the chicken, salt, onion, carrot, parsley, and seasonings. Cover and cook for 45 minutes, then turn heat down and let simmer till the chicken is tender.

2. Let the chicken cool in the Stock. Remove the scum that has floated to the surface. Remove the skin from the chicken and cut the meat in small pieces.

3. Heat the liquid and strain. Soak the gelatin in ¹/₂ cup cold water. Add hot Chicken Stock slowly to make about 1 quart.

4. Pour some of the Stock in a ring mold, just covering the bottom. Add tomato and cucumber slices. Pour on more Stock so that this first layer is covered. Place mold in refrigerator to set. Continue to layer pieces of chicken and tomato and cucumber slices. When all chicken has been added pour on the rest of the Stock.

5. Place mold in refrigerator till ready to serve.

6. To serve: dip the mold quickly in hot water so that the aspic loosens from the bottom and turn upside down on a serving dish. Serve with horseradish cream in the middle and sour cream potato salad.

Capon Roasted in Salt

SERVES 4

1 capon (about	in quarters
5 pounds)	2 sprigs parsley
Salt	6 to 7 pounds coarse
1 carrot, cut in 1-inch	kosher salt
pieces	Watercress
1 medium onion, cut	

1. Rinse capon; pat dry. Salt inside of cavity lightly; fill cavity with vegetables. *(continued)*

165

2. Line a deep Dutch oven (that will fit size of capon, allowing 1½ to 2 inches space on bottom, sides, and top) with heavy-duty aluminum foil, allowing 2 inches of foil to fold down over top edge of pan. Fill bottom of Dutch oven with a 1½-inch layer of salt. Place capon in Dutch oven. Carefully fill Dutch oven with salt, being careful not to get salt inside cavity of capon. Layer salt over top of capon.
3. Roast uncovered in a 400°F oven 2 hours. Remove from oven. Let stand 15 minutes.
4. Lay Dutch oven on its side. Using foil lining, gently pull salt-encased capon from Dutch oven. Break salt from capon, using an ice pick or screwdriver and hammer. Place capon on serving platter; remove vegetables from cavity. Garnish with watercress. Serve immediately.

Duck Bigarade

SERVES 4

2 limes, halved	extract
1 ready-to-cook duck (about 5 pounds)	½ cup orange peel strips
Salt, freshly ground pepper, and Cayenne or red pepper	4 small oranges, halved and seeded
	2 cups chicken broth
2 cups firmly packed brown sugar	¼ cup orange juice
1 cup water	½ cup amber rum
2 teaspoons vanilla	¼ cup butter
	¼ cup cornstarch

1. Squeeze lime juice over the entire duck. Season with salt, pepper, and Cayenne. Place on a rack in a roasting pan.
2. Roast, uncovered, in a 425°F oven 25 minutes. Turn oven control to 350°F and continue to roast 30 minutes.
3. Combine brown sugar, water, and vanilla extract in a large, heavy saucepan. Bring to a boil over high heat and boil about 6 minutes. Add orange peel and orange halves and continue boiling 1 minute. Remove from heat and cool. Set ¼ cup syrup aside in a small saucepan.
4. Transfer duck to a warm platter. Remove fat from roasting pan. Stir in chicken broth and orange juice to deglaze. Heat the rum, ignite it, and when flames die down, pour it into the chicken broth.
5. Heat the reserved syrup until it caramelizes. Add to chicken broth mixture and blend well.
6. Mix butter and cornstarch and add to roasting pan. Cook over medium heat, stirring constantly, until the gravy is slightly thicker.
7. Carve the duck. Sprinkle the glazed orange peel strips over the meat. Pour a little gravy over the

Chicken with Parsley Sauce.

meat. Serve remaining gravy separately. Arrange glazed orange halves around the duck, alternating with bouquets of watercress. Serve with Caribbean Rice.*
*Check index for recipe.

Chicken with Parsley Sauce

SERVES 6

5 pounds roasting chicken	¼ pound bacon
1 carrot, sliced	*Sauce:*
1 onion, quartered	1 large bunch parsley
2 stalks celery, chopped	2 cups milk
2 tablespoons parsley	1 bay leaf
1 bay leaf	¼ teaspoon mace
¼ teaspoon thyme	6 peppercorns
6 peppercorns	3 tablespoons butter
½ teaspoon salt	3 tablespoons flour
	½ teaspoon salt
	½ teaspoon pepper

1. In a large saucepan place bird, vegetables, herbs, and seasonings. Pour in enough cold water to cover thighs.
2. Cover pan and bring to a boil slowly. Simmer 1¼ hours or until tender. Turn bird over from time to time. Cool in pan.
3. Remove parsley sprigs from stalks. Boil sprigs. Reserve parsley stalks for 7 minutes in salted water. Drain, squeeze dry, and rub through a strainer to make 1 tablespoon parsley purée.
4. Heat milk, bay leaf, mace, peppercorns, and parsley stalks almost to boiling for 7 minutes. Strain.
5. Melt butter and stir in flour. Pour on milk and bring to a boil, stirring until sauce thickens. Simmer 2 minutes. Add parsley purée and season. Keep warm.
6. Cook bacon till crisp, drain on paper towels.
7. Drain chicken and carve, discarding skin. Serve with sauce. Garnish with bacon.

Honey-Glazed Chicken

SERVES 4-6

1 chicken (3 to 3½ pounds), cut in serving pieces	1 teaspoon salt
	¾ teaspoon garlic powder
2 tablespoons butter	1 teaspoon dry mustard
⅓ cup honey	¼ teaspoon pepper
1 teaspoon grated orange peel	

1. In a 2-quart glass baking dish, arrange chicken on
(continued)

a rack, if possible. Place meatier pieces in corners and small pieces in the center. Place giblets in the center tucked under back or wings. Cover with waxed paper.

2. Cook 15 minutes, rotating dish one-quarter turn halfway through cooking time.

3. In a 1-cup glass measure, heat butter 15 to 30 seconds. Add honey, orange peel, salt, garlic powder, dry mustard, and pepper; stir to blend. Heat mixture 30 seconds. Brush chicken pieces with honey-butter mixture.

4. Cook, uncovered, 4 minutes. Turn chicken pieces over and brush with remaining mixture. Return to oven and cook, uncovered, 3 to 4 minutes.

5. Remove chicken pieces to serving dish, pour drippings over chicken, and serve.

Conventional oven: Bake at 375°F 1¼ hours.

Cranberry Chicken

SERVES 4-6

1 broiler fryer (2½ to 3 pounds), cut in serving pieces	3 tablespoons brown sugar
2 tablespoons lemon juice	1 can (16 ounces) cranberry sauce

1. Arrange chicken pieces in a 2-quart glass baking dish with meatier pieces toward edge.

2. In a 1-cup glass measure, blend lemon juice, brown sugar, and cranberry sauce. Pour sauce evenly over chicken and cover dish with waxed paper.

3. Cook 20 minutes, basting with sauce and rotating dish one-quarter turn halfway through cooking time.

4. Rest, covered, 10 minutes before serving.

Canard à l'Orange

SERVES 8

2 ducklings (4 to 5 pounds each)	1 can (13¾ ounces) condensed chicken broth
2 teaspoons salt	
½ teaspoon pepper	½ cup orange marmalade
1 clove garlic, peeled and cut crosswise into halves	¼ cup dry white wine
	¼ cup orange juice
½ cup dry white wine	2 teaspoons cornstarch
½ cup orange marmalade	
Sauce:	2 teaspoons lemon juice
2 tablespoons butter or margarine	2 tablespoons slivered orange peel

1. If frozen, let ducklings thaw according to package directions. Remove giblets, necks, and livers from ducklings. Reserve livers for sauce; if desired, reserve giblets and necks for soup stock. Remove and discard excess fat. Wash, drain, and pat dry with paper toweling. Rub cavities with salt, pepper, and garlic. Fasten neck skin to back with a skewer. Tuck tail ends into cavities. Tie legs together and tuck wing tips under ducklings. Prick skin generously to release fat. Place ducklings, breast side up, on a rack in a large shallow roasting pan.

2. Roast at 350°F 2 to 2½ hours or until legs can be moved easily, basting several times during roasting and removing accumulated drippings about every 30 minutes. Remove ducklings from oven and spread surface with mixture of wine and marmalade. Return to oven and continue roasting for 10 minutes.

3. For sauce, melt butter in a skillet. Add duckling livers and sauté until lightly browned. Remove and chop livers. Add chicken broth, marmalade, wine, orange juice, and cornstarch blended with lemon juice. Cook, stirring constantly over low heat for 10 minutes or until sauce bubbles and thickens. Stir in chopped livers and orange peel.

4. Transfer ducklings to a heated platter. Remove skewers and twine. Garnish, if desired, with watercress and orange slices. Reheat sauce if necessary and serve with duckling.

Chicken Liver Pie

SERVES 4

Pie Dough:	crushed tomatoes
1 cup flour	1 tablespoon flour
½ teaspoon salt	1 small green pepper, cut in strips
4 ounces butter	
1 egg yolk	¾ teaspoon salt
½ tablespoon water	½ teaspoon pepper
Filling:	1 teaspoon crumbled marjoram
¾ pound chicken liver	¾ pound bacon
1 (1-pound) can	

1. Combine flour and salt. Rub in butter with fingertips, add egg yolk and water and work together quickly. Place in a cool place to rest, about 30 minutes.

2. Roll dough out about ⅛-inch thick and line the bottom and the sides of an ovenproof dish with it. Bake in oven at 350° for about 20 minutes.

3. Pour crushed tomatoes in a saucepan and thicken with flour. Boil for about 3 minutes. Stir in the green pepper, saving some for decoration, and season.

4. Cut the chicken livers in small pieces and lightly fry in butter for 3-5 minutes. They are then still light rosy inside.

5. Stir the liver into the tomato mixture.

6. Fry the bacon till crisp.

7. Pour the liver and tomato mixture in the warm pie crust and sprinkle with the bacon and the pepper strips. Serve pie immediately with a green salad and beer.

Chicken Liver Pie.

Chicken Rolls

SERVES 4

1 fried or grilled chicken (2 pounds)	cheese
2 small tomatoes	4 slices frozen puff pastry
1 tablespoon finely chopped chives	*For Brushing:*
4 ounces Gorgonzola	Beaten egg

1. Preheat the oven to 350°F.
2. Bone the chicken and cut the meat in small pieces.
3. Wash the tomatoes and cut them in 8 slices. Cut the Gorgonzola in 8 pieces.
4. Roll out the puff pastry slices according to the directions on the package.
5. Divide the puff pastry in half and spoon the chicken meat in the middle of the slices. Place the tomatoes with the chives and the Gorgonzola on the chicken meat.
6. Fold up the corners. Place the rolls on a greased baking sheet.
7. Brush the rolls with beaten egg.
8. Bake in the middle of the oven for about 15 minutes. Serve the rolls straight from the oven with a mixed salad.

Chicken Rolls.

Fried Chicken with Cabbage.

Fried Chicken with Cabbage

SERVES 4

1 broiler chicken (about 2 pounds)	³/₄ pound white cabbage
2 tablespoons butter	¹/₂ pound mushrooms
1 teaspoon salt	1¹/₂ tablespoons butter
¹/₂ teaspoon pepper	¹/₂ teaspoon paprika
1 teaspoon paprika	3 ounces plain yogurt
2 teaspoons soy sauce	
2 green peppers, sliced	

1. Preheat oven to 325°F.
2. Cut chicken, first along the backbone, then split in half lengthwise.
3. Melt the butter and stir in salt, seasonings, and soy sauce.

(continued)

4. Brush the chicken halves with mixture.

5. Place chicken in ovenproof dish and bake for approximately 45 minutes.

6. Heat the butter in a frying pan and sauté the peppers, white cabbage, and mushrooms with the paprika for about 10 minutes.

7. Stir any juices from the chicken into the vegetables, then add the yogurt.

8. Cut the baked chicken into serving pieces, and place them on a serving dish with the vegetables. Serve with boiled white rice.

Chicken à la Suisse

SERVES 4

1 broiler chicken, cut up	4 slices lean smoked ham (6 ounces)
2 tablespoons butter	½ cup light cream
½ teaspoon salt	1 cup Swiss cheese, grated
½ teaspoon pepper	

1. Brown chicken all over in butter. Season with salt and pepper and cook, covered, over low heat for 25 minutes.

2. Remove bones and put chicken in an ovenproof dish.

3. Pour on the cream.

4. Cut away all fat from the ham and chop finely. Distribute evenly over the chicken.

5. Pepper lightly and sprinkle with cheese. Bake in a preheated oven at 400°F for 15 minutes till the cheese has browned slightly. Serve with a tomato and onion salad.

Indonesian Chicken

SERVES 6

10-12 chicken legs (about 2½-3 pounds) or 3 chicken breasts	1 cup chicken bouillon
	Curry powder
	Paprika
1 chopped small yellow onion	Coconut flakes
	Roasted almonds
1 chopped green pepper	Chutney
	Garnish:
Sambal Badjek	1 banana, sliced
Sambal Oelek	1 pineapple, diced
2 tablespoons butter	

1. Sauté onions and paprika in butter till translucent.

2. Add the chicken bouillon and reduce a little by boiling. Season very carefully with Sambal Badjek and Sambal Oelek.

3. Fry the chicken parts in butter about 5 minutes per side, and transfer to a casserole. Add the chicken bouillon and let simmer, covered, for 20 minutes, or until tender. Garnish with banana slices and pineapple cubes. Serve the chicken with boiled rice, seasonings, coconut flakes, roasted almonds, and chutney.

Seasoned Georgia Chicken

SERVES 4

2 pounds chicken	crushed
2 cups fresh orange juice	1 cup canned peaches in slices
1 teaspoon salt	¼ teaspoon salt
½ teaspoon nutmeg	2 tablespoons flour (optional)
½ teaspoon ginger	¼ teaspoon pepper
1 teaspoon basil	
1 clove garlic,	

1. Cut chicken in portion sizes.

2. Place orange juice, salt, nutmeg, ginger, basil, garlic, and chicken pieces in saucepan. Bring to a boil and simmer until the chicken is tender, some 35 minutes.

3. Transfer the chicken pieces to a hot serving dish and garnish with the peach slices. Keep hot. Strain the sauce; thicken it with the flour stirred in 1½ ounces water if you find it too thin.

4. Taste and correct seasoning and boil the sauce on low heat for some 5 minutes until it thickens. Pour the sauce on the chicken pieces and the peaches. Serve with boiled rice and a salad.

Microwave Fried Chicken

SERVES 4-6

1 broiler-fryer (2½ to 3 pounds), cut up	¼ cup butter, melted
	Paprika
1 cup corn flake crumbs	

1. Wash chicken and coat with crumbs. In a 1-cup glass measure, heat butter 45 seconds.

2. On roasting rack in a 2-quart glass baking dish, arrange chicken with meatier pieces around edges of dish, and smaller pieces, such as wings, in the center. Pour a small amount of butter over each piece. Sprinkle with paprika.

3. Cook 10 to 12 minutes. Turn chicken pieces over and coat each piece with remaining butter and paprika. Cook 10 to 12 minutes. *(continued)*

Indonesian Chicken.

Seasoned Georgia Chicken.

4. Let rest 5 minutes before serving.

Note: The chicken may be covered during cooking, which will steam the chicken, producing a soft, not crisp, skin. If the chicken is in a glass ceramic baking dish or is transferred to a metal pan, additional browning can be achieved by placing cooked chicken under a conventional broiler 1 to 2 minutes.

Chicken Pontalba.

Chicken Pontalba

SERVES 4

2^{1}/$_{2}$-3 pound broiler chicken or 4 chicken breasts	3 tablespoons parsley, finely chopped
3 ounces butter	Water
2 yellow onions, thinly sliced	*Garnish:*
1 tablespoon garlic, finely chopped	1 red pepper, cut in strips
^{1}/$_{2}$ pound sliced mushrooms	*Coating:*
6 ounces smoked ham, finely chopped	^{1}/$_{3}$ cup flour
	1^{1}/$_{2}$ teaspoons salt
^{2}/$_{3}$ cup dry white wine	^{1}/$_{4}$ teaspoon pepper
	For Frying:
	2-4 tablespoons butter

1. Cut the chicken in breast and leg parts.
2. Combine flour, salt, and pepper.
3. Dredge chicken parts in flour mixture. Heat butter in skillet and brown parts. Add water and simmer for 40-50 minutes. Set aside.
4. Meanwhile melt the butter, add onion and garlic, and sauté till transparent. Add mushrooms and ham and sauté for another 5 minutes. Add the wine and bring to a boil. Keep mixture warm while chicken is cooking. Serve chicken parts on top of the ham and mushroom mixture garnished with pepper strips.

Oven-Fried Chicken

SERVES 4

1 broiler chicken (2^{1}/$_{2}$ pounds)	2 cloves garlic, pressed
4 ounces yogurt	1^{1}/$_{2}$ teaspoons salt
1 tablespoon fresh lemon juice	^{1}/$_{4}$ teaspoon freshly ground pepper
1 teaspoon Worcestershire sauce	1 cup fine bread crumbs
2 teaspoons paprika	2 teaspoons sage

1. Preheat the oven to 325°F.

Oven-Fried Chicken.

2. Divide the chicken in breast and leg parts.
3. Mix the yogurt with the lemon juice, the Worcestershire sauce, the paprika, and the pressed garlic.
4. Dip the chicken parts in the yogurt mixture and coat them in the bread crumbs combined with salt, pepper, and sage.
5. Place the coated chicken parts on well-greased aluminum foil on a baking sheet.
6. Cook the chicken parts in the oven for about 50 minutes. Serve with a green salad, lemon wedges, and fried or baked potatoes.

Creamed Chicken Casserole

SERVES 4

4 chicken breasts, halved	2 green onions, chopped
1 can (10^{1}/$_{2}$ ounces) condensed cream of chicken soup	Dash pepper
	^{1}/$_{4}$ cup cashews
2 tablespoons brandy	Parsley, chopped
^{1}/$_{2}$ cup sour cream	Paprika

1. Wash chicken and pat dry. Arrange in a 2-quart baking dish. Cook 10 to 12 minutes, rotating one-quarter turn halfway through cooking time.
2. In a mixing bowl blend soup, brandy, sour cream, onion, pepper, and cashews. Pour over chicken.
3. Cook, covered, 12 to 15 minutes, rotating one-quarter turn halfway through cooking time.
4. Garnish with parsley or paprika, if desired.

FISH and SHELLFISH

Planked Fish Fillet Dinner

SERVES 2

1 large fish fillet, weighing about 10 ounces (such as sole, flounder, whitefish, lake trout, or haddock)	Salt and pepper
	Seasoned instant potatoes
	2 broiled tomato halves
1 tablespoon melted butter or margarine	4 broiled mushroom caps (optional)
	Lemon slices
	Watercress or parsley

1. If fish is frozen, let thaw on refrigerator shelf or at room temperature. Brush seasoned plank lightly with melted butter.
2. Place fish fillet on plank and brush with remaining butter. Sprinkle lightly with salt and pepper. Bake at 350°F for 20 minutes, or just until fish flakes easily.
3. Remove from oven, and turn oven temperature up to 450°F. Pipe a border of hot mashed potatoes along sides of fish.
4. Return to oven for 10 minutes until potatoes are delicately browned. Place tomato halves and mushroom caps, if desired, on plank. Garnish with lemon slices and watercress. Serve at once.

Party Fish Florentine

SERVES 4

2¹/₂ pounds halibut	¹/₂ teaspoon white pepper
Equal amounts of white wine and water to cover fish	1 egg yolk
1¹/₂ teaspoons salt	*Garnish:*
6 white peppercorns per quart liquid	1 can mussels in water, cooked
Parsley stalks	¹/₂ pound shrimp, cooked
1 onion, sliced	1 pound spinach
¹/₄ cup carrots, sliced	¹/₂ teaspoon salt
Sauce:	1 tablespoon butter
1¹/₂ cups strained fish liquid	1¹/₂ pounds boiled parsley-sprinkled potatoes
2 tablespoons flour	
¹/₂ teaspoon salt	

1. In a heavy saucepan bring the water, wine, seasonings, onion, and carrots to a boil. Cover and simmer for 5-10 minutes.

2. Place the fish in an ovenproof dish and pour the liquid on top. Cover with foil and bake for 30-40 minutes at 300°F till the fish is flaky.
3. Meanwhile cook the spinach. Add salt and butter. Keep hot.
4. Prepare sauce. Remove the fish from the pan and keep hot.
5. Pour the strained fish bouillon into a saucepan and bring to a boil. Stir in the flour with a little cold water until smooth. Simmer for 35 minutes, seasoning with salt and pepper. Whip the egg yolk and add to the sauce. Remove from the heat.
6. Arrange the cooked spinach on a platter. Place the cooked halibut on top. Place the mussels and shrimp around the fish and put the sauce on top. Serve with a green salad and parsley-sprinkled potatoes.

Trout Amandine with Pineapple

SERVES 6

2 tablespoons butter	6 whole cleaned and boned trout (about 8 ounces each)
1 package (2¹/₄ ounces) slivered almonds	
¹/₄ cup (¹/₂ stick) butter	6 drained canned pineapple slices
1 tablespoon lemon juice	

1. Put 2 tablespoons butter and almonds into a glass pie plate. Cook uncovered in microwave oven 5 to 6 minutes; stir every minute just until almonds are lightly toasted. Set aside.
2. Melt remaining butter in a 2-cup glass measure in microwave oven (30 seconds). Add lemon juice.
3. Brush whole trout inside and out with lemon-butter mixture. Arrange fish around edge of a microwave-safe serving plate in a circular pattern. Fit a small piece of foil over each head to shield. Cover with plastic wrap.
4. Cook in microwave oven 6 to 7 minutes, or until fish flakes easily. (Be certain to check for doneness under shielded area.)
5. Remove from oven and allow to stand covered 2 minutes.
6. Meanwhile, arrange pineapple slices on toasted almonds. Cover with plastic wrap. Heat in microwave oven 2 minutes. Garnish fish with almonds and pineapple.

Party Fish Florentine.

174

Deviled Crab

SERVES 6

Mustard Sauce:
2 tablespoons dry
   mustard
2 tablespoons water
2 tablespoons olive oil
1 tablespoon ketchup
¼ teaspoon salt
¼ teaspoon Worces-
   tershire sauce

Crabmeat Mixture:
6 tablespoons butter
4 teaspoons finely
   chopped green
   pepper
2 teaspoons finely
   chopped onion
6 tablespoons flour
1 teaspoon salt

½ teaspoon dry
   mustard
1½ cups milk
1 teaspoon Worces-
   tershire sauce
2 egg yolks, slightly
   beaten
1 pound lump
   crabmeat, drained
2 teaspoons chopped
   pimiento
2 tablespoons dry
   sherry
1 cup fine dry en-
   riched bread
   crumbs
Paprika
Butter, melted

1. For Mustard Sauce, blend dry mustard, water, olive oil, ketchup, salt, and Worcestershire sauce in a small bowl; set aside.
2. For crabmeat mixture, heat butter in a large heavy saucepan. Add green pepper and onion; cook until onion is golden in color.

3. Blend flour, salt, and dry mustard; stir in. Heat until bubbly. Add milk gradually, stirring until smooth. Stir in Worcestershire sauce. Bring rapidly to boiling; cook 1 to 2 minutes.
4. Remove mixture from heat and stir a small amount of hot mixture into the egg yolks; return to saucepan and cook 3 to 5 minutes, stirring constantly.
5. Stir in crabmeat and pimiento; heat thoroughly. Remove from heat and blend in sherry and the Mustard Sauce.
6. Spoon into 6 shell-shaped ramekins, allowing about ½ cup mixture for each. Sprinkle top with bread crumbs and paprika; drizzle with melted butter.
7. Set in a 450°F oven about 6 minutes, or until tops are lightly browned and mixture is thoroughly heated. Serve hot.

Deep-Fried White Fish

SERVES 4

2 pounds white fish
¾ cup sifted all-
   purpose flour
2 eggs, beaten

½ cup milk
½ cup bread crumbs
Vegetable oil for
   frying

1. Wash fish, sprinkle with salt and pepper.
2. Mix milk and eggs.

Deep-Fried White Fish.

Deep-Fried Perch.

3. Dip fish in milk, then the flour, then the bread crumbs.

4. Heat oil to 375° and carefully put fish into oil, cooking until golden brown.

Serve with spinach and tartar sauce.

Stuffed Flounder

SERVES 6-8

¼ cup chopped green onion	2 pounds flounder fillets, cut in serving pieces
¼ cup butter	2 tablespoons butter
1 can (4 ounces) chopped mushrooms	2 tablespoons flour
1 can (16½ ounces) crabmeat, drained	¼ teaspoon salt
	Milk
½ cup cracker crumbs	⅓ cup sherry
2 tablespoons parsley flakes	1 cup shredded Cheddar cheese
½ teaspoon salt	½ teaspoon paprika
¼ teaspoon pepper	1 teaspoon parsley flakes

1. In a 2-quart glass casserole, combine green onion and butter and cook 2 to 3 minutes, stirring after every minute.

2. Drain mushrooms and reserve liquid. Combine mushrooms, crabmeat, cracker crumbs, 2 tablespoons parsley flakes, salt, and pepper with cooked onion. Spread mixture over fish fillets. Roll up each piece of fish and secure with a wooden pick. Place seam side down in a 10-inch glass baking dish.

3. In a 4-cup glass measure, heat butter 30 seconds. Stir in flour and salt.

4. Add enough milk to reserved mushroom liquid to make 1 cup. Gradually stir milk and sherry into flour mixture. Cook sauce 2 to 3 minutes, stirring every minute, until thickened. Pour sauce over flounder.

5. Cook flounder 6 to 8 minutes, rotating dish one-quarter turn halfway through cooking time.

6. Sprinkle cheese, paprika, and 1 teaspoon parsley flakes over fish. Cook 3 to 5 minutes, or until fish flakes easily with fork.

Deep-Fried Perch

SERVES 6

2 pounds perch, cut into bite-sized pieces	1 cup milk
	1 tablespoon butter, melted
1 cup all-purpose flour	Vegetable oil for frying
2 eggs, beaten	Tartar sauce with dill

1. In a large bowl combine the flour, eggs, milk, and butter and blend until smooth.

2. Dip fish into batter and coat all sides; then deep-fry in hot oil (350°F) until golden brown.

3. Remove and dry on paper towels.

Serve with tartar sauce to which some fresh dill has been added. Garnish with fresh dill.

177

Cod Provençale.

Curried Cod.

Cod Provençale

SERVES 4

1¹/₂ pounds fresh cod fillets	pepper
1 leek	3 tomatoes
1 tablespoon butter	*Parsley and Garlic Butter:*
¹/₂ teaspoon salt	2 tablespoons butter
¹/₄ teaspoon pepper	2 tablespoons chopped parsley
¹/₄ teaspoon garlic salt, or 1 clove garlic, minced	¹/₈ teaspoon garlic salt
1 large red or green	¹/₂ teaspoon salt

1. Preheat the oven to 450°F.
2. Wash and cut the leek in slices. Fry in the butter.
3. Add salt, pepper, and garlic.
4. Wash and slice pepper and tomatoes. Add to the leek in the frying pan and fry.
5. Place the vegetables in an ovenproof dish.
6. Wash and divide the fish fillets in small parts if they are large. Place on the vegetable bed in the dish.
7. Make the parsley and garlic butter and spoon out on the cod fillets. Cover with aluminum foil and bake for 20 minutes.

Serve with boiled potatoes or rice.

Salmonburgers

SERVES 3-4

1 can (16 ounces) salmon	2 eggs, beaten
¹/₂ cup chopped onion	1 teaspoon dry mustard
¹/₄ cup salad oil	¹/₂ teaspoon salt
¹/₃ cup dry bread crumbs	¹/₂ cup dry bread crumbs

1. Drain salmon, reserving ¹/₃ cup liquid; set aside.
2. In a 2-cup glass measure, cook onion in oil 2 to 2¹/₂ minutes. In a large mixing bowl, combine onion, ¹/₃ cup dry bread crumbs, reserved salmon liquid, eggs, mustard, salt, and salmon; mix well. Shape into 6 patties.
3. Roll patties in ¹/₂ cup bread crumbs. Place on roasting rack in a 2-quart baking dish. Cook patties 5 to 6 minutes, rotating dish one-quarter turn halfway through cooking time. Rest 5 minutes before serving.

Salmon Ring: Follow recipe for Salmonburgers. Form mixture into a ring in a 1¹/₂-quart glass baking dish. Place a glass, open end up, in center of ring. Cook 5 to 6 minutes, rotating dish one-quarter turn halfway through cooking time. Rest 5 minutes before serving.

Curried Cod

SERVES 4

2 pounds cod	peeled tomatoes
¹/₂ teaspoon salt	2¹/₂ tablespoons butter
1 large leek	2 teaspoons curry
1 can (1 pound)	

1. Trim the leek and cut in thin slices.
2. Pour the liquid from the tomatoes in a wide saucepan. Top with half the leek.
3. Divide the fish in 4 pieces and place the fish on the leek.
4. Mix the butter and curry and spread it on the fish. Cover with the rest of the leek and put the tomatoes all around. Simmer covered for 20 minutes. Serve with boiled potatoes.

African Rock Lobster en Casserole

SERVES 6

6 (3 ounces each) frozen South African rock lobster tails	water
¹/₄ cup butter or margarine	1 or 2 packages (10 ounces each) frozen asparagus spears, cooked following package directions
¹/₄ cup flour	
2 cups chicken broth	
2 egg yolks, fork beaten	1 package (8 ounces) spaghetti, cooked and drained
¹/₃ cup half-and-half	
2 to 3 teaspoons Worcestershire sauce	Parmesan-Romano cheese
1 teaspoon dry mustard blended with about 1 tablespoon cold	¹/₄ cup toasted slivered almonds

1. Drop frozen lobster tails into boiling salted water. Return to boiling and simmer 3 minutes.
2. Remove cooked lobster tails and place under running cold water until cool enough to handle. With scissors, cut along each edge of bony membrane on the underside of shell; remove meat.
3. Dice half of the meat and cut remainder into chunks; set aside.
4. Heat butter in a heavy saucepan; stir in flour. Cook until bubbly. Add broth gradually while blending thoroughly. Stirring constantly, bring rapidly to boiling, and cook 1 to 2 minutes. Immediately blend about 3 tablespoonfuls into egg yolks and stir into the hot sauce. Cook 3 to 5 minutes, stirring constantly.
5. Blend in half-and-half, Worcestershire sauce, mustard, and diced lobster. Heat thoroughly.

(continued)

Cod with Horseradish Sauce.

6. Divide cooked asparagus equally among 6 individual casseroles. Spoon over spaghetti and hot lobster sauce. Generously shake cheese over all. Top with lobster chunks and almonds.

Cod with Horseradish Sauce

SERVES 2

1 pound cod steaks	1/4 cup fish stock
3 tablespoons salt	1 cup milk
6 white peppercorns, coarsely ground	2 tablespoons grated horseradish
1 small yellow onion	2 tablespoons chili sauce
Sauce:	Salt and pepper
2 tablespoons butter	
2 tablespoons flour	

1. Place salt, pepper, and onion in 1 1/2 quarts water. Boil covered for 5 minutes. Add the fish, quickly let the mixture come to a boil again, then simmer slowly for 5 minutes. Arrange fish on a heated platter.
2. Mix butter and flour. Add 1/4 cup fish stock and milk. Add horseradish and chili sauce; add salt and pepper to taste. Simmer 5 minutes till hot.
3. Pour some of the sauce over the fish and serve with boiled potatoes and the rest of the sauce.

Bay Scallops with Cucumber Rings

SERVES 6

2 pounds bay scallops or sea scallops, cut in thirds	pared, sliced lengthwise, seeded, and cut in 1-inch slices
1 tablespoon minced onion	1/4 cup dry white wine
1/2 cup minced celery	1 tablespoon flour
1 cup minced carrot	Cold water
1 1/2 cups Chicken Stock*	Salt
1/2 teaspoon salt	*Check index for recipe
2 large cucumbers,	

1. Simmer scallops, onion, celery, and carrot in the Stock until scallops are tender (about 4 minutes). Strain Stock into a medium saucepan. Sprinkle 1/2 teaspoon salt over scallop mixture; keep warm.
2. Simmer cucumbers in Stock until just tender (about 4 minutes). Remove cucumbers with slotted spoon; keep warm.
3. Heat remaining Stock and wine to boiling. Mix flour with a little cold water; stir into Stock. Simmer, stirring constantly, until thickened (about 3 minutes). Season to taste with salt. Spoon half the cu-

Scampi Provençale.

cumbers into a clear glass serving bowl. Arrange scallops on top. Spoon remaining cucumbers over scallops; pour sauce over. Serve immediately.

Red Snapper Steaks California Style

SERVES 6

6 fresh or thawed frozen red snapper steaks (about 2 pounds)	1 tablespoon grated orange peel
Salt and pepper	¼ cup orange juice
¼ cup butter or margarine, melted	1 teaspoon lemon juice
	Dash nutmeg
	Fresh orange sections

1. Arrange red snapper steaks in a single layer in a well-greased baking pan; season with salt and pepper.
2. Combine butter, orange peel and juice, lemon juice, and nutmeg; pour over fish.
3. Bake at 350°F 20 to 25 minutes, or until fish flakes easily when tested with a fork.
4. To serve, put steaks onto a warm platter; spoon sauce in pan over them. Garnish with orange sections.

Scampi Provençale

SERVES 4

1½ pounds shrimp, cleaned and de-veined	1 small green pepper, cut in strips
2 tablespoons olive oil	2 cups long-grain rice
2 small yellow onions, chopped	2 teaspoon salt
1 clove garlic, chopped	1 cup Chicken Stock*
1 small sweet red pepper, cut in strips	4 tomatoes
	1 tablespoon paprika
	*Check index for recipe

1. Heat the oil in a large frying pan. Sauté onion and garlic until transparent, about 5 minutes. Add peppers and cook until soft.
2. Add 1 cup rice, Chicken Stock, paprika, and salt. Simmer covered 20 minutes.
3. Scald the tomatoes in boiling water. Skin them and cut in wedges. In another frying pan brown them lightly. Add the shrimp and cook until pink, about 5 minutes.
4. Add tomatoes and shrimp to rice and heat thoroughly.
5. Cook second cup of rice; arrange in a circle and pour scampi in center.

Serve with a crisp, green salad.

Fish Kabobs

SERVES 8

2 pounds fish fillets (haddock)	*Marinade:*
24 cherry tomatoes	1 small onion, sliced
4 green peppers, cut in pieces	1¹/₂ teaspoons salt
	Juice of 1 lemon
	Dill
	Oil for brushing

1. Cut the fish fillets into pieces.
2. Soak the fish in the marinade for 2 hours.
3. Alternate the fish, tomatoes, and green pepper on skewers. Grill while turning for about 4 minutes. Brush with the oil while on the grill.

Paprika Buttered Fish Fillets

SERVES ABOUT 4

1 package (1 pound) frozen fish fillets (perch, haddock, cod, or halibut), thawed	Flour
	Salt and pepper
	2 tablespoons butter
	Paprika

1. Dip fillets in flour seasoned with salt and pepper, coating well. Set aside.
2. Melt butter in an 11 × 7-inch baking dish. Dip fillets in butter and arrange in baking dish. Sprinkle with paprika.
3. Cook, uncovered, 2 to 4 minutes. Do not turn fish over, but do rotate dish one-quarter turn halfway through cooking time.
4. Serve garnished with cooked asparagus spears and carrots.

Sole Sauté Amandine

SERVES 3-4

3 tablespoons flour	¹/₄ cup butter
³/₄ teaspoon salt	¹/₄ cup sliced almonds
¹/₄ teaspoon pepper	1 tablespoon fresh lemon juice
1 pound sole or other white fish fillets	1 tablespoon chopped parsley
1 tablespoon oil	

1. Combine flour, salt, and pepper in a shallow dish. Dip fillets into mixture, coating on all sides.
2. In a 10-inch glass dish, heat oil and 1 tablespoon butter 1 minute. Place fillets in dish and cover.

3. Sauté 4 to 5 minutes, turning fillets over and rotating dish one-quarter turn halfway through cooking time. Rest, covered, 5 minutes.
4. In a 1-cup glass measure, combine 3 tablespoons butter, almonds, and lemon juice. Cook and stir 1 to 2 minutes, until brown.
5. Pour sauce over fillets, sprinkle with parsley, and serve immediately.

Baked Leftover Fish

SERVES ABOUT 4

3 boiled potatoes, sliced	Salt and pepper
1¹/₂ cups diced cooked fish	1 tablespoon flour
	1 cup sour cream
³/₄ cup sliced cooked cauliflower or mushrooms (optional)	¹/₄ cup water
	3 tablespoons bread crumbs
2 hard-cooked eggs, sliced	2 tablespoons grated Parmesan cheese
	2 tablespoons butter

1. Arrange layers of half the potatoes, fish, cauliflower, eggs, and remaining potatoes in a greased 1¹/₂-quart casserole. Lightly sprinkle salt and pepper over each layer.
2. Blend flour into sour cream; stir in water. Spoon over casserole mixture.
3. Mix bread crumbs, cheese, and butter together. Sprinkle over top of casserole.
4. Bake at 350°F 30 minutes.

Red Snapper à l'Orange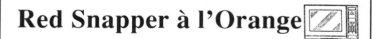

SERVES 4

1 pound red snapper, cut in serving pieces	1 teaspoon grated orange peel
2 tablespoons orange juice	1 tablespoon butter
	¹/₂ teaspoon lemon juice

1. In a 2-quart glass baking dish, arrange fish evenly around edge.
2. In a 1-cup glass measure, blend orange juice, orange peel, butter, lemon juice, salt, and pepper. Heat 30 seconds and pour over fish.
3. Cook fish, covered, 5 to 6 minutes, rotating dish one-quarter turn halfway through cooking time.
4. Rest, covered, 5 minutes before serving. Garnish with parsley.

Fish Kabobs.

Crab au Gratin

SERVES 4

1 large crab or 1 can crabmeat (about 1 pound)	½ teaspoon salt
1 can (6 ounces) artichoke bottoms	⅛ teaspoon freshly ground black pepper
1 can (8 ounces) asparagus	2 teaspoons brandy
2 tablespoons butter	*For frying:*
2 tablespoons flour	3 ounces grated Cheddar cheese
4 ounces heavy cream and the asparagus liquid and crab liquid (if any)	*Garnish:* Finely chopped parsley

1. Clean and cut the crabmeat in pieces. Place the artichoke bottoms in a greased ovenproof dish and distribute the crabmeat on the artichokes.
2. Melt the butter in a frying pan. Add the flour and the cream, asparagus, and crab liquid. Cook for 5 minutes. Add salt and pepper and the brandy.
3. Cut the asparagus in small pieces and mix into the liquid. Pour the asparagus mixture on the crabmeat and sprinkle with the cheese.
4. Bake in a 450°F oven until the cheese browns — about 5-10 minutes. Sprinkle with the finely chopped parsley and serve with boiled rice and a green salad.

Crab au Gratin.

Shrimp San Giusto

SERVES 3-4

1 pound large uncooked shrimp	2 tablespoons olive oil
½ teaspoon salt	1 tablespoon butter
⅛ teaspoon pepper	½ cup finely chopped onion
1 bay leaf	1 clove garlic, finely chopped
3 tablespoons lemon juice	1 teaspoon finely chopped parsley
2½ cups water	Flour
1 bay leaf	⅓ cup dry white wine
1 thick slice onion	1 large tomato, peeled, seeded, and chopped
Pinch each salt, pepper, thyme, and oregano	

1. Using scissors, cut the shells of the shrimp down middle of back; remove shells and set aside. Clean and devein shrimp.
2. Place cleaned shrimp in a bowl with salt, pepper, and a bay leaf; drizzle with lemon juice. Set shrimp aside to marinate 1 hour.
3. To make fish stock, place shrimp shells in a saucepan with water, a bay leaf, onion slice, salt, pepper, thyme, and oregano. Cover and simmer 30 minutes; strain.
4. Heat olive oil and butter in a skillet. Add chopped onion, garlic, and parsley; cook until soft. Coat marinated shrimp with flour, add to skillet with vegetables, and cook until lightly browned on both sides.
5. Add wine and simmer until it is almost evaporated. Stir in tomato and ½ cup or more of the strained fish stock. Simmer 15 to 20 minutes, or until the sauce is desired consistency.

Deep-Fried Squid

SERVES 3

12 squid, cleaned, with tentacles left on	and pepper Vegetable oil for deep frying
Flour seasoned generously with salt	3 lemons, cut in wedges

1. Rinse the cleaned squid in cold water and pat dry with paper towels. Dip the squid into the seasoned flour and coat all surfaces evenly.
2. Heat the oil in a deep fryer to 375°F. Drop in the squid, a few at a time. Fry until golden brown (about 5 minutes). Transfer the squid with a slotted spoon to a baking dish lined with paper towels. Keep in a 200°F oven until all the squid are fried.
3. Remove paper; serve squid with lemon.

Mussels Marinières.

Mussels Marinières

SERVES 4

60 mussels	leaves
¹/₂ teaspoon pepper	1 cup chopped onion
¹/₂ cup chopped	1 cup dry white wine
parsley	3 tablespoons butter
Pinch dried thyme	Parsley

1. Wash and rinse the mussels very carefully. Discard any that are not closed. Scrape them and rinse them again in running water. They must not remain in water because then they open and emit the tasty salty water that they contain.
2. Put the mussels in a saucepan with the pepper, parsley, thyme, raw chopped onions, and wine. Bring to a boil over high heat and continue cooking until they open completely. This works best if you shake the saucepan several times with the cover on, to get the mussels that are at the bottom of the saucepan to the top and vice versa.
3. Remove the mussels from the heat as soon as they open.
4. Pour the liquid into another saucepan and put it over high heat. Add the butter and parsley. Simmer until half of the liquid has evaporated. Serve the mussels in soup plates and pour the sauce on top.

Pike or Carp Stuffed with Anchovies

SERVES 6-8

1 can (2 ounces) flat	temperature)
anchovy fillets	2 eggs, separated
1 pike (3 pounds)	¹/₂ cup grated fresh
with milt and liver,	bread
or other white fish	¹/₄ cup melted butter
¹/₄ cup butter or	for basting
margarine (at room	1 cup sour cream

1. Cut half the anchovies in thin strips. Lard the fish with strips of anchovy.
2. Chop or mash remaining anchovies; cream with 2 tablespoons of butter. Divide in half.
3. For stuffing, beat egg yolks. Chop liver. Combine grated bread, egg yolks, milt, and liver. Add half of anchovy butter; mix well. Beat egg whites until stiff peaks are formed; fold into bread mixture.
4. Fill cavity of fish with stuffing. Close cavity with skewers or wooden picks. Place fish in roasting pan. Drizzle with half the melted butter.
5. Bake at 350°F 30 minutes. Baste with remaining anchovy butter over fish. Top with sour cream. Continue baking until fish is tender and flakes easily.

Stuffed Brook Trout with Shredded Almonds

SERVES 4

4 portion-sized fresh trout	*For Coating:*
4 tablespoons chopped dill	1 egg
4 tablespoons parsley	4 tablespoons flour
3/4 teaspoon salt	4 tablespoons fine bread crumbs
Pepper	*For Frying:*
1/2 teaspoon pounded tarragon	Butter
	1 bag shredded almonds
	1 tablespoon salad oil

1. Heat oil in a frying pan and put in the shredded almonds. Turn them when they start browning, about 3-5 minutes, and place on a paper towel.
2. Wipe the fish dry inside and outside with paper towel; season and stuff with the herbs.
3. Just before frying, coat the fish in beaten egg and then in a mixture of flour and bread crumbs.
4. Heat the butter in a frying pan over medium heat. Cover the frying pan and fry the fish slowly, about 5 minutes on each side, then 5-10 minutes on low heat. Turn the fish once or twice and sprinkle with the roasted almonds just before serving.

Savory Oysters

SERVES 6-8

1/3 cup butter or margarine	drained (reserve liquor)
1 can (4 ounces) sliced mushrooms, drained	1/4 cup cream
1/3 cup chopped green pepper	1 teaspoon Worcestershire sauce
1/2 clove garlic	1 teaspoon salt
2 cups coarse toasted enriched bread crumbs	1 teaspoon paprika
1 quart oysters,	1/8 teaspoon ground mace
	Few grains Cayenne pepper

1. Heat butter in a large skillet. Add mushrooms, green pepper, and garlic; cook about 5 minutes. Remove skillet from heat; discard garlic. Stir in toasted bread crumbs. Set aside.

Stuffed Brook Trout with Shredded Almonds.

186

2. Mix ¼ cup reserved oyster liquor, cream, and Worcestershire sauce.

3. Blend salt, paprika, mace, and Cayenne.

4. Use about a third of crumb mixture to form a layer in bottom of a greased 2-quart casserole. Arrange about half of oysters and half of seasonings over crumbs. Repeat crumb layer, then oyster and seasoning layers. Pour the liquid mixture over all. Top with remaining crumbs.

5. Bake at 375°F 20 to 30 minutes, or until thoroughly heated and crumbs are golden brown.

Deep-Fried Fillets of Sole

SERVES 4

1½ pounds fillets of sole	1 bottle (24 ounces) vegetable oil
Salt	1 bunch of parsley
⅓ cup all-purpose flour	Lemon wedges

1. Wipe the fillets dry and split lengthwise. Salt and roll together. Fasten with wooden picks.

2. Dip in flour and fry 4-5 rolls at a time in deep-fat fryer or a large deep pot.

3. Place parsley on a perforated ladle and quickly dip into oil.

Serve fish with parsley and lemon wedges.

Red Snapper Veracruz Style

SERVES ABOUT 6

¼ cup olive oil	¼ teaspoon pepper
1 cup chopped onion	2 pounds red snapper fillets
1 clove garlic, minced	¼ cup sliced pimiento-stuffed olives
2 cups (16-ounce can) tomatoes with liquid	2 tablespoons capers
1 teaspoon salt	Lemon wedges

1. Heat oil in a large skillet. Cook onion and garlic in hot oil until onion is soft, about 5 minutes. Add tomatoes, salt, and pepper and cook about 5 minutes to blend flavors; slightly chop tomatoes as they cook.

2. Arrange red snapper fillets in a 3-quart baking dish. Pour sauce over fish. Sprinkle with olives and capers.

3. Bake at 350°F 25 to 30 minutes, or until fish can be flaked easily with a fork. Serve with lemon wedges.

Deep-Fried Fillets of Sole.

Fried Clams

SERVES 8

2 quarts shucked clams	Few drops Tabasco
2 eggs, beaten	1 cup Italian bread crumbs
½ teaspoon salt	Vegetable oil for deep-frying
½ teaspoon pepper	(24 ounces)
½ teaspoon dill	

1. Clean sand from clams and drain.
2. Mix egg with salt, pepper, dill, and Tabasco.
3. Dip clams in egg mixture.
4. Put bread crumbs on a piece of wax paper and roll clams until coated.
5. Place clams in the basket of a deep fat fryer and fry till golden brown. Drain on paper towel and serve with cooked spinach.

Baked Halibut in Parchment Paper

SERVES 1

1 tablespoon olive oil	any other preferred steak)
Juice of ½ lemon	
Pinch basil	Salt and pepper
Pinch oregano	2 thin lemon slices
1 halibut steak (or	4 capers

1. Combine oil, lemon juice, basil, and oregano;

spoon over both sides of the fish. Season with salt and pepper.
2. Place the fish on a piece of parchment paper. Lay lemon slices and capers on top of fish. Seal paper and tie. Put into a baking dish.
3. Bake at 325°F 30 minutes.
4. Serve hot sealed in parchment.

Broiled Salmon

SERVES 6

6 salmon steaks, cut ½-inch thick	chopped green onion
1 cup sauterne	Seasoned salt
½ cup vegetable oil	Green onion, chopped (optional)
2 tablespoons wine vinegar	Pimiento strips (optional)
2 teaspoons soy sauce	
2 tablespoons	

1. Put salmon steaks into a large shallow dish. Mix sauterne, oil, wine vinegar, soy sauce, and green onion; pour over salmon. Marinate in refrigerator several hours or overnight, turning occasionally.
2. To broil, remove steaks from marinade and place on broiler rack. Set under broiler with top 6 inches from heat. Broil about 5 minutes on each side, brushing generously with marinade several times. About 2 minutes before removing from broiler, sprinkle each steak lightly with seasoned salt and, if desired, top with green onion and pimiento. Serve at once.

Fried Clams.

Scallop Ratatouille

SERVES 4

1 eggplant	1 (1-pound) can
1 green pepper	tomatoes
1 clove garlic	1 pound scallops
2 tablespoons vege-	1 teaspoon salt
table oil	

1. Peel and cut the eggplant in cubes. Seed the pepper and cut in pieces.
2. Chop the garlic very finely.
3. Heat the oil in a casserole and fry the eggplant, green pepper, and garlic for a few minutes. Add the tomatoes with liquid and the scallops. Add salt and heat over medium heat covered for 5 minutes.

Ancona Fish Stew

SERVES 6

2 pounds assorted fish	2 teaspoons salt
(mullet, sole, and	½ teaspoon pepper
halibut fillets)	Pinch saffron
1 large onion, thinly	Water (about 2 cups)
sliced	Dry white wine
½ cup olive oil	(about 2 cups)

1. Cut fish fillets in 2½-inch pieces; set aside.

Scallop Ratatouille.

2. Sauté onion in olive oil until golden. Sprinkle in salt, pepper, and saffron. Add the fish and enough water and wine to cover the fish. Bring to boiling and cook over high heat 10 to 15 minutes.
3. Serve very hot in warmed soup bowls with crust of fried bread, if desired.

Foil-Baked Pike or Perch

SERVES 4

1 pike or 2 perch	ground black
(2 pounds)	pepper
Stuffing:	2 ounces finely
2 tablespoons salad	chopped parsley
oil	2 ounces finely
1 tablespoon fresh	chopped chive
lemon juice	1 teaspoon crumbled
½ teaspoon salt	rosemary
¼ teaspoon freshly	

1. Clean fish and wash well. It is not necessary to scale it.
2. Mix the stuffing. Place the fish on greased extra-heavy aluminum foil and stuff it.
3. Wrap in foil.
4. Place fish on grill and cook for 30 minutes, turning after 15 minutes.

Serve with baked potatoes, chive- or anchovy-flavored butter, and green salad.

Tuna for Two

SERVES 2

1 can (2 ounces) sliced	room soup with
mushrooms,	wine
drained	1 can (6½ or
¼ cup sliced green	7 ounces) tuna,
onion	drained and flaked
¼ teaspoon dill weed	1 tablespoon chopped
2 tablespoons butter	pimiento
or margarine	1 package (10 ounces)
1 tablespoon lemon	frozen broccoli
juice or wine	spears, cooked and
1 can (7½ ounces)	drained
semicondensed	2 tablespoons grated
cream of mush-	Parmesan cheese

1. Sauté mushrooms, onion, and dill weed in butter in a saucepan. Stir in lemon juice, soup, tuna, and pimiento.
2. Arrange broccoli spears in 2 or 3 individual casseroles. Spoon tuna mixture over broccoli. Sprinkle with Parmesan cheese.
3. Bake, uncovered, at 350°F 20 minutes, or until heated through.

From left to right: Foil-Baked Pike; Grilled Scallops; Grilled Snapper.

Grilled Scallops with Trimmings

SERVES 4

1 pound sea scallops
1 small can mussels in
    water
2 tomatoes
1 green pepper

Barbecue Sauce:
1 tablespoon salad oil
2 teaspoons mustard
½ teaspoon salt
1 teaspoon basil,
    crumbled

1. Drain mussels.
2. Cut the tomatoes in wedges and the pepper in pieces.
3. Alternate fish, tomatoes, and peppers on skewers.
4. Mix the barbecue sauce and brush on the skewers.
5. Cook the skewers on the grill for 5 minutes, turning occasionally.
Serve with fresh corn.

Grilled Snapper

SERVES 4

2 pounds snapper
Marinade:
3 ounces salad oil
3 ounces wine vinegar
½ teaspoon salt
½ teaspoon freshly

ground black
pepper
1 tablespoon rose-
    mary, crumbled
2 teaspoons thyme,
    crumbled

1. Clean and wash the snapper. Place snapper on grill, brush with marinade, and cook for about 3 minutes on each side.

Serve with baked potatoes, parsley-flavored butter, and a green salad.

191

Microwave Turbot

SERVES 4-5

1 egg, slightly beaten	½ cup corn flake
1 tablespoon lemon	crumbs
juice	1 pound turbot fillets,
½ teaspoon salt	cut in serving
Dash pepper	pieces

1. In a small glass bowl, combine egg, lemon juice, salt, and pepper. Dip fish into mixture and coat with crumbs.
2. Arrange fish around edge of a 10-inch baking dish.
3. Cook, covered, 4 to 5 minutes, rotating dish one-quarter turn halfway through cooking time.

Sole Véronique in Parchment

SERVES 4

2 pounds sole fillets	lemon peel
¾ teaspoon salt	1½ cups seedless
3 tablespoons snipped	white grapes
parsley	⅔ cup dry white wine
2 teaspoons minced	Lemon wedges

1. Lay each fillet on a piece of parchment paper or aluminum foil, 12 × 12 inches. Sprinkle fillets with salt, parsley, and lemon peel. Divide grapes over fish; sprinkle with wine. Bring edges of parchment up, crimp edges and seal; place on a jelly-roll pan.
2. Bake at 350°F 20 minutes.
3. Place parchment packets on individual plates; let each person open packet. Serve with lemon wedges.

Fried Scampi

SERVES ABOUT 6

3 pounds fresh	minced
prawns or shrimp	1 teaspoon salt
with shells	½ teaspoon oregano
Fat for deep frying	¼ teaspoon pepper
heated to 360°F	1 teaspoon chopped
½ cup olive oil	parsley
4 cloves garlic,	

1. Wash prawns in cold water. Remove tiny legs, peel off shells, and devein prawns. Rinse in cold water, then pat dry with absorbent paper.
2. Put only as many prawns in fat as will float uncrowded one layer deep. Fry 3 to 5 minutes, or

until golden brown. Drain over fat before removing to absorbent paper. Turn fried prawns onto a warm platter.
3. Heat oil in a skillet. Add garlic, salt, oregano, and pepper and cook until garlic is lightly browned. Pour sauce over prawns and sprinkle with parsley.

Baked Halibut

SERVES 6

2 pounds halibut,	*For Baking:*
thickly sliced	1 (8-ounce) bottle
½ teaspoon salt	clam juice
Juice of ½ lemon	*For Garnish:*
3 tablespoons butter	1 can anchovies
	4 olives

1. Rub the halibut with lemon juice and salt. Place fish in an ovenproof baking dish. Add slices of butter and arrange the anchovies in a "grid" pattern over the fish. Slice the olives and place a slice in each square.
2. Place the fish in a preheated 450°F oven. Baste with clam juice. Cook for 15-20 minutes till fish flakes when pricked with a fork. Serve with boiled potatoes in parsley butter and a tossed green salad.

Flounder Surprise

SERVES 4

1 pound flounder	lemon juice
fillets	2 egg yolks
½ teaspoon salt	¼ cup heavy cream
Stuffing:	1 cup strained fish
¾ cup mushroom	liquid
soup	¼ teaspoon salt
¾ cup fish stock or	½ teaspoon pepper
clam juice	*Garnish:*
¾ cup white wine	1 package frozen
Sauce:	lobster tails
1 tablespoon butter	8 fresh mushrooms
1 tablespoon flour	Lemon slices
2 tablespoons fresh	Dill

1. Salt the flounder fillets. Spread the mushroom soup on the fillets; roll up and place in a greased ovenproof dish with the seam down.
2. Mix fish stock and wine and pour over the fish just to cover. Cover the fish with a cover or aluminum foil and bake in a 350°F oven for about 10 minutes.
3. Pour off the liquid carefully and reserve.
4. Melt the butter, then add the flour and some stock and simmer the sauce for about 5 minutes. Let sauce cool a little, then stir in the egg yolks mixed with the cream. Taste and correct seasonings.

5. Meanwhile cook the lobster tails in the reserved stock till they turn pink, about 5 minutes.

6. Place the fish in a serving dish and pour the sauce on top. Decorate with raw slices of mushroom, lemon slices, dill, and lobster tails. Serve with boiled potatoes.

Flounder Surprise.

Grilled Swordfish with Tomato Sauce

SERVES 6

2 pounds swordfish (cut into 1-inch cubes)	finely chopped
	1 clove garlic, minced
	$1/2$ teaspoon oregano
2 lemons (cut in thin slices)	$1/2$ teaspoon thyme
	1 bay leaf, crushed
1 can (1 pound 13 ounces) Italian plum tomatoes	Salt
	Ground pepper
	1 tablespoon olive oil
1 medium onion,	Tomato Sauce (below)

1. In a skillet heat the oil and sauté the onions and garlic.

2. Add the tomatoes and seasonings and continue cooking over low heat 15-20 minutes.

3. String the lemon slices and swordfish alternately on skewers.

4. Grill the swordfish over low charcoal heat, turning frequently until fish flakes easily.

5. Serve each skewer on a plate with Tomato Sauce.

Baked Halibut.

Grilled Swordfish with Tomato Sauce.

Tomato Sauce

3 CUPS

3 tablespoons butter	1 bay leaf
1 large onion, chopped	1 garlic clove, crushed in a garlic press
2 pounds fresh ripe tomatoes, peeled and chopped	1 teaspoon vinegar
	Salt and pepper to taste
2 teaspoons sugar	
2 whole cloves	

1. Melt butter in a saucepan; add onion and cook until translucent.

2. Add tomatoes and remaining ingredients.

3. Simmer uncovered 20 minutes.

Note: A variation served during Lent is Anchovy Tomato Sauce. To prepare, use **olive oil** instead of butter, decrease sugar to 1 teaspoon, increase vinegar to 2 teaspoons; and add $1/2$ **tube anchovy paste** or **1 can (2 ounces) anchovies,** drained and cut into small pieces.

Fish Stew

SERVES 8 (2 CUPS EACH)

3 pounds fish fillets, skinned *(see Note)*	2 garlic cloves, minced
5 medium tomatoes, peeled and chopped	1 teaspoon fennel seed, crushed
3 carrots, chopped	1 tablespoon minced orange peel
1 large onion, thinly sliced	1 cup dry white wine
2 teaspoons salt	1 quart fish stock*
1/4 teaspoon freshly ground pepper	*Check index for recipe

1. Cut fish into 1 1/2-inch pieces. Set aside.
2. Simmer tomatoes, carrots, onion, salt, pepper, garlic, fennel, and orange peel in a mixture of wine and stock 15 minutes. Add fish to stock mixture; simmer covered until fish is tender and flakes with a fork (about 20 minutes).
3. Serve immediately in large shallow soup bowls.

Note: Flounder, haddock, cod, whitefish, halibut, bass, or other fish can be used in this recipe. For maximum flavor and variety, select at least 3 kinds of fish.

Grilled Lobster

SERVES 1

1 live lobster (about 1 1/2 pounds)	Tabasco Butter

1. Purchase a lobster for each serving. Live lobsters may be killed and dressed for cooking at the market. If prepared at home, place the lobster on a cutting board with back or smooth shell up. Hold a towel firmly over the head and claws. Kill by quickly inserting the point of a sharp heavy knife into the center of the small cross showing on the back of the head. Without removing knife, quickly bear down heavily, cutting through entire length of the body and tail. Split the halves apart and remove the stomach, a small sac that lies in the head, and the spongy lungs that lie between meat and shell. Also remove the dark intestinal line running through the center of the body. Crack large claws with a nutcracker or mallet.
2. Brush meat with Tabasco Butter. Place shell side down on grill about 5 inches from coals. Grill about 20 minutes, or until shell is browned. Baste frequently with butter. Serve in shell with remaining butter.

Tabasco Butter: Melt **1/2 cup butter** and stir in **1/2 teaspoon Tabasco** and **1 tablespoon lime juice.**

Lobster Tails Flambées

SERVES 6

12 large lobster tails, frozen	tarragon, or chervil
3 tablespoons salad oil	1 ounce brandy
2 tablespoons finely chopped shallots	1 cup Pernod
1/2 pound fresh sliced mushrooms	6 ounces heavy cream, whipped
4 tablespoons finely chopped parsley,	5-8 tablespoons Hollandaise sauce
	1 can French lobster soup

1. Cook the lobster soup for 10 minutes till it reduces.
2. In a chafing dish sauté the shallots until golden. Add the mushrooms and herbs.
3. Drop frozen lobster tails into boiling salted water. Return to boiling and simmer 3 minutes.
4. Remove cooked lobster tails and place under running cold water until cool enough to handle. With scissors cut along each edge of bony membrane on the underside of shell; remove meat.
5. Add lobster tails and stir until they are thoroughly heated, about 2 minutes. Pour the liquor into 2 glasses, pour into the pan, and set aflame. Have a cover handy to quench the fire if necessary.
6. When the fire is out, add the soup and whipped cream.
7. Add seasonings. This must be done at great speed or the lobster will get tough.
8. Remove pan from heat and stir in the Hollandaise sauce. Serve immediately with boiled rice.

Cod Sailor Style

SERVES 4

2 pounds cod steaks, about 1 inch thick	2 tablespoons capers
2 cups canned tomatoes, sieved	1 tablespoon parsley
1/4 cup chopped green olives	1 teaspoon salt
	1/2 teaspoon pepper
	1/2 teaspoon oregano

1. Put cod steaks into a greased 1 1/2-quart casserole.
2. Combine tomatoes, olives, capers, parsley, salt, pepper, and oregano in a saucepan. Bring to boiling and pour over cod.
3. Bake at 350°F 25 to 30 minutes, or until fish flakes easily when tested with a fork.

Lobster Tails Flambées.

Beer Batter Shrimp.

Crab-Stuffed Sole

SERVES 6-8

3 tablespoons butter	minced
3 tablespoons flour	2 tablespoons butter
1¹/₂ cups milk	1 can (6¹/₂ ounces)
¹/₃ cup sherry	crabmeat
¹/₂ teaspoon salt	5 fresh mushrooms,
1 cup shredded Swiss	cleaned and
cheese	chopped
2 pounds sole fillets	¹/₂ cup cracker
Salt	crumbs
Pepper	Parsley flakes
1 medium onion,	

1. In a 4-cup glass measure, heat butter 30 seconds. Stir in flour, milk, sherry, and salt, blending well. Cook 2 to 3 minutes, stirring every minute until thickened. Stir in cheese and set aside.
2. Cut fish in serving pieces and sprinkle with salt and pepper.
3. In a 4-cup glass measure, cook onion in butter 2 to 3 minutes, stirring once, until tender. Add crabmeat, mushrooms, and cracker crumbs; mix well.
4. Spread crabmeat mixture evenly over each piece of fish. Roll up pieces of fish and secure with a wooden pick. Place seam side down in a 10-inch glass baking dish.
5. Cook, covered, 5 to 6 minutes, rotating dish one-quarter turn halfway through cooking time. Remove pan drippings and pour sauce over fish. Cook 2 to 3 minutes, sprinkle with parsley flakes, and serve.

Beer Batter Shrimp

SERVES 4

1 pound shrimp,	flour
cleaned and de-	*For Frying:*
veined	1 bottle (24 ounces)
Batter:	oil
4 ounces beer	Parsley
4 ounces all-purpose	Lemon wedges

1. Mix beer and flour together.
2. Dip shrimp in batter.
3. Heat oil to boiling in a deep fat fryer or large and deep pot.
4. Fry shrimp a few at a time for about 10 minutes and place on a folded paper towel to remove grease.
5. Place parsley on a perforated ladle and quickly dip into oil.
Serve shrimp with parsley and lemon wedges.

196

Stuffed Squid

SERVES 8

32 squid, cleaned and tentacles removed	2 cloves garlic, crushed in a garlic press
³/₄ cup olive oil	½ cup pine nuts
1 large onion, chopped	¼ cup dried black currants
1½ cups water	1 cup dry white wine
1 cup long-grain rice	Salt and pepper to taste
½ cup chopped parsley	Water
1 teaspoon mint	Juice of 2 lemons
1 teaspoon basil	

1. Reserve squid. Rinse tentacles in cold water. Drain and mince finely.
2. In a large saucepan, heat 2 tablespoons of the oil, add onion and minced tentacles and cook over low heat until tentacles turn pink. Add water. Heat to boiling. Reduce heat, add rice, parsley, mint, basil, garlic, pine nuts, currants, and ½ cup of the wine.
3. Simmer until liquid is absorbed. Season with salt and pepper. Cool.
4. Using a teaspoon, stuff each squid cavity loosely with the rice mixture. Arrange squid in rows in a large baking dish. Combine the remaining wine and olive oil with enough water to reach half the depth of the squid. Season with additional salt and pepper. Cover.
5. Bake at 325°F about 40 minutes, or until squid is tender. Drizzle with lemon juice just before serving.

Note: Stuffing may also be used as a side dish. Stuff 16 squid. Put remaining stuffing in a baking dish. Add a little water, salt, and pepper and cover. Bake at 325°F 30 minutes.

Scampi on Spit

SERVES 4

1½ pounds shrimp, cleaned and de-veined	½ teaspoon paprika
1 egg	½ teaspoon salt
½ teaspoon curry powder	3 tablespoons butter
	3 ounces bread crumbs

1. Cut the shrimp into bite-sized pieces.
2. Dip in beaten egg and sauté in browned butter. Season while frying. Sprinkle with the bread crumbs and continue to cook 4-5 minutes till pink.
3. Thread on spit with the help of a fork and serve.

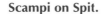

Scampi on Spit.

Summer Casserole.

Lobster Fritti.

Summer Casserole

SERVES 4

8 fillets of sole	1 can (1 pound) peeled
Salt	tomatoes
2 tablespoons corn oil	4 ounces white wine
1 tablespoon butter	Pepper
1 finely chopped	1 teaspoon crumbled
yellow onion	thyme
1 clove garlic,	2 tablespoons chopped
crushed	parsley (optional)

1. Rub the fillets with salt. Heat butter and oil in a casserole with a thick bottom and put in the onion and the fillets.
2. Add the tomatoes with their liquid and the wine. Season and add more salt if needed. Cover and let the fish braise in a 400°F oven for 15-20 minutes.
Serve with boiled potatoes or mashed potatoes.

Lobster Fritti

SERVES 4

8 lobster tails (frozen)	1 teaspoon salt
3 ounces flour	2 lemons
1 egg, beaten	*For Frying:*
4 bunches parsley	Vegetable oil

1. Pour the oil in a deep saucepan. The oil should reach about 2-inches above the bottom. Heat oil to 315°F.
2. Thaw lobster tails and remove from the shell.
3. Coat the lobster meat with the beaten egg and flour. Cook in the hot oil until pink (3-5 minutes). Remove and let drain on paper towel.
4. Meanwhile cook the washed and carefully dried parsley for a moment in the oil. Let the parsley drain on paper towel.
5. Salt and arrange the lobster tails and the parsley on a hot serving dish.
Serve with lemon wedges and butter stirred with finely chopped parsley and seasoned with fresh lemon juice.

Seviche

SERVES 6

1 pound pompano (or	1 or 2 canned jala-
other mild-flavored	peño chilies, seeded
fish fillets)	and finely chopped
Juice of 6 limes (or	$^{1}/_{4}$ cup olive oil
lemons)	1 tablespoon vinegar
2 medium tomatoes,	$^{1}/_{4}$ teaspoon oregano
peeled and chopped	Salt and pepper
2 tablespoons finely	Sliced green olives
chopped onion	Chopped parsley

1. Wash the fish very well. Cut into small chunks or strips and place in a glass jar or glass bowl with cover. Pour lime juice over fish; cover and refriger-

Brook Trout with Button Mushrooms.

ate about 6 hours. (Lime juice will "cook" raw fish until it is white and firm.)

2. At least a half hour before serving, add tomato, onion, chili, olive oil, vinegar, oregano, and salt and pepper to taste; stir gently until evenly mixed.

3. When read to serve, garnish with sliced olives and parsley.

Brook Trout with Button Mushrooms

SERVES 4

4 brook trout (8-inch each)	button mushrooms
¼ cup all-purpose flour	3 tablespoons butter
	Salt
1 (1-pound) can	Pepper

1. Clean, wash, and dry the trout. Cut off the fins. Coat fish lightly in flour and sauté in 3 tablespoons melted butter till firm and nicely browned.

2. Remove trout and sauté mushrooms in butter until golden brown.

3. Arrange trout on a serving dish with mushrooms on top and serve.

Serve with boiled spinach, skinned tomatoes, and a green salad.

Cold Poached Salmon

SERVES 5

5 salmon steaks or fillets	1½ teaspoons salt
2 cups water	2 tablespoons lemon juice
½ fresh lemon, thinly sliced	3 tablespoons vinegar
½ medium onion, thinly sliced	*Garnish:*
6 whole cloves	1 hard-cooked egg, sliced
1 bay leaf	1 lemon, sliced
1 stalk celery, cut in 1-inch pieces	Cucumber slices
	Dill

1. In a 2-quart glass baking dish, combine water, lemon, onion, cloves, bay leaf, celery, salt, lemon juice, and vinegar. Heat, covered, 5 to 6 minutes, stirring halfway through cooking time.

2. Arrange salmon in corners of baking dish. Cook, covered, 5 to 6 minutes, rotating dish one-quarter turn halfway through cooking time.

(continued)

3. Gently turn fish over in liquid and rest, covered, 2 to 3 minutes. Fish should flake easily when tested with a fork. Add more cooking time if desired.
4. Remove fish from liquid. Serve hot or refrigerate 3 to 4 hours and serve cold with tartar sauce.

Poached Striped Bass

SERVES 6-8

1 quart water	Salt to taste
1 quart dry white wine	10 coriander seeds
Juice of 3 lemons	8 whole peppercorns
2 cups olive oil	1 bay leaf
2 medium onions, quartered	4 parsley sprigs
1 large carrot, pared and left whole	1 thyme sprig
2 celery stalks with leaves	3 garlic cloves, peeled and left whole
2 leeks	5 pounds bass, cleaned, with gills removed and head and tail left on

1. Pour water, wine, lemon juice, and olive oil into a saucepot.
2. Wrap remaining ingredients, except fish, in cheesecloth and add. Bring to boiling and simmer, covered, 15 minutes.
3. Wrap fish in cheesecloth. Place in a fish poacher or a deep greased baking dish.
4. Pour in stock, discarding vegetables; cover and simmer 15 minutes. Remove from heat.
5. Let fish remain in the liquid for another 15 minutes. Lift out of pan and drain; reserve fish stock for other use. Remove cheesecloth and peel off skin.
6. Serve fish at room temperature with Vinegar and Oil Dressing with Tomato (below).

Vinegar and Oil Dressing with Tomato

1³/₄ CUPS

1 tablespoon imported mustard (Dijon, preferably)	and diced
	2 whole scallions, minced
2 tablespoons red wine vinegar, or more to taste	2 tablespoons minced parsley
¹/₂ cup olive oil	1 tablespoon chopped capers
1 large tomato, peeled	1 teaspoon dill

Put mustard and vinegar into a small bowl. Add olive oil while stirring with a whisk. Add remaining ingredients, mix well. Refrigerate several hours before serving.

Crab-Filled Fish Rolls Veracruz Style

SERVES 6

6 fish fillets (such as red snapper or sole), cut into long, thin slices	parsley
	1 teaspoon salt
	Dash of pepper
Juice of 1 lemon or lime	¹/₄ pound crabmeat, shredded
¹/₂ cup milk	¹/₄ pound shredded Monterey Jack cheese
2 tablespoons olive oil	
¹/₂ cup chopped onion	1 cup sour cream
1 clove garlic, minced	1 egg yolk
1 small tomato, peeled and chopped	¹/₄ pound butter or margarine
1 teaspoon minced	

1. Rinse fish; rub with lemon or lime juice; soak in milk.
2. Meanwhile, heat olive oil in a small skillet. Sauté onion and garlic in oil; add tomato and cook until no longer juicy. Remove from heat and stir in parsley, salt, and pepper. Add crabmeat and ¹/₃ of the cheese and mix well.
3. Remove fish from milk and pat dry with paper towels. Place a small amount of crabmeat filling on one end of fillet and roll up, as for a jelly roll. Place fish rolls in one layer in a greased baking dish.
4. Beat sour cream with egg yolk and pour over fish. Dot with butter. Sprinkle remaining cheese over top.
5. Bake at 350°F until golden brown and cheese is melted (about 20 minutes).

Baked Fish à la Spetses

SERVES 6-8

4 pounds fish fillets (turbot, whitefish, bass, mullet)	in a garlic press
	Salt and pepper to taste
4 fresh tomatoes, peeled and sliced	1 teaspoon basil (optional)
³/₄ cup olive oil	1 cup fresh bread crumbs
1 cup white wine	
2 tablespoons chopped parsley	1 slice feta cheese for each portion
1 garlic clove, crushed	

1. Put fillets into a baking dish.
2. In a bowl, combine tomatoes, olive oil, wine, parsley, garlic, salt, pepper, and basil. Pour over fillets. Sprinkle with bread crumbs.
3. Bake at 375°F 40 minutes.
4. Top fillets with feta cheese slices. Broil 1 or 2 minutes.

Flounder in Dill Sauce.

Scallops au Gratin

SERVES 4

1 pound spinach	sauce
1 pound scallops	*For Baking:*
2 tablespoons crumbled tarragon	4 cooked potatoes, mashed
1/8 teaspoon Cayenne pepper	1/4 cup Swiss cheese, grated
1/4 cup heavy cream	1 1/2 ounces grated
1 tablespoon chili	blue cheese

1. Spread the spinach in a lightly greased ovenproof dish. Spoon the mashed potatoes around the spinach. Distribute the scallops on the spinach. Whip the cream and season with chili sauce, tarragon, Cayenne pepper and cheese. Spread on scallops.
2. Bake in a 450°F oven for 10 minutes until brown.

Flounder in Dill Sauce

SERVES 2

1 pound fillets of flounder	or 4 tomatoes
1/2 teaspoon salt	Chopped dill
1/2 teaspoon pepper	1 can lobster or shrimp soup
1 small can crabmeat	

1. Season fish with salt and pepper.
2. Place crabmeat or tomatoes and dill in the center of each fillet. Roll fillets up. Close with toothpicks and place close together in a skillet.
3. Pour 2 cups lightly salted boiling water over fish. Cover and simmer for 10 minutes.
4. Meanwhile, prepare lobster or shrimp soup according to can directions. Place the fish in a serving dish and pour sauce on top.

201

PASTA and RICE

Spaghetti with Meatballs

SERVES 6

1 pound ground beef	chopped and sautéed
1/4 pound ground veal	1 teaspoon basil
1/4 pound ground pork	1 teaspoon garlic salt
1/2 teaspoon salt	3/4 cup heavy cream
1 teaspoon pepper	3 tablespoons butter
1/2 cup bread crumbs	2 cups Italian sauce for
1 egg	spaghetti
4 tablespoons onion,	

1. Mix the meats and salt and pepper. Stir in egg, onions, and bread crumbs. Add cream a little at a time.
2. Shape mixture into small meatballs.
3. Melt butter in a skillet and brown the meatballs over high heat. Shake the pan occasionally, turning the meatballs so that they brown all over. Lower the heat and continue to sauté for 5 minutes.
4. Heat the spaghetti sauce.
5. Put meatballs in spaghetti sauce and simmer for about 30 minutes.
Serve with spaghetti.

Rice and Crabmeat au Gratin

SERVES 4

4 ounces long-grain rice	2 eggs, beaten
1 small bunch dill	8 ounces plain yogurt
1 large can crab meat	1 teaspoon curry
1 red pepper, chopped	1 tablespoon ready-
1 green pepper,	made mustard
chopped	

1. Boil rice with dill stalks according to package directions. Substitute some liquid from the crabmeat for water.
2. Set rice aside.
3. Mix cooled rice with crabmeat and chopped peppers and stir in a mixture of beaten eggs, yogurt, curry, and mustard.
4. Pour into ovenproof shells and bake in oven at 350°F for 20 minutes.

Homemade Noodles

ABOUT 2 POUNDS NOODLES

3 cups semolina	1 1/2 teaspoons salt
3 eggs	1 1/2 teaspoons warm
3 tablespoons olive oil	water
(do not substitute)	

1. Combine all ingredients in a mixing bowl and work with fingers until dough holds together and can be shaped into a ball. A few drops of water may be added, if necessary, but do not let dough get sticky.
2. Knead dough on a board until smooth and shiny. Cover and let rest 15 minutes. Divide dough into 4 portions. Roll out each portion into a paper-thin sheet.
3. Lay sheets on a linen cloth and allow to dry for 1 to 2 hours.
4. Loosely fold sheets over jelly-roll fashion. Cut strips no more than 1/4 inch wide. Holding in place, cut again at right angles, the same width, to make square noodles. Noodles may be cooked right away or dried.
5. To dry, transfer to a large tray, and spread on a linen surface for about 3 days, turning occasionally.
6. To cook, bring a large quantity of water, with **salt** and **2 tablespoons oil** added, to a rolling boil. Add noodles and boil until they have doubled in size (about 5 minutes).
7. Serve hot with **browned butter** or **tomato sauce**. Sprinkle with **grated kefalotyri cheese**.

Beaten Noodles

SERVES ABOUT 6

1 tablespoon butter or	2 egg yolks
margarine (at room	3 tablespoons flour
temperature)	1/4 teaspoon salt
2 whole eggs	

1. Beat butter until fluffy. Beat in whole eggs and egg yolks, one at a time. Mix in flour and salt.
2. Spoon into **boiling soup or bouillon**. Cover; cook 2 minutes. Turn. Cover and cook a few seconds longer.
3. To serve, break noodles into separate portions with a spoon.

Spaghetti with Meatballs.

Rice and Crabmeat au Gratin.

Fettuccine Alfredo

SERVES 8

1 pound green noodles	1 clove garlic, minced
Boiling salted water	Grated Parmesan
2 tablespoons olive oil	cheese
1 teaspoon chopped	Butter
fresh basil	

1. Cook noodles in boiling salted water until just tender; drain.
2. In a chafing dish, heat olive oil, basil, and garlic. Toss the noodles in hot oil with a fork until they are very hot.
3. Sprinkle generously with Parmesan cheese, adding a generous piece of butter, and toss again a moment before serving.

Confetti Rice Ring

SERVES 4-6

4½ cups cooked rice	3 canned whole pimien-
6 tablespoons butter or	tos, drained and
margarine	chopped
¾ cup snipped parsley	

1. Prepare rice. While hot, stir in butter, parsley, and pimiento.
2. Pack rice mixture into a buttered 5-cup glass ring mold. Cover with plastic wrap.
3. Heat thoroughly in microwave oven (5 to 6 minutes). Uncover and allow to stand 3 minutes.
4. Unmold on a warm serving plate. Fill ring as desired.

Green Lasagne

ABOUT 1¼ POUNDS PASTA

½ pound spinach	1 teaspoon salt
4 cups all-purpose flour	2 large eggs, beaten

1. Wash spinach and place in heavy saucepan. Do not add water; cook only in moisture remaining on leaves from washing. Partially cover and cook 5 minutes, stirring occasionally with a fork.
2. Drain spinach, press out the water, chop it, and force it through a sieve; or drain, press out water, and purée in an electric blender. It should retain its fresh green color and become a smooth purée. If the purée is very wet, heat it in the saucepan, about a minute, over very high heat to evaporate some of the moisture. Allow it to cool.
3. Sift the flour and salt into a large mixing bowl. Make a well in the center of the flour and put the beaten eggs and puréed spinach in it. Mix gradually with one hand, or with a fork, until the paste is well blended. If the mixture is too dry, add some water until it forms a ball. If the dough is too sticky, add more flour.
4. Knead the dough at least 12 minutes, until it is smooth and elastic. Divide dough in 4 pieces and roll out to 1/16-inch thick. Cut the sheets of dough into 4 × 2-inch rectangles, or longer if desired. The dough may also be cut in squares. Let cut pieces of dough dry on towels for an hour. If not using immediately, store at room temperature.

Green Noodles: Follow recipe for Green Lasagne. Roll the sheets of dough up and cut in ¼-inch-wide strips. Unroll and place on towels for half an hour to dry. Place in **boiling salted water** and cook 5 minutes; drain. Served tossed with **butter**, or any sauce desired.

Rice Noodles

ABOUT 2 CUPS

1½ cups cooked rice	margarine
2 eggs	¼ teaspoon salt
1 tablespoon butter or	

1. Combine all ingredients. Beat until well mixed.
2. Drop by small spoonfuls into boiling soup or broth. Cook until noodles float, about 3 minutes.

Spaghetti Sicilian Style

SERVES ABOUT 6

½ cup olive oil	fresh basil or
2 cloves garlic, peeled	½ teaspoon dried
and quartered	sweet basil
½ medium-size egg-	1 tablespoon capers
plant, pared and	4 anchovy fillets, cut in
diced	small pieces
6 large ripe tomatoes,	12 ripe olives, pitted
peeled and coarsely	and halved
chopped	1 teaspoon salt
2 green peppers	¼ teaspoon pepper
1 tablespoon chopped	1 pound spaghetti

1. Heat olive oil in a skillet; stir in garlic. Remove garlic from oil when brown. Stir eggplant and tomatoes into skillet; simmer 30 minutes. *(continued)*

Fettuccine Alfredo.

Seafood and Rice Casserole.

in their liquid and discard the liquid. Mix cooked shrimp, mussels, chopped dill, and parsley with the rice.

Long-Grain Rice

SERVES 5-6

2½ cups water	**1 teaspoon salt**
1 cup long-grain rice	

1. In a covered 2-quart casserole, bring water to boiling, 5 to 6 minutes. Stir in rice and salt.
2. Cook, covered, 7 to 9 minutes, rotating dish one-quarter turn halfway through cooking time.
3. Rest, covered, 10 minutes before serving.

Seafood and Rice Casserole

SERVES 3-4

1 cup long-grain rice	**1½ pounds shrimp,**
1 onion, chopped	**cooked**
2 tablespoons butter	**1 can mussels in water**
½ teaspoon curry	**(8 ounces)**
½ teaspoon paprika	**1 bunch dill, chopped**
2 chicken bouillon	**1 bunch parsley,**
cubes	**chopped**
Salt	

1. Put chopped onion and rice in melted butter in a large casserole or saucepan and sprinkle curry and paprika on top.
2. Stir and fry the rice without letting it brown. Add 2 cups of water and the bouillon cubes, and cook slowly covered for 18-20 minutes. Meanwhile, heat the mussels

Fettuccine with Bacon

SERVES 4

1 pound fettuccine	**¼ cup red wine**
¼ pound sliced bacon	**1 bay leaf, crushed**
1 medium onion, finely	**¼ teaspoon oregano**
chopped	**¼ teaspoon ground**
1 clove garlic, minced	**pepper**
1 can Italian plum	**1 egg**
tomatoes (medium	**Parmesan cheese,**
size)	**grated**

1. Cook the bacon until crisp and brown in a skillet. Remove, pat dry, and put aside.
2. Put the onion and garlic into the same skillet and sauté until transparent. Add the tomatoes, red wine, and seasonings. Simmer for 15-20 minutes.
3. Cook the fettuccine in boiling water until *al dente*.

Curried Shrimp with Rice.

4. Drain fettuccine and place in a serving bowl. Add bacon pieces and tomato sauce, mixing thoroughly.
5. Put a raw egg on top and serve.
6. Sprinkle with Parmesan cheese.

Curried Shrimp with Rice

SERVES 6

¹/₂ teaspoon salt	3 tablespoons curry
1 small yellow onion,	powder
peeled and sliced	¹/₄ cup flour
1 lemon, sliced	¹/₂ teaspoon salt
6 whole black pepper-	¹/₄ teaspoon ground
corns	ginger
2 pounds shrimp,	¹/₄ teaspoon ground
cleaned and deveined	cardamom
¹/₄ cup chutney,	¹/₄ teaspoon pepper
chopped	2 cans (10¹/₂ ounces)
	condensed chicken
Sauce:	broth
3 tablespoons butter	2 tablespoons lime juice
1 cup onion, chopped	2 teaspoons lime peel,
1 cup apple, chopped	grated
1 clove garlic, minced	

1. Heat butter in a large frying pan. Sauté onion, apple, garlic, and curry powder about 5 minutes until onion is tender.
2. Remove from heat. Blend in flour, salt, ginger, cardamom, and pepper.
3. Gradually stir in chicken broth, lime juice, and lime peel.
4. Bring to a boil, stirring constantly. Reduce heat and simmer uncovered 20 minutes, stirring occasionally.
5. Boil salt, onion, lemon, and peppercorns in 1 quart of water. Add shrimp, reduce heat and let shrimp simmer till pink.
6. Drain shrimp and add to curry sauce. Stir in chopped chutney and heat just to boiling.
Serve immediately with rice.

Macaroni in Browned Butter with Grated Cheese

SERVES 4-6

1 pound macaroni	kefalotyri or
1 cup butter	Parmesan cheese (or
¹/₂ cup freshly grated	more to taste)

1. Cook macaroni according to directions on the

(continued)

package, adding ½ cup cooking oil and 1 tablespoon salt. Drain. Rinse under hot water.

2. Brown butter in a saucepan, stirring constantly.

3. Return the macaroni to the pot in which it was cooked, or place it in a warm serving dish. Drizzle the browned butter over it. With two spoons lift the macaroni to coat all the strands evenly. Cover with freshly grated kefalotyri. Serve at once.

Lemon Rice with Egg

SERVES ABOUT 4

1¾ cups chicken broth	1 tablespoon lemon
¾ cup uncooked long-	juice
grain rice	¼ cup grated
1 egg	Parmesan cheese

1. Bring broth to boiling in a saucepan. Stir in rice; cover tightly. Cook 15 to 20 minutes, or until rice is tender and liquid is absorbed.

2. Place egg, lemon juice, and cheese in a bowl; beat until foamy. Stir into rice over low heat. Serve immediately.

Ravioli au Gratin

SERVES 6

2 pounds cheese-filled	1 bay leaf, crushed
ravioli	1 teaspoon oregano
1 can (16 ounces) plum	¼ cup Parmesan
tomatoes	cheese, grated
1 small onion, chopped	¼ cup olive oil
1 clove garlic, chopped	⅔ cup Mozzarella
¼ cup red wine	cheese, grated

1. Heat the olive oil in a skillet and sauté the onion and garlic for 4-5 minutes.

2. Add the tomatoes, wine, and seasonings and simmer for 20-25 minutes.

Ravioli au Gratin.

3. Add the Parmesan cheese and let melt into the sauce.

4. In a large pot bring 2 quarts of water to a boil and cook ravioli according to package directions.

5. Drain ravioli and put in a casserole, then gently add the tomato sauce.

6. Spread the grated Mozzarella cheese over the top and bake in a 325°F oven for 20-25 minutes.

Beefy Rice

SERVES 4-6

1 beef bouillon cube	1/2 cup butter
1 3/4 cups water	1 teaspoon salt
1 cup uncooked white rice	1 tablespoon parsley flakes

1. In a 3-quart glass casserole, combine bouillon cube, water, rice, butter, and salt.

2. Cook, covered, 12 to 14 minutes, stirring halfway through cooking time.

3. Rest, covered, 10 minutes. Stir in parsley flakes.

Conventional oven: Bake at 375°F 1 hour.

Green Noodles

SERVES ABOUT 8

1/4 pound spinach	1 tablespoon salt
3 cups sifted all-purpose flour	3/4 cup grated Parmesan cheese
1/2 teaspoon salt	1/2 teaspoon salt
3 eggs	1/4 cup butter
6 quarts water	

1. Wash spinach and put into a heavy saucepan. Do not add water; cook only in moisture remaining on leaves from washing. Partially cover and cook 5 minutes, stirring occasionally with a fork.

2. Drain spinach, pressing out water, and chop finely.

3. Mix flour and 1/2 teaspoon salt in a bowl; make a well in center. Add eggs, one at a time, mixing slightly after each addition. Add the chopped spinach and mix well.

4. Turn dough onto a lightly floured surface and knead until smooth, adding flour if needed for a stiff dough.

5. Divide dough in half. Lightly roll each half into a rectangle, about 1/8 inch thick. Cover; let stand 1 hour. Beginning with a narrow end, gently fold over about 2 inches of dough and continue folding over so that final width is about 3 inches. (Dough must be dry enough so layers do not stick together.) Beginning at a narrow edge, cut dough into strips 1/4 inch wide. Unroll strips and arrange on waxed paper on a flat surface. Let stand until noodles are dry (2 to 3 hours).

6. Bring water to boiling in a large saucepot. Add 1 tablespoon salt. Add noodles gradually. Boil rapidly, uncovered, 8 to 10 minutes, or until tender.

7. Drain noodles and put a third of them into a greased 2-quart casserole. Top with a third each of the cheese and remaining salt. Dot with a third of the butter. Repeat layering twice.

8. Bake at 350°F 15 to 20 minutes, or until cheese is melted.

Egg Noodles Abruzzi

SERVES 4-6

1 tablespoon butter	1/4 teaspoon pepper
1/4 cup olive oil	1/2 cup dry white wine
1 pound ground lamb	2 large tomatoes, peeled and coarsely chopped
2 green peppers, chopped	
1 teaspoon salt	1 pound egg noodles

1. Heat butter and oil in a large skillet. Stir in lamb and green peppers; season with salt and pepper. Brown the meat slightly, stirring occasionally.

2. Add wine and simmer until liquid is almost evaporated. Stir in tomatoes and simmer mixture 30 minutes, or until sauce is thick.

3. Cook noodles according to package directions; drain. Place noodles on a hot platter, pour sauce over noodles, and serve.

Spaghetti à la King Crab

SERVES ABOUT 6

Parmesan Croutons	sliced
2 cans (7 1/2 ounces each) Alaska king crab or 1 pound frozen Alaska king crab	2 medium tomatoes, peeled and diced
	1/2 cup chopped parsley
	2 tablespoons lemon juice
2 tablespoons olive oil	1/4 teaspoon thyme
1/2 cup butter or margarine	1/2 teaspoon salt
4 cloves garlic, minced	1 pound enriched spaghetti
1 bunch green onions,	

1. Prepare Parmesan Croutons; set aside.

2. Drain canned crab and slice. Or, defrost, drain, and slice frozen crab.

3. Heat olive oil, butter, and garlic in a saucepan. Add crab, green onions, tomatoes, parsley, lemon juice, basil, thyme, and salt. Heat gently 8 to 10 minutes.

4. Meanwhile, cook spaghetti following package directions; drain.

5. Toss spaghetti with king crab sauce. Top with Parmesan Croutons. Pass additional grated Parmesan cheese.

(continued)

Parmesan Croutons: Put **3 tablespoons butter** into a shallow baking pan. Set in a 350°F oven until butter is melted. Slice **French bread** into small cubes to make about 1 cup. Toss with melted butter. Return to oven until golden (about 6 minutes). Sprinkle with **2 tablespoons grated Parmesan cheese** and toss.

Green Noodles Florentine

SERVES 4

1 pound green noodles	1 cup parsley, chopped
Water	¹/₃ cup chives, chopped
Salt	¹/₃ cup Monterey jack
¹/₄ cup butter	cheese, grated
¹/₃ cup brandy	Salt
Sauce:	Pepper
¹/₄ cup olive oil	2 teaspoons basil
2 cloves garlic, finely	*Garnish:*
chopped	Parmesan cheese,
1 package frozen	grated
spinach, thawed	Stuffed olives, sliced

1. Sauté the garlic in oil together with spinach, parsley, and cloves. Add cheese and seasonings. Keep warm.
2. Boil the noodles in salted water according to package directions. Drain.
3. Stir in the butter, pour on the brandy and set aflame. Let burn off by itself.

4. Place the noodles in a hot serving dish and pour on the green sauce. Dredge with Parmesan cheese and garnish with sliced olives.

Pasta with Beans Sorrento Style

SERVES 4-6

2 cups dried Great	6 ripe tomatoes, peeled
Northern beans	and diced
5 cups water	1 tablespoon chopped
1 teaspoon salt	Italian parsley
1 cup chopped celery	4 fresh basil leaves,
1 cup chopped onion	chopped, or 1 tea-
3 tablespoons olive oil	spoon dried basil
1 teaspoon salt	¹/₂ pound conchigliette

1. Rinse beans and put into a heavy saucepot or kettle. Add water and bring rapidly to boiling; boil 2 minutes and remove from heat. Cover; set aside 1 hour.
2. Stir 1 teaspoon salt into beans, cover, and bring to boiling. Cook until beans are nearly done, but still firm (about 2 hours). Drain and set aside.
3. Sauté the celery and onion in olive oil until soft. Sprinkle in 1 teaspoon salt, then stir in tomatoes, parsley, and basil.

Green Noodles Florentine.

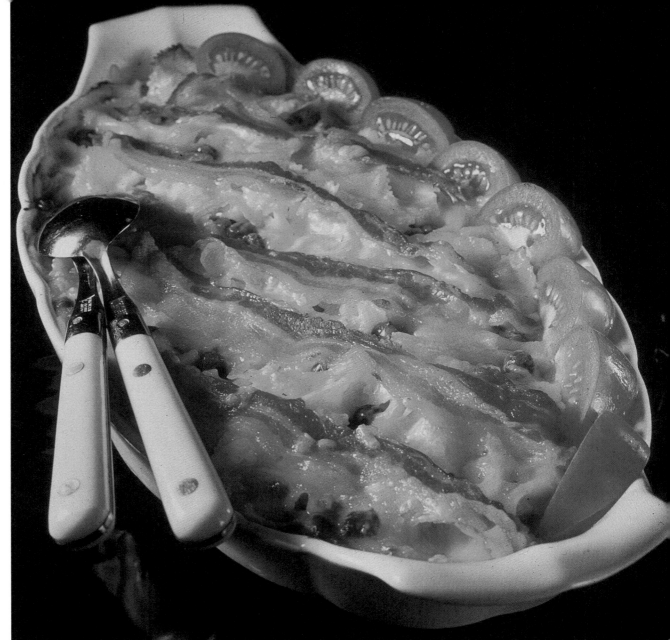

Baked Spaghetti
and Bacon.

4. Simmer 15 minutes, uncovered. Add the beans to tomato mixture; stir well. Cook the conchigliette according to package directions, drain, and stir into bean mixture. Serve in hot soup bowls.

Skillet Franks 'n' Noodles

SERVES 4-6

1 pound frankfurters, cut in half diagonally	celery or mushroom soup
1/2 cup chopped onion	1/2 cup milk
1/2 teaspoon basil or oregano leaves, crushed	1/2 cup chopped canned tomatoes
2 tablespoons butter or margarine	2 cups cooked wide noodles
1 can (10³/4 ounces) condensed cream of	2 tablespoons chopped parsley

1. In a skillet, brown frankfurters and cook onion with basil in butter until tender.
2. Stir in remaining ingredients. Heat, stirring occasionally.

Baked Spaghetti and Bacon

SERVES 4

³/4 pound spaghetti	1/2 teaspoon curry
³/4 cup Mozarella cheese	1¹/2 tablespoons flour
1 package frozen peas	1 cup milk
1 pound sliced bacon	³/4 teaspoon salt
Sauce:	1/4 teaspoon pepper
1 tablespoon butter	

1. Place the spaghetti in lightly salted boiling water. Boil rapidly until just soft, about 10-12 minutes.
2. Strain spaghetti and rinse with cold water.
3. Grate the cheese coarsely. Preheat the oven to 350°F.
4. To make sauce: Heat butter and add curry, flour, and then milk, a little at a time, while stirring. Add peas and half the cheese. Season with salt and pepper.
5. Place half the spaghetti in a wide greased ovenproof dish. Pour on the sauce. Add the rest of the spaghetti. Cover with remaining cheese and bacon.
6. Bake in oven for about 15 minutes until the bacon has turned brown. Arrange tomato wedges around the dish and serve with a green salad.

Cannelloni

SERVES 6

Pasta Dough:
1 cup flour
1 egg
1 egg white
1 tablespoon olive oil
1 teaspoon salt
A few drops of water

Stuffing:
2 tablespoons olive oil
2 ounces finely chopped
  onion
1 teaspoon finely
  chopped garlic
4 ounces squeezed
  spinach (whole
  leaves)
2 tablespoons butter
1/2 pound ground beef
2-4 chicken livers
5 tablespoons freshly
  ground Parmesan
  cheese
2 tablespoons heavy
  cream
2 eggs
1/2 teaspoon oregano
Salt
Black pepper

Tomato Sauce:
4 tablespoons olive oil
3/4 cup finely chopped
  onion
1 can (1 pound 13
  ounces) peeled
  tomatoes
6 tablespoons tomato
  purée
2 teaspoons dried basil
  or 2 tablespoons
  chopped fresh basil
2 teaspoons salt
1 1/2 teaspoons black
  pepper
1/2 teaspoon sugar

White Sauce:
4 tablespoons butter
4 tablespoons flour
1 cup milk
3/4 cup heavy cream
Salt
Pepper
1 teaspoon olive oil

Garnish:
1/3 cup Parmesan
  cheese

1. To make pasta: Place flour in a heap on a pastry board and make a depression in the middle. Add egg, egg white, oil, salt, and a few drops of water. Work the dough until smooth and shiny. Place in the refrigerator to rest before rolling it out.
2. To make stuffing: Fry the onion and garlic in the oil for 7 minutes till it is transparent.
3. Add the spinach and let it cook until all the moisture has evaporated. Transfer mixture into a saucepan.
4. Melt butter in a frying pan and brown the ground beef and the chopped chicken livers. Mix browned beef and chicken livers, grated cheese, spinach, cream, eggs, and seasoning in a saucepan. Taste and correct seasoning if necessary.
5. To make tomato sauce: Fry the chopped onions in the oil, add the peeled tomatoes and their liquid, the tomato purée, and seasonings. Simmer this sauce covered for about 40 minutes. Season to taste with salt and pepper.
6. To make white sauce: Place the butter and flour in a frying pan and mix.
7. Add the cream and the milk, a little at a time. Simmer the sauce, stirring, for some 5 minutes. Season with salt and pepper.
8. Roll the dough into thin squares 6" × 6". Place in a large pot of boiling water with 1 teaspoon olive oil. Boil 10 pieces at a time for about 5 minutes till medium soft. Drain the squares on paper towels.
9. Preheat the oven to 400°F. Place 1 tablespoon of the stuffing on the bottom of each paste piece and roll together.
10. Place the rolls side by side in an ovenproof dish, distribute the white sauce on top, and add pats of tomato sauce. Sprinkle with grated cheese.
11. Place the dish in the middle of the oven and cook until the cheese has melted and the sauce is bubbling. Serve immediately.

Caribbean Rice

SERVES 8

4 parsley sprigs
3 peppercorns
2 garlic cloves
2 scallions or green
  onions, cut in pieces
1 1/2 teaspoons salt
1/2 teaspoon thyme
2 tablespoons peanut

oil
2 cups rice
4 1/2 cups chicken broth
1 bay leaf
1 green hot pepper or
  1/2 teaspoon Cayenne
  or red pepper

1. In a mortar, pound parsley, peppercorns, garlic, scallions, salt, and thyme to a paste. Set aside.
2. Heat oil in a large, heavy saucepan; add rice. Stir until all the rice is coated with oil and turns chalky.
3. Add seasoning paste and chicken broth; bring to a boil. Reduce heat and add bay leaf and pepper. Cover saucepan and cook undisturbed for 20 minutes.

Cannelloni.

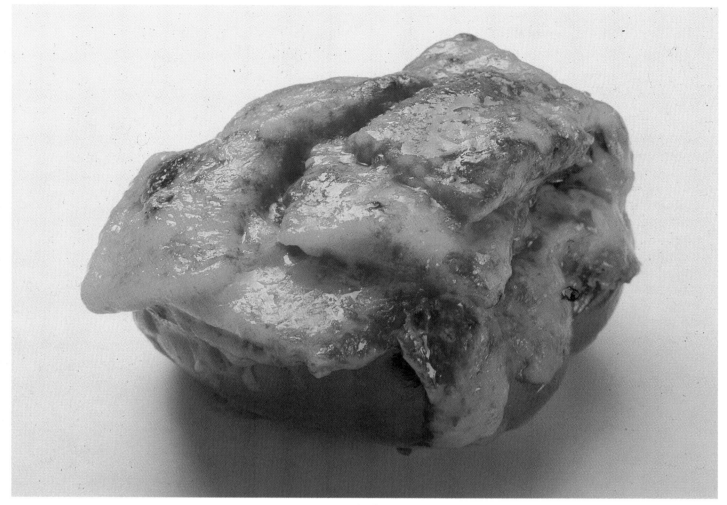

Ravioli-Stuffed Peppers.

4. Remove the cover; continue to cook over low heat for 5 minutes, or until no liquid remains.

5. Discard bay leaf and whole pepper. Fluff rice and serve.

Rice and Avocado: Follow recipe for Caribbean Rice. Place **cubed avocado** on top of the rice for the last 5 minutes of cooking. Mix in avocado when rice is fluffed.

Coconut and Rice: Follow recipe for Caribbean Rice, using **brown rice** and an additional ¹/₂ **cup chicken broth**. Add **1 cup freshly grated coconut** along with bay leaf and pepper. Proceed as directed.

Saffron Rice: Steep ¹/₂ **teaspoon Spanish saffron** in 2¹/₄ **cups boiling water** until it turns bright orange. Strain. Follow recipe for Caribbean Rice, using saffron water in place of some of the chicken broth to cook the rice.

New Peas in Rice Ring

SERVES ABOUT 6

1 package	white rice mix
(6 or 6³/₄ ounces)	3 pounds fresh peas
seasoned wild and	Butter

1. Cook rice mix according to package directions.

2. Meanwhile, rinse and shell peas just before cooking to retain their delicate flavor. Cook covered in boiling salted water to cover for 15 to 20 minutes or until peas are tender. Drain and add just enough butter so peas glisten.

3. Butter a 1-quart ring mold. When rice is done, turn into the mold, packing down gently with spoon. Invert onto a warm serving platter and lift off mold.

4. Spoon hot peas into center of rice ring just before serving.

Ravioli-Stuffed Peppers

SERVES 4

4 medium peppers	¹/₂ teaspoon basil or
1 large can ravioli	tarragon
¹/₂ teaspoon Italian	³/₄ cup Parmesan
salad seasoning	cheese

1. Remove seeds from the peppers. Wash well.

2. Parboil peppers for 5 minutes in boiling salted water. Peppers can also be stuffed raw but require longer oven time.

3. Fill the peppers with ravioli, season with Italian seasoning and basil or tarragon.

4. Sprinkle cheese on top of each pepper and place in a 350°F oven for 30 minutes till peppers are tender.

Fiesta Zucchini-Tomato Casserole

SERVES 6-8

1¹/₂ quarts water
2 packets dry onion soup mix
4 ounces enriched spaghetti, broken
¹/₃ cup butter or margarine
²/₃ cup coarsely chopped onion
1 cup green pepper strips
2 or 3 zucchini (about ³/₄ pound), washed, ends trimmed, and zucchini cut in about ¹/₂-inch slices
4 medium tomatoes, peeled and cut in wedges
¹/₄ cup snipped parsley
1 teaspoon seasoned salt
¹/₈ teaspoon ground black pepper
²/₃ cup shredded Swiss cheese

1. Bring water to boiling in a saucepot. Add onion soup mix and spaghetti to the boiling water. Partially cover and boil gently about 10 minutes, or until spaghetti is tender. Drain and set spaghetti mixture aside; reserve liquid.*
2. Heat butter in a large heavy skillet. Add onion and green pepper and cook about 3 minutes, or until tender. Add zucchini; cover and cook 5 minutes. Stir in tomatoes, parsley, seasoned salt, and pepper. Cover and cook about 2 minutes, or just until heated.
3. Turn contents of skillet into a 2-quart casserole. Add drained spaghetti and toss gently to mix. Sprinkle cheese over top. If necessary to reheat mixture, set in a 350°F oven until thoroughly heated before placing under broiler.
4. Set under broiler with top about 5 inches from heat until cheese is melted and lightly browned.

*The strained soup may be stored for future use as broth or for cooking vegetables, preparing gravy or sauce, as desired.

Rice-Vegetable Medley

SERVES ABOUT 8

3 tablespoons butter or margarine
³/₄ cup chooped onion
1¹/₂ pounds zucchini, thinly sliced
1 can (16 ounces) whole kernel golden corn, drained
1 can (16 ounces) tomatoes (undrained)
3 cups cooked enriched white rice
1¹/₂ teaspoons salt
¹/₄ teaspoon ground black pepper
¹/₄ teaspoon ground coriander
¹/₄ teaspoon oregano leaves

1. Heat butter in a large saucepan.
2. Add onion and zucchini; cook until tender, stirring occasionally. Add corn, tomatoes with liquid, cooked rice, salt, pepper, coriander, and oregano; mix well.
3. Cover and bring to boiling; reduce heat and simmer 15 minutes.

Ravioli with Tomato Sauce

SERVES 4

1 package ravioli (cheese-filled)
2 cups peeled tomatoes
2 tablespoons olive oil
1 medium onion, chopped
2 cloves garlic, minced
¹/₂ teaspoon oregano
¹/₂ teaspoon basil
¹/₄ teaspoon thyme
¹/₂ teaspoon parsley

1. Heat the oil and sauté the onion and garlic for 5 minutes.
2. Add the tomatoes and spices and simmer for another 15-20 minutes.

Ravioli with Tomato Sauce.

Spaghetti with Meat Sauce.

3. Cook the ravioli in boiling, salted water.
4. Drain the cooked ravioli and mix with the sauce. Serve with grated Parmesan cheese.

Spaghetti with Meat Sauce (Home Style)

SERVES 4

1 pound ground beef	1 tablespoon chili sauce
¹/₄ cup olive oil	¹/₄ teaspoon basil
1 onion, chopped	¹/₄ teaspoon oregano
2 cloves garlic, finely chopped	1 bay leaf, crushed
	1 teaspoon parsley
¹/₂ cup red wine	1 pound spaghetti
1 can (1 pound 12 ounces) plum tomatoes	¹/₄ cup Parmesan cheese, grated

1. In a large skillet heat the olive oil and sauté the onion and garlic.

2. Add the ground beef and brown thoroughly.
3. Add the tomatoes, wine, chili sauce, and seasonings and simmer for 30-35 minutes over low heat.
4. Cook the spaghetti in boiling water *al dente* and drain.
5. Mix the pasta with the sauce, sprinkle with Parmesan cheese, and serve.

Chiffon Noodles

SERVES ABOUT 4

2 eggs, separated	¹/₂ teaspoon salt
2 tablespoons flour	

1. Beat egg whites and salt until stiff, not dry, peaks form.
2. Beat yolks separately just until frothy. Fold into whites. Fold in flour.
3. Gently spoon onto **boiling soup or broth**. Cover; cook 2 minutes. Turn; cook a few seconds longer.
4. To serve, break into separate portions with a spoon.

Sicilian Rice Dish

SERVES 4

1¼ cups long-grain rice	margarine
2½ cups cold water	½ teaspoon basil
1½ teaspoons salt	1 (1-pound) can Italian
Dash of pepper	tomatoes
7 ounces ground pork	Parmesan cheese,
2 onions, sliced	grated
2 tablespoons butter or	

1. Bring rice, water, and salt to a boil while stirring and cook covered 20 minutes. Remove from heat immediately and stir rice with a fork.
2. Brown pork and onions well in butter and season with salt, pepper, and basil.
3. Add tomatoes with juice. Simmer covered over low heat. Butter an ovenproof dish and place alternately thin layers of rice and meat. Sprinkle each layer with Parmesan cheese. The first layer should be rice and the last layer meat. Bake in a 400-425°F oven until food is heated thoroughly, about 15 minutes.
Serve with grated cheese, parsley, and ketchup.

Ravioli

ABOUT 3 DOZEN RAVIOLI

Tomato Meat Sauce	¾ teaspoon salt
(below)	¼ teaspoon pepper
3 cups (about 1½	Basic Noodle Dough
pounds) ricotta	(below)
1½ tablespoons	7 quarts water
chopped parsley	2 tablespoons salt
2 eggs, well beaten	Grated Parmesan or
1 tablespoon grated	Romano cheese
Parmesan cheese	

1. Prepare Tomato Meat Sauce.
2. Mix ricotta, parsley, eggs, 1 tablespoon grated Parmesan, ¾ teaspoon salt, and pepper.
3. Prepare noodle dough. Divide dough in fourths. Lightly roll each fourth ⅛ inch thick to form a rectangle. Cut dough lengthwise with pastry cutter into strips 5 inches wide. Put 2 teaspoons filling 1½ inches from narrow end in center of each strip. Continuing along strip, put 2 teaspoons filling at 3½-inch intervals.
4. Fold each strip in half lengthwise, covering mounds of filling. To seal, press the edges together with the tines of a fork. Press gently between mounds to form rectangles about 3½ inches long. Cut apart with a pastry cutter and press cut edges of rectangles with tines of fork to seal.
5. Bring water to boiling in a large saucepot. Add 2 tablespoons salt. Add ravioli gradually; cook about half of ravioli at one time. Boil, uncovered, about 20 minutes, or until tender. Remove with slotted spoon and drain. Put on a warm platter and top with Tomato Meat Sauce. Sprinkle with grated cheese.

Ravioli with Meat Filling: Follow recipe for Ravioli. Prepare sauce. Omit ricotta and parsley. Heat **2 tablespoons olive oil** in a skillet. Add **¾ pound ground beef** and cook until no pink color remains. Cook **½ pound spinach** until tender; drain. Mix spinach and ground beef with egg mixture. Proceed as directed.

Tomato Meat Sauce

ABOUT 4 CUPS SAUCE

¼ cup olive oil	with liquid, sieved
½ cup chopped onion	1 tablespoon salt
½ pound beef chuck	1 bay leaf
½ pound pork shoulder	1 can (6 ounces) tomato
7 cups canned tomatoes	paste

1. Heat olive oil in a large saucepot. Add onion and cook until lightly browned. Add the meat and brown on all sides. Stir in tomatoes and salt. Add bay leaf. Cover and simmer about 2½ hours.
2. Stir tomato paste into sauce. Simmer, uncovered, stirring occasionally, about 2 hours, or until thickened. If sauce becomes too thick, add ½ cup water.
3. Remove meat and bay leaf from sauce (use meat as desired). Serve sauce over cooked spaghetti.

Tomato Sauce with Ground Meat: Follow recipe for Tomato Meat Sauce. Brown **½ pound ground beef** in **3 tablespoons olive oil,** breaking beef into small pieces. After removing meat from sauce, add ground beef and simmer 10 minutes longer.

Basic Noodle Dough

ABOUT 1¾ POUNDS DOUGH

4 cups sifted all-purpose	4 eggs
flour	6 tablespoons cold
½ teaspoon salt	water

1. Mix flour and salt in a bowl; make a well in center. Add eggs, one at a time, mixing slightly after each addition. Add water gradually, mixing to make a stiff dough.
2. Turn dough onto a lightly floured surface and knead until smooth.
3. Proceed as directed in recipes.

Sicilian Rice Dish.

217

Baked Rice Balls

SERVES 7-8

1¹/₂ pounds ground beef	cheese
1 small onion, chopped	¹/₄ cup butter
1 can (6 ounces) tomato paste	2 to 2¹/₂ cups all-purpose flour
³/₄ cup water	2 eggs, slightly beaten
1 teaspoon salt	3 eggs, slightly beaten
¹/₈ teaspoon pepper	2 cups fine dry bread crumbs
1 tablespoon chopped parsley	1 can (8 ounces) tomato sauce
6 cups cooked rice, hot	
¹/₂ cup grated Romano	

1. Brown ground beef with onion in a skillet. Add tomato paste, stir, and cook 5 minutes. Add water, salt, pepper, and parsley. Mix well and cool about 15 minutes.
2. Combine rice, cheese, butter, 1 cup flour, and 2 eggs. Mix until butter is melted and ingredients are well blended.
3. With well-floured hands, shape some rice into a small ball. Flatten slightly and top with 1 tablespoon of the meat mixture. Top with more rice to cover meat, and make into a ball size of a small orange.
4. Hold the ball over a shallow pan filled with about 1 cup flour; add more flour when needed. Sprinkle rice ball with flour while gently packing and turning in palm of hand.
5. Carefully dip ball in beaten eggs, then roll gently in bread crumbs to coat. Repeat with remaining rice.

Risotto with Bacon.

Place finished rice balls in a jelly-roll pan or baking sheet lined with aluminum foil.
6. Bake at 350°F 30 minutes. While rice balls are baking, stir tomato sauce into meat sauce and heat. Serve sauce over baked rice balls.

Rice Salad with Assorted Sausages

SERVES 6-8

¹/₃ cup white wine vinegar	white rice, cooled
1 teaspoon lemon juice	3 cups finely shredded red cabbage
¹/₄ teaspoon French mustard	¹/₂ cup raisins
1 teaspoon salt	¹/₂ cup walnut pieces
¹/₄ teaspoon ground black pepper	Greens
¹/₃ cup salad oil	Link sausage (such as bratwurst, smoky links, and frankfurters), cooked
3 cups cooked enriched	

1. Put vinegar into a bottle. Add lemon juice, mustard, salt, and pepper. Cover and shake. Add oil and shake well.
2. Combine rice, cabbage, raisins, and walnuts in a bowl; chill.
3. When ready to serve, shake dressing well and pour over salad; toss until well mixed.
4. Arrange greens on luncheon plates, spoon salad on greens, and accompany with assorted sausages.

Risotto with Bacon

SERVES 4

1 cup long-grain rice	1 large red pepper
2 cups water	Freshly ground black pepper
1 teaspoon salt	
About ³/₄ cup diced leftover meat	Garlic salt
1 small leek	¹/₄ pound bacon

1. Boil the rice according to the package directions. Cut the leek and pepper into strips.
2. Cut the bacon in strips, fry until crisp, drain on paper towel.
3. Sauté leek and pepper strips in bacon fat till soft.
4. Mix diced meat with the vegetables and rice.
5. Grind some black pepper and sprinkle over rice. Season with a dust of garlic salt.
6. Place on a serving dish and sprinkle the bacon on top.
Serve with lettuce leaves and tomato halves.

Paella.

Paella

SERVES 8

2 cups cooked chicken	¹/₂ teaspoon pepper
¹/₄ cup olive oil	2 teaspoons paprika
2 cloves garlic, chopped	¹/₈ teaspoon Cayenne
1 large yellow onion,	pepper
finely chopped	2 dozen clams, in shell
2 cups long-grain white	1 pound shrimp,
rice	shelled and deveined
4 cups chicken stock	2 red peppers
2 teaspoons saffron	1 green pepper
¹/₂ pound hard Spanish	12 asparagus spears
sausage, sliced	20 black olives
¹/₂ teaspoon salt	

1. Preheat oven to 350°F.
2. Cut chicken into 1¹/₂-inch pieces.
3. Pour olive oil into a large casserole or paella pan and heat. Add garlic and onion.
4. Add rice, chicken stock, and saffron. Bring to a boil, lower heat, and simmer covered for 25 minutes.
5. Add sausage, chicken, salt, pepper, paprika, and Cayenne pepper. Cover and bake for 15 minutes.
6. Add clams and shrimp and bake an additional 10 minutes. Serve in paella pan or large platter. Garnish with green and red peppers, olives, and asparagus.

Spaghetti au Gratin

SERVES 4

4 cups cooked spaghetti	*Garnish:*
or macaroni	¹/₂ pound green beans,
1 can lobster or clam	cooked and diced
soup	¹/₂ cup Parmesan
Black pepper	cheese
1 clove garlic, crushed	

1. Place spaghetti in a buttered ovenproof dish.
2. Cook soup according to can directions. Season with pepper. Add garlic and pour over spaghetti.
3. Garnish with green beans and sprinkle with cheese.
4. Bake in 475°F oven about 15 minutes until cheese melts.
Serve with grated raw carrots.

EGG and CHEESE DISHES

Shirred Eggs with Feta

SERVES 1

1 tablespoon butter	cheese
2 eggs	Dash pepper
1/4 cup crumbled feta	

1. Melt butter in a ramekin or baking dish. Add eggs. Sprinkle with cheese. Season with pepper.
2. Bake at 350°F about 10 minutes, or until eggs are done as desired.

Croustade Basket

1 CROUSTADE BASKET

1 loaf unsliced bread	or margarine
1/3 cup melted butter	

1. Neatly trim the crusts from top and sides of loaf. Using a sharp pointed knife, hollow out center, leaving 1-inch sides and bottom.
2. Brush inside and out with melted butter. Place on a baking sheet.
3. Toast in a 400°F oven 10 to 15 minutes, or until golden brown and crisp. Fill with **Scrambled Eggs** (double recipe), below, and serve with **Mushroom-Caraway Sauce,** below.

Miniature Croustades: Trim crusts from top and sides of loaf of unsliced bread; cut into cubes slightly larger than 1 inch. Using a serrated knife, hollow out centers. Brush cases inside and out with a mixture of **1/2 cup butter** and **1/4 teaspoon garlic salt.** Set on a baking sheet. Toast at 360°F.

Scrambled Eggs

SERVES 4

6 eggs	3/4 teaspoon salt
6 tablespoons milk, cream, or undiluted evaporated milk	1/8 teaspoon pepper
	3 tablespoons butter or margarine

1. Beat the eggs, milk, salt, and pepper together until blended.

2. Heat an 8- or 10-inch skillet until hot enough to sizzle a drop of water. Melt butter in skillet.
3. Pour egg mixture into skillet and cook over low heat. With a spatula, lift mixture from bottom and sides of skillet as it thickens, allowing uncooked portion to flow to bottom. Cook until eggs are thick and creamy.

Mushroom-Caraway Sauce

ABOUT 2 CUPS

1 can (10 1/2 ounces) condensed cream of mushroom soup	seed
	1/4 teaspoon onion salt
1 bottle (7 ounces) lemon-lime carbonated beverage	1/8 teaspoon freshly ground black pepper
1/4 cup heavy cream	1 3/4 teaspoons wine vinegar
3/4 teaspoon caraway	

1. Put mushroom soup into a heavy saucepan; stir until smooth.
2. Gradually add lemon-lime carbonated beverage and then cream, stirring constantly.
3. Blend in the remaining ingredients and heat until mixture begins to simmer.

Marvelous Eggs

SERVES 4

3 tablespoons butter	1/4 teaspoon lemon juice
1 tablespoon minced green onion	1 package (3 ounces) cream cheese, cut in 1/2-inch cubes
6 eggs, slightly beaten	
1/3 cup milk	
1/2 teaspoon salt	

1. In a 2-quart glass casserole, heat butter 30 seconds. Add onion and cook 2 minutes, stirring once. Stir in eggs, milk, salt, and lemon juice.
2. Cook, covered, 4 to 5 minutes, stirring every 2 minutes. When almost set, lightly fold in cream cheese.
3. Cook 1 minute longer, rest 5 minutes, and serve.

Cheese Pie with Olives.

Cheese Pie with Olives

SERVES 4

1 package puff-pastry, frozen	Salt
Filling:	Paprika
³/₄ cup heavy cream	Cayenne pepper
2 egg yolks	1 tablespoon brandy
1¹/₂ cups Swiss cheese, grated	*For Brushing:*
	1 egg
¹/₂ tablespoon all-purpose flour	*Garnish:*
	Black olives

1. Roll out the thawed puff-pastry and line a pie pan with it. (Reserve some dough for the lattice-work.) Prick bottom with a fork. Bake in a 400°F oven for about 10 minutes and let it cool.

2. Filling: Whip the cream, add yolks, cheese, and flour. Season with salt, paprika, and Cayenne pepper and add the brandy.

3. Spread the filling on the pie crust.

4. Cut out strips from the dough and arrange like a lattice across the pie. Brush with egg.

5. Bake the pie until golden brown in a 400°F oven for about 10 minutes. Garnish with black olives.

Confetti Eggs

SERVES 3-4

2 tablespoons butter	4 eggs
$^1/_2$ cup diced ham	Dash Tabasco
2 green onions,	$^1/_2$ teaspoon salt
including tops,	$^1/_4$ teaspoon pepper
chopped	

1. In a 2-quart casserole, cook butter, ham, and green onions 3 to 4 minutes, stirring every minute.
2. Add eggs, Tabasco, salt, and pepper; stir to blend.
3. Cook, covered, 3 to 4 minutes, stirring halfway through cooking time.
4. Rest, covered, 5 minutes.

Ham and Cheese Soufflé

SERVES 4

1$^1/_4$ cups all-purpose	1 onion
flour	3 eggs
3$^1/_2$ ounces butter	1$^1/_4$ cups milk
3 tablespoons water	1-1$^1/_4$ cups Cheddar
4 ounces smoked ham	cheese, grated

1. Mix the flour, butter, and water. Place in refrigerator for an hour.

Ham and Cheese Soufflé.

2. Roll out dough and place in a large, round, ovenproof dish.
3. Slice onion and brown lightly in butter. Slice ham. Place ham and onion on dough and bake in a 400°F oven for about 10 minutes.
4. Beat eggs with milk and cheese. Pour over pie and bake 20-25 minutes longer.

Serve with a green salad.

Cheese Soufflé

SERVES 4

6 eggs, separated	1 cup milk
4 tablespoons butter	$^1/_2$ teaspoon salt
1 cup Swiss cheese,	White pepper
grated	$^1/_2$ cup Cheddar
3 tablespoons all-	cheese, grated
purpose flour	

1. Preheat oven to 400°F. Grease a 2-quart soufflé dish with 1 tablespoon butter and sprinkle bottom and sides with 1 tablespoon grated Swiss cheese.
2. Melt 3 tablespoons butter in a heavy saucepan over moderate heat. Stir in flour and cook over low heat for 1 minute.
3. Remove pan and pour in hot milk, beating until mixed with flour mixture. Add salt and pepper, reheat, and cook till mixture boils and thickens.
4. Remove from heat and beat in egg yolks, one at a time. Set aside and let cool.

Cheese Soufflé.

Open Omelet.

5. Beat egg whites till stiff peaks form.

6. Stir grated cheeses into the sauce. Fold egg whites into mixture with a spatula.

7. Pour mixture into soufflé dish and place in the middle of the oven. Turn heat to 375°F. Bake for 25 minutes till soufflé puffs above rim of dish. Serve immediately.

Open Omelet

SERVES 4

8 eggs	ham, thinly sliced
16 tablespoons milk	1 small can mush-
Salt	rooms
Pepper	1 yellow onion, finely
2 tablespoons chives,	chopped
finely chopped	Paprika
½ pound smoked	3 tablespoons butter

1. Sauté the mushrooms and onion and add the ham when the onion is transparent. Sauté the ham about 5 more minutes. Season with paprika. Set aside.

2. Beat the eggs quickly, add milk, salt, pepper, and chives.

3. Brown butter in a frying pan. Pour in the egg batter and let it set while stirring a few times. Remove pan from heat when the omelet is set.

4. Top omelet with the mushroom-onion mixture and serve at once.

Cheese Rabbit Fondue

SERVES 4-6

1 small clove garlic	mustard
2 cups beer	2 tablespoons
1 pound sharp Ched-	chopped chives or
dar cheese, shred-	green onion top
ded (about 4 cups)	(optional)
3 tablespoons flour	1 loaf sourdough
1 teaspoon Worces-	French bread, cut
tershire sauce	into 1-inch cubes
½ teaspoon dry	

1. Rub inside of a nonmetal fondue pot with garlic; discard garlic. Heat beer in the pot until almost boiling.

(continued)

2. Dredge cheese in flour and add about ¹/₂ cup at a time, stirring until cheese is melted and blended before adding more.

3. When mixture is smooth and thickened, stir in Worcestershire sauce and dry mustard.

4. Sprinkle chives on top and serve with bread cubes. Keep fondue warm while serving.

Bacon and Egg Turbans

SERVES 6

6 slices bacon	2 tablespoons sour
6 eggs	cream

1. Arrange bacon on roasting rack in a 2-quart glass baking dish and cook as follows: 1 slice for 1 minute; 2 slices for 1¹/₂ minutes; 3 slices for 2¹/₂ minutes; 4 slices for 3 minutes; and 6 slices for 4 minutes. Limp, not crisp, bacon is desired.

2. Arrange a bacon slice in a circle in the bottom of a 6-ounce glass custard cup. Break egg in cup over bacon. Pierce yolk with fork, and top egg with 1 teaspoon sour cream.

3. Place cups in a circle on a 9-inch glass pie plate. Add 1 cup water to glass plate and cover with plastic wrap. Cook until done, as follows, rotating plate one-quarter turn halfway through cooking time: 1 egg, 1¹/₂ to 2 minutes; 2 eggs, 2 to 3 minutes; 3 eggs, 2¹/₂ to 3¹/₂ minutes; 4 eggs, 3 to 4 minutes; 6 eggs, 4 to 5 minutes.

4. Rest, covered, 1 minute after cooking. Invert custard cup on buttered toasted English muffin and serve immediately.

Spinach-Bacon Soufflé

SERVES 6

2 cups firmly packed, finely chopped fresh spinach leaves (dry the leaves before chopping)	or margarine ¹/₄ cup enriched all-purpose flour ¹/₂ teaspoon salt ¹/₄ to ¹/₂ teaspoon thyme
¹/₄ cup finely chopped green onions with tops	1 cup milk 3 egg yolks, well beaten
¹/₂ pound sliced bacon, cooked, drained and crumbled	4 egg whites 2 teaspoons shredded Parmesan cheese
3 tablespoons butter	

1. Toss the spinach, green onions, and bacon together in a bowl; set aside.

2. Heat butter in a saucepan over low heat. Blend in flour, salt, and thyme. Stirring constantly, heat until bubbly. Add milk gradually, continuing to stir. Bring rapidly to boiling and boil 1 to 2 minutes, stirring constantly.

3. Remove from heat and blend spinach-bacon mixture into the sauce. Stir in the beaten egg yolks; set aside to cool.

4. Meanwhile, beat egg whites until rounded peaks are formed (peaks turn over slightly when beater is slowly lifted upright); do not overbeat.

5. Gently spread spinach-bacon mixture over the beaten egg whites. Carefully fold together until ingredients are just blended.

6. Turn mixture into an ungreased 2-quart soufflé dish (straight-side casserole); sprinkle top with Parmesan cheese.

7. Bake at 350°F 40 minutes, or until a knife comes out clean when inserted halfway between center and edge of soufflé and top is lightly browned. Serve immediately.

Asparagus Omelet

SERVES 2

3 eggs	pepper
4 tablespoons milk	2 tablespoons butter
¹/₄ teaspoon white	5 stalks asparagus

1. Wash asparagus, place in a pot with cold water, and cook covered for 7-10 minutes. Asparagus should be crisp, not mushy.

2. Heat butter in a skillet. Beat eggs, milk, and pepper and pour into the hot skillet.

3. Cook eggs over medium heat until set, shaking the pan slightly so eggs do not stick.

4. Fold omelet onto a plate, top with asparagus and serve.

Cheese and Green Pepper Omelet

SERVES 2

3 eggs	1 tablespoon butter or
¹/₄ teaspoon salt	margarine for
¹/₄ teaspoon pepper	frying
2-3 tablespoons water or milk	2 slices Cheddar cheese
Nutmeg (optional)	1 green pepper, sliced
Onion or garlic powder (optional)	1 red pepper, sliced

1. Beat 3 eggs with a little salt, pepper, and 2-3 tablespoons water or milk. Nutmeg and onion or garlic powder can also be used as seasonings.

2. Cook in frying pan with butter or margarine. Place slices of cheese and sliced peppers on omelet and fold over.

**Cheese and
Green Pepper Omelet.**

Asparagus Omelet.

Quick Cheese Fondue

2 CUPS FONDUE

1 can (10¹/₂ ounces)
  condensed Cheddar
  cheese soup
¹/₃ cup milk
¹/₄ teaspoon garlic

powder
¹/₄ teaspoon nutmeg
1¹/₂ cups shredded
  Swiss cheese

1. In a 4-cup glass measure, blend soup and milk; cook 3 to 4 minutes, stirring halfway through cooking time.
2. Add garlic powder and nutmeg; stir to blend. Blend in cheese.
3. Cook 2 to 3 minutes, stirring every minute, until cheese is melted.
4. Serve immediately while warm.

Fried Eggs

2 EGGS PER SERVING

Eggs

1. Break egg into 10-ounce custard cup. Pierce yolk with a fork and cover cup with plastic wrap.
2. Cook as follows, rotating one-quarter turn halfway through cooking time: 1 egg, 25 to 35 seconds; 2 eggs, 1 minute to 1¹/₄ minutes; 3 eggs, 1¹/₂ to 1³/₄ minutes; 4 eggs, 2 to 2¹/₄ minutes If a soft yolk is preferred, cook the shorter time. If a firmer yolk is desired, cook the longer time.
3. Rest, covered, 5 minutes before serving, if desired.

Note: If cupcaker is used, place a small amount of butter in the bottom of paper baking cup in each well. Break egg into each cup and cover with plastic wrap. Cook as directed for fried eggs in custard cup, but reduce cooking time 5 to 10 seconds for each egg.

Note: Never cook an egg in its shell in the microwave oven. Steam forms readily, and the egg might explode the shell.

Onion Pie

SERVES 4

6 ounces butter
1¹/₄ cups all-purpose
  flour
3 tablespoons cold
  water
Filling:
3 large onions
2 tablespoons butter

Egg Mixture:
2 eggs
³/₄ cup milk
³/₄ cup Cheddar
  cheese, grated
1 teaspoon salt
White pepper

1. Mix butter, flour, and water and knead thoroughly. Refrigerate for 30 minutes.

Onion Pie.

226

Fried Sausage in Baking Dish.

2. Slice peeled onions and sauté in butter.
3. Roll out dough and place in a buttered pie pan.
4. Beat eggs and milk together. Mix in grated cheese, salt, and pepper.
5. Pour the egg mixture over dough and add the onions. Bake in 475°F oven for 25 minutes.

Poached Eggs

2 EGGS PER SERVING

Eggs	Water

1. Place ½ cup water in a 10-ounce custard cup and heat 30 seconds.
2. Break egg into hot water and cover with plastic wrap.
3. Cook, following times indicated for Fried Egg (above).
4. Rest, covered, 5 minutes before serving.

Fried Sausage in Baking Dish

SERVES 1

2 frankfurters, cubed	1 egg
1 tablespoon chopped onion	½ tablespoon flour
1 tomato, cubed	1½ ounces milk
2 tablespoons cubed potatoes	Salt
2 tablespoons butter	*Garnish:* Chopped parsley

1. Fry sausage till golden brown.
2. Fry onion, tomato, potato in butter. Transfer together with sausages to an ovenproof dish.
3. Beat together egg, flour, milk, and salt and pour the egg batter over the mixture.
4. Bake eggs at 425°F for 15-20 minutes till set. Garnish with chopped parsley.

Cheese Mousse

SERVES 4

³/₄ cup heavy cream
7 ounces cream
   cheese
1 package unflavored
   gelatin
¹/₂ teaspoon salt
¹/₂ teaspoon paprika

1 tablespoon chopped
   chives
Garnish:
Watercress
2 sliced cucumbers
6 radishes

1. Whip the heavy cream till stiff. Stir in the cream cheese until smooth and add half the cream to it.
2. Place the gelatin in 2 tablespoons water and dissolve over low heat. Stir the gelatin in the cream and cream cheese mixture and add the rest of the whipped cream. Add seasonings.
3. Pour the cheese cream into a water-rinsed ring mold. Place in refrigerator to set. Serve garnished with watercress, cucumbers and radishes.

Cheese Fondue

SERVES 3-4

¹/₂ pound Swiss
   cheese, shredded
2 tablespoons flour
¹/₂ teaspoon salt
¹/₄ teaspoon garlic
   powder
¹/₄ teaspoon nutmeg

¹/₄ teaspoon white
   pepper
¹/₂ cup milk
2 tablespoons kirsch
   (optional)
French bread, cut in
   1-inch cubes

1. In a 2-quart glass casserole, mix together the cheese, flour, salt, garlic powder, nutmeg, and white pepper. Add milk and, if desired, kirsch; stir to mix.
2. Cook, covered, 3 to 4 minutes, stirring once or twice. Rest, covered, 5 minutes.
3. Spear cubes of bread and dip in fondue. If fondue cools, reheat 1 to 2 minutes.

Danish Omelet

SERVES 6

12 slices of bacon
8 eggs
1¹/₂ teaspoons all-
   purpose flour
16 tablespoons milk
2 ounces chives, finely

chopped
¹/₂ teaspoon salt
¹/₂ teaspoon freshly
   ground black
   pepper

1. Beat the eggs and flour together. Add the milk and seasonings.

2. Cut the bacon slices in half and brown in a frying pan. Turn the head down and pour in the egg and milk batter. Increase the heat a little and stir with a fork so that the eggs set without burning. Serve with the surface still creamy.

Mushroom Eggs on Toast

SERVES 3-4

1 pound fresh mush-
   rooms, cleaned and
   sliced
¹/₄ cup butter
4 slices hot buttered
   toast
2 tablespoons butter
2 tablespoons flour

1 cup milk
¹/₂ cup grated Parme-
   san cheese
¹/₄ teaspoon dry
   mustard
4 poached eggs (*see
   above*)
Paprika (optional)

1. In a 1-quart glass casserole, cook mushrooms in ¹/₄ cup butter 3 to 4 minutes, stirring halfway through cooking time. Cover each slice toast with one-fourth of the mushrooms.
2. In a 2-cup glass measure, heat 2 tablespoons butter 30 seconds. Stir in flour to blend. Stir in milk and cook 2 to 3 minutes, stirring every minute, until sauce becomes thick. Add cheese and dry mustard; stir to blend.
3. Place an egg on top of mushrooms on each toast slice and cover with sauce. Sprinkle with paprika, if desired.

Fluffy Cheese Potatoes

SERVES 6

6 medium-size (about
   2 pounds) baking
   potatoes
1 tablespoon fat
2 ounces process
   Swiss cheese (about
   ¹/₂ cup, shredded)
4 tablespoons butter
   or margarine
¹/₂ cup hot milk or
   cream

³/₄ teaspoon salt
¹/₄ teaspoon paprika
¹/₄ teaspoon pepper
8 slices crisp,
   panbroiled bacon,
   crumbled
1 tablespoon finely
   chopped onion
Finely chopped
   parsley

1. Wash and scrub potatoes with a vegetable brush.
2. Dry potatoes with absorbent paper and rub with fat.
3. Place potatoes on rack in oven.
4. Bake at 425°F 45 to 60 minutes, or until potatoes are soft when pressed with the fingers (protected by paper napkin).
5. While potatoes bake, shred cheese and set aside.

Danish Omelet.

6. Remove potatoes from oven. To make each potato mealy, gently roll potatoes back and forth on a flat surface. Cut large potatoes into halves lengthwise or cut a thin lengthwise slice from each smaller potato. With a spoon, scoop out inside without breaking skin. Mash thoroughly or rice. Whip in, in order, butter or margarine, milk or cream (adding gradually) and a mixture of salt, paprika, and pepper until mixture is fluffy.

7. Mix in the shredded cheese and bacon and onion.

8. Pile mixture lightly into potato skins, leaving tops uneven.

9. Return potatoes to oven for 8 to 10 minutes, or until thoroughly heated.

10. Sprinkle with parsley.

Cheddar Cheese Potatoes: Follow recipe for Fluffy Cheese Potatoes. Substitute $1/3$ cup grated **sharp Cheddar cheese** for the Swiss cheese.

Cheddar Cheese-Olive Potatoes: Follow recipe for Fluffy Cheese Potatoes. Substitute $1/3$ cup grated **sharp Cheddar cheese** for the Swiss cheese. Omit the bacon and onion and add 8 to 10 **stuffed olives,** finely chopped, with the cheese. If desired, omit parsley and top potatoes with $1/3$ cup crushed buttered **corn flakes** or **crumbs** before baking.

Bacon and Egg Casserole.

Bacon and Egg Casserole

SERVES 6

6 eggs, beaten	2 tablespoons butter
1 pound bacon	¹/₂ tablespoon flour
1 large onion, chopped	1 cup milk
4 tomatoes, quartered	4 ounces Cheddar cheese, shredded
2 medium potatoes, cooked and cubed	4 ounces cooked peas
	Parsley

1. Fry bacon till brown, then set aside.
2. Sauté onion, tomatoes, and potatoes till brown, then transfer to baking dish.
3. Heat milk, add cheese, and stir over a low flame until cheese is melted; add flour and continue stirring till dissolved.
4. Pour milk mixture over onions in baking dish, add bacon and peas. Add 6 eggs to top of casserole.
5. Bake in a 400°F oven for 15-20 minutes, remove, and sprinkle with chopped parsley.

Eggs Florentine à l'Orange

SERVES 4

1 tablespoon butter or margarine	and drained
¹/₂ cup chopped onion	1 teaspoon salt
¹/₄ pound mushrooms, cleaned and sliced	¹/₈ teaspoon pepper
1 package (10 ounces) frozen chopped spinach, thawed	1 cup Florida orange sections*
	4 eggs
	Salt
	Pepper

1. Melt butter in medium saucepan. Add onions and cook until tender; add mushrooms and cook 5 minutes. Stir in spinach, salt, pepper, and orange sections.
2. Divide equally among 4 buttered ramekins or individual shallow baking dishes, making a depression in the center of each.
3. Bake in a 350°F oven 15 to 20 minutes, or until hot.
4. Add 1 egg to the depression in each dish; sprinkle with additional salt and pepper. Bake 7 to 10 minutes longer, or until egg white is set.

*To section Florida oranges, cut off peel round and round spiral fashion. Go over fruit again, removing any remaining white membrane. Cut along side of each dividing membrane from outside to middle of core. Remove section by section over a bowl; reserve juice for other use.

Egg Foo Yong

SERVES 4

1 cup finely diced cooked ham, roast pork, or chicken	¹/₄ to ¹/₂ teaspoon salt (reduce if using ham)
1 cup drained canned bean sprouts	6 eggs, slightly beaten
³/₄ cup chopped onion	Fat or cooking oil (about 2 tablespoons or enough to form an ¹/₈-inch layer)
1 tablespoon soy sauce	
¹/₂ teaspoon monosodium glutamate	Foo Yong Sauce

1. Mix ham, bean sprouts, onion, soy sauce, monosodium glutamate, and salt. Stir in eggs.
2. Heat fat in a large wok. Drop a fourth of the mixture into the hot fat to form a patty. Cook about 5 minutes, or until browned on one side; turn and brown other side.
3. Remove patty from wok; drain over fat a few seconds. Transfer to a warm heat-resistant platter; keep warm in a 200°F oven while cooking remaining patties.

230

4. Pour hot sauce over the patties and serve with hot fluffy rice and additional soy sauce.

Foo Yong Sauce: Blend **2 tablespoons cornstarch, 1 tablespoon cold water, 2 teaspoons soy sauce,** and **1 teaspoon molasses** in a small saucepan. Stir in **1 cup chicken broth.** Bring to boiling, stirring constantly. Boil 3 minutes, or until sauce is thickened. Keep hot.

³/₄ Cup Sauce

Smoked Ham Omelet

SERVES 4

---

6 ounces smoked ham	**4 eggs**
4 tomatoes	**1¹/₂ tablespoons flour**
1 green pepper	**¹/₂ teaspoon salt**
2 tablespoons butter	**¹/₂ teaspoon paprika**
³/₄ cup milk	

---

1. Slice ham in strips. Slice tomatoes and cube green pepper. Sauté in butter.
2. Bring milk to boil and let cool.
3. Combine milk, eggs, flour, and seasonings and mix with ham mixture. Cook while stirring 5-7 minutes.
4. Sprinkle with paprika.

Serve with bread and a raw vegetable salad.

Welsh Rabbit

SERVES 4-6

1¹/₂ teaspoons butter	**¹/₄ teaspoon dry mustard**
2 cups shredded pasteurized process sharp Cheddar cheese	**Few grains Cayenne pepper**
¹/₄ teaspoon Worcestershire sauce	**¹/₃ cup milk**
	Toast

---

1. Melt butter in a 1-quart glass casserole in microwave oven (about 15 seconds). Add cheese and heat uncovered in microwave oven about 1 minute, or until cheese begins to melt; stir after 30 seconds.
2. Add Worcestershire sauce, dry mustard, and Cay-

(continued)

enne pepper to cheese. Add milk gradually, stirring constantly. Heat uncovered in microwave oven to serving temperature (1½ to 2½ minutes); stir occasionally.

3. Serve immediately on hot toast.

Onion Pie with Anchovies

SERVES 4-6

Dough:
¾ cup butter
1 egg
1½ cups flour
1 teaspoon salt

Filling:
4 yellow onions
2 tablespoons butter
½ cup light cream

2 eggs
½ teaspoon salt
⅛ teaspoon pepper
½ teaspoon tarragon

Topping:
8 anchovy fillets
2 ounces Swiss cheese, grated

1. Mix the ingredients for the dough and line a 9-inch pie pan with the dough. Put in a cool place.
2. Preheat oven to 350°F.
3. Peel and slice the onions and sauté in butter until golden brown.
4. Remove pan from heat, add the cream, and stir in the eggs, one at a time.
5. Season with salt, pepper, and tarragon.
6. Pour the mixture in the pie shell and bake for 30 minutes until the filling has set.
7. Increase oven heat to 400°F.

8. Sprinkle pie with the cheese and garnish with the anchovy fillets.
9. Bake for another 5 minutes until the pie has turned brown.

Serve with green salad.

Cheese-Tomato Supper Dish

SERVES ABOUT 8

⅔ cup butter or margarine
¼ cup minced onion
1 cup mushrooms, cleaned and sliced
2 tablespoons flour
½ teaspoon dry mustard
¼ teaspoon salt
Few grains Cayenne pepper
½ cup milk
½ teaspoon Worces-

tershire sauce
1 can (10¾ ounces) condensed tomato soup
¾ pound sharp Cheddar cheese, shredded (about 3 cups)
6 hard-cooked eggs, cut into quarters lengthwise
1 tablespoon minced parsley

1. Heat butter in cooking pan of chafing dish over medium heat. Add onion and mushrooms. Cook over medium heat, stirring occasionally, until mushrooms are tender. With a slotted spoon, remove mushrooms to a bowl; set aside.
2. Blend a mixture of flour, dry mustard, salt, and Cayenne pepper into cooking pan. Heat until mixture bubbles and remove from heat.
3. Gradually add milk, Worcestershire sauce, and condensed soup while stirring. Place cooking pan

Onion Pie with Anchovies.

Luxurious Omelet.

over simmering water. Add cheese all at once, and stir until cheese is melted.

4. Blend in the hard-cooked eggs and reserved mushrooms. Garnish with parsley and serve with toast fingers or bread sticks.

Luxurious Omelet

SERVES 4

1 medium onion, chopped	cream
6 ounces smoked ham	Salt
4 boiled potatoes, diced or sliced	Freshly ground pepper
2 tablespoons butter	1 package mixed vegetables
6 eggs	3 tomatoes, sliced
6 tablespoons light	Chopped parsley

1. Cut the ham in strips and fry it in the butter together with onion and potatoes until the onion is soft and all ingredients are lightly browned.

2. Meanwhile, boil the vegetables. Drain.

3. Beat eggs and cream, season with salt and pepper, and pour the batter on the ingredients in the frying pan. Add the vegetables and the tomatoes.

4. Cook the omelet on a low flame. Lift the omelet with a fork as it sets, allowing batter to reach the bottom of the pan and set. The omelet is ready when it has set and has a creamy surface. Sprinkle with parsley and serve straight from the pan or place omelet on a serving dish.

Serve with bread, butter, cheese, and a green salad.

Shirred Eggs with Sausage and Cheese

SERVES 6

Salami or bologna, thinly sliced	cheese, thinly sliced
2 tablespoons butter or margarine	6 eggs
Swiss or Cheddar	Salt
	Pepper
	Worcestershire sauce

1. Brown salami lightly in the butter in a skillet; reserve drippings in skillet.

2. Line a 9-inch pie plate with salami and add an even layer of cheese.

3. Break and slip eggs, one at a time, onto the cheese. Pour drippings over all. Season with salt and pepper and drizzle with Worcestershire sauce.

4. Bake at 325°F about 22 minutes, or until eggs are as firm as desired. Serve immediately with parsley-buttered toast.

233

VEGETABLES and SALADS

Fresh Vegetable Medley

SERVES 10-12

1 pound broccoli, cut in thin stalks	5 or 6 fresh mushrooms, cleaned and cut in half
1 small head cauliflower (about 1 pound), cut in flowerets	1 medium sweet red pepper, cut in strips
1 large zucchini, sliced ¼ inch thick	1 medium sweet green pepper, cut in strips
1 large crookneck squash, sliced ¼ inch thick	¼ cup butter
1 large pattypan squash, sliced ¼ inch thick	½ teaspoon garlic salt ¼ teaspoon pepper

1. In a 2-quart glass baking dish or on a large glass serving platter, arrange broccoli around edge of dish; place cauliflower next to broccoli, and squash, mushrooms, and peppers alternately near the center of the dish.
2. In a 1-cup glass measure, combine butter, garlic salt, and pepper; heat 30 to 45 seconds. Drizzle butter over vegetables.
3. Cook, covered, 15 to 20 minutes or until vegetables are done as desired, rotating dish one-quarter turn every 5 minutes.
4. Rest, covered, 5 minutes before serving.

Cooked Fresh Broccoli

SERVES 4

1 small bunch
  (1 pound) broccoli

1. Wash and remove dried leaves.
2. Add 2 tablespoons water and ½ teaspoon salt, if desired, to 1-quart glass dish.
3. Add broccoli to dish and cook, covered. Rotate dish one-quarter turn halfway through cooking time.

Chicken Salad with Lychees

SERVES 5-6

3 cups cooked diced chicken	*Dressing:*
2-3 stalks celery, chopped	¾ cup mayonnaise
1 green pepper, chopped	¼ cup sour cream
¾ cup French dressing	2 teaspoons curry powder
Salad greens	2 tablespoons grated onion
1 can lychees	2 tablespoons chopped parsley
1 small can mandarins	

1. Combine the chicken, celery, and green pepper. Add salt, pepper, and the French dressing. Toss lightly together and chill for about ½ hour.
2. Arrange salad greens around a large platter and pile the chicken mixture in the center.
3. Drain the lychees and mandarins. Place a mandarin segment in each lychee and arrange around the edge or down the center.
4. Blend all the ingredients for the dressing together and chill well. Serve the dressing separately.

Stuffed Peppers

SERVES 6

6 medium-sized red or green peppers	1 cup cooked hot rice
Butter or margarine	Salt, paprika
3 tablespoons finely chopped onion	¼ teaspoon curry powder
1½ cups ground cooked poultry or meat	1 teaspoon Worcestershire sauce
	Bread crumbs

1. Remove a slice from the stalk end of the peppers and scoop out seeds and pithy veins. Put peppers into boiling salted water, cook for about 10 minutes, then drain.

(continued)

Stuffed Peppers.

Chicken Salad with Lychees.

2. Heat 2 tablespoons butter, sauté the onion for a few minutes, add the meat, and sauté together until the onion is lightly colored.

3. Add all the other ingredients, check the seasoning, and fill the pepper cases.

4. Arrange in a greased baking pan, brush with melted butter, sprinkle with bread crumbs and, finally, sprinkle with a little more melted butter.

5. Bake for about 20 minutes.

Spinach and Mushroom Salad

SERVES 4-6

4 slices cooked bacon	²/₃ cup orange juice
1 pound fresh spinach	1 tablespoon lemon juice
2 hard-cooked eggs, finely chopped	¹/₃ cup bacon drippings
¹/₂ pound fresh mushrooms, cleaned and sliced	2 tablespoons soy sauce
2 teaspoons grated orange peel	¹/₂ teaspoon garlic powder

1. Crumble bacon into small pieces.

2. Wash spinach and remove tough stems. Dry with paper towel. Tear leaves into bite-size pieces and arrange in salad bowl.

3. Add eggs, mushrooms, and bacon. Cover tightly and refrigerate until serving time.

4. In a 1-quart glass measure, blend orange peel, orange juice, lemon juice, bacon drippings, soy sauce, and garlic powder. Cook 1 to 2 minutes, stirring every 30 seconds, until mixture boils.

5. Pour hot dressing over spinach just prior to serving.

Cabbage Pudding

SERVES 6

3 cups finely chopped cabbage	¹/₂ teaspoon salt
¹/₂ cup onions, chopped	¹/₂ teaspoon pepper
	¹/₄ pound boiled ham, chopped
1 cup cooked rice	Parsley
2 cups tomatoes	

1. Preheat oven to 325°F. Layer tomatoes and rice in the bottom of a casserole dish.

Cabbage Pudding.

2. Mix cabbage, onion, salt, pepper, and ham.

3. Place on top of tomatoes and rice. Bake for 45 minutes. Sprinkle with parsley. Serve from the bottom of the dish.

Serve with sliced salami or liverwurst.

Butter-Sauced Asparagus

SERVES ABOUT 6

2 pounds fresh asparagus, washed, or 2 packages (10 ounces each) frozen asparagus spears, cooked	¹/₄ cup chopped pecans
	¹/₄ cup finely chopped celery
	1 tablespoon lemon juice
¹/₄ cup butter	

1. Put fresh asparagus into a small amount of boiling salted water in a skillet, bring to boiling, reduce heat, and cook 5 minutes, uncovered; cover and cook 10 minutes, or until just tender.

2. Meanwhile, heat butter in a small saucepan. Add pecans and celery and cook 5 minutes. Stir in lemon juice. Pour over asparagus and serve immediately.

Broccoli Florentine

SERVES 4

1 pound broccoli, washed and trimmed	2 cloves garlic, sliced thin
2 tablespoons olive oil	¹/₄ teaspoon salt
	¹/₄ teaspoon pepper

1. Split the heavy broccoli stalks (over ¹/₂ inch thick) lengthwise through stalks up to flowerets. Put into a small amount of boiling salted water. Cook, uncovered, 5 minutes, then cover and cook 10 to 15 minutes, or until broccoli is just tender.

2. Meanwhile, heat oil and garlic in a large skillet until garlic is lightly browned.

3. Drain broccoli and add to skillet; turn to coat with oil. Cook about 10 minutes, stirring occasionally. Season with salt and pepper. Serve hot.

Broccoli Roman Style: Follow recipe for Broccoli Florentine. Omit cooking broccoli in boiling water. Cook broccoli in oil only 5 minutes. Add 1¹/₂ **cups dry red wine** to skillet. Cook, covered, over low heat about 20 minutes, or until broccoli is tender; stir occasionally.

Spinach Sautéed in Oil: Follow recipe for Broccoli Florentine; substitute **2 cups chopped cooked spinach** for broccoli. Add spinach, **1 tablespoon chopped pinenuts or almonds,** and **1 tablespoon raisins** to oil mixture.

Cold Shellfish Salad.

Red Cabbage Casserole.

Cold Shellfish Salad

SERVES 4

1 cup long-grain rice	1 tablespoon lemon
2 tablespoons butter	juice
1 small yellow onion,	3 tablespoons salad
finely chopped	oil
2 (8-ounce) bottles	1½ ounces dill, finely
clam juice	chopped
¾ pound mussels	*Garnish:*
1 pound shrimp	Lemon wedges
Dressing:	Dill sprigs
1 can anchovy fillets	

1. Sauté onion in butter till transparent. Add the rice and clam juice. Simmer, covered, for 25 minutes until all liquid is absorbed.
2. Mash the anchovy fillets and mix with lemon juice, salad oil, and dill. Pour dressing on the rice and mix well. Place the rice in a cold place for a few hours.
3. Clean the mussels; shell and devein the shrimp. Cook the shrimp in a large pot of boiling water for 5 minutes or until they turn pink. Cook the mussels separately in a large pot of boiling water for 6-8 minutes till the shells open.
4. Mix the shellfish with the rice and arrange on a serving dish. Serve with a bowl of cherry tomatoes or tomato wedges and hot French bread.

Red Cabbage Casserole

SERVES 4

½ package bacon,	1 apple, chopped
chopped	2 cups beef bouillon
½ head red cabbage,	White pepper
shredded	½ teaspoon salt
1 leek, chopped	

1. In a large heavy saucepan, brown bacon, add cabbage and onion, and cook 5-10 minutes.
2. Cook apple in bouillon and add to cabbage. Cook, covered, about 10 minutes.
Serve casserole as it is or with rice or sausages.

Asparagus Parmesan

SERVES ABOUT 6

1½ pounds asparagus	cheese
½ cup butter, melted	1 teaspoon salt
½ cup grated Parme-	½ teaspoon pepper
san or Romano	

1. Wash asparagus. Put into a small amount of boiling salted water in a skillet. Bring to boiling, reduce heat, and cook 5 minutes, uncovered; cover and cook 10 minutes, or until just tender.
2. Pour melted butter into a greased 1½-quart casserole. Put cooked asparagus into casserole and

Barbecued Corn.

sprinkle with mixture of grated cheese, salt, and pepper.

3. Bake at 450°F 5 to 10 minutes, or until cheese is melted.

Eggplant Casserole

SERVES 4-6

1 eggplant (about 1¹/₂ pounds)	2 cans (8 ounces each) tomato sauce
Salt	1 cup thinly sliced
Flour	mozzarella cheese
¹/₂ cup salad oil for skillet	¹/₂ cup grated Parmesan cheese

1. Peel eggplant and cut in ¹/₂-inch-thick slices. Sprinkle both sides with salt, and set aside 20 to 30 minutes.
2. Dip eggplant slices in flour. Brown eggplant in hot microwave browning dish or in hot salad oil in hot skillet on a conventional range. Drain slices on paper towel.
3. Pour 1 can tomato sauce in a 10-inch glass baking dish. Lay eggplant slices in sauce, and cover with other can of sauce. Place mozzarella cheese

over the sauce and sprinkle Parmesan cheese on top.

4. Cover with waxed paper or lid. Cook 12 to 14 minutes, rotating dish one-quarter turn halfway through cooking time.
5. Rest, covered, 5 minutes.

Barbecued Corn

SERVES 4

4 fresh or quick-
frozen corn on the
cob

1. Remove husk and silk from the corn and spread generously with softened butter.
2. Sprinkle with salt and pepper and wrap each cob in double thickness of foil, or use heavy-duty foil. Twist the ends to seal.
3. Place on the grid of the barbecue over the hot coals and cook for about 20 minutes, turning frequently.

Note: If using frozen corn, less time will be required for cooking.

Acorn Squash

SERVES 2

1 small acorn squash	sugar
1¹/₂ tablespoons butter	¹/₄ teaspoon salt
1¹/₂ teaspoons brown	¹/₈ teaspoon ginger

1. Pierce squash and place whole on dish or rack. Cook, 6 to 8 minutes, rotating dish one-quarter turn and turning squash over halfway through cooking time.
2. When done, cut in half and remove seeds.
3. Divide butter, brown sugar, salt, and ginger in squash cavities. Cover with plastic wrap.
4. Cook in microwave oven at high temperature for 2 minutes. Allow to stand 5 minutes before serving.

Parsley-Buttered New Potatoes

SERVES ABOUT 6

18 small new potatoes	2 tablespoons butter
Boiling water	1 tablespoon snipped
1¹/₂ teaspoons salt	parsley

1. Scrub potatoes and put into a saucepan.
2. Pour in boiling water to a 1-inch depth. Add salt; cover and cook about 15 minutes, or until tender. Drain and peel.
3. Return potatoes to saucepan and toss with butter and parsley.

Wilted Lettuce

SERVES ABOUT 8

1 large head lettuce	2 tablespoons heavy
6 slices bacon, diced	cream
¹/₂ cup water	1 tablespoon sugar
¹/₄ cup cider vinegar	¹/₄ teaspoon salt

1. Tear lettuce into pieces into a bowl; set aside.
2. Fry bacon until crisp in a skillet; reserve ¹/₄ cup drippings. Drain bacon on absorbent paper; set aside.
3. Stir the remaining ingredients into drippings in skillet. Heat mixture just to boiling, stirring constantly.
4. Immediately pour vinegar mixture over the lettuce and toss lightly to coat thoroughly. Top with the bacon.

Green Salad

SERVES ABOUT 6

1 large head lettuce, or an equal amount of another salad green (curly endive, romaine, escarole,	chicory, or dandelion greens)
	1 clove garlic
	Italian Dressing (below)

1. Wash lettuce in cold water, removing core, separating leaves, and removing any bruised leaves. Drain; dry thoroughly and carefully. Tear lettuce into bite-size pieces, put into a plastic bag, and chill 1 hour.
2. Just before serving, cut garlic in half and rub a wooden bowl. Put greens in bowl and pour on desired amount of dressing. Turn and toss the greens until well coated with dressing and no dressing remains in the bottom of the bowl.

Mixed Salad: Follow recipe for Green Salad. Add ¹/₄ **cup chopped cucumber,** ¹/₄ **cup chopped celery,** ¹/₄ **cup sliced radishes,** and ¹/₄ **cup chopped ripe olives** to lettuce before tossing with dressing.

Italian Dressing

ABOUT 1¹/₂ CUPS DRESSING

6 tablespoons olive oil	crushed in a garlic
3 tablespoons wine vinegar	press
	¹/₄ teaspoon salt
1 clove garlic,	¹/₈ teaspoon pepper

1. Place all ingredients in a screw-top jar, shake well, and chill.
2. Just before serving, beat or shake thoroughly.

Anchovy Dressing: Follow recipe for Italian Dressing. Add **1 teaspoon prepared mustard** and **2 finely chopped anchovy fillets** to jar before shaking.

Green Beans with Onion Rings

SERVES 6

1 cup water	beans sliced
1 onion, thinly sliced	¹/₂ cup butter
2 pounds green beans, ends snipped off and	Salt and pepper to taste
	Lemon juice to taste

1. Bring water to boiling.

2. Separate onion slices into rings and add. Add green beans, butter, salt, pepper, and lemon juice.
3. Boil until beans are tender (about 20 minutes).

Baked Carrots au Gratin

SERVES 8

3 pounds carrots, blanched and sliced
1 small onion, minced
2 cups light cream
½ cup Cheddar

cheese, grated
½ cup all-purpose flour
1 tablespoon butter
⅛ teaspoon nutmeg

1. Sauté the onion in butter for 4-5 minutes over low heat.
2. Slowly add the flour and light cream, stirring constantly until mixture is smooth.
3. Mash the carrots in a food processor or force through a medium sieve.
4. Mix the onion mixture with the carrots and nutmeg and put the mixture in a shallow baking dish. Sprinkle with grated Cheddar cheese and bake in a preheated 325°F oven for 30-35 minutes.

Serve with salami and cheese or tongue.

Stuffed Vegetables

SERVES 6

6 turnips, kohlrabi, cucumbers, or celery roots (about 1½ pounds)
2 cups boiling water or chicken broth
1½ teaspoons salt
½ teaspoon sugar (optional)
¼ pound ground beef or pork

¼ cup sliced mushrooms
¼ cup chopped onion
1 tablespoon grated Parmesan cheese (optional)
¼ teaspoon salt
⅛ teaspoon pepper
1 egg, beaten
2 tablespoons fine dry bread crumbs

1. Trim and pare vegetables. Cook in boiling water with 1½ teaspoons salt and sugar, if desired, until tender.
2. Scoop out centers of vegetables until a thick, hollow shell is left.
3. Fry ground beef with mushrooms and onion in a skillet until onion is golden. Add cheese, salt, and pepper; mix well. Remove from heat. Blend in egg.
4. Mash scooped-out portion of vegetables. Combine with meat mixture. *(continued)*

Baked Carrots au Gratin.

5. Fill vegetable shells with stuffing. Sprinkle bread crumbs on top.
6. Place stuffed vegetables in a shallow casserole or baking dish.
7. Bake at 400°F 10 to 15 minutes, or until lightly browned on top.

Beans Plaki

SERVES ABOUT 12

3 cups dried white beans	tomato sauce
½ cup olive oil	2 celery stalks, diced
2 medium onions, chopped	1 carrot, diced
2 garlic cloves, crushed in a garlic press	1 bay leaf
	1 teaspoon oregano
	1 teaspoon sugar
1 can (8 ounces)	Salt and pepper to taste
	Wine vinegar

1. Place beans in a pot and cover with water. Bring to a boil. Simmer covered 2 to 3 hours, until just tender. Drain.
2. Heat oil in a saucepan, add onion, and cook until translucent. Add garlic, tomato sauce, celery, carrot, bay leaf, oregano, sugar, salt, and pepper. Simmer 5 minutes. (If sauce is too thick, add a little water.)
3. Add beans to sauce and simmer, covered, about 20 minutes, or until tender.
4. Serve hot or cold with a cruet of wine vinegar.

Braised Leeks au Gratin.

Braised Leeks au Gratin

SERVES 4

2 pounds leeks	purpose flour
2 tablespoons butter	1 cup milk
1 egg	¼ pound Cheddar cheese, diced
2 tablespoons all-	

1. Clean and wash leeks and cook in water over low heat for about 30 minutes.
2. In a separate saucepan, melt the butter and combine the egg, milk, and flour, stirring over low heat until thoroughly blended.
3. Put the cooked leeks in an ovenproof dish, pour on the sauce, and top with the Cheddar cheese.
4. Bake in a preheated 325°F oven for 15-20 minutes. Remove, let cool, and serve.

Yams or Sweet Potatoes

1 YAM OR SWEET POTATO PER PERSON

Yams or sweet potatoes	Salt
	Butter (optional)

Boil yams and serve plain sprinkled with salt and, if desired, topped with butter. Or barbecue yams on a grill 4 inches from ash-covered coals, turning frequently, until soft. Or bake yams until tender.

Mixed Vegetable Salad

SERVES ABOUT 8

1 cup diced cooked potatoes	salad dressing
	Lettuce
1½ cups cooked sliced carrots	1 cup sliced celery
1½ cups cooked whole or cut green beans (fresh, frozen, or canned)	1 small onion, chopped
	2 hard-cooked eggs, chopped
1½ cups cooked green peas (fresh, frozen, or canned)	¾ cup small pimiento-stuffed olives
	¾ cup mayonnaise
1 cup sliced or diced cooked beets	¼ cup chili sauce
Bottled Italian-style	1 teaspoon lemon juice

1. Put potatoes, carrots, beans, peas, and beets into separate bowls. Pour salad dressing over each vegetable; chill thoroughly.
2. To serve, drain vegetables and arrange in a let-

Ratatouille Salad.

tuce-lined salad bowl along with celery, onion, eggs, and olives.
3. Blend mayonnaise, chili sauce, and lemon juice. Pass with the salad.

Ratatouille Salad

SERVES 4

2 eggplants	small pieces
A little coarse salt	4 tomatoes, peeled
Olive oil, about	and chopped
¹/₂ cup	2 cloves garlic,
1 onion, peeled and	crushed
chopped	12 coriander seeds
1 large red pepper,	Chopped basil or
seeded and cut into	parsley

1. Wipe the eggplants, cut into ¹/₂-inch squares, and put into a colander. Sprinkle with coarse salt and leave to drain.
2. Heat some of the oil in a skillet and sauté the onion for about 10 minutes or until it begins to soften. Add a little more oil, put in the eggplant and red pepper, cover, and simmer for 30-40 minutes.
3. Add tomatoes, garlic, and coriander and continue to cook until the tomatoes are soft and mushy, adding a little more oil if necessary. Adjust the seasoning, then chill.
4. Drain off any excess oil and sprinkle with basil or parsley.

Creamed Corn Casserole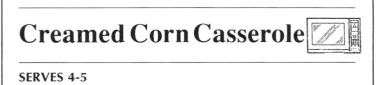

SERVES 4-5

2 tablespoons butter	1 can (17 ounces)
1 egg	cream-style corn
¹/₃ cup soda cracker	¹/₂ teaspoon salt
crumbs	¹/₄ teaspoon pepper

1. In a 1-quart glass casserole, heat butter 30 seconds. Add egg, cracker crumbs, corn, salt, and pepper; blend evenly.
2. Cook 4 to 6 minutes, stirring halfway through cooking time.
3. Rest 5 minutes before serving.

Macaroni Salad.

Cucumber Salad

SERVES 6-8

2 medium-size (about 1¼ pounds) cucumbers, washed and pared	½ teaspoon sugar
	¼ teaspoon paprika
	¼ teaspoon pepper
2 teaspoons salt	½ clove garlic, minced
3 tablespoons vinegar	¼ teaspoon paprika
3 tablespoons water	

1. Slice cucumbers thinly into a bowl.
2. Sprinkle salt over the cucumber slices.
3. Mix lightly and set cucumbers aside for 1 hour.
4. Meanwhile, mix vinegar, water, sugar, ¼ teaspoon paprika, pepper, and garlic together and set aside.
5. Squeeze cucumber slices, a few at a time (discarding liquid), and put into a bowl. Pour the vinegar mixture over the cucumbers and toss lightly. Sprinkle ¼ teaspoon paprika onto cucumbers.
6. Chill the salad in refrigerator for 1 to 2 hours.

Cucumber Salad with Sour Cream: Follow recipe for Cucumber Salad. Blend in 1 cup **thick sour cream** after the vinegar mixture.

Cucumber Salad with Onions: Follow recipe for Cucumber Salad or variation. Omit garlic. Cut off root ends from 3 or 4 fresh **green onions or scallions.** Trim green tops down to 2- or 3-inches, removing any wilted or bruised parts; peel and rinse. Slice onions by holding on hard surface and cutting across all with sharp knife. Add sliced onions to cucumber slices before adding the vinegar mixture.

Macaroni Salad

SERVES 6

2 cups shell or ring macaroni	½ cup very finely chopped onion
2 tablespoons butter	2 cups cooked peas
1 cup cubed Cheddar cheese	½ cup mayonnaise
1 cup sliced gherkins	Seasoning
	Lettuce

1. Cook the macaroni in boiling salted water, drain well, add the butter, and toss lightly.
2. Add cheese, gherkins, onion, and peas.
3. Stir in the mayonnaise and blend carefully, making sure the macaroni is well mixed with the mayonnaise.
4. Check the seasoning and set aside to chill.
5. Serve individually in lettuce leaves or on a bed of shredded lettuce.

Austrian Potato Stew.

Soy Pilaf with Fresh Vegetables

SERVES 4-6

1½ cups chopped
   onion
½ cup soy grits or
   granules *(see Note)*
1 small eggplant,
   pared and cut in
   ½-inch cubes
1½ cups Chicken
   Stock*
½ teaspoon curry
   powder
¼ teaspoon salt
½ teaspoon paprika
½ teaspoon cumin
¼ teaspoon chili
   powder

⅛ teaspoon garlic
   powder
¼ teaspoon salt
2 medium tomatoes,
   chopped
1 green onion,
   chopped
1½ tablespoons
   lemon juice
¼ teaspoon salt
⅛ teaspoon freshly
   ground pepper
1 tablespoon snipped
   parsley

*Check index for
   recipe

1. Spread onion in a 9 × 5 × 2-inch baking dish; sprinkle with soy. Layer eggplant over top. Mix stock with curry, salt, paprika, cumin, chili powder, and garlic; pour over eggplant.
2. Bake covered at 350°F 1 hour. Mound mixture on a serving platter; sprinkle with ¼ teaspoon salt.

3. While eggplant mixture is baking, mix tomatoes and remaining ingredients in a small bowl. Refrigerate covered. Spoon around pilaf on platter.

Note: Soy grits can be purchased in specialty or health food stores. They have a flavor similar to cracked wheat. Cracked wheat can be used in this recipe. You will need 2 cups cooked cracked wheat; cook according to package directions.

Austrian Potato Stew

SERVES 4

8 medium potatoes
4 ounces smoked ham
1 large finely chopped
   yellow onion
1 tablespoon flour
1½ cups Beef Stock*
1 tablespoon wine
   vinegar
½ teaspoon salt
Freshly ground
   pepper

1 bay leaf
½ teaspoon marjo-
   ram or thyme
1 tablespoon capers
Grated rind of
   ¼ lemon
Parsley
Watercress

*Check index for
   recipe

1. Boil the potatoes in their skins for about 8 minutes.

(continued)

2. Peel and cut into ¹/₂-inch thick slices.

3. Cut ham in strips or cubes.

4. Brown the ham and the onion over low heat while stirring. Sprinkle in the flour and add the stock.

5. Add wine vinegar, salt, pepper, marjoram or thyme, grated lemon rind, and capers.

6. Taste and correct seasoning of the stew, if necessary, and add the potato slices and bay leaf.

7. Boil potatoes until soft and serve the dish piping hot, sprinkled with parsley or watercress.

Sweet-and-Sour Cabbage

SERVES 4-6

1 small onion, chopped	1 small tart apple, cored and diced
3 tablespoons butter	3 tablespoons vinegar
1 cup meat stock or water	1 tablespoon brown sugar
1 small head cabbage, shredded	¹/₄ teaspoon allspice
	¹/₂ teaspoon salt

1. In a 2-quart glass casserole, sauté onion in butter 2 minutes, stirring after 1 minute. Stir in stock, cabbage, and apple.

2. Cover casserole and cook 6 to 8 minutes, stirring halfway through cooking time.

3. Add vinegar, brown sugar, allspice, and salt to cabbage; mix well. Cook 3 to 4 minutes.

4. Rest, covered, 5 minutes before serving.

Rainbow Salad

SERVES 4

¹/₄ pound cooked ham, diced	juice
	Lettuce
1 cup cottage cheese	2 hard-cooked eggs
Pinch of Cayenne pepper	Parsley or watercress
¹/₄ teaspoon salt	*Dressing:*
¹/₂ cucumber	¹/₂ cup yogurt
4 stalks celery, chopped	1 teaspoon lemon juice
2 red dessert apples, cored and chopped but not peeled	Pinch of garlic salt
	1 teaspoon prepared mustard
2 carrots, grated	Black pepper, paprika
2 tablespoons lemon	

1. Combine the ham, cottage cheese, pepper, and salt.

2. Arrange thin slices of cucumber around the edge

of a large platter and cut the rest into ¹/₄ inch dice.

3. Put the diced cucumber, celery, apples, and carrots into a bowl, add the lemon juice, and mix well. Arrange on the platter, put lettuce leaves in the center, and place the ham and cheese mixture on top.

4. Cut the eggs in halves lengthwise and arrange on top. Place a sprig of parsley or watercress in the center.

5. Serve with the dressing.

Smothered Mixed Vegetables

SERVES 8

8 small carrots, sliced	oil
8 small potatoes	1 large Spanish onion, sliced
4 medium white turnips, pared and sliced	1 cup Beef Stock*
	¹/₄ cup peanut oil
4 medium tomatoes, peeled, seeded, and quartered	1 tablespoon salt
	Freshly ground pepper
2 small chayote or zucchini, sliced	1 garlic clove, crushed in a garlic press
1 green and 1 red sweet pepper, cut in strips	4 dried Italian pepper pods or 1 pink hot pepper
1 small eggplant (unpeeled), diced	1 tablespoon tomato paste
Cauliflower chunks	
¹/₂ cup green peas	*Check index for recipe
¹/₂ cup lima beans	
2 tablespoons peanut	

1. Arrange in a top-of-range casserole with lid the sliced carrot, potatoes, turnip slices, tomato quarters, sliced chayote, pepper strips, diced eggplant, cauliflower chunks, peas, and beans.

2. Heat 2 tablespoons oil in a skillet over medium heat. Add onion and sauté until golden. Add stock, ¹/₄ cup oil, salt, pepper, and garlic; pour over vegetables in casserole. Lay pepper pods over vegetables; cover and cook over low heat 45 minutes.

3. Remove cover, increase heat, and cook off most of the liquid. Remove peppers and stir tomato paste into vegetable mixture. Serve with pepper steak or well-browned spareribs or pork chops.

Rainbow Salad.

Red Cabbage with Apples.

Red Cabbage with Apples

SERVES 6-8

1 head red cabbage
  (about 3 pounds)
4 cooking apples
1 tablespoon cider
  vinegar

2 tablespoons brown
  sugar
1 teaspoon salt
1/2 cup water

1. Core cabbage and shred coarsely.
2. Peel and core apples and slice in thin strips.
3. Pour water into a large pot; add salt and then cabbage, apples, vinegar, and sugar.
4. Cook rapidly for 6-8 minutes, drain, and serve.

Red Kidney Bean Salad

SERVES ABOUT 4

1 can (16 ounces)
  kidney beans
1/4 cup wine vinegar
3 tablespoons olive oil
1/4 teaspoon oregano
1/4 teaspoon salt

1/8 teaspoon pepper
1/4 cup sliced celery
2 tablespoons
  chopped onion
Lettuce cups

1. Thoroughly rinse and drain kidney beans.
2. Combine vinegar, oil, oregano, salt, and pepper; mix with beans. Blend in celery and onion; chill.
3. Serve in crisp lettuce cups.

Spinach Casserole

SERVES 8-12

4 packages (10 ounces each) frozen spinach, defrosted	taste
	2 tablespoons dill weed
7 slices day-old whole wheat bread with crusts removed	1 tablespoon oregano
	1/2 teaspoon cinnamon
Water	1 tablespoon mint
1/4 cup olive oil	6 eggs, beaten
3 garlic cloves, crushed in a garlic press	3/4 cup grated kefalotyri cheese
	1 1/2 cups water or chicken broth
2 bunches scallions, minced	1 cup freshly toasted coarse bread crumbs
1 leek, minced	
1/2 pound mushrooms	Olive oil
Salt and pepper to	

1. Squeeze excess liquid from spinach. Sprinkle bread slices with water. Squeeze water out.
2. Heat olive oil in a large skillet. Sauté garlic, scallions, leek, and mushrooms for 3 minutes. Remove from heat. Add salt, pepper, dill, oregano, cinnamon, mint, and spinach. Sauté the mixture for 3 minutes. Add bread, eggs, cheese, and water; mix well.
3. Oil a 3 1/2-quart baking dish and sprinkle bottom with bread crumbs. Pour in the spinach mixture.
4. Bake at 350°F 40 to 50 minutes, or until mixture is firm.

Salade Niçoise

SERVES 6-8

Salad Dressing (below)	tuna, drained
	1 mild onion, quartered and thinly sliced
3 medium-sized cooked potatoes, sliced	
	2 ripe tomatoes, cut in wedges
1 package (9 ounces) frozen green beans, cooked	2 hard-cooked eggs, quartered
1 clove garlic, cut in half	1 can (2 ounces) rolled anchovy fillets, drained
1 small head Boston lettuce	
	3/4 cup pitted ripe olives
2 cans (6 1/2 or 7 ounces each)	1 tablespoon capers

1. Pour enough salad dressing over warm potato slices and cooked beans (in separate bowls) to coat vegetables.
2. Before serving, rub the inside of a large shallow salad bowl with the cut surface of the garlic. Line the bowl or a large serving platter with the lettuce.
3. Unmold the tuna in center of bowl and separate into chunks.
4. Arrange separate mounds of the potatoes, green beans, onion, tomatoes, and hard-cooked eggs in colorful grouping around the tuna. Garnish with anchovies, olives, and capers.
5. Pour dressing over all before serving.

Salad Dressing: Combine in a jar or bottle 1/2 cup olive oil or **salad oil, 2 tablespoons red wine vinegar,** a mixture of **1 teaspoon salt, 1/2 teaspoon pepper,** and **1 teaspoon dry mustard, 1 tablespoon finely chopped chives,** and **1 tablespoon finely chopped parsley.** Shake vigorously to blend well before pouring over salad.
About 2/3 Cup

Fried Artichoke Hearts

SERVES 4

3/4 cup beer	3/4 cup all-purpose flour
1/2 teaspoon salt	
1 egg, beaten	Oil for deep frying
8 canned artichoke hearts	

1. Mix beer, salt, and egg.
2. Dip artichokes in beer batter, then in flour.
3. Fry in hot oil for 5 minutes until brown all over.
4. Drain on paper towels and serve hot with lemon wedges.

Cauliflower au Gratin

SERVES 3-4

1/2 cup butter	1/4 cup seasoned bread crumbs
1 medium head cauliflower, cut in flowerets	
	1/4 cup grated Parmesan cheese
1/4 teaspoon garlic salt	
1/4 teaspoon salt	1/2 cup shredded Swiss cheese
1/4 teaspoon pepper	
2 large tomatoes, cut in wedges	

1. In a 1 1/2-quart glass casserole, heat butter 30 seconds. Add cauliflower, garlic salt, salt, and pepper, and stir to coat cauliflower with butter.
2. Cover cauliflower and cook 5 to 6 minutes, rotating dish one-quarter turn halfway through cooking time.
3. Arrange tomatoes on top of cauliflower and cook 2 minutes. *(continued)*

249

4. Add bread crumbs, Parmesan cheese, and Swiss cheese. Cook 1 to 2 minutes until cheese begins to melt.
5. Rest, covered, 5 minutes before serving.

Shrimp and Avocado Salad

SERVES ABOUT 8

1 cup wine vinegar	tard
1/3 cup water	1 teaspoon thyme, crushed
1/2 cup lemon juice	
1 cup salad oil	1 teaspoon oregano, crushed
1/4 cup chopped parsley	
	2 pounds large cooked shrimp, peeled and deveined
2 cloves garlic, minced	
1 tablespoon salt	
1/4 teaspoon freshly ground black pepper	3 small onions, sliced
	1/3 cup chopped green pepper
1 tablespoon sugar	2 ripe avocados, peeled and sliced
1 teaspoon dry mus-	

1. For marinade, combine vinegar, water, lemon juice, oil, parsley, and garlic in a bowl or a screwtop jar. Add a mixture of salt, pepper, sugar, dry mustard, thyme, and oregano; blend thoroughly.
2. Put shrimp, onions, and green pepper into a large shallow dish. Pour marinade over all, cover and refrigerate 8 hours or overnight.
3. About 1 hour before serving, put avocado slices into bowl. Pour enough marinade from shrimp over the avocado to cover completely.
4. To serve, remove avocado slices and shrimp from marinade and arrange on crisp lettuce in a large serving bowl.

Orange-Glazed Carrots

SERVES 6-8

6 to 8 medium carrots, pared and diagonally sliced	juice
	1 teaspoon grated orange peel
2 tablespoons butter	1 teaspoon lemon juice
1/4 cup brown sugar	
2 tablespoons orange	1/4 teaspoon salt

1. In a 1 1/2-quart glass casserole, combine carrots, butter, brown sugar, orange juice, orange peel, lemon juice, and salt.
2. Cover carrots and cook 10 to 12 minutes, stirring halfway through cooking time.
3. Rest, covered, 10 minutes before serving.

Marinated Fruit Salad

SERVES 8

2 apples	Confectioners' sugar
3 pears	1/4 cup rum or Cointreau
3 peaches	
1 pineapple	

1. Pare, core, and slice apples and pears. Halve, pit, peel, and slice peaches. Cut pineapple into chunks.
2. Place fruit in a bowl and sprinkle with confectioners' sugar to taste. Sprinkle with rum or Cointreau.
3. Cover the bowl tightly and chill for at least 6 hours so the sugar draws out fruit juices.

Zesty Beets

SERVES ABOUT 4

1 can or jar (16 ounces) small whole beets	pared horseradish
	1/2 teaspoon prepared mustard
2 tablespoons butter or margarine	1/2 teaspoon seasoned salt
2 tablespoons pre-	

1. Heat beets in liquid; drain.
2. Add butter, horseradish, prepared mustard, and seasoned salt; stir gently.

Potato Pancakes with Meat Filling

SERVES 4

7-8 potatoes	1 can mushrooms, chopped
1 large onion	
1-2 eggs	Leftover sauce (optional)
Water or milk	
1 teaspoon salt	*Garnish:*
Black pepper	1/4 cup grated cheese
Filling:	
3/4-1 1/4 cups leftover meat	

1. Peel and chop potatoes and onion. Mix with eggs and add water or milk if mixture looks dry. Season with salt and pepper.
2. Make patties out of mixture.
3. Brown meat with chopped mushrooms. Add juice from mushrooms and leftover sauce. Season with salt and pepper.

4. Add filling to pancakes and bake in a 475°F oven for 10 minutes till brown.
5. Serve as is or sprinkle with grated cheese.

Potato Pancakes with Meat Filling.

Cauliflower Pudding

SERVES 6

1 cup Chicken Stock*	**¹/₂ teaspoon lemon**
¹/₂ cup cream	**juice**
4 eggs	**1¹/₂ cups cooked**
¹/₂ teaspoon paprika	**cauliflower,**
¹/₂ teaspoon celery	**chopped**
salt	***Check index for**
1 tablespoon parsley,	**recipe**
chopped	

1. Preheat oven to 325°F.
2. Beat all ingredients except cauliflower with a wire whisk until well blended.
3. Add well-chopped cauliflower to mixture and pour into a well-greased mold or baking dish, ²/₃ full. Place on a rack in a roasting pan of hot water. Fill water as high as mixture in mold. Bake for 20-50 minutes till a knife inserted in the center comes out clean.

Serve with cold cuts.

Cauliflower Pudding.

Baked Stuffed Peppers.

Baked Stuffed Peppers

SERVES 4

3 large green peppers	**1 (1-pound) can**
Stuffing:	**peeled tomatoes**
¹/₂ pound boned neck	**3 ounces chopped**
of lamb in small	**parsley**
cubes	**Salt**
2 bacon strips	**Pepper**
1 chopped yellow	**¹/₂ teaspoon oregano**
onion	**¹/₂ teaspoon basil**
3 cubes beef bouillon	*For Frying:*
1 cup parboiled	**1¹/₂ tablespoons**
mushrooms	**butter**

1. Wash the peppers, cut in halves, and remove all seeds.
2. Fry lamb cubes, bacon strips, and chopped onion in the butter. Add tomatoes, mushrooms, parsley, and bouillon. Season and simmer for about 15 minutes.
3. Distribute the stuffing in the pepper halves and place them in an ovenproof dish. Dot with butter and pour on the liquid from the canned tomatoes.
4. Bake in a 400°F oven for about 30 minutes, basting with the tomato liquid a few times.

Serve with boiled rice or potatoes.

Garbanzo Salad

SERVES ABOUT 6

1 can (15 ounces) garbanzos, drained	3 green onions, chopped
1/4 cup chopped parsley	1/4 cup wine vinegar
1 can or jar (4 ounces) pimientos, drained and chopped	2 tablespoons olive or salad oil
	1 teaspoon salt
	1/2 teaspoon sugar
	1/4 teaspoon pepper

Combine all ingredients in a bowl; cover and refrigerate until chilled.

Baked Beans

SERVES 8

1 1/2 pounds dried navy beans	1/2 teaspoon salt
3/4 pound salt pork	1/4 cup brown sugar
1 medium yellow onion	2 teaspoons dry mustard
	1 cup light molasses

1. Wash beans and cover with 2 quarts of cold water. Refrigerate overnight, covered.
2. Place beans and water in a large kettle. Bring to a boil. Reduce heat to simmer and cook, covered, for 30 minutes. Drain. Reserve liquid.
3. Preheat oven to 300°F.
4. Trim rind from salt pork and cut into 1-inch cubes.
5. Chop onion and place in casserole. Add beans, pork, and 1 1/2 cups reserved liquid, mustard, and molasses. Cover and cook for 6 hours. Stir every hour.
6. Remove cover a half hour before baking time is up.

Creamed Green Beans

SERVES 6-8

1 jar (8 ounces) pasteurized process cheese spread	5 fresh mushrooms, cleaned and chopped
1 can (10 1/2 ounces) condensed cream of mushroom soup	1 can (8 ounces) water chestnuts, drained and sliced
Tabasco	2 cans (16 ounces each) French-style green beans, drained
1 tablespoon soy sauce	
1 medium onion, chopped	Slivered almonds
3 tablespoons butter	

1. In a 4-cup glass measure, blend cheese spread, soup, Tabasco, and soy sauce. Cook 3 to 5 minutes, stirring halfway through cooking time.
2. In a 1 1/2-quart glass casserole, cook onion and butter 3 to 4 minutes, stirring halfway through cooking time until onions are transparent. Stir in mushrooms and water chestnuts and cook 1 minute.

Baked Beans.

Fruity Cole Slaw.

3. Add green beans and soup mixture to mushroom mixture; stir to blend. Garnish with almonds.
4. Cook 5 minutes, rotating dish one-quarter turn halfway through cooking time.
5. Rest 5 minutes before serving.

Fruity Cole Slaw

SERVES 4-5

1 lettuce	$^{1}/_{2}$ cup chopped celery
3 cups finely shredded cabbage	10 marshmallows
1 can pineapple pieces (about 1 cup), drained and chopped	2 dessert apples
	Lemon juice
	$^{1}/_{2}$ cup mayonnaise

1. Line a bowl with the lettuce.
2. Mix the cabbage, pineapple, celery, and marshmallows, cut into pieces. Peel, core, and chop one apple and add to the cabbage mixture.
3. Core but do not peel the second apple, cut into slices, and brush with lemon juice.
4. Add mayonnaise to the cabbage mixture, toss all together lightly, and put into the bowl.
5. Garnish with the apple slices.
This goes well with barbecued ham or pork.

Mushrooms Parmesan

SERVES 6-8

1 pound mushrooms with 1- to 2-inch caps	crumbs
	3 tablespoons grated Parmesan cheese
2 tablespoons olive oil	1 tablespoon chopped parsley
$^{1}/_{4}$ cup chopped onion	
$^{1}/_{2}$ clove garlic, finely chopped	$^{1}/_{2}$ teaspoon salt
	$^{1}/_{8}$ teaspoon oregano
$^{1}/_{3}$ cup fine dry bread	2 tablespoons olive oil

1. Clean mushrooms and remove stems. Place caps open-end up in a shallow greased 1$^{1}/_{2}$-quart baking dish; set aside. Finely chop mushroom stems.
2. Heat 2 tablespoons olive oil in a skillet. Add mushroom stems, onion, and garlic. Cook slowly until onion and garlic are slightly browned.
3. Combine bread crumbs, cheese, parsley, salt, and oregano. Mix in the onion, garlic, and mushroom stems. Lightly fill mushroom caps with mixture. Pour 2 tablespoons olive oil into the baking dish.
4. Bake at 400°F 15 to 20 minutes, or until mushrooms are tender and tops are browned.

Anchovy-Stuffed Mushrooms: Follow recipe for Mushrooms Parmesan. Omit cheese. Mix in **4 anchovy fillets,** finely chopped.

Braised Cucumbers

SERVES 8

1/4 cup parsley, cleaned and trimmed (2 tablespoons chopped)	Salt and pepper to taste
	Pinch sugar
2 medium onions, peeled and quartered	2 tablespoons lemon juice
	1 teaspoon dried dill
4 tablespoons butter	1/2 cup sour cream
6 large cucumbers	Dash nutmeg
2 tablespoons flour	*Check index for recipe
1/2 cup Chicken Stock*	

1. Using **steel blade of food processor,** separately process parsley and onions until chopped. Set aside.
2. In a saucepan, sauté chopped onion in butter until transparent.
3. Pare cucumbers, cut in half lengthwise, and remove seeds. Cut into 3-inch lengths.
4. Add cucumbers to sautéed onions and cook until lightly browned. Add flour and cook for 2 minutes. Add chicken stock, salt, pepper, sugar, and lemon juice. Sprinkle with chopped parsley and dill and simmer for 10 minutes. Just before serving, add sour cream and nutmeg. Bring to a boil and reduce heat. Simmer for 5 minutes.

Apple-Stuffed Acorn Squash

SERVES 4

2 acorn squash	1/3 cup firmly packed brown sugar
2 tart apples	
1 1/2 teaspoons grated fresh lemon peel	Salt
	Cinnamon
1 tablespoon fresh lemon juice	Apple and lemon slices for garnish (optional)
1/4 cup butter or margarine, melted	

1. Cut squash into halves lengthwise and scoop out seedy centers. Place cut side down in baking dish and pour in boiling water to a 1/2-inch depth. Bake at 400°F 20 minutes.
2. Pare, core, and dice apples; mix with lemon peel and juice, 2 tablespoons butter, and brown sugar.
3. Invert squash halves and brush with remaining 2 tablespoons butter; sprinkle with salt and cinnamon.
4. Fill squash halves with apple mixture. Pour boiling water into dish to a 1/2-inch depth; cover and bake 30 minutes.
5. Before serving, spoon pan juices over squash. If desired, garnish with apple and lemon slices.

Danish Cabbage

SERVES 6

2 pounds cabbage	seed
3 cups boiling water	1/2 teaspoon salt
1 cup sour cream	1/2 teaspoon white pepper
1 teaspoon caraway	

1. Slice cabbage into small pieces and cook in boiling water, covered, 6 to 8 minutes until tender, but still crisp. Drain very well.
2. In the top of a double boiler toss cabbage with sour cream, caraway seed, salt, and pepper. Cover and cook for 15 minutes.

Orange and Onion Salad

SERVES 4

3 oranges	4 tablespoons salad oil
1 Spanish onion	
2 tablespoons tarragon or white wine vinegar	A pinch of paprika
	A pinch of sugar
	Chopped parsley

1. Peel the oranges, removing all the white pith, and cut into thin slices.
2. Peel the onion, slice thinly, and separate the slices into rings.
3. Arrange the orange and onion slices alternately in a serving dish.
4. Combine the vinegar and oil, and add seasoning of salt, black pepper, and a pinch each of paprika and sugar. Shake well, and pour over the orange and onion.
5. Marinate for at least one hour, and before serving sprinkle with chopped parsley.

Tomato and Herb Salad

SERVES 4

2 large tomatoes	Wine vinegar or lemon juice
Salt	
Olive oil	Herbs, chopped

1. Peel some firm tomatoes, cut them into fairly thick slices, and arrange them on a platter. Sprinkle with a little salt, a few drops of olive oil and wine vinegar or lemon juice.
2. Sprinkle thickly with chopped herbs as available—parsley, chives, dill, basil, tarragon, etc.
3. Chill before serving.

Orange and Onion Salad, left; Tomato and Herb Salad, right.

Puffed Cauliflower Cheese.

Puffed Cauliflower Cheese

SERVES 4

1 medium-sized head of cauliflower	the cauliflower has been cooked
¹/₄ cup margarine	¹/₄ cup fine white bread crumbs
2 tablespoons flour	
1 cup milk, or milk and water in which	3 eggs (separated)
	1 cup grated cheese

Preheat oven to 400°F.

1. Wash the cauliflower, remove stalk end, cut into quarters, and remove the hard stalk. Divide into flowerets, and cook in boiling salted water until tender. Then drain.

2. Heat the fat in a pan, add flour, and stir over low heat for 2 minutes. Remove from the heat, add milk gradually, and stir until smooth. Return to the heat and stir until boiling. Add salt and pepper and most of the bread crumbs.

3. Stir in egg yolks, grated cheese, and the cauliflower. Adjust the seasoning to taste.

4. Beat egg whites until stiff and fold into the mixture. Put into a greased ovenproof dish, sprinkle with the remaining bread crumbs, and bake for about 30 minutes until well risen and brown.

255

Steamed Yellow Squash

SERVES 6

1 can (10 ounces) plum tomatoes	Salt and pepper to taste
1 large onion, minced	1 cup chicken stock
1 tablespoon minced parsley	3 tablespoons butter
1 teaspoon mint	2 pounds small yellow squash, sliced in half lengthwise
1 teaspoon oregano	

1. Combine all ingredients except squash.
2. Bring to a boil. Add squash.
3. Reduce heat and simmer about 15 minutes, or until squash is tender.

Baked Sweet Potatoes in Foil

SERVES 4

4 sweet potatoes	sugar
Vegetable shortening	4 teaspoons butter or margarine
4 teaspoons brown	

1. Wash, scrub, and dry sweet potatoes. Rub short-ening over entire surface of potatoes and wrap each loosely in aluminum foil. Seal open ends with a double fold.
2. Place on grill and bake about 45 minutes, or until tender. Turn several times for even baking.
3. Loosen foil. Make a slit in top of each. Put brown sugar and butter on top.

Cauliflower and Avocado Salad

SERVES 4-6

1 medium size cauli-flower	2-3 tomatoes, peeled and cut into eighths
½ cup French dress-ing	½ cup crumbled cheese (Roquefort or blue)
1 ripe avocado pear	Lettuce or endive
½ cup sliced stuffed olives	

1. Divide the cauliflower into flowerets, cover with iced water, and chill for 1 hour.
2. Drain and dry cauliflower. Then chop coarsely, and put into a bowl. Pour over the French dressing, and leave for 2 hours.
3. Just before serving, add the peeled and diced avocado, olives, tomatoes, and cheese.
4. Serve on a bed of lettuce.

Cauliflower and Avocado Salad.

Greek Salad

SERVES 8

Salad Dressing:
⅓ cup olive oil
¼ cup wine vinegar
½ teaspoon salt
1 teaspoon oregano

Salad:
1 large head romaine, trimmed and torn in pieces
1 cucumber, pared and cut in 3½-inch pieces
1 small bunch rad-ishes, cleaned and trimmed
2 small green peppers, trimmed and cored
1 can (8 ounces) whole beets, drained
4 tomatoes
⅓ pound feta cheese
Greek olives
Anchovy fillets (optional)

1. For salad dressing, mix all ingredients and refrigerate.
2. For salad, put romaine pieces in a large salad bowl.
3. Using **slicing disc** of food processor, slice cucumber, radishes, green pepper, and beets.
4. Cut tomatoes into quarters.
5. Using **plastic blade** of food processor, process feta cheese, using quick on/off motions, until crumbled.
6. Combine prepared salad ingredients with romaine in a bowl, sprinkle with crumbled feta cheese, and top with olives and, if desired, anchovy fillets. Pour salad dressing over salad and serve.

Anchovy and Tuna Salad

SERVES 4

4 tomatoes, peeled and quartered
2 small green peppers, seeded and sliced thinly
4 stalks celery, chopped
1 small cooked beet
2 hard-cooked eggs, cut into quarters
1 can anchovy fillets
1 can tuna fish, drained and flaked
Green and black olives

Dressing:
2 tablespoons white wine vinegar
6 tablespoons olive oil
Salt
Freshly ground black pepper
½ teaspoon prepared mustard
1 teaspoon tarragon, chives, chervil, and parsley, each finely chopped

1. Arrange the tomatoes, green peppers, celery, beet, and eggs in a salad bowl or on a large platter.
2. Combine all the ingredients for the dressing and blend well.
3. Arrange the anchovy fillets, tuna, and olives attractively on top and pour the dressing over.

Anchovy and Tuna Salad.

Greek-Style Lamb-and-Olive Salad

SERVES 6

*Greek-Style Salad
    Dressing:*
$^1/_2$ cup olive or salad
    oil
1 cup red wine vine-
    gar
3 to 4 tablespoons
    honey
$1^1/_2$ teaspoons salt
$^1/_8$ teaspoon dry
    mustard
2 teaspoons crushed
    dried mint leaves
$^1/_4$ teaspoon crushed
    oregano

$^1/_4$ teaspoon crushed
    thyme
$^1/_4$ teaspoon anise seed
Salad:
$1^1/_2$ pounds roast
    lamb, trimmed of
    fat and cut in strips
Curly endive
1 large cucumber,
    pared and sliced
4 medium tomatoes,
    sliced and quar-
    tered
1 cup pitted ripe
    olives

1. For dressing, mix oil, vinegar, honey, salt, dry mustard, mint, oregano, thyme, and anise.
2. Pour the dressing over cooked lamb in a bowl, cover, and marinate in refrigerator at least 1 hour, or until thoroughly chilled.
3. To serve, arrange curly endive in a large salad bowl. Toss cucumber, tomatoes, and olives with some of the dressing and turn into salad bowl. Spoon meat over vegetables and pour more dressing over all.

Asparagus Vinaigrette

SERVES 6

1 envelope herb-
    flavored oil-and-
    vinegar salad
    dressing mix
Tarragon-flavored
    white wine vinegar
Water
Salad oil
2 tablespoons

chopped parsley
1 tablespoon finely
    chopped chives
2 teaspoons capers
1 hard-cooked egg,
    finely chopped
Cooked asparagus
    spears, chilled

1. Prepare salad dressing mix as directed on package, using vinegar, water, and salad oil.
2. Using 1 cup of the dressing, mix well with parsley, chives, capers, and egg. Chill thoroughly.

3. To serve, arrange chilled asparagus in six bundles on a chilled serving plate lined with Boston lettuce. Garnish each bundle with a pimiento strip. Complete platter with cucumber slices and radish roses. Mix dressing well before spooning over asparagus.

German Potato Salad

SERVES ABOUT 6

12 slices bacon, diced
    and fried until
    crisp (reserve
    6 tablespoons drip-
    pings)
3 medium-sized
    onions, chopped
    (2 cups)
1 cup less 2 table-

spoons cider vinegar
$1^1/_2$ tablespoons sugar
$1^1/_2$ teaspoons salt
$^1/_4$ teaspoon pepper
2 to 3 pounds pota-
    toes, cooked, peeled,
    and cut in $^1/_4$-inch
    slices

1. Heat bacon drippings in a skillet. Add onion and cook until tender, stirring occasionally. Stir in vinegar, sugar, salt, and pepper; heat to boiling. Mix in bacon.
2. Pour over potato slices in a serving dish and toss lightly to coat evenly. Garnish with snipped parsley and paprika. Serve hot.

Onion Charlotte

SERVES 4

4 Bermuda onions,
    peeled and thickly
    sliced
1 cup milk
2 tablespoons corn-
    starch
3 tablespoons marga-
    rine
$^1/_8$ teaspoon grated
    nugmeg

$^1/_8$ teaspoon ground
    cinnamon
4-5 slices stale bread
$^1/_4$ cup oil or cooking
    fat
3 tablespoons grated
    cheese
2 tablespoons fine
    bread crumbs

Preheat oven to 400°F.
1. Put the onions into a pan, just cover with cold water, cover, and boil for 2-3 minutes. Then drain off the water. Return the onions to the pan, add milk and 4 tablespoons water. Cover and simmer until the onions are tender — 10 to 15 minutes.
2. Mix cornstarch to a smooth paste with a little extra milk, add to the onions and stir until boiling. Add 2 tablespoons of the margarine, salt, pepper, nutmeg, and cinnamon.
3. Remove the crusts from the bread, and fry in the oil until brown on both sides. Arrange the fried

Pear and Grape Salad.

Onion Charlotte.

bread in the bottom and around the sides of a baking dish. Pour in the onion mixture.

4. Sprinkle with cheese and bread crumbs mixed together. Melt the remaining tablespoon of margarine and dribble over the top. Bake until well browned.

Pear and Grape Salad

SERVES 4

4 ripe dessert pears	½ pound black
1 cup cream cheese	grapes
1-2 tablespoons	Crisp lettuce
French dressing	

1. Peel the pears, cut in half, and scoop out the core with a teaspoon.
2. Blend the cream cheese with enough French dressing to make it spreadable and coat the rounded side of each pear half.
3. Halve and seed the grapes and press them into the cheese, close together so that each pear half resembles a small bunch of grapes.
4. Serve on crisp lettuce leaves.

Brussels Sprouts in Herb Butter

SERVES ABOUT 8

2 pounds fresh Brussels sprouts	juice
	³/₄ teaspoon salt
¹/₃ cup butter	¹/₄ teaspoon thyme
1 tablespoon grated onion	¹/₄ teaspoon marjoram
1 tablespoon lemon	¹/₄ teaspoon savory

1. Cook Brussels sprouts in boiling salted water until just tender.
2. Put butter, onion, lemon juice, salt, thyme, marjoram, and savory into a saucepan. Set over low heat until butter is melted, stirring to blend.
3. When Brussels sprouts are tender, drain thoroughly and turn into a warm serving dish. Pour the seasoned butter mixture over the Brussels sprouts and toss gently to coat sprouts evenly and thoroughly.

Baked Zucchini

SERVES 6-8

2 pounds zucchini	crumbs
1 cup shredded mild Cheddar cheese	3 tablespoons chopped parsley
¹/₂ cup cottage cheese	1¹/₂ teaspoons salt
4 eggs, beaten	¹/₂ teaspoon pepper
³/₄ cup dry bread	3 tablespoons butter

1. Wash zucchini and slice crosswise into ¹/₄-inch slices. (It is not necessary to peel zucchini, unless skin seems very tough.)
2. Combine cheeses, eggs, bread crumbs, parsley, salt, and pepper until evenly mixed. Layer into baking dish, alternating zucchini with sauce. Dot top with butter.
3. Bake at 375°F about 45 minutes, or until slightly set.

Fried Eggplant

SERVES ABOUT 6

2 medium eggplants	2 cups all-purpose flour
Salt	
³/₄ cup olive oil	Salt and pepper to taste
³/₄ cup vegetable oil	

1. Slice eggplants horizontally ¹/₃ inch thick. Sprinkle both sides generously with salt. Arrange in a single layer in baking dish. Allow to stand 1 hour.
2. Squeeze each eggplant slice firmly between palms of hands or use a heavy weight wrapped in aluminum foil to press out excess liquid.
3. Heat oils together to smoking.
4. Meanwhile, season flour with salt and pepper. Dip each slice in the flour. Fry the eggplant slices until golden brown, turning once. Remove. Serve immediately.

Lobster Salad

SERVES ABOUT 12

6 cups diced fresh lobster meat, chilled	¹/₂ teaspoon thyme
	2 garlic cloves, crushed in a garlic press
3 hard-cooked eggs, mashed through a sieve	2 cups mayonnaise
	1 tablespoon capers
1 large scallion, minced	Juice of 1 lemon
1 small leek, finely chopped	Cucumber, sliced paper thin
2 teaspoons tarragon	Tomato wedges for garnish

1. Combine all ingredients except cucumber and tomato. Adjust seasoning.
2. Spoon into heated pastry shells, a lobster cavity, or on a bed of lettuce. Garnish with cucumber slices and tomato wedges.

Molded Grapefruit Salad

SERVES 4

1 can (about 16 ounces) grapefruit	1 dessert apple, peeled, cored, and chopped
2 envelopes unflavored gelatin	2-3 stalks celery, chopped
2 tablespoons lemon juice	Lettuce

1. Drain the syrup from the grapefruit and add sufficient water to make 1 cup.
2. Soften the gelatin in a little of the syrup for 5-10 minutes. Then stir over hot water until melted. Add the rest of the syrup and lemon juice and leave in a cold place until it begins to thicken.
3. Stir in the grapefruit, apple, and celery. Pour into a prepared mold or into individual molds and refrigerate until set.
4. Serve on a bed of lettuce.

Molded Grapefruit Salad.

DESSERTS

Basic Mousse with Variations

SERVES 6

1 envelope unflavored gelatin
1/2 cup cold water
1 cup instant nonfat dry-milk solids
1/4 cup sugar or honey
1 teaspoon vanilla extract
10 to 12 ice cubes
Mint sprigs or strawberries for garnish

1. Sprinkle gelatin over cold water in a saucepan; let stand 5 minutes. Set over low heat, stirring constantly until gelatin is dissolved (about 3 minutes).
2. Pour gelatin mixture into a food processor or blender container; add remaining ingredients except ice cubes. Process 10 seconds. Add ice cubes one at a time until mixture has consistency of heavy whipped cream.
3. Pour mixture into a serving bowl or individual stemmed glasses. Refrigerate until set (about 1/2 hour). Garnish with mint or strawberries.

Note: Mousse can be unmolded, if desired. Run knife around side of bowl; dip briefly in hot water. Invert on serving plate.

Coffee Mousse: Follow recipe for Basic Mousse, adding **1 tablespoon instant coffee crystals** and **1/4 teaspoon ground cinnamon** to ingredients.

Rum-Pineapple Mousse: Follow recipe for Basic Mousse, adding **1 tablespoon dark rum** to ingredients. When mousse is almost consistency of heavy whipped cream, add **1 cup crushed pineapple**. Continue adding ice cubes until desired consistency is achieved.

Ricotta Mousse: Prepare half the Basic Mousse recipe. When desired consistency is reached, add **1 tablespoon apple concentrate, 1 cup low-fat ricotta cheese,** and **1/4 teaspoon cinnamon.** Turn food processor on and off 2 times so ingredients are just blended.

Fruit Mousse: Follow recipe for Basic Mousse, adding **1 cup sliced fruit or berries** to ingredients.

Fruit Concentrate Mousse: Follow recipe for Basic Mousse; omit sugar and add **3 tablespoons natural fruit concentrate** to ingredients. Garnish with slices of fresh fruit or **1 to 2 cups prepared fruit.**

Note: Natural fruit concentrates can be purchased in specialty sections of the supermarket or in gourmet food shops. Many flavors, such as peach, apple, blackberry, and strawberry, are available.

Port Wine Mousse.

Coconut Flan

SERVES 6

Caramel Topping:
1/2 cup granulated sugar
2 tablespoons water
Custard:
2 cups milk
4 eggs
1/4 cup sugar
1/8 teaspoon salt
1/2 teaspoon vanilla extract
1/3 cup shredded or flaked coconut

1. For caramel topping, heat sugar and water in a small skillet, stirring constantly, until sugar melts and turns golden brown.
2. Pour syrup into a 1-quart baking dish or 6 custard cups, tipping to coat bottom and part way up sides. Set dish aside while preparing custard.
3. For custard, scald milk. Beat eggs; beat in sugar, salt, and vanilla extract. Gradually beat scalded milk into egg mixture. Strain into prepared baking dish or custard cups. Sprinkle top with coconut.
4. Place baking dish in pan containing hot water that comes at least 1 inch up sides of dish.
5. Bake at 325°F about 45 minutes for individual custard cups, or 1 hour for baking dish.

Port Wine Mousse

SERVES 4

1 envelope unflavored gelatin
3 eggs, separated
4 tablespoons sugar
Grated rind of 3 oranges
3 ounces port (or other dessert wine)
6 ounces heavy cream
3 ounces shelled walnuts

1. Place gelatin in a bowl with cold water.
2. Beat egg yolks and sugar for about 5 minutes and add wine and grated orange rind.
3. Melt the gelatin in 1/4 cup water over low heat and let cool.
4. Meanwhile beat the egg whites and the cream separately to stiff peaks. Stir the gelatin into the egg, sugar, and wine mixture. Then stir in the cream and the egg whites. Stir gently till everything is mixed.
5. Pour mousse in a bowl or individual cups and top with shelled walnuts. Chill till mousse is firm, about 3 hours.

Individual Fruit Puddings

SERVES 8

Pudding:
2 medium oranges
1¹/₂ cups sifted en-
  riched all-purpose
  flour
1 teaspoon baking
  soda
¹/₄ teaspoon salt
¹/₄ teaspoon ground
  cinnamon
¹/₄ teaspoon ground
  cloves
¹/₄ teaspoon ground
  nutmeg
¹/₄ cup shortening
1 cup firmly packed
  brown sugar
1 egg, well beaten

1 cup dark seedless
  raisins
¹/₂ cup pitted dates, cut
  in pieces
¹/₂ cup walnuts,
  coarsely chopped

Orange Sauce:
³/₄ cup sugar
2 tablespoons corn-
  starch
¹/₈ teaspoon salt
³/₄ cup orange juice
¹/₂ cup water
1 teaspoon grated
  orange peel
1 tablespoon butter or
  margarine

1. For pudding, grease eight 5-ounce custard cups. Set aside.
2. Peel oranges; slice into cartwheels, and cut into pieces; reserve juice as it collects.
3. Blend flour, baking soda, salt, cinnamon, cloves, and nutmeg. Set aside.
4. Beat shortening; add brown sugar gradually, beating until fluffy. Add egg and beat thoroughly.

5. Mix in the orange pieces, reserved juice, raisins, dates, and walnuts. Blend in the dry ingredients.
6. Fill custard cups about two-thirds full with mixture; cover tightly with aluminum foil. Set in a pan and fill pan with water to a 1-inch depth. Cover pan with aluminum foil.
7. Cook in a 325°F oven 2 hours.
8. For Orange Sauce, mix sugar, cornstarch, and salt in a saucepan. Add orange juice and water gradually, stirring constantly. Bring to boiling, stirring constantly until thickened; cook over low heat 6 to 8 minutes, stirring occasionally.
9. Remove from heat. Blend in orange peel and butter. Keep warm.
10. Unmold puddings while hot onto dessert plates and spoon sauce over each.

Father's Molds

SERVES 6

4 ounces butter
3 ounces sugar
1 teaspoon confection-
  ers' sugar
2 eggs
3 ounces wheat flour
³/₄ teaspoon baking

  powder
1 tablespoon potato
  flour
bread crumbs
Decoration:
Whipped cream
Berries

1. Beat butter and sugar until foamy.

Father's Molds.

Cheese Soufflé with Strawberry Sauce.

2. Add the eggs, one at a time, and continue to beat.
3. Mix the wheat and potato flour with the baking powder and stir into the egg mixture.
4. Distribute batter in well-greased cake molds sprinkled with fine bread crumbs.
5. Bake in a 350°F oven for 15 minutes. Decorate the cold cakes with whipped cream and berries.

Cheese Soufflé with Strawberry Sauce

SERVES 8-10

Crust:	3 tablespoons flour
1 cup graham cracker crumbs	1¹/₂ teaspoons lemon peel
2 tablespoons sugar	1¹/₂ teaspoons orange peel
¹/₃ cup butter, melted	1 teaspoon vanilla extract
Cake:	5 egg whites
1³/₄ cups sugar	¹/₄ cup heavy cream
2 egg yolks	2 packages frozen strawberries
5 packages (8 ounces) cream cheese	

1. Crust: Mix crumbs, sugar, and butter. Press into bottom of soufflé dish. Refrigerate.

2. Preheat oven to 500°F. In a large bowl mix cheese, sugar, flour, lemon and orange peel, and vanilla. Beat at high speed until blended.
3. Beat in egg whites and egg yolks, one at a time. Add cream, beat until mixed. Pour on crust in soufflé dish.
4. Bake 10 minutes. Reduce oven temperature to 250°F and bake for another hour.
5. Refrigerate.
Serve with thawed strawberries.

Rhubarb Compote

SERVES 4

1¹/₂ pounds rhubarb	2 ounces sliced almonds
³/₄ cup sugar	³/₄ cup heavy cream, whipped
3 tablespoons butter	
1 cup bread crumbs	

1. Rinse rhubarb and cut into 1-inch pieces. Place in an ovenproof dish and pour sugar on top. Cover with aluminum foil and bake in a 400°F oven for 20 minutes. Remove from oven and let cool.
2. Heat butter in a skillet and brown bread crumbs and almonds. Let cool.
3. Place bread crumb mixture in the bottom of 4 dessert dishes. Spoon rhubarb on top and garnish with whipped cream.

Lemon Delight.

Frozen Chocolate Mousse

SERVES 10-12

$^2/_3$ cup sugar	2 cups chilled whipping cream
$^1/_4$ cup water	
4 ounces (4 squares) unsweetened chocolate	$^1/_2$ cup confectioners' sugar
1$^1/_2$ teaspoons unflavored gelatin	1 teaspoon vanilla extract
$^1/_4$ cup cold water	$^1/_2$ cup chilled whipping cream

1. Put sugar and $^1/_4$ cup water into top of a double boiler. Place over direct heat and stir until sugar is dissolved.
2. Set over simmering water and add chocolate. Heat until chocolate is melted. Remove from heat and set aside to cool.
3. Soften gelatin in cold water in a small saucepan. Stir over low heat until gelatin is dissolved.
4. Rinse a fancy 1$^1/_2$-quart mold with cold water and set aside to drain.
5. Beat whipping cream, 1 cup at a time, in a chilled bowl using a chilled rotary beater, until it piles softly. Beat the confectioners' sugar and vanilla extract into the whipped cream until blended.
6. Stir dissolved gelatin into chocolate mixture and gently mix chocolate into whipped cream until thoroughly blended. Spoon into mold, and place in freezer about 3 hours, or until firm.
7. Beat $^1/_2$ cup whipping cream, using a chilled bowl and chilled beaters, until cream stands in stiff peaks when beater is lifted.
8. Just before ready to serve, remove mousse from freezer. To unmold, loosen top edge of mold with a knife. Wet a clean towel in hot water and wring it almost dry. Place a chilled serving plate on mold and invert. Wrap towel around mold for a few seconds only. Gently remove mold. If mousse does not loosen, repeat.
9. Force whipped cream through a pastry bag and a No. 27 star tube, to decorate center and sides of mousse.

Lemon Delight

SERVES 4

3 egg yolks	1 teaspoon gelatin
3 egg whites	Juice of 1 lemon
2 tablespoons sugar	Peel of 1 lemon

1. Beat egg yolks and sugar with electric mixer till light and airy.
2. Soak gelatin in 3 tablespoons hot water. Mix with egg yolks and add lemon juice and lemon peel.
3. Beat egg whites until they form stiff peaks.

Almond Paste Bombe.

4. Fold egg whites into egg yolks and pour mixture into 4 dessert dishes. Refrigerate for 2-3 hours till firm. Garnish with grapes and serve with cookies.

Almond Paste Bombe

SERVES 6-8

3 pints ice cream (various flavors)	14 ounces almond paste
1½ cups heavy cream, whipped	2 tablespoons cocoa

Buy 3 flavors of ice cream and mix each with ⅓ cup whipped cream. Flavor each with strained berries, juice, etc. and color with different shades of food coloring. Layer the ice creams in a large, round, plastic bowl and put in the freezer for at least 6 hours. Also put into freezer the dish on which the ice cream is to be served.

1. Between two sheets of wax paper roll out 14 ounces almond paste to form a large, round, flat cake.
2. Take the bowl of ice cream from the freezer, turn upside-down, and slide the ice cream onto the serving dish.
3. Quickly cover the ice cream with the almond paste, pinching corners together.
4. Cut away superfluous almond paste, flatten the joints with a flat knife, and trim the bottom.

5. Brush the paste shell with water, powder with cocoa, and brush with a wet brush to make a smooth, brown surface.
6. Decorate with whipped cream, topped with a triangular piece of leftover almond paste.
7. Place bombe in the freezer for a few hours.
8. Powder the top with confectioners' sugar and decorate the serving dish with butter cookies.

Year-Round Fruit Compote

SERVES 8-10

1 cup dried apricots	apple chunks (undrained)
1 cup golden raisins	Lemon peel from ¼ lemon
1 package (12 ounces) pitted prunes	1 cinnamon stick, broken in half
1 can (20 ounces) unsweetened pine-	

1. Put fruits, lemon peel, and cinnamon sticks into a 1½-quart glass casserole. Cover with an all-glass lid or plastic wrap.
2. Cook in microwave oven 8 minutes; rotate dish one-quarter turn once.
3. Remove lemon peel and cinnamon before serving.

Molded Cheese Dessert

SERVES 4

2 envelopes unfla-vored gelatin	1 teaspoon vanilla extract
1 cup cold water	1/4 cup sugar
1 cup double-strength coffee	2 bay leaves, broken in half
1 pound pot cheese or low-fat cottage cheese	Mint leaves or water-cress

1. Sprinkle gelatin over cold water in a small skillet; let stand 5 minutes. Heat, stirring occasionally, over low heat until dissolved (about 3 minutes). Pour gelatin mixture into a food processor or blender; add remaining ingredients except bay leaves and mint. Purée mixture.
2. Spoon mixture into a 1-quart mold. Push bay leaf pieces into mixture. Refrigerate covered 4 to 6 hours; unmold. Garnish with mint.

Lemon Egg Fluff

SERVES 12

3 envelopes unfla-vored gelatin	frozen lemonade concentrate, thawed
1/2 cup sugar	10 egg whites
Few grains salt	1/2 cup sugar
1 cup water	Cherry-Cinnamon Sauce, below
10 egg yolks, beaten	
1 can (6 ounces)	

1. Thoroughly blend gelatin, sugar, and salt in a heavy saucepan. Mix in water. Stir over low heat until gelatin is dissolved.
2. Gradually add a small amount of hot gelatin mixture to egg yolks, stirring constantly. Blend into mixture in saucepan; cook and stir 2 minutes without boiling.
3. Remove from heat. Stir in lemonade concentrate. Chill until mixture is slightly thickened.
4. Beat egg whites until frothy. Gradually add sugar, continuing to beat until stiff peaks are formed; fold in gelatin mixture. Turn into a 2 1/2-quart tower mold and chill until firm.
5. Unmold onto a chilled serving plate and serve with Cherry-Cinnamon Sauce.

Sauce: Combine 1/2 **cup sugar** and **2 tablespoons cornstarch** in a saucepan; mix thoroughly. Drain **1 can (about 16 ounces) tart red cherries,** reserving the liquid. Add cherry liquid and **3 tablespoons red cinnamon candies** to sugar mixture. Bring to boiling, stirring constantly; continue cooking until mixture is thickened and clear. Remove from heat. Stir in **1 tablespoon lemon juice** and the cherries. Cool. Makes about 2 1/4 cups sauce.

Pears on Pineapple Slices

SERVES 6-7

7-8 pears	raspberries
1 can pineapple slices	White wine
1 package frozen	

1. Drain pineapple slices, reserving juice. Add wine to juice and bring to a boil.
2. Meanwhile peel, halve, and core pears.
3. Put pears in boiling wine and juice. Simmer until pears are soft.
4. Arrange pineapple slices on serving dish and put a pear half on top of each slice.
5. Fill center of pears with half-thawed raspberries and place remainder of berries in center of serving dish.
6. Pour cooled pineapple-wine juice over pears and refrigerate.
You can also serve cored pears with shredded walnuts or whole pears with walnuts and maraschino cherries.

Napoleon

SERVES 8-10

1 1/2 cups puff pastry	2 tablespoons water
1/2 cup raspberry jam	1/2 teaspoon vanilla
1 cup lemon pudding	1 tablespoon rasp-berry jelly
Icing:	
1 cup confectioners' sugar	

1. Preheat oven to 425°F.
2. Roll out dough into a rectangle about 1/8-inch thick. Put on a dampened baking sheet. Prick dough with a fork and chill for 10 minutes.
3. Bake the dough for 10-15 minutes till brown. Loosen with a spatula and turn over. Bake for another 5 minutes.
4. Place on a wire rack to cool.
5. Cut and trim edges into 3-inch wide strips.
6. Spread the jam on one strip and then the lemon pudding. Cover with another strip. Press down lightly.
7. Make icing: Mix the confectioners' sugar with enough water so that it spreads easily. Add vanilla and raspberry jelly.
8. Heat icing to tepid. Spread on immediately and serve.

Pears on Pineapple Slices.

Napoleon.

Chocolate Fondue

ABOUT 4 CUPS

4 packages (6 ounces each) milk chocolate pieces or semisweet chocolate pieces

2 cups (1 pint) light corn syrup

1 tablespoon vanilla extract

½ cup cream, brandy, or rum

Assorted dippers (marshmallows, strawberries with hull, apple slices, banana chunks, pineapple chunks, mandarin orange segments, cherries with stems, cake cubes, melon balls)

1. Combine chocolate pieces and corn syrup in a heavy saucepan. Heat and stir until chocolate melts and mixture is smooth.

2. Add vanilla extract (omit if using brandy or rum) and cream; stir until well blended. Turn into a fondue pot and keep hot.

3. To serve, surround fondue pot with small bowls of dippers. Provide fondue forks for guests to spear dippers, then dip into fondue.

269

Blueberry-Orange Parfaits

SERVES 6

2 tablespoons corn-
  starch
1 cup sugar
1/2 teaspoon salt
2 cups orange juice
2 eggs, beaten
1/2 teaspoon grated
  lemon peel

2 tablespoons sugar
2 cups fresh blueber-
  ries
Whipped cream
  (optional)

1. Mix cornstarch, 1 cup sugar, and salt in a heavy saucepan. Add a small amount of the orange juice and blend until smooth. Stir in remaining orange juice.
2. Bring mixture to boiling, stirring constantly, and cook 3 to 5 minutes.
3. Stir about 3 tablespoons of the hot mixture into beaten eggs; immediately blend with mixture in saucepan.
4. Cook and stir about 3 minutes. Remove from water and cool. Stir in lemon peel. Chill.
5. Meanwhile, sprinkle 2 tablespoons sugar over blueberries and allow to stand at least 30 minutes. Spoon alternating layers of custard and blueberries in parfait glasses, beginning with a layer of custard and ending with blueberries. Top with whipped cream, if desired.

Almendrado

SERVES 12

1 tablespoon unfla-
  vored gelatin
1/2 cup sugar
1 cup cold water
4 egg whites
1/2 teaspoon almond
  extract

Red and green food
  coloring
1 cup finely ground
  almonds
Custard Sauce with
  Almonds, below

1. Mix gelatin and sugar in a saucepan. Stir in water. Set over low heat and stir until gelatin and sugar are dissolved. Chill until slightly thickened.
2. Beat egg whites until stiff, not dry, peaks are formed. Fold into gelatin mixture along with almond extract. Beat until mixture resembles whipped cream. Divide equally into 3 portions. Color one portion red, another green, and leave the last one white.
3. Pour red mixture into an 8-inch square dish or pan. Sprinkle with half of the almonds. Pour in white mixture and sprinkle with remaining almonds. Top with green layer. Chill thoroughly.
4. Cut into portions and serve with Custard Sauce.

Custard Sauce with Almonds: Scald **2 cups milk.** Mix **4 egg yolks** and 1/4 **cup sugar** in the top of a double boiler. Add scalded milk gradually, stirring constantly.

Cook over boiling water, stirring constantly until mixture coats a spoon. Remove from water and stir in 1/4 **teaspoon almond extract** and 1/2 **cup toasted sliced almonds.** Cool; chill thoroughly. Makes about 2 1/2 cups.

Marinated Fruit Salad

SERVES 8

2 apples
3 pears
3 peaches
1 pineapple

Confectioners' sugar
1/4 cup rum or Coin-
  treau

1. Pare, core, and slice apples and pears. Halve, pit, peel, and slice peaches. Cut pineapple into chunks.
2. Place fruit in a bowl and sprinkle with confectioners' sugar to taste. Sprinkle with rum or Cointreau.
3. Cover the bowl tightly and chill for at least 6 hours so the sugar draws out fruit juices.

Vanilla Soufflé

SERVES ABOUT 6

1 tablespoon confec-
  tioners' sugar
1/4 cup butter or
  margarine
3 tablespoons flour
1 cup milk

4 egg yolks
1/2 cup sugar
1 tablespoon vanilla
  extract
4 egg whites

1. Butter bottom of a 1 1/2-quart soufflé dish (straight-sided casserole) and sift confectioners' sugar over it.
2. Heat butter in a saucepan. Stir in flour. Gradually add milk, stirring until thickened and smooth. Remove from heat.
3. Beat egg yolks, sugar, and vanilla extract together until mixture is very thick. Spoon sauce gradually into egg-yolk mixture while beating vigorously. Cool to lukewarm.
4. Using clean beater, beat egg whites until rounded peaks are formed. Spread egg-yolk mixture gently over egg whites and fold until thoroughly blended. Turn mixture into prepared soufflé dish. Set dish in a pan of very hot water.
5. Bake, uncovered, at 400°F 15 minutes. Turn oven control to 375°F and bake 30 to 40 minutes, or until a knife inserted halfway between center and edge comes out clean. Serve immediately.
6. Accompany with pureed thawed frozen strawberries or raspberries.

Marinated Fruit Salad.

Apple Pudding.

Twelve-Fruit Compote

SERVES ABOUT 12

3 cups water	¹/₂ cup cranberries
1 pound mixed dried	1 cup sugar
fruits including	1 lemon, sliced
pears, figs, apricots,	6 whole cloves
and peaches	2 cinnamon sticks
1 cup pitted prunes	(3 inches each)
¹/₂ cup raisins or	1 orange
currants	¹/₂ cup grapes, pome-
1 cup pitted sweet	granate seeds, or
cherries	pitted plums
2 apples, peeled and	¹/₂ cup fruit-flavored
sliced or 6 ounces	brandy
dried apple slices	

1. Combine water, mixed dried fruits, prunes, and raisins in a 6-quart kettle. Bring to boiling. Cover; simmer about 20 minutes, or until fruits are plump and tender.
2. Add cherries, apples, and cranberries. Stir in sugar, lemon, and spices. Cover; simmer 5 minutes.
3. Grate peel of orange; reserve. Peel and section orange, removing all skin and white membrane. Add to fruits in kettle.
4. Stir in grapes and brandy. Bring just to boiling. Remove from heat. Stir in orange peel. Cover; let stand 15 minutes.

Apple Pudding

SERVES 6

6 large apples	¹/₂ cup butter or
Juice of ¹/₂ lemon	margarine
(optional)	*Decoration:*
1 (6-8 ounce) can	2¹/₄ ounces almonds,
almond paste	sliced

1. Grease an ovenproof dish or pie plate. Pare and coarsely grate the apples. Place in bottom of dish. (If you wish, squeeze juice of ¹/₂ lemon on top.)
2. Coarsely grate almond paste and butter. Gently mix together.
3. Place mixture over apples and top with sliced almonds.
4. Bake in a 400°F oven for 15 minutes.
Serve warm with whipped cream or vanilla ice cream.

Swiss Jelly Roll

SERVES 6-8

3 eggs	jam *or*
4 ounces sugar	2 pints mashed straw-
³/₄ cup flour	berries
1 teaspoon baking	¹/₄ cup confectioners'
powder	sugar
Filling:	
6 ounces strawberry	

1. Beat eggs and sugar very foamy. Combine flour and baking powder and stir into the egg batter.

2. Spread the batter evenly on greased wax paper. Place on a 12" × 14" cookie sheet and bake in a 400°F oven for 10-15 minutes. Place cake on sugared wax paper.

3. Remove the paper and spread on jelly. Roll up cake lengthwise. Place the roll with the joint down back on the wax paper and store in a cold place until ready to serve. Sift on confectioners' sugar before serving.

Zuppa Inglese

SERVES 8

Sponge cake:
6 eggs, separated
6 ounces sugar
1 cup flour
Green curaçao
Brandy
Fresh orange juice
   (optional)
Bread crumbs
Cream:
3 egg yolks

3 ounces sugar
2 ounces flour
2 cups milk or half
   and half
Finely grated rind of
   ½ lemon
Meringue:
3 egg whites
3 ounces sugar

1. Preheat the oven to 325°F.
2. Beat egg yolks for the sponge cake and sugar until foamy. Add the flour and beat until smooth.

3. Beat the egg whites to stiff peaks and carefully fold into the sponge cake batter.
4. Pour batter into a well-greased 9-inch spring form sprinkled with fine bread crumbs. Bake for about 45 minutes. Cool the cake and place on a cake rack to cool completely.
5. Beat the ingredients for the cream in a heavy saucepan. Simmer over low heat while beating until cream thickens. Chill and add the grated lemon rind.
6. Fold two 23-inch sheets of aluminum foil double and place them crosswise in a 9-inch pan. Smooth the foil and let it hang over the edges of the pan. This will make it easy to lift the cake when it is ready.
7. Cut the sponge cake horizontally in ½-inch slices. Spread a thin layer of cream on the bottom of the foil-lined pan. Soak 3 sponge cake slices in green curaçao. Use liqueur sparingly; otherwise the slices will absorb too much. Soak 2 slices of sponge cake in brandy diluted with orange juice.
 Stack slices of sponge cake alternately on the cream in the pan, with cream between layers. The top layer should be a slice of sponge cake soaked in curaçao. Spread the rest of the cream on top. Refrigerate at least 2-3 hours.
8. Preheat the oven to 225°F.
9. Beat the 3 egg whites for the meringue to stiff peaks. Add the sugar while beating rapidly. Spread the meringue on the cake, top with sugar, and bake until the meringue is light brown. Take the cake out and let it cool. Lift the cake from the mold with the aid of the foil strips and place it on a serving dish.
Serve with black coffee and whipped cream.

Zuppa Inglese.

DESSERTS

Bread Pudding

SERVES 6

2 cups firmly packed	and sliced
dark brown sugar	1 cup raisins
1 quart water	1 cup chopped
1 stick cinnamon	blanched almonds
1 clove	½ pound Monterey
6 slices toast, cubed	Jack or similar
3 apples, pared, cored,	cheese, cubed

1. Put brown sugar, water, cinnamon, and clove into a saucepan and bring to boiling; reduce heat and simmer until a light syrup is formed. Discard spices and set syrup aside.
2. Meanwhile, arrange a layer of toast cubes in a buttered casserole. Cover with a layer of apples, raisins, almonds, and cheese. Repeat until all ingredients are used. Pour syrup over all.
3. Bake at 350°F about 30 minutes.
4. Serve hot.

Strawberry Pancakes

SERVES 3

1 quart fully ripe	½ teaspoon vanilla
strawberries	extract
1¼ cups sifted all-	2 egg whites
purpose flour	4 teaspoons sugar
⅛ teaspoon salt	2 tablespoons sugar
2 eggs, well beaten	Confectioners' sugar
½ cup milk	

1. Set out a griddle or a heavy 10-inch skillet.
2. Wash and remove blemishes from strawberries.
3. Set 18 berries aside to garnish serving plates; hull and slice remaining berries, place them in refrigerator.
4. Sift together flour and salt into a bowl and set aside.
5. Beat with rotary beater to blend eggs, milk, and vanilla extract.
6. Set griddle over low heat.
7. Make a well in center of dry ingredients. Add egg mixture, stirring batter only until blended; set batter aside.
8. Beat egg whites until frothy.
9. Add 4 teaspoons of sugar gradually, beating well after each addition.
10. Beat until stiff peaks are formed. Carefully fold egg whites into batter.
11. Test griddle; it is hot enough for baking when drops of water sprinkled on surface dance in small beads. Lightly grease griddle if manufacturer so directs. For each pancake pour about 1 cup of the batter onto griddle. Immediately tilt griddle back and forth to spread batter evenly. If necessary, use spatula to spread batter. Cook until pancake is puffy, full of bubbles, and

golden brown on underside. Turn only once and brown other side. Transfer pancakes to a warm platter and keep them warm by placing between folds of absorbent paper in a 350°F oven.
12. When all the pancakes are cooked, remove strawberries from refrigerator. Mix one-half of the sliced berries with sugar.
13. Spoon about ½ cup of the sweetened strawberries onto each pancake and roll. Place pancakes onto individual plates. Sprinkle each with confectioners' sugar.
14. Arrange remaining sliced strawberries over the top of pancakes. Garnish plates with leaf lettuce and the whole strawberries. Serve immediately.

Almond Apples

SERVES 4

4 medium apples	Grated rind of
8 ounces almond paste	1 lemon
1 egg white	1 egg yolk, beaten
	Shredded almonds

1. Pare and core the apples and place in a greased ovenproof dish.
2. Grate the almond paste coarsely. Mix the almond paste with the egg white and lemon rind. Divide the mixture into four parts and shape each part into a round cake. Place a cake on each of the apples and press it down a little.
3. Brush with the egg yolk and sprinkle on the shredded almonds. Bake in a 400°F oven for 30 minutes or until the apples are soft and brown. Serve with vanilla ice cream.

Stuffed Peaches

SERVES 6

½ cup almond maca-	1 tablespoon chopped
roon crumbs	candied orange peel
6 large firm peaches	⅓ cup sherry or
½ cup blanched	marsala
almonds, chopped	2 tablespoons sugar
2 tablespoons sugar	

1. Using an electric blender, grind enough almond macaroons to make ½ cup crumbs. Set crumbs aside.
2. Rinse, peel, and cut peaches into halves. Remove pit and small portion of the pulp around cavity.
3. Combine and mix macaroon crumbs, chopped almonds, 2 tablespoons sugar, and orange peel.
4. Lightly fill peach halves with mixture. Put two halves together and fasten with wooden picks. Place in baking dish.

274

Dessert Crêpes.

5. Pour sherry over peaches and sprinkle remaining sugar over peaches.
6. Bake at 350°F 15 minutes and serve either hot or cold.

Dessert Crêpes

SERVES 6

2 eggs
1 cup flour
2 cups milk
1/2 teaspoon salt
3 teaspoons sugar
Grated rind of
   1 lemon
2 tablespoons melted
   butter

Filling and Decoration:
1 1/2 cups heavy cream,
   whipped
2 tablespoons sugar
1/2 tablespoon confec-
   tioners' sugar
1 package frozen
   blueberries
2 packages frozen
   raspberries

1. Beat the milk and the eggs together.
2. Add the flour, salt, sugar, and grated lemon rind while continuing to beat.
3. Cook crêpes, adding the melted butter just before they are golden brown on both sides.
4. Stack crêpes, putting whipped cream and berries between each layer. Top with the rest of the cream and berries.

Cream Puffs with Banana Slices

SERVES 6

1 cup water
1/8 teaspoon salt
1/2 cup sweet butter
1 cup flour
3 eggs

1 egg yolk, beaten
4 bananas, sliced
2 cups heavy cream,
   whipped
Grated chocolate

1. Preheat oven to 350°F. Pour water and salt into a heavy saucepan. Cut the butter into small pieces and add to water. Heat over low heat, stirring with a wooden spoon, until mixture comes to a boil.
2. Put flour in all at once. Stir until blended and dough forms a ball. Remove dough to a bowl and beat in 3 eggs, one at a time. Continue beating until dough is very shiny. Refrigerate for 30 minutes.
3. Drop large tablespoons of dough 2 inches apart on an ungreased cookie sheet. Brush with beaten egg yolk.
4. Bake 35-40 minutes until puffed and golden brown. Cool puffs on a wire rack. Cut off tops and fill with whipped cream and banana slices. Sprinkle with grated chocolate.

Beignets

SERVES 6-8

²/₃ cup all-purpose
   flour
¹/₄ teaspoon salt
²/₃ cup water

¹/₃ cup butter
4 eggs
Confectioners' sugar
Raspberry jam

1. Sift flour and salt together.
2. Pour the water into a heavy saucepan and add butter. Bring to a boil. Remove pan from heat and add the flour.
3. Beat vigorously for a few seconds until mixture is smooth and forms a ball. Cool about 5 minutes.
4. Beat in eggs one at a time. Beat for 1-2 minutes till dough is glossy.
5. Place batter in a pastry tube and pipe into circles.
6. Heat the deep fat fryer to 350°F.
7. Dip a metal spatula in the oil and then carefully pick up the beignets and drop them in the oil. Drop only a few at a time so they will have room to puff. Once the dough is added increase the temperature to 375°F and continue cooking about 5-6 minutes until golden brown and firm.
8. Remove the beignets with a slotted spoon and drain on paper towels. Sprinkle with confectioners' sugar and serve with heated raspberry jam.

Spiked Watermelon

SERVES 12

1 large ripe water-
   melon

2 cups amber rum

1. Cut a hole 2¹/₂ inches wide and 2 inches deep in the watermelon rind. Pour rum through hole and replace rind.
2. Chill 24 hours. Serve ice-cold slices.

Mexican Custard

SERVES ABOUT 10

1 quart milk
1 cup sugar
3 or 4 cinnamon sticks
¹/₈ teaspoon salt

4 eggs
1 teaspoon vanilla
   extract

1. Combine milk, sugar, and cinnamon sticks in saucepan. Bring to scalding point, stirring constantly. Remove from heat and cool to lukewarm.
2. Meanwhile, beat eggs in a 1¹/₂-quart casserole.

Beignets.

Gradually beat in milk-sugar mixture; stir in vanilla extract. Place in a shallow pan of water.
3. Bake at 325°F about 1 hour, or until custard is set.
4. Serve warm or cooled.

Pasta Flora

SERVES 10

¹/₂ **cup unsalted butter (at room temperature)**	**flour**
	1 tablespoon baking powder
2 eggs	**1 pint jam or preserves**
1 teaspoon vanilla extract	**1 egg yolk, beaten with ¹/₂ teaspoon water**
1 cup sugar	
3 cups all-purpose	

1. Beat butter 4 minutes, using an electric mixer. Add eggs, vanilla extract, and sugar. Beat until fluffy. Mix flour and baking powder. Slowly work into mixture until well blended.
2. Divide dough into 2 parts; one a ball using three fourths of the total, and one using one fourth of the total.
3. Line the bottom of a 13 × 9-inch baking pan with the larger portion of the dough. Spread the preserves evenly over dough.
4. Roll the remaining quarter of the dough on a lightly floured board to fit the size of the pan. Cut into strips. Form a lattice over the preserves. Brush dough with the egg yolk and water.
5. Bake at 350°F about 45 minutes until pastry is golden brown or a wooden pick comes out clean when inserted. Cool. Cut into squares.

Quick Vanilla Pudding

SERVES 4

1 package vanilla pudding	**syrup**
¹/₂ cup butterscotch	**Cherries**

1. Mix and cook vanilla pudding according to package directions. Pour into individual molds and let cool and set.
2. Before completely firm, make a well in the center of each serving and pour in butterscotch syrup. Garnish with a cherry and serve chilled.

Quick Vanilla Pudding.

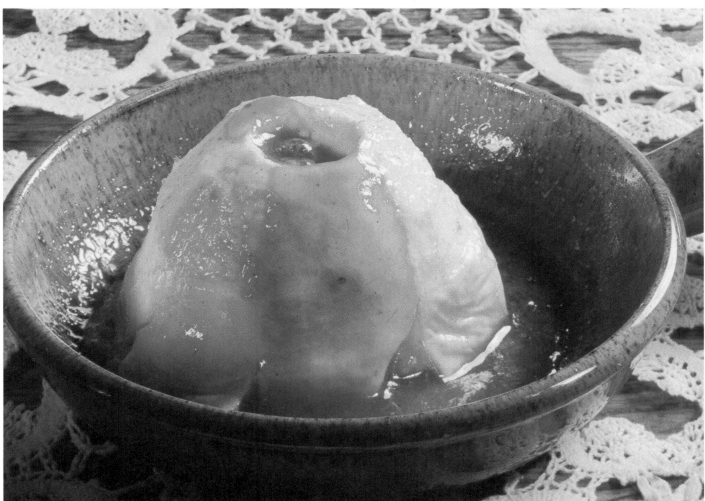

277

Spumone

SERVES 6-8

1/2 cup sugar	2 drops green food
1/8 teaspoon salt	coloring
1 cup milk, scalded	1/2 cup whipping
3 egg yolks, beaten	cream, whipped
1 cup whipping cream	1 maraschino cherry
1/2 ounce (1/2 square)	1 tablespoon sugar
unsweetened choco-	6 unblanched al-
late, melted	monds, finely
2 teaspoons rum	chopped
extract	1/4 teaspoon almond
1 tablespoon sugar	extract
1/8 teaspoon pistachio	1/2 cup whipping
extract	cream, whipped

1. Stir 1/2 cup sugar and salt into scalded milk in the top of a double boiler. Stir until sugar is dissolved.
2. Stir about 3 tablespoons of the hot milk into the egg yolks. Immediately return to double boiler top. Cook over boiling water, stirring constantly, about 5 minutes, or until mixture coats a spoon. Remove from heat and cool.
3. Stir in 1 cup whipping cream and divide mixture equally into two bowls.
4. Add melted chocolate to mixture in one bowl and mix thoroughly. Set in refrigerator.
5. Add rum extract to remaining mixture and pour into refrigerator tray. Freeze until mushy.
6. Turn into a chilled bowl and beat until mixture is smooth and creamy. Spoon into a chilled 1-quart mold and freeze until firm.
7. Fold 1 tablespoon sugar, pistachio extract, and food coloring into 1/2 cup whipping cream, whipped. Spoon over firm rum ice cream; freeze until firm.
8. When pistachio cream becomes firm, place the maraschino cherry in the center and return to freezer.
9. Fold 1 tablespoon sugar, chopped almonds, and almond extract into remaining 1/2 cup whipping cream, whipped. Spoon over firm pistachio cream. Freeze until firm.
10. When almond cream is firm, pour chocolate ice cream mixture into refrigerator tray and freeze until mushy.
11. Turn into a chilled bowl and beat until mixture is smooth and creamy. Spoon mixture over firm almond cream. Cover mold with aluminum foil or waxed paper. Return to freezer and freeze 6 to 8 hours, or until very firm.
12. To unmold, quickly dip mold into warm water and invert. Cut spumone into wedge-shaped pieces.

Pears with Tea Sauce

SERVES 4

1 (12 ounces) can	2 tablespoons tea
pears	leaves
1 package slivered	2 egg yolks
almonds	3/4 cup heavy cream,
Sauce:	whipped
3/4 cup pear juice	

1. Roast almonds in a shallow pan in a 350°F oven until lightly browned (about 15 minutes). Drain pears, reserving juice. Bring 3/4 cup pear juice to a boil. Remove from heat and let tea leaves soak in juice for about 3 minutes. Drain and discard the tea leaves.
2. Beat in egg yolks and let boil until sauce thickens, stirring constantly. Place pot in cold water and let cool while stirring. Whip cream and mix with sauce. Place pears in serving dish and sprinkle with almonds. Serve with ice-cold tea sauce.

Raspberry Charlotte

SERVES 12

4 eggs, separated	1/2 teaspoon salt
3/4 cup sugar	1/2 cup raspberry jelly
1 teaspoon vanilla	2 cups heavy cream
3/4 cup all-purpose	1 package raspberries,
flour	frozen
3/4 teaspoon baking	2 teaspoons gelatin
powder	

1. Preheat oven to 375°F. Grease a 10 1/2" × 15 1/2" jelly roll pan and place waxed paper on top.
2. Beat egg yolks and sugar together till creamy. Add vanilla.
3. Sift together flour, baking powder, and salt.
4. Add flour gradually to the egg mixture. Beat until smooth.
5. Whip egg whites till stiff peaks form. Fold into flour batter.
6. Pour into jelly roll pan and bake for 13 minutes.
7. Loosen edges as soon as cake comes from the oven. Place a sheet of waxed paper on top of the pan and turn over. Let cool.
8. When cool, spread on jelly and roll up.
9. Melt gelatin in two tablespoons hot water.
10. Whip 1 cup cream to stiff peaks. Add raspberries and gelatin.
11. Cut jelly roll in 1/4" slices. Line a round mold or bowl and pour in the raspberry cream. Put the mold in the refrigerator till cream has set.
12. Loosen mold and turn upside down. Serve with cold whipped cream.

Raspberry Charlotte.

Pears with Tea Sauce.

Mocha Mousse.

Mocha Mousse

SERVES 4

3 tablespoons un-sweetened cocoa	whipped
2 teaspoons instant coffee	2 egg whites
3 tablespoons sugar	*Decoration:*
1½ cups heavy cream,	3 ounces heavy cream, whipped

1. Mix cocoa, coffee, and sugar with the whipped cream.
2. Beat the egg whites till stiff and stir into the cream.
3. Distribute the mousse in individual cups.
4. Top with a spoonful of whipped cream.

Cocoa Pillows.

Cocoa Pillows

SERVES 8

¾ pound all-purpose flour	*Filling:*
1½ ounces butter or margarine	3 egg whites
3 egg yolks	1½ ounces granulated sugar
	1 tablespoon cocoa powder

1. Mix flour, butter, and egg yolks. Let stand. Roll out and cut in squares.
2. Filling: beat egg whites and carefully mix in sugar and cocoa powder. Put filling on each square and press sides together.
3. Bake in 300°F oven.

Pineapple Frappé.

Pineapple Frappé

SERVES 4

1 can (1 pound) crushed pineapple	(about 2 ounces)
3 teaspoons gelatin	3 tablespoons orange marmalade
Juice of 1 lemon	

1. Mix gelatin with about 2 ounces of pineapple syrup in a saucepan, add ¼ cup boiling water, and let the gelatin dissolve.
2. Meanwhile mix the rest of the crushed pineapple in a large bowl with the lemon juice and the orange marmalade.
3. Pour the melted gelatin in a thin stream into the pineapple mixture, beating rapidly all the time.
4. Put the bowl in the refrigerator.
5. The frappé is ready to be served in about ½ hour. Decorate with lemon or orange slices.

Pineapple Boat

SERVES 4-6

1 small pineapple	½ cup whipped cream
2 cups whipping	mixed with chopped
cream	flaked coconut
1 cup sugar	Chopped cashews
1 tablespoon lime juice	

1. Cut pineapple in half lengthwise, a little off center. Remove pulp, keeping larger shell intact, and discard core. Chop pineapple finely or process in an electric blender. Measure 2 cups of pineapple and juice. Add to whipping cream along with sugar and the lime juice.
2. Cut the leafy top off the pineapple shell and reserve for decoration. Spoon pineapple mixture into the shell and freeze until firm.
3. To serve, pipe large rosettes of the whipped cream around the shell and sprinkle with cashews. Decorate with leafy top.

Apples in Blankets

ABOUT 14

1 pound apples, pared	⅓ cup sour cream
and cored	¼ cup buttermilk
2 eggs	Fat for deep frying
⅓ cup sugar	heated to 365°F
Dash salt	Confectioners' sugar
1¼ cups all-purpose	Nutmeg or cinnamon
flour	(optional)

1. Slice apples crosswise to make rings about ⅜-inch thick.
2. Beat eggs with sugar until thick and foamy. Add salt. Beat in small amounts of flour alternately with sour cream and buttermilk. Beat until batter is well mixed.
3. Coat apple slices with batter. Fry in hot fat until golden.
4. Drain on paper towels. Sprinkle with confectioners' sugar. Add a dash of nutmeg or cinnamon, if desired.

Cantaloupe Sherbet

ABOUT 1½ PINTS SHERBET

2 cups ripe cantaloupe	½ cup sugar
pieces	2 tablespoons fresh
1 egg white	lime juice

1. Put melon pieces, egg white, sugar, and lime juice into an electric blender container. Cover and blend until smooth.

2. Turn into a shallow baking dish. Set in freezer; stir occasionally during freezing.
3. To serve, spoon into chilled dessert dishes.

Pineapple Sherbet: Follow recipe for Cantaloupe Sherbet; substitute **2 cups fresh pineapple pieces** for cantaloupe.

Watermelon Sherbet: Follow recipe for Cantaloupe Sherbet; substitute **2 cups watermelon pieces** for cantaloupe and, if desired, decrease sugar to ¼ cup.

Apricot Ice Cream

SERVES 6

1 cup light cream	diced
4 egg yolks	1 teaspoon gelatin
Grated rind from	½ teaspoon vanilla
½ lemon	6 dried, finely
3 ounces sugar	chopped apricots
6 ounces dried and	1 cup heavy cream,
soaked apricots,	whipped

1. Beat the egg yolks in the cream in a heavy saucepan. Add grated lemon rind and sugar and whip the cream continuously while heating slowly. Remove from heat when cream starts to simmer, but go on whipping while it cools down.
2. Mix gelatin with 2 tablespoons hot water.
3. Add gelatin and vanilla to diced apricots. Chill until about to set.
4. Fold cream into gelatin mixture.
5. Freeze the cream for at least 3 hours and whip it a few times during that time. The apricot ice cream is spooned up in tall glasses and decorated with finely chopped dried apricots and whipped cream.

Italian Strawberry Water Ice

ABOUT 2 QUARTS WATER ICE

2 cups sugar	and hulled
1 cup water	⅓ cup orange juice
4 pints fresh ripe	¼ cup lemon juice
strawberries, rinsed	

1. Combine sugar and water in a saucepan; stir and bring to boiling. Boil 5 minutes; let cool.
2. Purée the strawberries in an electric blender or force through a sieve or food mill. Add juices to a mixture of the cooked syrup and strawberries; mix well.
3. Turn into refrigerator trays, cover tightly, and freeze.
4. About 45 minutes before serving time, remove trays from freezer to refrigerator to allow the ice to soften slightly. Spoon into sherbet glasses or other serving dishes.

Ice Cream Caesar

SERVES 4

1 pint vanilla ice cream	chopped
3 ounces shredded chocolate	¼ cup raisins
¼ cup walnuts,	¼ cup rum or orange liqueur

1. Soak raisins in rum or orange liqueur for 2-6 hours.
2. Divide ice cream between 4 dessert dishes.
3. Garnish with chocolate, nuts, and raisins.

Indian Pudding

SERVES 6

3 cups milk	½ cup light molasses
½ cup cornmeal	½ teaspoon salt
1 tablespoon butter or margarine	½ teaspoon ginger
	1 cup cold milk

1. Scald 2½ cups milk in top of double boiler over boiling water.
2. Combine cornmeal and the remaining ½ cup milk. Add to scalded milk, stirring constantly. Cook about 25 minutes, stirring frequently.
3. Stir in butter, molasses, salt, and ginger.
4. Pour into a greased 1½-quart baking dish. Pour the 1 cup cold milk over pudding.
5. Set in a baking pan. Pour boiling water around dish to within 1 inch of top.
6. Bake, covered, at 300°F about 2 hours. Remove cover and bake an additional 1 hour. Serve warm or cold with cream or ice cream.

Baklava

50 TO 60 PIECES

Syrup:	walnuts or blanched
2 cups honey	almonds
2 cups sugar	1 tablespoon cinnamon
3 cups water	
2 whole cloves	*Filo:*
1 stick cinnamon	¾ pound unsalted
Filling:	butter, melted
2 pounds chopped	2 packages filo

1. For syrup, combine all the ingredients in a large saucepan. Bring to a boil. Lower heat at once, cover, and simmer for 20 minutes. Remove from heat and cool to room temperature.
2. For filling, combine walnuts and cinnamon in a bowl. Set aside.
3. For filo, melt butter in a saucepan, being careful not to let it brown. Reheat it if it cools and does not spread easily.
4. Remove the layers of filo from their plastic wrapper and lay them flat on a large sheet of aluminum foil. Cover with another sheet of foil. (Filo must be kept completely covered at all times or it will dry out.)
5. Separate the filo layers one at a time. Brush with butter the bottom and sides of an 18 × 12-inch baking pan. Line the bottom of the pan with 4 filo layers, brushing each layer with melted butter before adding the next. After the fourth filo layer has been buttered, sprinkle it evenly with one third of the chopped nuts. Add 2 more filo layers, buttering each. Sprinkle with the remainder of the nuts. Cover with remaining filo, buttering each layer.
6. With a very sharp knife or a single-edge razor blade, using a ruler as a guide, cut into the topmost layers, tracing diamond shapes by making vertical cuts from one end of the pan to the other 1 inch apart, and diagonal cuts slightly less than ½ inch apart.
7. Bake at 250°F 1 hour and 50 minutes, or until golden. Cool 5 minutes. Pour the cooled syrup over it. Let stand overnight so syrup can be completely absorbed. Using a sharp knife, cut through each piece completely.
8. Remove the baklava slices with a fork to paper cupcake cups. Store no more than several weeks at room temperature. Baklava does not retain its crispness if stored in the refrigerator.

Peach Sherbet

SERVES 8

¾ pound well-ripened peaches	4 ounces sugar
	Juice of 1 lemon
½ bottle white wine	½ cup heavy cream
8 ounces water	2 ripe peaches, sliced

1. Bring water and sugar to a boil and let boil for a couple of minutes.
2. Remove pits from peaches and cut fruit in thin slices. Place in a large bowl. Pour warm sugared water over peach slices and let cool. Add wine. Let stand overnight.
3. Strain peaches and mix or purée with wine and syrup in a blender. Add lemon juice.
4. Place bowl in freezer for 1 hour or until it starts to set. Remove from freezer at half hour intervals for three hours and beat rapidly each time.
5. After last whipping, serve frozen sherbet immediately in large wine glasses.
6. Top with whipped cream and fresh peach slices.

Ice Cream Caesar.

Cassata.

Cassata

SERVES 8

White Layer:
1 pint vanilla ice cream
2 tablespoons rum or
  brandy
Red Layer:
1 pint strawberry ice
  cream
1 package frozen
  strawberries

Green Layer:
1 pint pistachio ice
  cream
10 maraschino cherries
2 tablespoons chopped
  candied melon
1 tablespoon chopped
  candied orange
  rind

1. You need three bowls of various sizes.
2. Start with the white layer: Stir the ice cream until soft and flavor with rum or brandy. Place the ice cream in the largest bowl. Press a medium size bowl into the ice cream, press hard, and place in the freezer.
3. When the vanilla ice cream is hard (about 2-3 hours) mix the red layer: Slice the strawberries. Mix with the strawberry ice cream. Remove medium bowl from the vanilla ice cream. Place strawberry ice cream on top of vanilla and press in with the smallest bowl. Place in freezer till it sets.
4. Mix the pistachio ice cream with the candied fruits. Remove the smallest bowl and place pistachio ice cream on top of strawberry ice cream. Place in the freezer till it sets.
5. Lower the bowl in warm water to remove the Cassata. Serve on a chilled serving dish.

Currant-Apple Fritters

ABOUT 30 FRITTERS

1 cup all-purpose flour
1¹/₂ teaspoons baking
  powder
¹/₄ teaspoon cinnamon
¹/₄ teaspoon salt
¹/₂ cup beer
¹/₂ cup currants

¹/₂ cup chopped pared
  apple
2 eggs, slightly beaten
1 teaspoon oil
Fat for deep frying
Confectioners' sugar

1. Combine flour, baking powder, cinnamon, and salt. Add beer, currants, apple, eggs, and oil. Stir to blend well.
2. Drop by rounded teaspoonfuls into hot deep fat heated to 365°F. Fry until browned. Drain on paper towels.
3. Keep hot in oven until serving time. While still hot, roll in confectioners' sugar.

Ice Cream Tarts

SERVES 6

1 cup water	1$^1/_2$ pints vanilla ice
$^1/_8$ teaspoon salt	cream, brick
8 tablespoons sweet	1 cup raspberries
butter	2 ounces semisweet
1 cup all-purpose flour	chocolate, melted
4 eggs	

1. Preheat oven to 350°F.
2. Pour water and salt into a heavy saucepan. Cut the butter into small pieces and add to water. Heat over low heat, stirring with a wooden spoon till mixture comes to a boil.
3. Add flour all at once. Stir until blended and dough forms a ball.
4. Remove dough to a bowl and beat in 3 eggs, one at a time till dough is very shiny.
5. Place in refrigerator for 30 minutes.
6. Put large tablespoons of dough onto an ungreased cookie sheet 2 inches apart. Brush with beaten egg yolk.
7. Bake for 35-40 minutes until puffed and golden brown.
8. Cool on a wire rack.

9. Cut the top off the pastries and fill with vanilla ice cream and raspberries.
10. Replace the top and drizzle hot chocolate on top.

Vanilla Ice Cream Surprise

SERVES 6-8

1 pound cake	2 tablespoons sugar
1 quart (brick) vanilla	2 ounces almonds,
ice cream	sliced
$^1/_3$ cup raspberry or	2 tablespoons brandy,
strawberry jam	heated
3 egg whites	

1. Place the pound cake on an ovenproof serving dish.
2. Cut the pound cake so that it is $^1/_2$ inch wider and longer than the ice cream brick.
3. Beat the egg whites to soft peaks, stir in the sugar, and beat till peaks are stiff.
4. Put the ice cream on top of the pound cake. Work quickly so that the ice cream does not melt.
5. Spread jam on top of the ice cream. Spread egg whites on top of the jam. Sprinkle with almonds and bake in a 450°F oven for about 3-4 minutes until the meringue has turned light brown. *(continued)*

**Vanilla
Ice Cream Surprise.**

6. Pour the brandy in the middle of the meringue and ignite.
Serve immediately.

Banana Fan

SERVES 3-4

4 ripe bananas	½ cup amber rum,
1 cup water	warmed and flamed
½ cup sugar	1 cup whipped cream
1 cup maraschino	¼ teaspoon vanilla
cherries	extract

1. Peel bananas and halve them lengthwise. Arrange halves flat side down in the shape of an open fan on a round silver or glass dish.
2. Boil water and sugar together at a rolling boil 4 minutes. Add cherries, reduce heat, and simmer 2 minutes. Remove some of the cherries with a perforated spoon and arrange in a design on upper portion of fan.
3. Put the remaining fruit with syrup into an electric blender along with flamed rum; process until puréed. Or force mixture through a food mill. Spoon over upper part of fan.
4. Blend whipped cream and vanilla extract. Using a pastry bag and decorating tube, make a thick border around upper portion of fan to simulate lace. Serve well chilled.

Zabaglione di Marsala.

Zabaglione di Marsala

SERVES 4

8 egg yolks	sherry)
½ cup confectioners'	Juice of ½ lemon
sugar	1 lemon rind, grated
½ cup marsala (or	

1. Beat yolks and sugar to a light foam.
2. Place yolks in top of a hot but not boiling double boiler. Add the wine and continue beating until the mixture starts to thicken. It should be light and foamy when ready.
3. Remove mixture from double boiler. Beat in lemon juice and grated lemon rind.
Serve warm.

Raspberry Foam

SERVES 4

4 egg whites	frozen raspberries,
2 tablespoons sugar	thawed
1 cup heavy cream	½ teaspoon lemon
1 (10-ounce) package	juice

1. In a bowl whip the egg whites, adding the sugar slowly, until stiff peaks are formed.
2. Whip the cream until stiff and fold into the egg whites.
3. Let the raspberries thaw completely and then fold into the cream mixture (both berries and syrup). Add the lemon juice.
4. Divide into individual serving cups and chill until serving.

Baked Banana and Orange Compote

SERVES 6

2 large navel oranges,	and cut in 1½-inch
peeled	pieces
½ teaspoon cinnamon	½ cup orange juice
4 large bananas, peeled	Cherries with stems

1. Cut oranges into ¼-inch slices; cut slices in half. Arrange orange slices in bottom of a shallow casserole; sprinkle with cinnamon.
2. Dip bananas in orange juice; arrange over oranges. Spoon remaining orange juice over fruit.
3. Bake at 400°F 15 minutes. Serve warm in compote dishes; garnish with cherries.

Baked Alaska.

Baked Alaska

SERVES 8

1 (9-inch round)   8 tablespoons sugar
   spongecake   2 tablespoons al-
1 quart ice cream   monds, slivered
Meringue:
4 egg whites

1. Soften the ice cream and place it in a 8" × 12" loaf pan. Return to freezer and freeze until hard.
2. Beat the egg whites till soft peaks form. Add the sugar a tablespoon at a time and beat till stiff peaks form.
3. Place the hard ice cream on top of the cake and cover the top of the ice cream and sides of the cake with the meringue. Sprinkle with slivered almonds and bake in a preheated 450°F oven till the meringue is lightly browned, about 5 minutes. Serve immediately.

Cherry-Pineapple Cobbler

SERVES 8

1 can (21 ounces)   3 tablespoons honey
   cherry pie filling   1 egg, slightly beaten
1 can (13¼ ounces)   ½ cup sour cream
   pineapple tidbits,   1½ cups unflavored
   drained   croutons
¼ teaspoon allspice

1. Combine cherry pie filling, pineapple tidbits, allspice, and 1 tablespoon honey. Put into a 1½-quart baking dish.
2. Blend egg, sour cream, and remaining 2 tablespoons honey. Stir in croutons. Spoon over cherry-pineapple mixture.
3. Bake, uncovered, at 375°F 30 minutes, or until heated through. If desired, top with ice cream.

Cheese-Stuffed Strawberries

SERVES 4

¹/₂ cup low-fat ricotta cheese	lemon juice
1 teaspoon grated lemon peel	1 teaspoon honey or sugar
1 teaspoon fresh	48 large strawberries
	Mint sprigs (optional)

1. Mix cheese, lemon peel, lemon juice, and honey in a food processor or blender until fluffy; refrigerate until chilled (about 1 hour).
2. Gently scoop centers from strawberries with melon-baller or fruit knife. Fill with cheese mixture.
3. Arrange filled strawberries on small individual plates. Garnish with mint.

Hot Spicy Fruit Pot

SERVES 8

1 can (16 ounces) pear halves	1 cinnamon stick
1 can (16 ounces) peach halves	¹/₄ teaspoon nutmeg
	¹/₄ teaspoon allspice
1 can (16 ounces) purple plums, halved and pitted	¹/₈ teaspoon ginger
	¹/₄ cup lemon juice
1 cup firmly packed brown sugar	2 teaspoons grated orange peel
	2 tablespoons butter or margarine

1. Drain fruits, reserving 1 cup liquid. Put fruit into a buttered 2-quart casserole.
2. Combine reserved liquid with remaining ingredients, except butter. Pour over fruit. Dot with butter.
3. Bake, covered, at 350°F 30 minutes, or until bubbly. Serve hot or cold. If desired, spoon over ice cream or cake.

Quick Applesauce Whip

SERVES ABOUT 6

1 can (16 ounces) applesauce	¹/₂ teaspoon ground cinnamon
¹/₂ teaspoon grated lemon peel	3 egg whites
	¹/₈ teaspoon salt
2 teaspoons lemon juice	6 tablespoons sugar
	Ground nutmeg

1. Combine applesauce, lemon peel, juice, and cinnamon.
2. Beat egg whites and salt until frothy. Add sugar gradually, beat well. Continue beating until rounded peaks are formed. Fold beaten egg whites into applesauce mixture.
3. Spoon immediately into dessert dishes. Sprinkle nutmeg over each serving.

Semisweet Chocolate Pudding

SERVES 6

1 package (6 ounces) semisweet chocolate pieces	extract
	4 egg whites
¹/₄ cup water	1 cup chilled whipping cream
¹/₂ cup firmly packed golden brown sugar	2 tablespoons golden brown sugar
4 egg yolks	Sliced almonds
1 teaspoon vanilla	

1. Combine chocolate pieces, water, and ¹/₂ cup brown sugar in the top of a double boiler. Heat over simmering water until chocolate is melted. Beat until smooth. Cool.
2. Beat egg yolks with vanilla extract. Stir into chocolate mixture. Beat egg whites until stiff. Fold chocolate mixture into egg whites. Spoon into individual serving dishes. Chill 3 hours.
3. Combine whipping cream and 2 tablespoons brown sugar. Whip until stiff. Top pudding with the whipped cream and sprinkle with almonds.

Spicy Fruit Gelatin "with a Head"

SERVES 4-5

1 can or bottle (12 ounces) beer	1 package (3 ounces) orange-flavored gelatin
2 tablespoons packed brown sugar	1 can (8¹/₄ ounces) crushed pineapple
1 stick cinnamon	
4 whole cloves	Water

1. Place beer, brown sugar, cinnamon, and cloves in a saucepan. Heat to boiling. Add gelatin; stir until dissolved.
2. Let stand at room temperature until lukewarm to mellow flavors. Remove spices.
3. Drain pineapple thoroughly, reserving liquid. Add water to liquid to measure ¹/₂ cup. Stir into gelatin mixture. Chill until partially thickened.
4. Fold in pineapple. Spoon into pilsner or parfait glasses. Chill until firm.
5. To serve, top with a "head" of whipped cream or prepared whipped topping.

Wine-Glazed Pears.

Wine-Glazed Pears

SERVES 8

8 pears of uniform size with stems	**1 cup whipped cream**
8 tablespoons white wine	*Syrup.*
	1¹/₂ cups water
10 ounces almond paste	**6 ounces sugar**
	Juice of ¹/₂ lemon

1. Peel pears.
2. Combine water, sugar, and lemon juice in a saucepan. Set over medium heat and stir until sugar is dissolved. Increase heat and bring mixture to boiling.

3. Boil pears in syrup until they are half soft. Place them in an ovenproof dish and pour 1 tablespoon white wine over each pear.
4. Cut the almond paste in slices and put 1 slice on each pear.
5. Bake the pears in a 350°F oven for 15 minutes. Serve with cold whipped cream.

CAKES, PIES, COOKIES and CANDIES

Melba Cake

SERVES 8

16 ounces almond paste	raspberries
4 eggs	1/2 can pears
Bread crumbs	Shredded almonds
1 tablespoon salad oil	1-2 pints vanilla ice cream
2 packages frozen	3 ounces rum

1. Grate the almond paste and place in a bowl. Add the eggs and stir the batter as smooth as possible. Pour into a round cake pan that has been sprinkled with bread crumbs.
2. Bake the cake in 300°F oven for about 45 minutes. Let the cake cool before it is carefully loosened and placed on a serving dish.
3. Heat 1 tablespoon salad oil in a frying pan over low heat and pour in the shredded almonds to brown, turning them often. Place the shredded almonds on paper towel.
4. Decoration: Mash one package thawed raspberries and spread over the cake. Cut the pears in wedges and arrange fan-shaped.
5. Sprinkle on the rest of the raspberries. Finally sprinkle on the roasted almonds.
The cake round can be baked several days before cake is to be served. It will keep well in the refrigerator if wrapped in plastic or foil.

Peanut Butter Coffee Cake

SERVES 4-6

2 cups all-purpose biscuit mix	2/3 cup milk
2 tablespoons sugar	1 egg
1/4 cup peanut butter, chunky or smooth	1/2 cup jelly or jam (optional)

1. Combine biscuit mix and sugar; cut in peanut butter with a fork. Stir in milk and egg; blend evenly. Pour into a buttered 9-inch glass dish. Swirl jelly through batter, if desired.
2. Cook 8 to 10 minutes, rotating dish one-quarter turn halfway through cooking time.
3. Rest 5 minutes before serving.

Irish Fruitcake

ONE 3³/₄-POUND FRUITCAKE

1¹/₂ cups walnuts (7 ounces)	2 cups sifted all-purpose flour
³/₄ cup dark seedless raisins (4 ounces)	1/2 teaspoon baking powder
³/₄ cup golden raisins (4 ounces)	1 teaspoon salt
³/₄ cup currants (3 ounces)	1 teaspoon cinnamon
³/₄ cup diced citron (4 ounces)	1/2 teaspoon nutmeg
³/₄ cup diced candied orange peel (4 ounces)	1/2 teaspoon allspice
	³/₄ cup butter or margarine
³/₄ cup halved candied cherries (6 ounces)	1 cup packed brown sugar
1/2 cup Irish whiskey or bourbon	3 eggs
1 tablespoon molasses	Confectioners' sugar
1 teaspoon grated lemon peel	Water
	Green food coloring
	Green decorator sugar
	Walnut halves

1. Chop walnuts coarsely and set aside.
2. Combine raisins, currants, and candied fruits and peels with 1/3 cup whiskey, molasses, and lemon peel. Mix well, cover, and let stand overnight.
3. The next day, sift flour with baking powder, salt, and spices.
4. Cream butter and brown sugar well. Add eggs, one at a time, beating thoroughly after each addition (mixture will look curdled). Blend flour mixture into creamed mixture. Add fruits and walnuts and mix well.
5. Turn into a well-greased 9-inch Bundt pan.
6. Place a shallow pan of hot water on oven floor. Set filled Bundt pan on lowest rack of oven.
7. Bake at 300°F about 1³/₄ hours, or until cake tests done. Let cool 10 minutes in pan, then invert cake onto wire rack and spoon remaining whiskey slowly over cake so it soaks in. Cool cake completely.
8. To decorate, mix a small amount of confectioners' sugar with enough water to thin to pouring consistency. Tint lightly with food coloring; drizzle over top of cake. Sprinkle with green sugar and arrange walnut halves on top.

Melba Cake.

Three-Tier Cake.

Strawberry-Peach
Cake.

Three-Tier Cake

YIELDS 10 PIECES

3 eggs	Bread crumbs
1 cup sugar	*Filling:*
1 cup flour	6 ounces heavy cream
1½ tablespoons potato flour	1 bag raspberries, frozen
2¼ teaspoons baking powder	*Decoration:*
4 tablespoons boiling water	Confectioners' sugar
Butter	3 ounces heavy cream
	Raspberries

1. Beat eggs and sugar until foamy. Add flour combined with the baking powder and the boiling water. Pour batter in a well-greased cake pan (1½ quarts) sprinkled with bread crumbs. Bake the cake in a 350°F oven for 30 minutes.
2. Let the cake cool. Cut the cake horizontally in two rounds.
3. Put one round cake layer on a serving dish. Place a saucer in the middle of the other layer and cut around the saucer, making a "ring" out of this layer.
4. Spread ¾ of the whipped cream on the bottom layer.
5. Place the "ring" on the whipped cream and fill the inside of the "ring" with raspberries.
6. Put the small round on top of the raspberries and sift confectioners' sugar over the entire cake. Then add the rest of the whipped cream and the raspberries as decoration.

Strawberry-Peach Cake

ONE 10-INCH CAKE

2 cups heavy cream	1 teaspoon vanilla extract
1 (1-pound) can halved peaches	1 cup sugar
1 quart strawberries, sliced	½ teaspoon cream of tartar
6 eggs, separated	1 cup all-purpose flour
2 tablespoons lemon juice	

1. Beat egg yolks with lemon juice and vanilla, slowly adding ½ cup sugar until mixture is thick.
2. Beat egg whites until stiff peaks form. Slowly add cream of tartar. Add ½ cup of sugar, a little at a time until stiff.
3. Fold in the yolk mixture.
4. Sift the flour and fold into the mixture.
5. Pour into a 10-inch tube pan and bake in a 325°F oven for about 50 minutes.
6. Release from pan and let cool.

7. Beat cream until stiff.
8. Slice cake horizontally in half and spread half of the whipped cream on the bottom half of the cake.
9. Place half the peaches over the whipped cream, then add the strawberries.
10. Put the top layer of the cake back, decorating it with the remaining whipped cream, strawberries, and peaches.

Strawberry Shortcake

SERVES 6-8

2 cups all-purpose flour	¾ cup milk
¼ cup sugar	Sweetened strawberries or other fresh fruit
1 tablespoon baking powder	Sweetened whipped cream
½ teaspoon salt	
½ cup (1 stick) butter	

1. Line two 8-inch round glass cake dishes with 2 layers of paper towels cut to fit dish.
2. Combine flour, sugar, baking powder, and salt in a bowl. Cut in butter until mixture resembles coarse crumbs. Add milk and mix only until the dry ingredients are moistened. Dough will be thick and lumpy.
3. Divide dough into two portions. Drop one-half of dough by teaspoonfuls into each lined cake dish. Spread evenly with moistened fingers.
4. Cook, uncovered, one dish at a time, in microwave oven 2½ to 3 minutes, or until done.
5. Remove shortcake from dishes and peel off paper.
6. Serve shortcake warm, filled and topped with fruit and whipped cream.

Irresistible Chocolate Cake

MAKES 2 9-INCH LAYERS

2½ cups sifted cake flour	margarine
½ teaspoon baking soda	1½ teaspoons vanilla
½ teaspoon salt	1½ cups sugar
1½ teaspoons baking powder	2 eggs, beaten
⅛ teaspoon nutmeg	3 squares (3 ounces) unsweetened chocolate, melted
¾ cup butter or	1¼ cups cold water

1. Sift together first 5 ingredients.
2. Cream together butter, vanilla, and sugar until creamy.
3. Add eggs; beat until fluffy.
4. Add chocolate; blend well. *(continued)*

293

5. Add dry ingredients and water alternately in thirds; beat after each addition.

6. Pour into 2 greased 9-inch layer pans.

7. Bake at 350°F 30 to 35 minutes.

Chocolate-Walnut Roll

1 CAKE ROLL

2 tablespoons fine dry bread crumbs	chilled
1 cup walnuts, ground	2 tablespoons sugar
$^{1}/_{4}$ cup sifted cake flour	$^{1}/_{2}$ teaspoon vanilla extract
$^{1}/_{4}$ cup unsweetened cocoa	1 tablespoon brandy
1 teaspoon baking powder	$^{1}/_{4}$ cup chopped walnuts
$^{1}/_{2}$ teaspoon salt	$^{1}/_{4}$ cup chopped candied cherries (half red and half green)
$^{1}/_{4}$ cup sugar	
4 eggs	
$^{1}/_{4}$ teaspoon cream of tartar	2 ounces (2 squares) semisweet chocolate
$^{1}/_{2}$ cup sugar	
2 tablespoons coffee beverage	2 teaspoons vegetable shortening
1 cup heavy cream,	2 teaspoons light corn syrup
	Granulated sugar

1. Set out a 15 × 10 × 1-inch pan. Line with greased waxed paper. To prevent sticking and for a slightly heavier crust, sprinkle greased paper with bread crumbs.

2. Sift together the cake flour, unsweetened cocoa, baking powder, salt, and sugar. Combine with walnuts, mixing well.

3. Separate the eggs and beat egg whites with cream of tartar in large mixer bowl until foamy. Beating constantly, add $^{1}/_{2}$ cup sugar gradually until very stiff peaks are formed.

4. Using same beater, beat the egg yolks until thick. Beat in coffee beverage.

5. Blend in the walnut-flour mixture. Turn batter over beaten egg whites and fold gently with spatula until no streaks of white remain. Turn into the baking pan and spread batter evenly into corners.

6. Bake at 400°F 10 minutes. Turn out onto sheet of waxed paper sprinkled with granulated sugar (about 2 tablespoons). Carefully peel off paper from cake. Cover cake with the pan and cool.

7. Meanwhile, prepare Walnut Cream Filling. Combine heavy cream and 2 tablespoons sugar in a small mixer bowl. Beat until stiff peaks are formed, then blend in vanilla extract and brandy.

8. Fold in chopped walnuts and candied cherries. Spread cooled cake with the filling and roll up lengthwise. Place roll on serving plate.

9. Prepare Chocolate Glaze. Melt semisweet chocolate and vegetable shortening over hot water. Remove from heat and stir in light corn syrup.

10. Cool slightly, then spread over top and sides of cake roll. Decorate with walnut halves and candied red cherries.

Chocolate-Walnut Roll.

Mocha and Nut Cake.

Mocha and Nut Cake

ONE 10-INCH CAKE

Nut Cake Rounds:
1 cup shelled hazel-
    nuts
1 cup confectioners'
    sugar
5 egg whites

Mocha Cream Filling:
1¹/₂ cups heavy cream
3 tablespoons confec-
    tioners' sugar
5 tablespoons strong
    coffee (preferably
    French roast)
2 teaspoons gelatin

1. Preheat the oven to 300°F.
2. Grease and flour three baking sheets and draw three rounds, about 9 inches in diameter. Use a plate for size.
3. Grind the nuts and mix with the sugar.
4. Beat the egg whites to very stiff peaks and fold them into the nut and sugar mixture.
5. Spread the batter evenly into three rounds on the sheets.
6. Bake for 10-15 minutes until rounds are light brown. Remove from oven and loosen immediately with a thin knife. Let the rounds cool.
7. Place the gelatin in ¹/₄ cup cold water for some 20 minutes. Melt gelatin on low heat and let cool.
8. Whip the cream with the confectioners' sugar to a light foam, add the cold coffee mixed with the gelatin and beat the mixture until thick.

9. Sandwich together the rounds with mocha-cream between them, spread a thin layer on top, and use the rest of the cream for decoration.
10. Put the cake in the refrigerator for at least two hours and dust with finely ground coffee just before serving.

Marble Tube Cake

MAKES 1 10-INCH TUBE CAKE

3¹/₂ cups sifted cake
    flour
3 teaspoons baking
    powder
¹/₂ teaspoon salt
1 cup butter or
    margarine
1 teaspoon almond

extract
2 cups sugar
4 eggs, well beaten
1 cup milk
¹/₄ cup cocoa
1 teaspoon rum
    flavoring

1. Sift flour, baking powder, and salt together.
2. Cream butter and almond extract together.
3. Gradually add 1¹/₂ cups sugar, creaming well after each addition.
4. Add eggs and beat until light and fluffy.
5. Add dry ingredients alternately with milk, beating just until blended after each addition.

(continued)

295

6. Blend remaining $1/2$ cup sugar and cocoa together.
7. Divide batter in half and add cocoa mixture and rum extract to half the batter; blend well.
8. Grease bottom of a 10-inch pan; line with waxed paper.
9. Spoon batters in alternate layers into pan; cut through gently with a spatula to marble the batters.
10. Bake at 350°F 60 minutes.
11. Cool 15 minutes; remove to rack.

Apricot Cake

YIELDS 8 PIECES

4 eggs	Butter (to grease
$1^1/4$ cups granulated	baking dish)
sugar	Bread crumbs
$1^1/4$ cups all-purpose	*Filling:*
flour	$3/4$ cup apricot jam
2 tablespoons potato	$3/4$ cup whipped
flour	cream
2 teaspoons baking	*Garnish:*
powder	1 can preserved
5 tablespoons boiling	apricots
water	

1. Beat eggs and sugar until foamy.
2. Mix flour, potato flour, and baking powder. Add to egg mixture.
3. Add boiling water to batter.
4. Butter baking dish and sprinkle with bread crumbs. Put in batter.
5. Bake in 350°F oven for 30-35 minutes.
6. Cut cake in two layers when cooled. Put whipped cream and jam between layers. Garnish with apricots.

Old English Cheesecake

10 PIECES

Crust:	$1/3$ cup almonds
$1^1/4$ cups all-purpose	(2 ounces), finely
flour	chopped
$1/4$ cup sugar	1 tablespoon grated
$1/3$ cup butter or	lemon peel
margarine	1 pound cottage
4 tablespoons cold	cheese
beer	$1/2$ cup flour
Filling:	4 eggs
$1/2$ cup golden raisins	1 cup sugar
($2^1/2$ ounces),	$3/4$ cup beer
chopped	$1/8$ teaspoon nutmeg

1. For crust, mix flour and sugar; cut in butter until crumbly. Add beer 1 tablespoon at a time, stirring with a fork. Shape dough into a ball. Chill.

2. Roll out on floured surface to a 13- to 14-inch circle. Fold in quarters. Gently unfold in a 9-inch springform pan ($1^1/2$ inches up sides if using a 10-inch pan). Prick all over with fork.
3. Bake at 425°F 10 minutes. Prick again and press to sides. Bake 10 minutes more, or until slightly golden.
4. For filling, mix chopped raisins, almonds, and peel.
5. Process cottage cheese, flour, and eggs until smooth, using food processor or electric blender. (Do in several batches in blender.)
6. Add sugar, beer, and nutmeg; blend until smooth. Stir in raisin mixture. Pour into cooled shell.
7. Bake at 300°F $1^1/4$ to $1^1/2$ hours, or until set. Cool to room temperature for serving. Dust with confectioners' sugar and top with whole unblanched almonds.

Baba with Raisins

1 BABA

1 cup butter or	powder
margarine (at room	$1^1/2$ cups all-purpose
temperature)	flour
$1^1/2$ cups confection-	1 cup cornstarch
ers' sugar	$1/3$ cup confectioners'
4 eggs, separated	sugar
$1/4$ cup orange juice	$1/2$ teaspoon salt
4 teaspoons lemon	$1/2$ cup raisins
juice	Fine dry bread
1 tablespoon grated	crumbs
orange or lemon	1 tablespoon whip-
peel	ping cream (op-
4 teaspoons baking	tional)

1. Cream butter. Gradually add $1^1/2$ cups confectioners' sugar, beating at high speed of electric mixture. Beat in egg yolks, one at a time. Beat in orange juice, lemon juice, and orange peel.
2. Mix flour, cornstarch, and $1/3$ cup confectioners' sugar.
3. With clean beaters, beat egg whites with salt until stiff, not dry, peaks form.
4. Fold half the flour mixture into the butter mixture. Fold in egg whites.
5. Add raisins to remaining flour mixture; mix well. Fold into batter.
6. Generously grease an 11-cup ring mold or baba pan. Coat with bread crumbs.
7. Turn batter into prepared pan. Brush top with cream.
8. Bake at 350°F about 40 minutes.

Apricot Cake.

296

Layer Cake with Two Fillings.

Layer Cake with Two Fillings

YIELDS 8 PIECES

For Cake Rounds:
4 eggs
6 ounces sugar
3 ounces potato flour
3 ounces wheat flour
1/2 teaspoon baking powder

Filling:
About 6 ounces currant jelly

Cream:
4 ounces light cream
2 tablespoons butter
4 ounces fresh orange juice

2 tablespoons honey or sugar
1 large egg or 2 egg yolks
1 tablespoon potato flour
1 tablespoon flour

Decoration:
7 ounces almond paste (not marzipan, which would be too sweet here)
1 egg
1 can mandarin oranges

1. Preheat the oven to 325°F. Separate egg whites and yolks. Beat the whites till stiff. Add the yolks and the sugar, beating rapidly all the time.

2. Sift together the two flours and the baking powder and stir this carefully into the batter. Mix well but avoid stirring so much that batter loses its foaminess.

3. Pour batter in a well-greased 2-quart cake pan with straight edges, sprinkled with bread crumbs. Bake for about 30 minutes. Place cake on cake rack and let it get cold. Cut the cake horizontally into 3 rounds.

4. Heat the cream in a saucepan with a heavy bottom. Add all ingredients except the butter. Simmer the mixture, beating it constantly until it thickens. Remove saucepan from heat and stir in the butter. Assemble the cake rounds on an ovenproof dish with 1 layer jelly and 1 layer cream between the rounds.

5. Grate the almond paste coarsely and mix with the egg in a bowl to a smooth batter. Place batter in a pastry bag with round tube and pipe a latticework pattern on top of the cake. Also pipe around the top. Let the cake stand for about 1 hour. The almond paste must dry a little.

6. Preheat the oven to 350°F. Leave the cake for 6-8 minutes in the oven until the almond paste has turned light brown. Let the cake cool and refrigerate. Decorate just before serving with well-drained mandarin oranges.

Black Forest Torte.

Black Forest Torte

ONE 8-INCH TORTE

1¹/₂ cups toasted filberts, grated	6 tablespoons kirsch
¹/₄ cup flour	6 egg whites
¹/₂ cup butter or margarine	Cherry Filling, (below)
1 cup sugar	3 cups chilled heavy cream
6 egg yolks	¹/₃ cup confectioners' sugar
4 ounces (4 squares) semisweet chocolate, melted and cooled	Chocolate curls or thin chocolate wafers

1. Grease and lightly flour an 8-inch springform pan; set aside.
2. Blend grated filberts and flour; set aside.
3. Cream butter until softened. Beat in sugar gradually until mixture is light and fluffy. Add egg yolks, one at a time, beating thoroughly after each addition.
4. Blend in the chocolate and 2 tablespoons of the kirsch. Stir in nut-flour mixture until blended.

5. Beat egg whites until stiff, not dry, peaks are formed. Fold into batter and turn into the pan.
6. Bake at 375°F about 1 hour, or until torte tests done. (Torte should be about 1¹/₂ inches high and top may have a slight crack.)
7. Cool 10 minutes in pan on a wire rack; remove from pan and cool.
8. Using a long sharp knife, carefully cut torte into 3 layers. Place top layer inverted on a cake plate; spread with Cherry Filling.
9. Whip cream (1¹/₂ cups at a time) until soft peaks are formed, gradually adding half of the confectioners' sugar and 2 tablespoons of the kirsch to each portion.
10. Generously spread some of the whipped cream over the Cherry Filling. Cover with second layer and remaining Cherry Filling. Spread generously with more whipped cream and top with third torte layer. Frost entire torte with remaining whipped cream.
11. Decorate torte with reserved cherries and chocolate curls or thin chocolate wafers.

Cherry Filling: Drain **1 jar** (16 ounces) **red maraschino cherries,** reserving ¹/₂ cup syrup. Set aside 13 cherries for decoration; slice remaining cherries. Set aside. Combine reserved syrup and **4 tablespoons kirsch.** In a saucepan, gradually blend syrup mix-

(continued)

ture into **1¹/₂ tablespoons cornstarch.** Mix in **1 tablespoon lemon juice.** Stir over medium heat until mixture boils ¹/₂ minute. Mix in sliced cherries and cool.

1¹/₃ Cups Filling

Bavarian Chocolate Cake

YIELDS 14-16 PIECES

4 ounces butter	*Chocolate Milk:*
4 ounces sugar	**3 ounces cocoa powder**
2 eggs	
1 teaspoon vanilla	**6 ounces half-and-half**
1 cup flour	
1¹/₂ teaspoons baking powder	**3 ounces sugar**

1. Bring the mixture of cocoa powder, the half-and-half, and the sugar to a boil in a saucepan and let it cool.
2. Beat butter and sugar until foamy. Add the eggs, one at a time, and the vanilla and beat until mixed.
3. Combine flour and baking powder and sift into the egg batter alternately with the cold chocolate milk.

Bavarian Chocolate Cake.

Juicy Almond Cake.

4. Pour the batter in a greased cake pan sprinkled with bread crumbs and bake at 325°F for about one hour.

Sally Lunn with Strawberries

ONE 10-INCH RING LOAF

1 cup milk, scalded	**3 eggs, beaten**
¹/₂ cup sugar	**5 cups all-purpose flour**
2 teaspoons salt	
¹/₂ cup butter or margarine, melted	**¹/₂ teaspoon ground nutmeg**
1 package active dry yeast	**3 pints fresh strawberries, sliced and sweetened**
¹/₂ cup warm water	

1. Combine milk, ¹/₄ cup of the sugar, salt, and butter; cool to lukewarm.
2. Soften yeast in the warm water in a large bowl. Blend with the milk mixture and eggs.
3. Gradually beat in the flour until smooth. Cover; let rise in a warm place until doubled, about 1 hour.
4. Stir dough down and turn into a greased and sugared 10-inch tube pan. Cover; let rise again until doubled, about 30 minutes.
5. Mix remaining ¹/₄ cup sugar with the nutmeg and sprinkle over top of dough.
6. Bake at 400°F about 40 minutes. Remove from oven and cool 5 minutes. Turn out Sally Lunn and serve warm or cooled with the strawberries mounded

Confetti Coffee Cake.

in the center of the ring. Accompany with a bowl of whipped cream or a pitcher of cream.

Note: If desired, the strawberries may be left whole and unhulled to be dipped into the cream as they are eaten.

Juicy Almond Cake

YIELDS 10 LARGE PIECES

3¹/₂ ounces butter	Melted butter
3 eggs	2 teaspoons baking
³/₄ cup sugar	powder
3 tablespoons light	Grated rind of
cream	1 orange
1 cup fine bread	*For the Cake Pan:*
crumbs	Butter
2 ounces almonds,	¹/₂ bag shredded
shredded	almonds

1. Melt the butter and let it get cool.
2. Beat eggs and sugar until foamy.
3. Add the butter and cream.
4. Stir in the bread crumbs combined with grated orange rind and the baking powder.
5. Pour the batter in a well-greased cake pan sprinkled with shredded almonds. Bake the cake in a 350°F oven for 30-35 minutes.

Confetti Coffee Cake

YIELDS 12 LARGE PIECES

10¹/₂ ounces marga-rine	*Frosting:*
1¹/₂ cups sugar	2¹/₂ cups confection-ers' sugar, sifted
4 eggs	4 tablespoons water
2¹/₂ cups all-purpose flour	*Garnish:*
2 teaspoons baking powder	4 tablespoons pre-served mixed fruit, chopped
¹/₂ cup water	
Peel of ¹/₂ lemon, finely chopped	

1. Mix sugar and margarine until foamy. Add eggs one at a time.
2. Add mixture of flour and baking powder. Then add water and lemon peel.
3. Put batter in buttered baking dish sprinkled with bread crumbs. Bake in 350°F oven about 40 minutes.
4. Let cake cool and cut in squares.
5. Mix confectioners' sugar and water until smooth.
6. Frost cake and sprinkle with chopped fruit.

Strawberry Cake.

Strawberry Cake

YIELDS 8 PIECES

4 eggs
¾ cup sugar
3 ounces wheat flour
4 ounces potato flour
2 teaspoons baking
  powder
Bread crumbs
Vanilla Cream:
1 egg
2 egg yolks
2 ounces sugar

3 ounces milk
1 vanilla stick
1 teaspoon potato
  flour
¾ cup heavy cream
Filling:
1½ quarts strawber-
  ries
Decoration:
1 cup heavy cream
1 pint strawberries

1. Beat eggs and sugar until white and foamy.

2. Sift in wheat flour, potato flour, and baking powder and stir until well mixed.
3. Pour the batter into a well-greased round cake pan of about 1½ quarts and sprinkle with fine bread crumbs. Bake in a 350°F oven for about 30 minutes.
4. Place the cake on a cake rack and cool.
5. Meanwhile make the vanilla cream. Mix egg, egg yolks, sugar, milk, potato flour in a thick saucepan and put in the vanilla stick after making a slit in it lengthwise.
6. Heat and stir continuously until the cream is thick and foamy.
7. Place the saucepan in cold water and beat until it is cold.
8. Whip the cream till thick.
9. Slice the strawberries and add to the vanilla cream.
10. Cut the cake in three rounds and sandwich together with strawberries and vanilla cream between them.

302

11. Cover the top of the cake with the whipped cream. Decorate with strawberries. Put cake in the refrigerator for a few hours before serving.

Pineapple Upside-Down Cake

SERVES 6-8

2 tablespoons butter	brown sugar
1 can (8 ounces)	6 maraschino cherries
crushed pineapple	1 package (9 ounces)
¹/₂ cup firmly packed	yellow cake mix

1. Heat butter 30 seconds in an 8-inch round glass baking dish.
2. Drain pineapple, reserving juice.
3. Blend together butter, brown sugar, and drained pineapple; spread evenly in bottom of pan. Arrange maraschino cherries in bottom of pan.
4. Prepare cake mix as directed on package, substituting the reserved pineapple juice for water. Pour batter evenly over pineapple mixture.
5. Cook 5 to 7 minutes, rotating dish one-quarter turn halfway through cooking time. Rest 5 minutes until cake pulls away from sides of pan.
6. Invert onto serving dish.

Note: If desired, pineapple slices may be used. Blend the melted butter and the brown sugar in baking dish and arrange slices on top. Other fruits, such as apricots or peaches, may be used, also.

Devil's Food Cake

MAKES 2 9-INCH LAYERS

2 cups sifted cake	1 teaspoon salt
flour	³/₄ cup cocoa
1³/₄ cups sugar	²/₃ cup soft shortening
¹/₂ teaspoon baking	1 cup water
powder	1¹/₂ teaspoons vanilla
1¹/₄ teaspoons baking	3 eggs (¹/₂ to ²/₃ cup)
soda	

1. Sift flour, sugar, baking powder, soda, salt, and cocoa together.
2. Add shortening, a little over half the water, and vanilla.
3. Beat vigorously with a spoon for 2 minutes (or with mixer at medium speed).
4. Add remaining water and eggs; beat vigorously with spoon 2 minutes (or with mixer at medium speed).
5. Turn into prepared pans; bake at 350°F 30 to 40 minutes.

Angel Food Cake

MAKES 1 9-INCH TUBE CAKE

1 cup sifted cake flour	tartar
1¹/₄ cups sugar	¹/₂ teaspoon salt
1 cup egg whites	1 teaspoon vanilla
(8-10 eggs)	¹/₄ teaspoon almond
1 teaspoon cream of	extract

1. Sift flour and ¹/₄ cup sugar together 4 times.
2. Beat egg whites, cream of tartar, and salt until frothy throughout.
3. Add remaining sugar in small amounts and beat after each addition, preferably with a rotary beater. Egg whites should have fine, even texture and be stiff enough to hold a peak but not be dry.
4. Add flavorings.
5. Sift ¹/₄ of flour at a time over mixture and fold in lightly.
6. Pour into 9-inch ungreased tube pan; cut through batter with spatula to remove large air bubbles.
7. Bake in moderate oven (375°F) 35-40 minutes.
8. Invert pan and let cake stand until cold.

Lemon Chiffon Cake

MAKES 1 10-INCH TUBE CAKE

2¹/₄ cups sifted cake	when using all-
flour or 2 cups	purpose flour)
sifted all-purpose	³/₄ cup cold water
flour	1 tablespoon grated
1¹/₂ cups sugar	lemon rind
3 teaspoons baking	1¹/₂ teaspoons vanilla
powder	¹/₄ teaspoon lemon
1 teaspoon salt	extract
¹/₂ cup salad oil	7 egg whites
5 egg yolks, unbeaten	¹/₂ teaspoon cream of
(use 7 egg yolks	tartar

1. Sift first 4 ingredients together into large bowl; make a well in center.
2. Measure into this in order listed — salad oil, yolks, water, rind, and extracts.
3. Beat with electric mixer (medium speed) or with spoon until smooth; set aside.
4. Beat egg whites with cream of tartar in large bowl until stiff peaks are formed.
5. Pour yolk mixture slowly over whites, folding gently until just blended (do not overmix).
6. Turn into ungreased 10-inch tube pan.
7. Bake at 325°F 55 minutes, then at 350°F 10 minutes.
8. Invert pan; let stand until cool.

Spice Chiffon Cake. Follow recipe for Lemon Chif-

(continued)

fon Cake except: omit lemon rind and lemon extract; sift only 1 cup sugar with dry ingredients; add **1/2 cup firmly packed brown sugar** to sifted dry ingredients; add **1 teaspoon cinnamon, 1/2 teaspoon each of nutmeg and allspice, and 1/4 teaspoon cloves to dry ingredients.**

Orange Chiffon Cake. Follow recipe for Lemon Chiffon Cake except: substitute **3/4 cup orange juice** for the cold water and **2 teaspoons grated orange rind** for lemon rind.

Chocolate Torte

ONE 10-INCH TORTE

8 eggs, separated	2 ounces (2 squares)
1 1/4 cups sugar	semisweet choco-
3/4 cup all-purpose	late, grated
flour	1 1/2 teaspoons vanilla
1/4 cup fine dry bread	extract
crumbs	Filling (*see below*)
1/4 teaspoon salt	Frosting (*see below*)

1. Beat egg yolks until very thick and lemon-colored, about 5 minutes. Gradually beat in sugar.
2. Combine flour, bread crumbs, and salt. Add chocolate and mix thoroughly but lightly.
3. Add flour mixture to egg yolks and sugar in 4 portions, folding until well mixed after each addition.
4. With clean beaters, beat egg whites with vanilla extract until stiff, not dry, peaks are formed. Fold into flour mixture.
5. Turn into a well-greased 10-inch springform pan or deep, round layer cake pan.
6. Bake at 325°F 50 to 60 minutes. Remove from pan and cool completely.
7. Split cake in half.
8. Spread filling on bottom half. Replace top. Spread frosting over sides and top. Refrigerate 4 hours or longer for torte to mellow.

Filling: Whip **1/2 cup whipping cream** until cream piles softly. Fold in **1/4 cup ground almonds or walnuts** and **3 tablespoons sugar.**

Frosting: Melt **4 ounces (4 squares) unsweetened chocolate** and **3 tablespoons butter** together in a saucepan. Remove from heat. Stir in **1 tablespoon brandy.** Add **2 to 2 1/2 cups confectioners' sugar** and **2 to 3 tablespoons milk or cream** until frosting is of spreading consistency.

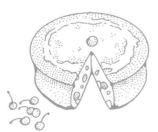

Champs Elysées Apple Pie

SERVES 6

Pie Dough:	6 firm, sourish apples
4 ounces butter	(pared, cored, in
2 cups all-purpose	wedges)
flour	**2 tablespoons sugar**
1 tablespoon cold	**1/2 tablespoon cinna-**
water	**mon**
Filling:	**Shredded almonds**
1 cup vanilla cream	

1. Combine the flour and the butter on the pastry board to a fine grainy mixture, add water, and work the pastry together quickly. Place in refrigerator for 30 minutes.
2. Roll out the pastry and line the bottom and the sides of a pie mold with it. Prick the bottom with a fork. Bake the pie crust in a 400°F oven for about 15 minutes. Let it cool.
3. Pour the vanilla cream into the mold and top with apple wedges. Sprinkle on sugar, cinnamon, and shredded almonds.
4. Bake the pie in a 400°F oven for about 20 minutes.

Serve fresh from the oven with icy-cold whipped cream.

Rhubarb Pie with Vanilla Cream

SERVES 4

1 pound rhubarb	**1 egg yolk**
4 ounces sugar	**2 teaspoons sugar**
Puff Pastry:	**2 teaspoons confec-**
1 1/2 cups all-purpose	**tioners' sugar**
flour	**2 teaspoons potato**
3 ounces sugar	**flour**
1/2 teaspoon salt	**3 ounces whipped**
6 ounces butter	**heavy cream**
2 egg yolks	*For Brushing:*
Vanilla Cream:	**Egg**
3/4 cup light cream	

1. Cut the rhubarb in 1-inch long pieces and layer them with the sugar in a saucepan. Let the sugar melt over low heat until the rhubarb is soft.
2. Mix the ingredients for the pastry on a pastry board. Add the egg yolks and work the pastry together quickly. Place in the refrigerator to set.
3. Roll out half the pastry and line a greased pie pan. Add in the rhubarb.
4. Roll out the rest of the pastry, cut it in strips, and

(continued)

**Rhubarb Pie
with Vanilla Cream.**

Champs Elysées Apple Pie.

cover the rhubarb lattice-style. Put a thin strip around the edges.

5. Brush with a lightly beaten egg and bake in the oven at 350°F for about 30 minutes.

6. Meanwhile make the vanilla cream. Mix all ingredients except the whipped cream and simmer until it thickens. Let the cream get cold. Stir in the whipped cream and serve on the side.

Shoofly Pie

ONE 8-INCH PIE

1 cup all-purpose flour	5 tablespoons molasses
²/₃ cup firmly packed dark brown sugar	1 tablespoon dark brown sugar
¼ teaspoon salt	½ teaspoon baking soda
5 tablespoons butter or margarine	1 unbaked 8-inch pie shell
²/₃ cup very hot water	

1. Combine flour, ²/₃ cup brown sugar, and salt in a bowl. Cut in butter until particles resemble rice kernels; set aside.

2. Blend hot water with the molasses, 1 tablespoon brown sugar, and baking soda.

3. Reserving 3 tablespoons crumb mixture for topping, stir molasses mixture into remaining crumb mixture. Pour into unbaked pie shell. Sprinkle reserved crumbs over filling.

4. Bake at 350°F 35 to 40 minutes, or until top springs back when touched lightly.

Dutch Apple Pie

ONE 9-INCH PIE

3 to 4 (about 1 pound) tart cooking apples	3 tablespoons flour
	½ teaspoon cinnamon
1 unbaked 9-inch pie shell	¼ teaspoon nutmeg
	⅛ teaspoon salt
1 egg, slightly beaten	4 teaspoons butter or margarine
1 cup whipping cream	½ cup walnuts, coarsely chopped
1½ teaspoons vanilla extract	¾ cup shredded sharp Cheddar cheese
1 cup sugar	

1. Wash, quarter, core, pare, and thinly slice apples. Turn slices into unbaked pie shell.

2. Blend the egg, cream, and vanilla extract. Gradually add a mixture of sugar, flour, nutmeg, cinnamon, and salt, mixing well. Pour over apples in pie shell. Dot with butter, sprinkle walnuts over top.

3. Bake at 450°F 10 minutes; turn oven control to

350°F and bake 35 to 40 minutes, or until apples are tender and top is lightly browned.

4. Remove from oven and sprinkle cheese over top. Serve warm.

Apricot Cheese Pie

ONE 9-INCH PIE

1 cup dried apricots	juice
1 unbaked 9-inch pie shell	¾ cup sugar
	1 tablespoon flour
3 eggs	½ teaspoon salt
½ teaspoon grated lemon peel	1½ cups creamed cottage cheese, sieved
1 teaspoon lemon	

1. Rinse and drain apricots; cut into small pieces and distribute over bottom of pie shell.

2. Combine eggs and lemon peel and juice; beat slightly. Gradually add a mixture of sugar, flour, and salt, beating constantly. Add the cottage cheese and mix until blended. Pour over apricots.

3. Bake at 375°F about 35 minutes, or until a knife inserted near center comes out clean.

4. Set pie on wire rack to cool before serving.

Blueberry Lattice-Top Pie

ONE 9-INCH PIE

1 package pie crust mix	1 cup sugar
	¾ cup cold water
4 cups fresh blueberries, washed and drained	1 peeled orange, coarsely chopped
	¼ cup cornstarch

1. Prepare pie crust following package directions. Roll out two-thirds of pie crust; line a 9-inch pie pan. Set aside.

2. Turn blueberries into a saucepan. Add sugar, ½ cup water, and orange; mix. Set over low heat and bring to boiling.

3. Mix cornstarch with remaining ¼ cup water. Stir into boiling mixture. Remove from heat. Cool.

4. Spoon cooled filling into pie crust.

5. Roll out remaining pie crust and cut into strips. Arrange strips in a lattice design over filling. Crimp edge of pie crust.

6. Bake at 400°F 35 to 40 minutes, or until browned. Cool.

Gooseberry Pie.

Gooseberry Pie

SERVES 4

Filling:
3 cups gooseberries, cleaned and rinsed
3 tablespoons sugar
1 tablespoon potato flour

Dough:
1 cup all-purpose flour
5¼ ounces margarine
3 tablespoons water
Egg whites
Sugar

1. Mix flour and margarine. Add water and place in cool place for ½ hour.
2. Preheat oven to 425°F. Roll ⅔ of dough out and place in bottom of pie form.
3. Mix sugar and potato flour. Add gooseberries and fill in pie form.
4. Separate rest of dough into 6 pieces and roll out into strips. Place crosswise on top of pie.
5. Brush with egg whites and sprinkle with sugar. Bake in 425°F oven for 30-40 minutes.
Serve cooled with vanilla ice cream or whipped cream.

Butternut Pie

ONE 9-INCH PIE

3 eggs
1 cup sugar
1 teaspoon salt
1 teaspoon vanilla extract
1 cup maple syrup

1 cup coarsely chopped butternuts*
1 unbaked 9-inch pie shell

1. Beat the eggs, sugar, salt, and extract together

(continued)

307

until thick and piled softly. Beat in the maple syrup, then stir in butternuts. Pour the filling into unbaked pie shell.

2. Bake at 350°F about 40 minutes, or until a knife inserted near center comes out clean.

*If butternuts are not available, substitute walnuts.

Pecan Pie

ONE 9-INCH PIE

3 tablespoons butter or margarine	pecans
2 teaspoons vanilla extract	1 cup dark corn syrup
³/₄ cup sugar	¹/₈ teaspoon salt
3 eggs	1 unbaked 9-inch pie shell
¹/₂ cup chopped	¹/₂ cup pecan halves

1. Cream butter with extract. Gradually add sugar, creaming well. Add eggs, one at a time, beating thoroughly after each addition.

2. Beat in chopped pecans, corn syrup, and salt. Turn into unbaked pie shell.

3. Bake at 450°F 10 minutes; reduce oven temperature to 350°F. Arrange pecan halves over top of filling. Bake 30 to 35 minutes, or until set. Cool on wire rack.

Lemon Meringue Pie

SERVES 6-7

1¹/₂ cups sugar	3 egg yolks, slightly beaten
¹/₄ teaspoon salt	
1¹/₂ cups boiling water	1 baked 9-inch pastry pie shell
2 tablespoons butter	
6 tablespoons cornstarch	3 egg whites
	6 tablespoons sugar
¹/₃ cup lemon juice	¹/₂ teaspoon lemon juice
1 tablespoon grated lemon peel	

1. In a 4-cup glass measure, combine 1¹/₂ cups sugar, salt, water, and butter. Cook 3 to 4 minutes, stirring halfway through cooking time until sugar is dissolved.

2. Blend cornstarch with 3 tablespoons water and stir into hot sugar mixture. Cook 2 to 3 minutes, stirring after every minute.

3. Stir in ¹/₃ cup lemon juice and lemon peel. Gradually add egg yolks, taking care to avoid overcooking them. Cook mixture 3 to 4 minutes, stirring after every minute. Cool and pour into pie shell.

4. Using an electric mixer, beat egg whites until stiff. Continue beating while adding 6 tablespoons

sugar, 1 tablespoon at a time, until rounded peaks are formed. Beat in ¹/₂ teaspoon lemon juice.

5. Spread meringue evenly over cooked filling, sealing to edges of pie shell.

6. Bake in a conventional oven at 450°F 5 to 6 minutes, or until lightly browned.

English Gingered Brandy Snaps

15 COOKIES

¹/₄ cup butter or margarine	ginger
¹/₄ cup sugar	¹/₈ teaspoon ground nutmeg
2 tablespoons light corn syrup	1 tablespoon brandy
1 teaspoon molasses	*Filling:*
¹/₂ cup all-purpose flour	1 cup whipping cream, whipped
¹/₂ teaspoon ground	1 tablespoon sugar

1. Combine butter, sugar, corn syrup, and molasses in a medium saucepan. Heat mixture over medium heat just until butter is melted.

2. Combine flour, ginger, and nutmeg in a small bowl. Stir this mixture into the butter mixture. Stir in the brandy.

3. Drop the mixture by teaspoonfuls 6 inches apart on greased cookie sheets.

4. Bake at 350°F 8 to 10 minutes. Let cool for 30 seconds. Ease cookies off the cookie sheets with a spatula; then immediately roll loosely around a 6-inch tapered metal tube with the upper surface of each brandy snap on the outside. Cool on wire racks.

5. Shortly before serving, whip cream, add sugar, and mix well. Using a pastry bag fitted with a star tip, fill the cavity in the rolled brandy snap from each end.

Note: If brandy snaps begin to harden before they are rolled, return them to the oven for 30 seconds to soften them.

Puff-Paste Twists

YIELDS ABOUT 40

4 egg yolks	1 lemon
3 ounces confectioners' sugar	1 cup flour
	2 ounces melted butter
¹/₂ teaspoon salt	
2 tablespoons brandy	*For Frying:*
Finely grated rind of	1 quart vegetable oil

1. Mix egg yolks, sugar, brandy, and lemon rind.

Add the flour and work together. Leave it in a cold place to set.

2. Roll out the flour and trim out strips about ¹/₂ inch wide and 4 inches long.

3. Make a slit along part of the middle of each strip and pull one end of it through the strip. Place a few twists at a time in the heated (300°F) fat and fry them until golden brown, about 1¹/₂-2 minutes. Let them drain on paper towel.

Sprinkle with confectioners' sugar just before serving.

Puff-paste Twists.

Rhubarb Pillows

YIELDS 12

1¹/₄ pounds rhubarb	10 ounces butter
1 cup granulated sugar	1 tablespoon sugar
	1 egg
12 slices almond paste	*For Brushing:*
Batter:	1 egg
2¹/₂ cups flour	

1. Cut rhubarb in 1-inch pieces. Place in a pot, add sugar. Cover and simmer for 10-15 minutes. Remove from heat and let cool.

2. Mix flour, butter, sugar, and egg. Knead thoroughly. Place in refrigerator for 1 hour.

3. Roll the dough out into 12 thin squares. Place almond paste and a tablespoon of rhubarb on each square and press sides firmly together.

4. Brush with egg and bake in 400°F oven for 15 minutes.

5. Serve with vanilla sauce, ice cream, or whipped cream.

Rhubarb Pillows.

Lemon Stars.

Lemon Stars

YIELDS ABOUT 36 COOKIES

¹/₂ cup soft margarine or butter	1¹/₂ cups flour
Grated rind of 1 small lemon	1 tablespoon brandy
	1 egg, beaten
	Granulated sugar

1. Cut margarine into flour. Add lemon rind and brandy. Quickly knead together. Refrigerate for 2 hours.

2. Roll out the dough and cut out cookies with a star-shaped cookie cutter.

3. Brush with egg and heavily coat with granulated sugar.

4. Bake in a 375°F oven for 12-15 minutes.

Assorted Small Cakes

YIELDS ABOUT 60 SMALL CAKES

Puff pastry:	melted
7 ounces butter	**Vanilla**
3 ounces sugar	**Brandy**
2 cups wheat flour	*For Brushing:*
3 ounces potato flour	**Egg**
1 egg yolk	*Decoration:*
Flavoring:	**Granulated sugar**
Grated lemon rind	**Jam**
Sweet chocolate,	**Berries**

1. Chop the butter into the flour and sugar, add the egg yolk, and work together quickly.
2. Place in the refrigerator to rest.
3. Divide the pastry into 4 equal parts and make the 4 different kinds of small cakes described below. Bake cakes in a 325°F oven for 10-12 minutes.
A. Jam cakes: Add 1 teaspoon finely grated lemon rind to the pastry. Roll out the pastry and cut out round cakes with a cookie cutter. Place a pat of jam on each cake and fold. Brush with egg, sprinkle with chopped almond and granulated sugar. Bake.
B. Brandy rings: Flavor the pastry with ¹/₂ tablespoon brandy. Roll pastry into thin lengths. Twist them together two and two, shape into rings, and bake.
C. Cakes with chocolate-coated granulated sugar: Flavor the pastry with 1 teaspoon vanilla. Roll out the pastry and cut out round cakes with a cookie cutter. Bake cakes. Cover the cold cakes with 3 ounces melted sweet chocolate and sprinkle with granulated sugar.
D. Berry tartlets: Flavor the pastry with 1 tablespoon finely grated lemon rind. Roll out pastry and line greased tart molds. Bake. Fill the cold cakes with berries.

Spritz

ABOUT 5 DOZEN COOKIES

1 cup butter	**2 cups sifted all-**
1 teaspoon vanilla	**purpose flour**
extract	**¹/₂ teaspoon baking**
¹/₂ cup sugar	**powder**
1 egg yolk	**¹/₄ teaspoon salt**

1. Cream butter with extract; add sugar gradually, beating until fluffy. Add egg yolk and beat thoroughly.
2. Sift flour, baking powder, and salt together; add to creamed mixture in fourths, mixing until blended after each addition.
3. Following manufacturer's directions, fill a cookie press with dough and form cookies of varied shapes directly onto ungreased cookie sheets.
4. Bake at 350°F 12 minutes.

Chocolate Spritz: Follow recipe for Spritz. Thoroughly blend. **¹/₄ cup boiling water** and **6 table-**

Assorted
Small Cakes.

Cherry Cookies.

spoons cocoa; cool. Mix in after addition of egg yolk.

Nut Spritz: Follow recipe for Spritz. Stir in **¹/₂ cup finely chopped nuts** (black walnuts or toasted blanched almonds) after the last addition of dry ingredients.

Chocolate-Tipped Spritz: Follow recipe for Spritz. Dip ends of cooled cookies into Chocolate Glaze *(below)*. If desired, dip into finely chopped **nuts,** crushed **peppermint stick candy,** or **chocolate shot.** Place on wire racks until glaze is set.

Marbled Spritz: Follow recipe for Spritz. Thoroughly blend **2 tablespoons boiling water** and **3 tablespoons cocoa;** cool. After the addition of egg yolk, remove half of the creamed mixture to another bowl and mix in half of the dry ingredients. Into remaining half of creamed mixture, stir cocoa mixture; blend in remaining dry ingredients. Shape each half of dough into a roll and cut lengthwise into halves. Press cut surfaces of vanilla and chocolate flavored doughs together before filling cookie press.

Spritz Sandwiches: Spread **chocolate frosting** or **jam** on bottom of some cookies. Cover with unfrosted cookies of same shape to form sandwiches.

Jelly-Filled Spritz: Make slight impression at center of cookie rounds and fill with **¹/₄ teaspoon jelly** or **jam** before baking.

Chocolate Glaze: Partially melt **3 ounces (¹/₂ cup)** **semisweet chocolate pieces** in the top of a double boiler over hot (not simmering) water. Remove from heat and stir until chocolate is melted. Blend in **3 tablespoons butter.**

Cherry Cookies

YIELDS 25 COOKIES

3¹/₂ ounces butter	*For Brushing and*
¹/₄ cup sugar	*Decoration:*
Grated rind of	1 egg, beaten
¹/₂ lemon	Maraschino cherries
1 egg	Chopped almonds
1³/₄ cups flour	

1. Stir butter and sugar until foamy. Add lemon rind, egg, and flour and work together.
2. Roll into small balls the size of walnuts. Roll the balls in beaten egg, then in chopped almonds.
3. Put them on a greased baking sheet and make a small dent in the middle. Place half a well-drained maraschino cherry in the center. Bake in a 350°F oven until the cookies are golden brown, about 10 minutes.

Almond Balls with Pineapple.

2. Grate the almond paste or crumble it in a bowl. Add the egg whites and work the mixture until smooth. It should not be too loose and thin.

3. Take teaspoonfuls of the dough and shape into small balls. Roll them in the sliced almonds and put them on the baking sheets. Cut the pineapple in small pieces and press one piece into each ball.

4. Place in a 350°F oven. Allow the cookies to rest while the oven gets warm.

5. Bake 10-15 minutes. Watch carefully. The cookies should be light yellow and the almond slices lightly browned.

6. Let cookies cool on the sheets, then loosen them.

Toffee-Covered Cookies.

Almond Balls with Pineapple

YIELDS 30 COOKIES

20 ounces almond paste	3 slices pineapple
2 egg whites	7 ounces sliced almonds

1. Cover one or two baking sheets with lightly greased aluminum foil.

Toffee-Covered Cookies

YIELDS 35 COOKIES

2 eggs	melted
4 ounces sugar	*Toffee Icing:*
3 ounces flour	3 ounces butter,
1 tablespoon finely ground coffee	melted
1 tablespoon cocoa	3 ounces sugar
1 teaspoon baking powder	3 ounces hazelnuts, coarsely chopped
4 ounces butter,	1 tablespoon milk
	1 tablespoon flour

1. Beat eggs and sugar until foamy. Combine flour, coffee, and cocoa.

2. Sprinkle a 10 × 10-inch greased cake pan with fine bread crumbs.

3. Sift the dry mixture into the egg batter. Stir in the melted butter. Pour the batter into the pan and bake in a 350°F oven for about 10 minutes.

4. Pour on the icing and bake another 8 minutes in a 400°F oven until the icing has turned light brown.

5. Let cool before cutting into 35 squares.

6. To make the icing: Simmer all ingredients in a saucepan, beating until mixture is smooth.

Chocolate Chip Cookies

ABOUT 4 DOZEN COOKIES

1 cup sifted all-purpose flour	extract
1/2 teaspoon baking powder	3/4 cup firmly packed light brown sugar
1/8 teaspoon baking soda	1 egg
1/8 teaspoon salt	1 package (6 ounces) semisweet chocolate pieces
1/2 cup butter	1/2 cup chopped nuts
1 teaspoon vanilla	

1. Blend flour, baking powder, baking soda, and salt.

2. Cream butter with vanilla extract. Add brown sugar gradually, creaming well. Add egg and beat thoroughly. Mix in dry ingredients, then chocolate pieces and nuts.

3. Drop batter by teaspoonfuls onto ungreased baking sheets.

4. Bake at 375°F 10 to 12 minutes.

5. Cool cookies on wire racks.

Coconut Macaroons

ABOUT 3 DOZEN COOKIES

2/3 cup (1/2 of a 14-ounce can) sweetened condensed milk	roasted almonds
	1/4 cup chopped maraschino cherries, drained
2 cups flaked coconut	1 1/2 teaspoons vanilla extract
1/2 to 3/4 cup coarsely chopped dry	

1. Mix all ingredients thoroughly. Drop by rounded teaspoonfuls onto well-greased cookie sheet. To speed removal of cookies from cookie sheet, bake no more than 12 at a time.

2. Bake at 350°F 10 to 12 minutes, or until delicately browned.

3. Immediately loosen all cookies from cookie sheet and remove cookies to wire rack at once.

Southern Brownies

ABOUT 2 DOZEN COOKIES

3 tablespoons shortening	1 teaspoon vanilla extract
2 ounces (2 squares) unsweetened chocolate	1 cup sugar
	1/2 cup all-purpose flour
2 egg yolks, well beaten	1/2 cup chopped nuts
	2 egg whites

1. Melt shortening and chocolate together in a large saucepan; cool.

2. Stir in egg yolks, then extract, sugar, flour, and nuts.

3. Beat egg whites until stiff, not dry, peaks are formed. Blend into chocolate mixture.

4. Spread batter in a well-greased 8 × 8 × 2-inch pan.

5. Bake at 350°F 30 minutes, or until a wooden pick comes out clean.

6. Cool completely before cutting.

Old-Fashioned Spice Cookies

ABOUT 5 DOZEN COOKIES

2 cups sifted all-purpose flour	brown sugar
	1/2 cup granulated sugar
3/4 teaspoon salt	
1/2 teaspoon baking soda	1 egg
1 teaspoon cinnamon	2 tablespoons water
1/2 teaspoon nutmeg	2 cups uncooked rolled oats, quick or old-fashioned
1/4 teaspoon cloves	
1 cup soft vegetable shortening	3/4 cup currants
	Confectioners' sugar
1 cup firmly packed	

1. Blend flour, salt, baking soda, and spices in a bowl. Add shortening, sugars, egg, and water; beat with electric mixer until smooth (about 2 minutes). Stir in oats and currants.

2. Chill dough thoroughly.

3. Roll only a small portion of chilled dough at a time to 1/8-inch thickness on a pastry canvas or board lightly sprinkled with confectioners' sugar. Cut with a floured 3-inch round cutter. Put onto ungreased cookie sheets. Sprinkle with granulated sugar.

4. Bake at 375°F 8 to 10 minutes.

Sour Apricot Roll

YIELDS 1 ROLL

7 ounces almond paste	10 dried apricots, finely chopped
2 teaspoons lemon juice	1/4 cup shelled walnuts or hazelnuts, chopped
3-4 drops yellow food coloring	

1. Grate the almond paste coarsely. Mix it with lemon juice and food coloring.
2. Roll out to a rectangle of 8 × 5 inches.
3. Sprinkle with the chopped apricots.
4. Roll together and coat the roll in chopped nuts.

Almond Paste "Chestnuts"

YIELDS 30

7 ounces almond paste	2 ounces butter
4 ounces sweet chocolate	1 tablespoon chocolate milk powder
1 egg yolk	1/2 teaspoon confectioners' sugar

1. Grate the almond paste coarsely.
2. Grate the chocolate bar very finely.
3. Mix the almond paste and chocolate and stir in the egg yolk and butter.
4. Shape the mixture into chestnut-size balls. Coat the balls with chocolate milk powder and confectioners' sugar. Put the balls in the refrigerator to set.

Chocolate Marshmallow Fudge

YIELDS 75 PIECES

1 1/2 cups sugar	2 teaspoons instant coffee
3/4 cup heavy cream	6 ounces dark sweet chocolate
4 ounces butter	
25 large marshmallows, halved	

1. Mix butter, cream, and halved marshmallows in a saucepan.
2. Stir over high heat until marshmallows have melted, about 10 minutes.
3. Add the coffee powder and the chocolate, cut in small pieces. Let the chocolate melt.
4. Pour the batter into an oiled small baking pan about 12 × 9 inches.
5. Let set overnight and cut the fudge into pieces.

Jelly Apples

YIELDS 2

1 cup sugar	*Garnish:*
1/2-3/4 cup water	Coconut
Dash cream of tartar	M & Ms
Food coloring of any color	Almonds
	Sprinkles
2 apples on sticks	Chopped nuts

1. Pour sugar, water, cream of tartar, and food coloring into a heavy saucepan and heat over low heat until sugar is dissolved.
2. Cover and cook about 3 minutes till syrup reaches 300°F.
3. Remove pan from heat and and place over hot water in a double boiler.
4. Quickly dip in apples on sticks.
5. Place the garnish of coconut, sprinkles, or nuts on wax paper and roll the apples in it. Decorate with M & Ms and almonds. Place on a well-buttered surface to harden or on a metal flower holder.

Chocolate Marshmallow Devils

15 COATED MARSHMALLOWS

1 package (6 ounces) semisweet chocolate pieces	15 large marshmallows
15 wooden skewers	3/4 cup crushed corn chips

1. In a 2-cup glass measure, heat chocolate pieces 3 to 4 minutes, stirring well after heating.
2. Place wooden skewer in center of each marshmallow. Dip marshmallow in melted chocolate, spread with knife to coat evenly, and roll in corn chips until well covered. Chill, remove skewers, and serve.

Walnut Brittle

ABOUT 2 POUNDS CANDY

2 cups sugar	2 tablespoons butter
1 cup light or dark corn syrup	3 cups coarsely chopped walnuts
1/2 cup water	2 teaspoons baking soda
1 teaspoon salt	

1. Combine sugar, corn syrup, water, salt, and butter

(continued)

Jelly Apples.

Clockwise from top left: Sour Apricot Roll; Almond Paste "Chestnuts"; Chocolate Marshmallow Fudge.

in a saucepan. Cook over moderate heat, stirring until sugar is dissolved. Cover and simmer 5 minutes to wash down sugar crystals from side of pan.

2. Uncover and boil to 300°F (hard crack stage).

3. While syrup is cooking, spread walnuts in a shallow pan and toast lightly in a 300°F oven. When candy reaches 300°F, quickly stir in the warm walnuts and baking soda. Turn at once into an oiled 15 × 1 × 1-inch jelly-roll pan (or two oiled cookie sheets if thinner brittle is desired) and spread thin.

4. Let stand until cold, then break into pieces.

lumps from forming. Reduce heat to very low and cook uncovered, stirring occasionally, until a candy thermometer registers 220°F. Stir in rosewater, mastic, lemon juice, and pistachios.

3. Pour the hot mixture into a square pan lined on bottom and sides with a heavy cotton cloth dusted with cornstarch. Spread mixture and dust top with cornstarch. Cover with a cloth and let it stand 24 hours.

4. Cut the layer into small squares with a sharp knife, roll the pieces in confectioners' sugar, and put into candy paper cups. This confection will keep for weeks.

Choco-Butterscotchies

ABOUT 5 DOZEN PIECES

1 cup sugar	semisweet choco-
1 cup light corn syrup	late pieces
1 cup peanut butter	1 package (6 ounces)
6 cups oven-toasted	butterscotch-
rice cereal	flavored pieces
1 package (6 ounces)	

1. In a large glass mixing bowl, blend together sugar and corn syrup. Cook 3 to 4 minutes until mixture is boiling.

2. Stir peanut butter into hot mixture. Add cereal; stir to blend well. Press mixture into a buttered 11 × 7-inch glass dish.

3. In a 2-cup glass measure, heat semisweet chocolate and butterscotch-flavored pieces 2 to 2½ minutes. Stir to blend well.

4. Spread melted mixture over cereal pressed in dish. Cool about 30 minutes. Cut into 1½-inch squares, then cut each square diagonally, forming triangular pieces.

Turkish Delight

ABOUT 3 DOZEN PIECES

2 cups granulated	⅛ teaspoon ground
sugar	mastic
½ cup light corn syrup	2 tablespoons fresh
½ cup cornstarch plus	lemon juice
3 tablespoons extra	¾ cup unsalted pista-
for dusting	chios
3 cups water	Confectioners' sugar
1 tablespoon rosewater	for rolling

1. Combine granulated sugar and corn syrup in a saucepan and bring to boiling, stirring constantly. Cook for 30 seconds. Cool.

2. In another saucepan, combine ½ cup cornstarch with water. Simmer mixture until thick. Mix cornstarch into syrup and bring slowly to boiling. Stir to prevent

Almond Bark

ABOUT 1 POUND

¾ cup blanched	1 package (12 ounces)
whole almonds	semisweet choco-
1 teaspoon butter	late pieces

1. Place almonds and butter in a 9-inch glass pie plate. Cook 3 to 4 minutes, stirring after every minute. Add more time if needed to toast almonds.

2. In a 4-cup glass measure, heat chocolate pieces 2 to 4 minutes; stir to blend. Add almonds and mix well.

3. Pour onto waxed paper and spread to desired thickness. Chill about 1 hour until firm. Break into pieces.

Walnut Toffee

ABOUT 2½ POUNDS CANDY

2¼ cups walnut pieces	1 cup butter
2 cups granulated	1 package (6 ounces)
sugar	semisweet or milk
½ cup water	chocolate pieces
½ cup light corn	(may use half of
syrup	each)

1. Coarsely chop 1½ cups walnuts for the toffee. Finely chop the remaining walnuts and set aside for the topping.

2. Combine sugar, water, corn syrup, and butter. Bring to boiling, stirring until sugar is dissolved. Cover and cook 5 minutes. Uncover and boil to 300°F (hard crack stage). Remove from heat.

3. Stir in the coarsely chopped walnuts and quickly spread in a buttered 15 × 1 × 1-inch jelly-roll pan. Let stand until cooled.

4. Melt chocolate pieces over warm (not hot) water. Spread over cooled toffee. Sprinkle finely chopped walnuts over chocolate. Let stand until chocolate is set (about 30 minutes). Break into pieces.

Filled Marzipan and Marzipan Rolls.

Filled Marzipan

YIELDS 1 LOAF

24 ounces marzipan	1³/₄ cups confection-
1 cup maraschino	ers' sugar
cherries	3 tablespoons hot
1 cup walnuts	water
3 squares un-	3 egg yolks
sweetened choco-	¹/₄ cup butter
late	

1. Place marzipan, cherries, and walnuts in a bowl. Mix well.
2. Melt chocolate in the top of a double boiler.
3. Remove from heat and stir in sifted confectioners' sugar and hot water. Mix until smooth.
4. Beat in egg yolks one at a time, beating hard after each addition. Beat in butter.
5. Form marzipan into a loaf and spread chocolate on top and sides. Chill until ready to serve.

Marzipan Rolls

YIELDS 3 ROLLS

18 ounces marzipan	walnuts or ¹/₂ cup
¹/₂ cup chopped	chocolate sprinkles

1. Roll marzipan into long cylinders.
2. Place nuts or chocolate sprinkles on wax paper. Roll marzipan in nuts or sprinkles.

INDEX